Mometrix
TEST PREPARATION

Praxis II

Special Education: Teaching Students with Behavioral Disorders/Emotional Disturbances (5372) Exam

Secrets Study Guide

Dear Future Exam Success Story

First of all, **THANK YOU** for purchasing Mometrix study materials!

Second, congratulations! You are one of the few determined test-takers who are committed to doing whatever it takes to excel on your exam. **You have come to the right place.** We developed these study materials with one goal in mind: to deliver you the information you need in a format that's concise and easy to use.

In addition to optimizing your guide for the content of the test, we've outlined our recommended steps for breaking down the preparation process into small, attainable goals so you can make sure you stay on track.

We've also analyzed the entire test-taking process, identifying the most common pitfalls and showing how you can overcome them and be ready for any curveball the test throws you.

Standardized testing is one of the biggest obstacles on your road to success, which only increases the importance of doing well in the high-pressure, high-stakes environment of test day. Your results on this test could have a significant impact on your future, and this guide provides the information and practical advice to help you achieve your full potential on test day.

Your success is our success

We would love to hear from you! If you would like to share the story of your exam success or if you have any questions or comments in regard to our products, please contact us at **800-673-8175** or **support@mometrix.com**.

Thanks again for your business and we wish you continued success!

Sincerely,
The Mometrix Test Preparation Team

Need more help? Check out our flashcards at:
http://MometrixFlashcards.com/PraxisII

TABLE OF CONTENTS

Introduction

Thank you for purchasing this resource! You have made the choice to prepare yourself for a test that could have a huge impact on your future, and this guide is designed to help you be fully ready for test day. Obviously, it's important to have a solid understanding of the test material, but you also need to be prepared for the unique environment and stressors of the test, so that you can perform to the best of your abilities.

For this purpose, the first section that appears in this guide is the **Secret Keys**. We've devoted countless hours to meticulously researching what works and what doesn't, and we've boiled down our findings to the five most impactful steps you can take to improve your performance on the test. We start at the beginning with study planning and move through the preparation process, all the way to the testing strategies that will help you get the most out of what you know when you're finally sitting in front of the test.

We recommend that you start preparing for your test as far in advance as possible. However, if you've bought this guide as a last-minute study resource and only have a few days before your test, we recommend that you skip over the first two Secret Keys since they address a long-term study plan.

If you struggle with **test anxiety**, we strongly encourage you to check out our recommendations for how you can overcome it. Test anxiety is a formidable foe, but it can be beaten, and we want to make sure you have the tools you need to defeat it.

Secret Key #1 – Plan Big, Study Small

There's a lot riding on your performance. If you want to ace this test, you're going to need to keep your skills sharp and the material fresh in your mind. You need a plan that lets you review everything you need to know while still fitting in your schedule. We'll break this strategy down into three categories.

Information Organization

Start with the information you already have: the official test outline. From this, you can make a complete list of all the concepts you need to cover before the test. Organize these concepts into groups that can be studied together, and create a list of any related vocabulary you need to learn so you can brush up on any difficult terms. You'll want to keep this vocabulary list handy once you actually start studying since you may need to add to it along the way.

Time Management

Once you have your set of study concepts, decide how to spread them out over the time you have left before the test. Break your study plan into small, clear goals so you have a manageable task for each day and know exactly what you're doing. Then just focus on one small step at a time. When you manage your time this way, you don't need to spend hours at a time studying. Studying a small block of content for a short period each day helps you retain information better and avoid stressing over how much you have left to do. You can relax knowing that you have a plan to cover everything in time. In order for this strategy to be effective though, you have to start studying early and stick to your schedule. Avoid the exhaustion and futility that comes from last-minute cramming!

Study Environment

The environment you study in has a big impact on your learning. Studying in a coffee shop, while probably more enjoyable, is not likely to be as fruitful as studying in a quiet room. It's important to keep distractions to a minimum. You're only planning to study for a short block of time, so make the most of it. Don't pause to check your phone or get up to find a snack. It's also important to **avoid multitasking**. Research has consistently shown that multitasking will make your studying dramatically less effective. Your study area should also be comfortable and well-lit so you don't have the distraction of straining your eyes or sitting on an uncomfortable chair.

 The time of day you study is also important. You want to be rested and alert. Don't wait until just before bedtime. Study when you'll be most likely to comprehend and remember. Even better, if you know what time of day your test will be, set that time aside for study. That way your brain will be used to working on that subject at that specific time and you'll have a better chance of recalling information.

Finally, it can be helpful to team up with others who are studying for the same test. Your actual studying should be done in as isolated an environment as possible, but the work of organizing the information and setting up the study plan can be divided up. In between study sessions, you can discuss with your teammates the concepts that you're all studying and quiz each other on the details. Just be sure that your teammates are as serious about the test as you are. If you find that your study time is being replaced with social time, you might need to find a new team.

2

Secret Key #2 – Make Your Studying Count

You're devoting a lot of time and effort to preparing for this test, so you want to be absolutely certain it will pay off. This means doing more than just reading the content and hoping you can remember it on test day. It's important to make every minute of study count. There are two main areas you can focus on to make your studying count.

Retention

It doesn't matter how much time you study if you can't remember the material. You need to make sure you are retaining the concepts. To check your retention of the information you're learning, try recalling it at later times with minimal prompting. Try carrying around flashcards and glance at one or two from time to time or ask a friend who's also studying for the test to quiz you.

To enhance your retention, look for ways to put the information into practice so that you can apply it rather than simply recalling it. If you're using the information in practical ways, it will be much easier to remember. Similarly, it helps to solidify a concept in your mind if you're not only reading it to yourself but also explaining it to someone else. Ask a friend to let you teach them about a concept you're a little shaky on (or speak aloud to an imaginary audience if necessary). As you try to summarize, define, give examples, and answer your friend's questions, you'll understand the concepts better and they will stay with you longer. Finally, step back for a big picture view and ask yourself how each piece of information fits with the whole subject. When you link the different concepts together and see them working together as a whole, it's easier to remember the individual components.

Finally, practice showing your work on any multi-step problems, even if you're just studying. Writing out each step you take to solve a problem will help solidify the process in your mind, and you'll be more likely to remember it during the test.

Modality

Modality simply refers to the means or method by which you study. Choosing a study modality that fits your own individual learning style is crucial. No two people learn best in exactly the same way, so it's important to know your strengths and use them to your advantage.

For example, if you learn best by visualization, focus on visualizing a concept in your mind and draw an image or a diagram. Try color-coding your notes, illustrating them, or creating symbols that will trigger your mind to recall a learned concept. If you learn best by hearing or discussing information, find a study partner who learns the same way or read aloud to yourself. Think about how to put the information in your own words. Imagine that you are giving a lecture on the topic and record yourself so you can listen to it later.

For any learning style, flashcards can be helpful. Organize the information so you can take advantage of spare moments to review. Underline key words or phrases. Use different colors for different categories. Mnemonic devices (such as creating a short list in which every item starts with the same letter) can also help with retention. Find what works best for you and use it to store the information in your mind most effectively and easily.

3

Secret Key #3 – Practice the Right Way

Your success on test day depends not only on how many hours you put into preparing, but also on whether you prepared the right way. It's good to check along the way to see if your studying is paying off. One of the most effective ways to do this is by taking practice tests to evaluate your progress. Practice tests are useful because they show exactly where you need to improve. Every time you take a practice test, pay special attention to these three groups of questions:

- The questions you got wrong
- The questions you had to guess on, even if you guessed right
- The questions you found difficult or slow to work through

This will show you exactly what your weak areas are, and where you need to devote more study time. Ask yourself why each of these questions gave you trouble. Was it because you didn't understand the material? Was it because you didn't remember the vocabulary? Do you need more repetitions on this type of question to build speed and confidence? Dig into those questions and figure out how you can strengthen your weak areas as you go back to review the material.

 Additionally, many practice tests have a section explaining the answer choices. It can be tempting to read the explanation and think that you now have a good understanding of the concept. However, an explanation likely only covers part of the question's broader context. Even if the explanation makes perfect sense, **go back and investigate** every concept related to the question until you're positive you have a thorough understanding.

As you go along, keep in mind that the practice test is just that: practice. Memorizing these questions and answers will not be very helpful on the actual test because it is unlikely to have any of the same exact questions. If you only know the right answers to the sample questions, you won't be prepared for the real thing. **Study the concepts** until you understand them fully, and then you'll be able to answer any question that shows up on the test.

It's important to wait on the practice tests until you're ready. If you take a test on your first day of study, you may be overwhelmed by the amount of material covered and how much you need to learn. Work up to it gradually.

On test day, you'll need to be prepared for answering questions, managing your time, and using the test-taking strategies you've learned. It's a lot to balance, like a mental marathon that will have a big impact on your future. Like training for a marathon, you'll need to start slowly and work your way up. When test day arrives, you'll be ready.

Start with the strategies you've read in the first two Secret Keys—plan your course and study in the way that works best for you. If you have time, consider using multiple study resources to get different approaches to the same concepts. It can be helpful to see difficult concepts from more than one angle. Then find a good source for practice tests. Many times, the test website will suggest potential study resources or provide sample tests.

Practice Test Strategy

If you're able to find at least three practice tests, we recommend this strategy:

UNTIMED AND OPEN-BOOK PRACTICE

Take the first test with no time constraints and with your notes and study guide handy. Take your time and focus on applying the strategies you've learned.

TIMED AND OPEN-BOOK PRACTICE

Take the second practice test open-book as well, but set a timer and practice pacing yourself to finish in time.

TIMED AND CLOSED-BOOK PRACTICE

Take any other practice tests as if it were test day. Set a timer and put away your study materials. Sit at a table or desk in a quiet room, imagine yourself at the testing center, and answer questions as quickly and accurately as possible.

Keep repeating timed and closed-book tests on a regular basis until you run out of practice tests or it's time for the actual test. Your mind will be ready for the schedule and stress of test day, and you'll be able to focus on recalling the material you've learned.

Secret Key #4 – Pace Yourself

Once you're fully prepared for the material on the test, your biggest challenge on test day will be managing your time. Just knowing that the clock is ticking can make you panic even if you have plenty of time left. Work on pacing yourself so you can build confidence against the time constraints of the exam. Pacing is a difficult skill to master, especially in a high-pressure environment, so **practice is vital**.

Set time expectations for your pace based on how much time is available. For example, if a section has 60 questions and the time limit is 30 minutes, you know you have to average 30 seconds or less per question in order to answer them all. Although 30 seconds is the hard limit, set 25 seconds per question as your goal, so you reserve extra time to spend on harder questions. When you budget extra time for the harder questions, you no longer have any reason to stress when those questions take longer to answer.

Don't let this time expectation distract you from working through the test at a calm, steady pace, but keep it in mind so you don't spend too much time on any one question. Recognize that taking extra time on one question you don't understand may keep you from answering two that you do understand later in the test. If your time limit for a question is up and you're still not sure of the answer, mark it and move on, and come back to it later if the time and the test format allow. If the testing format doesn't allow you to return to earlier questions, just make an educated guess; then put it out of your mind and move on.

On the easier questions, be careful not to rush. It may seem wise to hurry through them so you have more time for the challenging ones, but it's not worth missing one if you know the concept and just didn't take the time to read the question fully. Work efficiently but make sure you understand the question and have looked at all of the answer choices, since more than one may seem right at first.

Even if you're paying attention to the time, you may find yourself a little behind at some point. You should speed up to get back on track, but do so wisely. Don't panic; just take a few seconds less on each question until you're caught up. Don't guess without thinking, but do look through the answer choices and eliminate any you know are wrong. If you can get down to two choices, it is often worthwhile to guess from those. Once you've chosen an answer, move on and don't dwell on any that you skipped or had to hurry through. If a question was taking too long, chances are it was one of the harder ones, so you weren't as likely to get it right anyway.

On the other hand, if you find yourself getting ahead of schedule, it may be beneficial to slow down a little. The more quickly you work, the more likely you are to make a careless mistake that will affect your score. You've budgeted time for each question, so don't be afraid to spend that time. Practice an efficient but careful pace to get the most out of the time you have.

Secret Key #5 – Have a Plan for Guessing

When you're taking the test, you may find yourself stuck on a question. Some of the answer choices seem better than others, but you don't see the one answer choice that is obviously correct. What do you do?

The scenario described above is very common, yet most test takers have not effectively prepared for it. Developing and practicing a plan for guessing may be one of the single most effective uses of your time as you get ready for the exam.

In developing your plan for guessing, there are three questions to address:

- When should you start the guessing process?
- How should you narrow down the choices?
- Which answer should you choose?

When to Start the Guessing Process

Unless your plan for guessing is to select C every time (which, despite its merits, is not what we recommend), you need to leave yourself enough time to apply your answer elimination strategies. Since you have a limited amount of time for each question, that means that if you're going to give yourself the best shot at guessing correctly, you have to decide quickly whether or not you will guess.

Of course, the best-case scenario is that you don't have to guess at all, so first, see if you can answer the question based on your knowledge of the subject and basic reasoning skills. Focus on the key words in the question and try to jog your memory of related topics. Give yourself a chance to bring the knowledge to mind, but once you realize that you don't have (or you can't access) the knowledge you need to answer the question, it's time to start the guessing process.

It's almost always better to start the guessing process too early than too late. It only takes a few seconds to remember something and answer the question from knowledge. Carefully eliminating wrong answer choices takes longer. Plus, going through the process of eliminating answer choices can actually help jog your memory.

Summary: Start the guessing process as soon as you decide that you can't answer the question based on your knowledge.

7

How to Narrow Down the Choices

The next chapter in this book (**Test-Taking Strategies**) includes a wide range of strategies for how to approach questions and how to look for answer choices to eliminate. You will definitely want to read those carefully, practice them, and figure out which ones work best for you. Here though, we're going to address a mindset rather than a particular strategy.

Your odds of guessing an answer correctly depend on how many options you are choosing from.

Number of options left	5	4	3	2	1
Odds of guessing correctly	20%	25%	33%	50%	100%

You can see from this chart just how valuable it is to be able to eliminate incorrect answers and make an educated guess, but there are two things that many test takers do that cause them to miss out on the benefits of guessing:

- Accidentally eliminating the correct answer
- Selecting an answer based on an impression

We'll look at the first one here, and the second one in the next section.

To avoid accidentally eliminating the correct answer, we recommend a thought exercise called **the $5 challenge**. In this challenge, you only eliminate an answer choice from contention if you are willing to bet $5 on it being wrong. Why $5? Five dollars is a small but not insignificant amount of money. It's an amount you could afford to lose but wouldn't want to throw away. And while losing

$5 once might not hurt too much, doing it twenty times will set you back $100. In the same way, each small decision you make—eliminating a choice here, guessing on a question there—won't by itself impact your score very much, but when you put them all together, they can make a big difference. By holding each answer choice elimination decision to a higher standard, you can reduce the risk of accidentally eliminating the correct answer.

The $5 challenge can also be applied in a positive sense: If you are willing to bet $5 that an answer choice *is* correct, go ahead and mark it as correct.

Summary: Only eliminate an answer choice if you are willing to bet $5 that it is wrong.

Which Answer to Choose

You're taking the test. You've run into a hard question and decided you'll have to guess. You've eliminated all the answer choices you're willing to bet $5 on. Now you have to pick an answer. Why do we even need to talk about this? Why can't you just pick whichever one you feel like when the time comes?

The answer to these questions is that if you don't come into the test with a plan, you'll rely on your impression to select an answer choice, and if you do that, you risk falling into a trap. The test writers know that everyone who takes their test will be guessing on some of the questions, so they intentionally write wrong answer choices to seem plausible. You still have to pick an answer though, and if the wrong answer choices are designed to look right, how can you ever be sure that you're not falling for their trap? The best solution we've found to this dilemma is to take the decision out of your hands entirely. Here is the process we recommend:

Once you've eliminated any choices that you are confident (willing to bet $5) are wrong, select the first remaining choice as your answer.

Whether you choose to select the first remaining choice, the second, or the last, the important thing is that you use some preselected standard. Using this approach guarantees that you will not be enticed into selecting an answer choice that looks right, because you are not basing your decision on how the answer choices look.

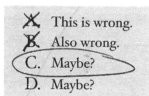

This is not meant to make you question your knowledge. Instead, it is to help you recognize the difference between your knowledge and your impressions. There's a huge difference between thinking an answer is right because of what you know, and thinking an answer is right because it looks or sounds like it should be right.

Summary: To ensure that your selection is appropriately random, make a predetermined selection from among all answer choices you have not eliminated.

9

Test-Taking Strategies

This section contains a list of test-taking strategies that you may find helpful as you work through the test. By taking what you know and applying logical thought, you can maximize your chances of answering any question correctly!

It is very important to realize that every question is different and every person is different: no single strategy will work on every question, and no single strategy will work for every person. That's why we've included all of them here, so you can try them out and determine which ones work best for different types of questions and which ones work best for you.

Question Strategies

⊘ READ CAREFULLY

Read the question and the answer choices carefully. Don't miss the question because you misread the terms. You have plenty of time to read each question thoroughly and make sure you understand what is being asked. Yet a happy medium must be attained, so don't waste too much time. You must read carefully and efficiently.

⊘ CONTEXTUAL CLUES

Look for contextual clues. If the question includes a word you are not familiar with, look at the immediate context for some indication of what the word might mean. Contextual clues can often give you all the information you need to decipher the meaning of an unfamiliar word. Even if you can't determine the meaning, you may be able to narrow down the possibilities enough to make a solid guess at the answer to the question.

⊘ PREFIXES

If you're having trouble with a word in the question or answer choices, try dissecting it. Take advantage of every clue that the word might include. Prefixes and suffixes can be a huge help. Usually, they allow you to determine a basic meaning. *Pre-* means before, *post-* means after, *pro-* is positive, *de-* is negative. From prefixes and suffixes, you can get an idea of the general meaning of the word and try to put it into context.

⊘ HEDGE WORDS

Watch out for critical hedge words, such as *likely, may, can, sometimes, often, almost, mostly, usually, generally, rarely,* and *sometimes*. Question writers insert these hedge phrases to cover every possibility. Often an answer choice will be wrong simply because it leaves no room for exception. Be on guard for answer choices that have definitive words such as *exactly* and *always*.

⊘ SWITCHBACK WORDS

Stay alert for *switchbacks*. These are the words and phrases frequently used to alert you to shifts in thought. The most common switchback words are *but, although,* and *however*. Others include *nevertheless, on the other hand, even though, while, in spite of, despite,* and *regardless of*. Switchback words are important to catch because they can change the direction of the question or an answer choice.

⊘ Face Value

When in doubt, use common sense. Accept the situation in the problem at face value. Don't read too much into it. These problems will not require you to make wild assumptions. If you have to go beyond creativity and warp time or space in order to have an answer choice fit the question, then you should move on and consider the other answer choices. These are normal problems rooted in reality. The applicable relationship or explanation may not be readily apparent, but it is there for you to figure out. Use your common sense to interpret anything that isn't clear.

Answer Choice Strategies

⊘ Answer Selection

The most thorough way to pick an answer choice is to identify and eliminate wrong answers until only one is left, then confirm it is the correct answer. Sometimes an answer choice may immediately seem right, but be careful. The test writers will usually put more than one reasonable answer choice on each question, so take a second to read all of them and make sure that the other choices are not equally obvious. As long as you have time left, it is better to read every answer choice than to pick the first one that looks right without checking the others.

⊘ Answer Choice Families

An answer choice family consists of two (in rare cases, three) answer choices that are very similar in construction and cannot all be true at the same time. If you see two answer choices that are direct opposites or parallels, one of them is usually the correct answer. For instance, if one answer choice says that quantity x increases and another either says that quantity x decreases (opposite) or says that quantity y increases (parallel), then those answer choices would fall into the same family. An answer choice that doesn't match the construction of the answer choice family is more likely to be incorrect. Most questions will not have answer choice families, but when they do appear, you should be prepared to recognize them.

⊘ Eliminate Answers

Eliminate answer choices as soon as you realize they are wrong, but make sure you consider all possibilities. If you are eliminating answer choices and realize that the last one you are left with is also wrong, don't panic. Start over and consider each choice again. There may be something you missed the first time that you will realize on the second pass.

⊘ Avoid Fact Traps

Don't be distracted by an answer choice that is factually true but doesn't answer the question. You are looking for the choice that answers the question. Stay focused on what the question is asking for so you don't accidentally pick an answer that is true but incorrect. Always go back to the question and make sure the answer choice you've selected actually answers the question and is not merely a true statement.

⊘ Extreme Statements

In general, you should avoid answers that put forth extreme actions as standard practice or proclaim controversial ideas as established fact. An answer choice that states the "process should be used in certain situations, if..." is much more likely to be correct than one that states the "process should be discontinued completely." The first is a calm rational statement and doesn't even make a definitive, uncompromising stance, using a hedge word *if* to provide wiggle room, whereas the second choice is far more extreme.

11

⊘ BENCHMARK

As you read through the answer choices and you come across one that seems to answer the question well, mentally select that answer choice. This is not your final answer, but it's the one that will help you evaluate the other answer choices. The one that you selected is your benchmark or standard for judging each of the other answer choices. Every other answer choice must be compared to your benchmark. That choice is correct until proven otherwise by another answer choice beating it. If you find a better answer, then that one becomes your new benchmark. Once you've decided that no other choice answers the question as well as your benchmark, you have your final answer.

⊘ PREDICT THE ANSWER

Before you even start looking at the answer choices, it is often best to try to predict the answer. When you come up with the answer on your own, it is easier to avoid distractions and traps because you will know exactly what to look for. The right answer choice is unlikely to be word-for-word what you came up with, but it should be a close match. Even if you are confident that you have the right answer, you should still take the time to read each option before moving on.

General Strategies

⊘ TOUGH QUESTIONS

If you are stumped on a problem or it appears too hard or too difficult, don't waste time. Move on! Remember though, if you can quickly check for obviously incorrect answer choices, your chances of guessing correctly are greatly improved. Before you completely give up, at least try to knock out a couple of possible answers. Eliminate what you can and then guess at the remaining answer choices before moving on.

⊘ CHECK YOUR WORK

Since you will probably not know every term listed and the answer to every question, it is important that you get credit for the ones that you do know. Don't miss any questions through careless mistakes. If at all possible, try to take a second to look back over your answer selection and make sure you've selected the correct answer choice and haven't made a costly careless mistake (such as marking an answer choice that you didn't mean to mark). This quick double check should more than pay for itself in caught mistakes for the time it costs.

⊘ PACE YOURSELF

It's easy to be overwhelmed when you're looking at a page full of questions; your mind is confused and full of random thoughts, and the clock is ticking down faster than you would like. Calm down and maintain the pace that you have set for yourself. Especially as you get down to the last few minutes of the test, don't let the small numbers on the clock make you panic. As long as you are on track by monitoring your pace, you are guaranteed to have time for each question.

⊘ DON'T RUSH

It is very easy to make errors when you are in a hurry. Maintaining a fast pace in answering questions is pointless if it makes you miss questions that you would have gotten right otherwise. Test writers like to include distracting information and wrong answers that seem right. Taking a little extra time to avoid careless mistakes can make all the difference in your test score. Find a pace that allows you to be confident in the answers that you select.

12

⊘ Keep Moving

Panicking will not help you pass the test, so do your best to stay calm and keep moving. Taking deep breaths and going through the answer elimination steps you practiced can help to break through a stress barrier and keep your pace.

Final Notes

The combination of a solid foundation of content knowledge and the confidence that comes from practicing your plan for applying that knowledge is the key to maximizing your performance on test day. As your foundation of content knowledge is built up and strengthened, you'll find that the strategies included in this chapter become more and more effective in helping you quickly sift through the distractions and traps of the test to isolate the correct answer.

Now that you're preparing to move forward into the test content chapters of this book, be sure to keep your goal in mind. As you read, think about how you will be able to apply this information on the test. If you've already seen sample questions for the test and you have an idea of the question format and style, try to come up with questions of your own that you can answer based on what you're reading. This will give you valuable practice applying your knowledge in the same ways you can expect to on test day.

Good luck and good studying!

Development and Characteristics of Students with EBD

Development and Characteristics of Students with Disabilities

TYPES OF DISABILITY CATEGORIES

Specific Learning Disabilities (SLD) is the umbrella term for children who struggle with issues in their abilities to read, write, speak, listen, reason, or do math. **Other Health Impairment (OHI)** is another umbrella term for a disability that limits a child's strength, energy, or alertness. **Autism Spectrum Disorder (ASD)** is a disability that mostly affects a child's social and communication skills, and sometimes behavior. **Emotional Disturbance (ED)** is a disability category for a number of mental disorders. **Speech or Language Impairment** covers children with language impairments. **Visual Impairment or Blindness** is a disability category for children with visual impairments that significantly impair their abilities to learn. **Deafness, Hearing Impairment**, and **Deaf-Blindness** cover children diagnosed with these disabilities. Children with **Orthopedic Impairments** have impairments to their bodies. An **Intellectual Disability** is the diagnosis for students with below-average intellectual abilities. **Traumatic Brain Injury (TBI)** covers children who have suffered from TBIs. A diagnosis of **Multiple Disabilities** means a child has more than one disability defined by IDEA.

INTERVENTIONS FOR STUDENTS WITH PHYSICAL DISABILITIES

A physical disability refers to any disability that limits **gross mobility** and prevents **normal body movement**. For example, muscular dystrophy is a physical disability that weakens the muscles of the human body over time. Students with physical disabilities require early interventions before grade school, if applicable. When students with physical disabilities enter grade school, they may receive interventions and related services if they qualify for special education and receive **Individualized Education Programs** or **504 Plans**. When physical disabilities do not affect the students' academic success, they may be put on 504 Plans to receive appropriate related services, accommodations, or modifications. When physical disabilities are present with other disabilities, or the physical disabilities affect academic performance, students may be put on Individualized Education Programs. They may also receive appropriate related services, accommodations, and modifications. Teachers, intervention specialists, physiotherapists, occupational therapists, and speech language pathologists are all team members that work with students with physical disabilities by assisting and implementing appropriate accommodations, modifications, and related services.

DYSLEXIA AND DYSGRAPHIA DISORDERS

Students with dyslexia are eligible for special education with a specific learning disability under the Individuals with Disabilities Education Act if their educational performances are significantly impacted by their disabilities. **Dyslexia** is a permanent condition that makes it difficult for people to read. This affects reading accuracy, fluency, and comprehension. Dyslexia also generalizes to difficulties in the content areas of writing, mathematics, spelling, and reading comprehension. Children who have dyslexia often have difficulties with **phonemic awareness skills** and **decoding**. It is not a disability that affects vision or the way people see letters. Dyslexia may coexist with other conditions such as **dysgraphia**, which is a disorder that causes issues with written expression. With dysgraphia, children often struggle with holding pencils and writing letters accurately. It is difficult

15

for students with dysgraphia to distinguish shapes, use correct letter spacing, read maps, copy text, understand spelling rules, and more.

BEHAVIORAL ISSUES FOR STUDENTS WITH AUTISM

Autism is a **spectrum disorder**, which means the characteristics associated with the disability vary depending on the student. However, there are common repetitive and patterned behaviors associated with communication and social interactions for this population of students. Students with autism may demonstrate delayed or different speech patterns, the inability to understand body language or facial expressions, and the inability to exhibit appropriate speech patterns, body language, or facial expressions. In a classroom environment, students with autism may demonstrate **repetitive behaviors** that are distracting, such as hand flapping or making vocalizations. Some students with autism demonstrate **preoccupation** with doing activities, tasks, or routines in certain ways. This preoccupation can lead to difficulties when the students are asked to make changes to the activities, tasks, or routines. Furthermore, some students with autism prefer to **participate** in a limited range of activities and may get upset when asked to participate in activities outside of their self-perceived ranges. Repetitive behaviors may translate into obsessions or excessive knowledge relating to one particular topic. Extreme interests in one topic can turn into disruptions when students with autism are asked to speak or write about different topics.

EFFECT OF HEARING LOSS ON LANGUAGE DEVELOPMENT

Hearing language is part of learning language. Children with **hearing loss** miss out on sounds associated with language, and this can affect their listening, speaking, reading, social skills, and overall school success. Hearing loss can sometimes lead to delayed speech and language, learning disabilities in school, insecurities, and issues with socialization and making friends. Children with hearing loss may:

- have trouble learning abstract vocabulary (i.e. since, before).
- omit article words in sentences (i.e. a, an).
- fall behind on core components of learning and development without early interventions.
- have difficulty speaking in and/or understanding sentences.
- speak in shorter sentences.
- have difficulty including word endings (i.e. -ing, -s).
- have issues speaking clearly because they cannot accurately hear sounds.
- omit quiet sounds, like *p, sh,* or *f.*
- be unable to hear what their own voices sound like.

Children with hearing loss are more likely to fall behind in school due to their hearing deficits. They can easily fall behind without support from interventions, teachers, and their families. Early **hearing testing** is essential to ensure that interventions, such as sign language, can be introduced to promote school and life success for children with hearing loss.

RECEPTIVE LANGUAGE DISORDERS

Children with receptive language disorders often demonstrate appropriate expressive language skills and hear and read at age-appropriate levels. They may seem like they are not paying attention or engaging in activities, or appear to have difficulties following or understanding directions. They may refrain from asking questions or interrupt frequently during activities, especially during read aloud activities. It may appear as if they are not listening, but children with receptive language disorders cannot perceive **meaning** from what they hear. Children with this disorder may consistently leave tasks incomplete unless the tasks are broken down into smaller steps. This is due to issues with directions, especially **verbal directions**. Children with receptive language disorders may not respond appropriately or at all to questions from peers or adults. Answers to comprehension questions, especially when texts are read aloud, may be off topic or incorrect. Children with receptive language disorders have trouble gathering and connecting meaning to what they hear. A receptive language disorder is not exclusively a learning disability. However, children who have receptive disorders may have learning disabilities.

TYPES OF DISABILITIES

Medical disabilities include problems related to diseases, illnesses, and trauma. Medical disabilities can also include problems related to genetics. **Physical disabilities** include problems related to fine and gross motor skills and can include sensory input or sensory perception disorders. Medical and physical disabilities often manifest with other disabilities, such as **learning disabilities**. Medical disabilities, such as a student whose health issue affects educational performance, are usually categorized under the *Other Health Impaired* or *Traumatic Brain Injury* eligibility categories under the Individuals with Disabilities Education Act (IDEA). People with physical disabilities, such as cerebral palsy, can be eligible for special education under IDEA under the Orthopedic Impairment category. However, for both medical and physical disabilities to qualify, a student's medical or physical disability must **adversely affect educational performance**. For example, a student with cerebral palsy may not be eligible for special education or an Individualized Education Program if the disability does not affect educational performance. The student would receive accommodations and modifications under a 504 Plan.

EDUCATIONAL IMPLICATIONS OF A DIAGNOSIS OF SLD, OHI, ASD, AND ED

Students with **Specific Learning Disability** (SLD) may struggle with instruction in general education classrooms and require specific instruction fine-tuned to their individual needs. Their annual IEP goals may target specific skills that are not age appropriate but are appropriate to their unique learning needs. An **OHI (Other Health Impairment)** diagnosis can include children with ADHD, diabetes, HIV/AIDS, heart conditions, and more. Students with OHI receive accommodations for their unique health or educational needs on a case-by-case basis. Students with **Autism Spectrum Disorder (ASD)** may rely on the use of visuals or access to other ways to express feelings or communicate. Students with ASD may not respond to everyday conversations or classroom situations the same ways their peers do. They require supports to learn how to express their needs within the general education classroom. Students with **emotional disturbances (ED)** exhibit an inability to learn that is not due to intellectual, sensory, or health problems. Students with ED also exhibit inability to form and maintain appropriate relationships with peers and adults, demonstrate inappropriate behaviors, and may exhibit depression or general unhappiness.

EARLY CHARACTERISTICS INDICATING A CHILD HAS A SPECIFIC LEARNING DISABILITY

Early characteristics that indicate a specific learning disability (**SLD**) include factors like medical history, speech acquisition, problems with socialization, academic delays, and behavioral delays. Delays in certain milestones may indicate learning disabilities, but these delays may also be due to other causes. Premature birth, serious childhood illnesses, frequent ear infections, and sleep disorders are **medical factors** that can influence the development of learning disabilities. Children that develop SLDs may demonstrate early delays in **oral speech**. For example, late speech development, pronunciation problems, and stuttering may indicate SLDs, but these issues may also sometimes be addressed by individualized speech instruction. Students with SLDs may also have problems adjusting **socially**. They may demonstrate social skills that are not age appropriate. Depending on when the children enter academic settings, they may demonstrate academic delays compared to similar-aged peers. These delays are usually determined using formal and informal assessments in educational settings. **Behaviors** such as hyperactivity or difficulty following directions may also indicate a child has a SLD. However, these indicators do not definitely mean that a child has a learning disability, and some of the indicators overlap with characteristics of other disabilities.

INSTRUCTIONAL STRATEGIES FOR TEACHING STUDENTS WITH SPECIFIC LEARNING DISABILITIES

While there is no one strategy that works effectively with all students with specific learning disabilities, there are some strategies that tend to produce **positive outcomes** for these students. Direct instruction, learning strategy instruction, and a multi-sensory approach are three large-scale interventions that can be used to promote student learning. **Direct instruction** is teacher-driven instruction that targets specific skills. Direct instruction is sometimes delivered in resource rooms. **Learning strategy instruction** is a method for teaching students with disabilities different tools and techniques useful for learning new content or skills. Learning strategy instruction includes techniques like chunking the content, sequencing tasks, and small group instruction. A **multi-sensory approach** ensures that students are receiving and interacting with new information and skills using more than one sense at a time. This approach is helpful for students with learning disabilities because it targets many different ways of learning.

CHILDREN WITH EMOTIONAL DISTURBANCES

A diagnosis of an emotional disturbance can also be referred to as a **behavioral disorder** or **mental illness**. Causes of emotional disturbances are generally unclear. However, heredity, brain disorders, and diet are some factors that influence the development of emotional disturbances. Emotional disturbance is the general term for children with anxiety disorders, bipolar disorder, eating disorders, obsessive-compulsive disorder, or any other psychotic disorders. The Individuals with Disabilities Education Act states that emotional disturbances can affect children beyond emotion and make them eligible for **special education** with this diagnosis. Children's cognitive, physical, or social behaviors may also be affected. Indicators of emotional disturbances include hyperactivity, aggression, withdrawal, immaturity, and academic difficulties. While many children demonstrate these indicators throughout their development, a strong indicator of an emotional disturbance is a **prolonged demonstration** of these behaviors. Children who have emotional disorders demonstrate behaviors associated with particular disorders. For example, a child with obsessive-compulsive disorder will demonstrate uncontrolled, reoccurring thoughts and behaviors.

ISSUES STUDENTS WITH ED EXPERIENCE IN THE INSTRUCTIONAL SETTING

Students with the diagnosis of emotional disturbance (ED) as defined by the Individuals with Disabilities Education Act require **emotional and behavioral support** in the classroom. Students with ED may also require **specialized academic instruction** in addition to behavioral and emotional support. The amount of support given varies according to the needs of individual students. These students also need **scaffolded instruction** in social skills, self-awareness, self-esteem, and self-control. Students with ED often exhibit behaviors that impede their learning or the learning of others. **Positive Behavioral Support (PBS)** is a preventative instructional strategy that focuses on promoting positive behaviors in students. With PBS, teachers or other professionals make changes to students' environments in order to decrease problem behaviors. PBS involves the process of collecting information on the behavior, identifying positive ways to support the behavior, and implementing a support to decrease the behavior. Supports can be implemented schoolwide or in the classroom. However, for students with ED, **classroom supports** are more effective because they can be individualized.

SIGNS INDICATING A CHILD HAS A SPEECH OR LANGUAGE IMPAIRMENT

Speech and language impairments, sometimes referred to as **communication disorders**, are disabilities recognized by the Individuals with Disabilities Education Act. Students diagnosed with communication disorders are eligible for special education if they qualify for services. Early indicators of communication disorders include but are not limited to:

- not smiling or interacting with others.
- lack of babbling or cooing in infants.
- lack of age-appropriate comprehension skills.
- speech that is not easily understood.
- issues with age-appropriate syntax development.
- issues with age-appropriate social skills.
- deficits in reading and writing skills.

Stuttering, beginning or ending words with incorrect sounds, and hearing loss are also indicators of possible communication disorders. These are symptoms of communication disorders, but they can also be linked to other disabilities, such as hearing impairments or autism. A prolonged demonstration of these indicators may suggest communication disorders. However, children can demonstrate delays and self-correct as they grow.

QUALIFICATIONS TO BE ELIGIBLE FOR SPECIAL EDUCATION UNDER THE CATEGORY OF OHI

The category of **Other Health Impaired** (OHI) under the Individuals with Disabilities Education Act (IDEA) indicates that a child has **limited strength, vitality, or alertness**. This includes hyper-alertness or hypo-alertness to environmental stimuli. In order to be eligible for special education under this category according to IDEA, the disability must **adversely affect educational performance**. It must also be due to **chronic or acute health problems**, such as attention deficit disorder (ADD), attention deficit hyperactivity disorder (ADHD), diabetes, epilepsy, heart conditions, hemophilia, lead poisoning, leukemia, nephritis, rheumatic fever, sickle cell anemia, or Tourette's Syndrome. It is important to note that in order to be eligible under this category, the disability must be affecting a child's academic performance. Since the OHI category encompasses a number of different disabilities, teachers and parents must rely on a student's Individualized Education Program to ensure that individual academic needs are met and appropriate accommodations and modifications are provided.

EDUCATIONAL IMPLICATIONS AND LIMITATIONS OF STUDENTS ELIGIBLE FOR SPECIAL EDUCATION

According to the Individuals with Disabilities Education Act (IDEA), students who are eligible for special education under the category of **Intellectual Disability** have significantly lower intellectual abilities, along with adaptive behavior deficits. Previously, intellectual disability was referred to as mental retardation. In 2010, President Obama signed **Rosa's Law**, which changed the term to *intellectual disability*. The definition of the disability category remained unchanged. Educational implications of a diagnosis of an intellectual disability differ depending on students' needs as determined by their Individualized Education Programs (IEPs). Students with intellectual disabilities often display **limitations to mental functioning** in skills like communication, self-care, and social skills (adaptive behavior). In many cases, these skills must be addressed in the educational environments in addition to any academic skill deficits. Learning adaptive behaviors and academic skills takes longer for students with intellectual disabilities, so their special education placements depend upon what environments are least restrictive. This depends on the individual student and is determined in the IEP.

COMPONENTS OF THE MULTIPLE DISABILITY ELIGIBILITY CATEGORY ACCORDING TO IDEA

A diagnosis of multiple disabilities according to the Individuals with Disabilities Education Act (IDEA) indicates two or more disabilities occurring simultaneously. The difference between a diagnosis of intellectual disability and **multiple disabilities** is that students with multiple disabilities present with such **severe educational needs** that they cannot be accommodated in special education settings that address only one disability. Students with multiple disabilities require assistance for more than one disability. Their educational performances are adversely affected by their disabilities. Placement in special education programs is determined by students' **least restrictive environments** and defined in their **Individualized Education Programs**. The multiple disability category does not encompass deaf-blindness, which has its own category under IDEA. Students with multiple disabilities often present with communication deficits and difficulties, mobility challenges, deficits in adaptive behavior, and the need for one-on-one instruction or assistance when performing daily activities.

QUALIFICATIONS TO RECEIVE SPECIAL EDUCATION FOR ORTHOPEDIC IMPAIRMENT

A student who qualifies to receive special education under the Individuals with Disabilities Education Act category for **Orthopedic Impairment** has a disability that adversely affects educational performance. This includes children with congenital anomalies, impairments caused by disease, or impairments from other causes, such as cerebral palsy or amputations. An orthopedic impairment alone does not qualify a student for special education and an Individualized Education Program. Once a student's educational performance is proven to be affected by the orthopedic impairment, the student can be eligible for special education and placed on an **IEP**. The IEP determines the student's least restrictive environment, individualized goals for academic skills or adaptive behavior, and any appropriate accommodations or modifications. Students with orthopedic impairments whose educational performances are not affected may receive accommodations and modifications on **504 Plans** if appropriate for their disabilities. Strategies for instruction should be determined and implemented on a case-by-case basis, as the orthopedic impairment category covers a broad range of disabilities.

STRATEGIES FACILITATING LEARNING IN STUDENTS WITH SPEECH OR LANGUAGE IMPAIRMENTS

In order to teach students with speech or language impairments, also referred to as **communication disorders**, special educators and professionals can use certain strategies to ensure learning takes place. Teachers and other professionals can use the **strategies** listed below:

- Use visuals and concrete examples to help students with communication disorders take in new information visually. Link the visuals with spoken words or phrases.
- Use visuals or photographs to introduce or reinforce vocabulary.
- Use repetition of spoken words to introduce or reinforce vocabulary.
- Model conversational and social skills, which helps students with communication disorders become familiar with word pronunciation.
- Speak at a slower rate when necessary, especially when presenting new information.
- Consistently check for understanding.
- Be aware that communication issues may sometimes result in other issues, such as behavioral or social skill issues.
- Pair actions and motions with words to emphasize meaning, especially for students with receptive language disorders.

DETERMINING IF A CHILD MAY HAVE AN INTELLECTUAL DISABILITY

Students diagnosed with intellectual disabilities (**ID**) demonstrate deficits in academic skills, abstract thinking, problem solving, language development, new skill acquisition, and retaining information. Students with intellectual disabilities do not adequately meet developmental or social milestones. They demonstrate **deficits in functioning** with one or more basic living skills. Students with intellectual disabilities struggle conceptually and sometimes demonstrate delays in language development. They may also have difficulties with time and money concepts, short-term memory, time management skills, pre-academic and academic skills, planning, and strategizing. Socially, this population of students may also grasp concrete concepts over abstract concepts, but in a process that is significantly behind their similar-aged, regular education peers. Students with ID demonstrate poor social judgement and decision-making skills because they have trouble understanding social cues and rules. These students also tend to struggle with self-care skills, household tasks, and completing tasks that may be easy for similar-aged peers.

PROMOTING A POSITIVE EDUCATIONAL PERFORMANCE FOR STUDENTS WITH INTELLECTUAL DISABILITIES

Students with intellectual disabilities often present skills that are far below the skill levels of similar-aged peers. Due to skill deficits in academic, behavioral, and social skills, these students require **specialized instruction** to address specific skills. The skills addressed vary depending on the needs of each individual student. An effective strategy for promoting a positive educational performance is to collect observations and data on the academic, behavioral, and social skill levels of the individual student. Teachers usually work with related services members, like speech language pathologists, to address needs and implement educational interventions that work for this population of students. These students can benefit from **communication interventions** focused on interactions the students may have with adults and peers. Students may benefit from augmentative communication devices, visual activity schedules, visual supports, and computer-based instruction to teach communication and social skills. Students with ID may also require **behavioral interventions** to teach appropriate behaviors or decrease negative behaviors. They may also benefit from increased **peer interactions** through structured social groups in order to promote appropriate communication skills.

EARLY INDICATIONS OF VISUAL IMPAIRMENT OR BLINDNESS

A visual impairment ranges from low vision to blindness. The Individuals with Disabilities Education Act defines a **visual impairment** as an impairment in vision that is great enough to affect a child's educational performance. **Blindness** is defined as a visual acuity of 20/200 or less in the dominant eye. Some people diagnosed with blindness still have minimal sight. Early indicators of a visual impairment or blindness for children include:

- holding things closely to their eyes or faces.
- experiencing fatigue after looking at things closely.
- misaligned eyes or squinting.
- tilting heads or covering eyes to see things up close or far away.
- demonstrating clumsiness.
- appearing to see better during the day.

Students who are diagnosed with visual impairments or blindness who are also eligible for special education benefit the most from early interventions, especially when the impairments are present with other disabilities. Appropriate interventions vary based on each student and whether or not the impairments are paired with other disabilities. Modifications, such as magnified text, Braille, auditory support, and text-tracking software, also help level the learning plane for these students.

EARLY COMMUNICATION AND SOCIAL SKILL DELAYS IN STUDENTS WITH ASD

Students with delays in communication development often need and receive some type of assistance or instruction with communication and social skills. For students with **Autism Spectrum Disorder (ASD)**, the need for communication and social skill instruction varies depending on the individual student. Early intervention for these students is key, as communication difficulties are an early symptom of Autism Spectrum Disorder. Key characteristics of **early communication difficulties** for a student with ASD may include not responding to his/her name, not pointing at objects of interest, avoiding eye contact, not engaging in pretend play, delayed speech or language skills, or repeating words or phrases. Children with ASD may also exhibit overreaction or underreaction to environmental stimuli. Key characteristics of **early social skill difficulties** for a student with ASD may include preferring to play alone, trouble understanding personal feelings or the feelings of others, not sharing interests with others, and difficulty with personal space boundaries. Infants with ASD may not respond to their names and demonstrate reduced babbling and reduced interest in people. Toddlers with ASD may demonstrate decreased interest in social interactions, difficulty with pretend play, and a preference for playing alone.

CHARACTERISTICS OF SOCIAL SKILL DELAYS IN STUDENTS WITH ASD

Autism Spectrum Disorder (ASD) is a disability that can affect a student's social, communication, and behavioral abilities. **Social skill delays and deficits** are common for students with ASD. Characteristics of social skill delays go hand-in-hand with **communication limitations** for students with ASD. This includes conversational focus on one or two narrow topics or ideas. This limits their conversations to one or two subject areas, and it is difficult for them to hold two-way conversations about things that do not interest them. Some students with ASD engage in repetitive language or echolalia or rely on standard phrases to communicate with others. Their **speech and language skills** may be delayed compared to their similar-aged peers. This may also affect their abilities to engage in effective, two-way conversations. The **nonverbal skills** of students with ASD may also be misinterpreted, such as avoiding eye contact while speaking or being spoken to.

EARLY SIGNS OF A CHILD HAVING ASD

Early signs of **Autism Spectrum Disorder** (ASD) include impairments or delays in social interactions and communication, repetitive behaviors, limited interests, and abnormal eating habits. Students with ASD typically do not interact in conversations in the same ways as similar-aged peers without ASD. They may demonstrate inability to engage in pretend play and may pretend they don't hear when being spoken to. Hand flapping, vocal sounds, or compulsive interactions with objects are repetitive behaviors sometimes demonstrated by students with ASD. They may only demonstrate interest in talking about one topic or be interested in interacting with one object. They may also demonstrate self-injurious behavior or sleep problems, in addition to having a limited diet of preferred foods. **Early intervention** is key for these students in order to address and improve functioning. These students may also benefit from **applied behavior analysis** to target specific behaviors and require speech and language therapy, occupational therapy, social skills instruction, or other services geared toward improving intellectual functioning.

LOW-INCIDENCE DISABILITIES AND HIGH-INCIDENCE DISABILITIES

Low-incidence disabilities account for up to 20% of all students' disabilities. Students with low-incidence disabilities have sometimes received assistance for their disabilities starting from an early age. This group includes students with intellectual disabilities and significant developmental delays. **Low-incidence disabilities** can include intellectual disabilities, multiple disabilities, hearing impairments, orthopedic impairments, other health impairments, visual impairments, autism, deaf-blindness, traumatic brain injury, and developmental delays. **High-incidence disabilities** account for up to 80% of all students' disabilities. Students with high-incidence disabilities present with academic, social, and/or behavioral problems and can often be held to the same standards as their regular education peers. Children with high-incidence disabilities may perform at the same capacities as their similar-aged peers but have deficits in reading, math, writing, handwriting, or maintaining attention. They may also present with limitations in communication, adaptive behavior, and social skills. Examples of high-incidence disabilities include speech and language impairments, learning disabilities, attention deficit hyperactivity disorder, emotional disorders, mild intellectual disabilities, certain spectrums of autism, and cognitive delays.

SENSORY PROCESSING DISORDERS

When a person experiences a deficit with handling sensory information interpreted by the brain, this is called a **sensory processing disorder (SPD)**. In brains without SPD, people can experience sensory input, and their brain receptors can interpret them to demonstrate appropriate reactions. In brains of people with SPD, the brains experience sensory input, but the brains' receptors are blocked, resulting in abnormal reactions. Previously known as a sensory integration disorder, SPD is not a disability specifically defined or eligible under the Individuals with Disabilities Education Act (IDEA). However, many students with disabilities defined by IDEA, like autism, also experience some sort of sensory processing disorder. Students with SPD may display **oversensitive or under-sensitive responses** to their environments, stimuli, and senses. Students with SPD may not understand physical boundaries, such as where their bodies are in space. They may bump into things and demonstrate clumsiness. These students may get upset easily, throw tantrums, demonstrate high anxiety, and not handle changes well.

CHARACTERISTICS AND CAUSES OF ADHD AND ADD

Children with **Attention Deficit Hyperactivity Disorder** (ADHD) may demonstrate hyperactivity, inattention, and impulsivity. However, they may demonstrate hyperactivity and inattention only or hyperactivity and impulsivity. Children with **Attention Deficit Disorder** (ADD) demonstrate inattention and impulsivity, but not hyperactivity. Students with either ADHD or ADD may have difficulties with attention span, following instructions, and concentrating to the point that educational performance is affected. Since ADD and ADHD symptoms are common among children, their presence does not necessarily indicate that a child needs a diagnosis of ADD or ADHD. ADD and ADHD are not caused by certain environmental factors, such as diet or watching too much television. Symptoms may be exacerbated by these factors, but the real causes can be heredity, chemical imbalances, issues with brain functions, environmental toxins, or prenatal trauma, such as the mother smoking or drinking during pregnancy.

IMPORTANCE OF ADAPTIVE BEHAVIOR SKILLS INSTRUCTION FOR STUDENTS WITH DISABILITIES

Adaptive behavior skills refer to age-appropriate behaviors that people need to live independently and function in daily life. **Adaptive behavior skills** include self-care skills, following rules, managing money, making friends, and more. For students with disabilities, especially severely limiting disabilities, adaptive behavior skills may need to be included in daily instruction. Adaptive behavior skills can be separated into conceptual skills, social skills, and practical life skills. **Conceptual skills** include academic concepts, such as reading, math, money, time, and communication skills. **Social skills** instruction focuses on teaching students to get along with others, communicate appropriately, and maintain appropriate behavior inside and outside the school environment. **Practical life skills** are skills needed to perform the tasks of daily living. Adaptive behavior assessments are useful in assessing what adaptive behavior skills need to be addressed for each student. These assessments are usually conducted using observations and questionnaires completed by parents, teachers, or students.

EFFECT OF ENVIRONMENTAL FACTORS ON SOCIAL-EMOTIONAL DEVELOPMENT

A person's **environment** has a large impact on social-emotional environment. Factors that impact a child's social-emotional development include:

- family relationships and environment.
- play-based learning.
- a nurturing environment.
- verbal skills.

Children who grow up with strong, solid family relationships in stable environments tend to develop appropriate **social-emotional skills**. Children who experience family or environmental stress and trauma, such as divorce or constant fighting, may demonstrate deficits in their social-emotional growth. **Play-based learning** fosters important skills and brain development when children observe adults demonstrating acceptable social behavior. In positive, nurturing environments, children learn by watching adults interacting appropriately with one another. They learn skills that foster social and emotional well-being. The first sounds infants hear are voices. Children first grasp a sense of spoken language in their home environments. Caregivers that speak to their children consistently help them develop **strong verbal skills**.

PHYSICAL STAGES OF GROSS MOTOR DEVELOPMENT IN CHILDREN

Gross motor skills refer to larger motor skills that require movement of the body as a whole. Gross motor skills begin developing in **infancy** as children learn to crawl and walk. At ages **two to three**, children transition from toddling to walking, then learn to jump, run, hop, throw, catch, and push themselves in riding toys with their feet. Children ages **three to four** become skilled at stair climbing. They also jump higher and develop better upper body mobility. Additionally, they develop the ability to ride a small bike or tricycle and kick large balls accurately. At ages **four to five**, children can go up and down stairs with ease. They also develop running mobility skills and speed and have more control when riding bikes or tricycles. Children ages **five to six** fine tune previously learned gross motor skills. They are more adept at physical play skills, such as those needed to play on jungle gyms or swings independently. Children in this age range demonstrate interest in organized sports and other extracurricular activities. Children develop and refine their gross motor skills as they grow. Sometimes a child will demonstrate a **delay** in a gross motor skill, but this does not always indicate a disability. Some disabilities are characterized by specific delays in gross motor skills. Parents and educators should be familiar with **gross motor skill milestones** in order to pinpoint any significant delays in students.

FINE MOTOR ABILITIES OF CHILDREN

Fine motor skills are skills focused on smaller movements, usually involving the hands and fingers. Children ages **two to three** begin to make things using their hands, such as block towers. They can scribble with writing utensils and manipulate playdough. They demonstrate conceptual knowledge of basic puzzles, fitting appropriate pieces into their correct locations. At this age, children begin to demonstrate a right or left-hand dominance. Adjusting fasteners, such as buttons and snaps, independently dressing and undressing, and cutting paper with scissors are fine motor milestones for children ages **three to four**. These children also fine tune their eating skills and use larger writing tools, maintaining a specific grip instead of a grasp. Children ages **four to five** refine their fine motor skills. Their artistic skills become more refined as they become more confident in hand dominance and drawing. Children ages **five to seven** begin to demonstrate fine motor abilities, such as writing letters and numbers and creating shapes. They use utensils and writing tools with greater ease. Children in this age range can complete self-care tasks independently, such as teeth brushing. A child with a **fine motor delay** would demonstrate a significant deficit in one or more fine motor skills at one or more stages of development.

CLASSROOM STRATEGIES PROMOTING SOCIAL-EMOTIONAL DEVELOPMENT AND GROWTH

Classroom environments should emanate **positivity** and **growth**. Classrooms that promote **social-emotional development and growth** provide security for students and create environments where learning takes place. Teachers can promote social-emotional development and growth by creating predictable classroom routines with visual reminders, keeping classrooms free of dangerous objects and materials, and arranging for learning to take place in large and small groups. They can also rotate activities and materials to keep students engaged, provide appropriate materials for learning centers, and create opportunities for children to engage socially. Teachers can act as nurturing adults by encouraging social interactions and problem solving, modeling appropriate language and social skills, encouraging and validating children's thoughts and feelings, and using clear signals to indicate transitions between activities. Teachers should build community environments in their classrooms, build appropriate relationships with students by getting to know their strengths and weaknesses, and demonstrate good conflict resolution and problem-solving abilities.

EDUCATIONAL IMPLICATIONS OF INSTRUCTING CHILDREN WITH ADHD OR ADD

The Individuals with Disabilities Education Act (IDEA) does **not** recognize Attention Deficit Hyperactivity Disorder (ADHD) or Attention Deficit Disorder (ADD) in any of its 13 major disability categories. Students may be diagnosed with ADHD or ADD only by a physician, but this diagnosis is not enough to qualify the student for **special education services**. When ADHD or ADD are present with another disability, such as a learning disability, the student qualifies for special education services under the learning disability. A student whose ability to learn is affected by ADHD or ADD can receive services with a 504 Plan in place. Section 504 provides services for any child whose disability affects a major life activity and makes the child eligible for accommodations and modifications in the classroom. This ensures that the child receives appropriate **accommodations** and/or **modifications** in the learning environment in order to be successful. Parents who think a child's disability adversely affects educational functioning may request a formal evaluation to be performed by the school. If a child is found to qualify for special education services, the child receives services under the **Other Health Impaired** category of IDEA.

EFFECT OF EMOTIONAL AND PSYCHOLOGICAL NEEDS ON STUDENTS WITH A DISABILITIES

When a child is diagnosed with a disability, educators often primarily focus on the educational implications. However, students with disabilities also have **emotional needs** associated with their disabilities. These needs vary by student and disability. Generally, students with disabilities struggle emotionally. Symptoms may include low self-esteem, anxiety, acting out, reduced intrinsic motivation, and physical symptoms like headaches. Educators, parents, and other professionals can manage the emotional needs of students with disabilities by talking about the disability diagnoses and educational implications of the diagnoses with the students. Educators can increase their **awareness** of how students might be feeling about the diagnoses and identify situations that may cause anxiety or acting out. Educators can also help by praising students consistently, even for small actions, which can help with confidence. Parents, educators, and other professionals can also work together to ensure that the students receive instruction in the most appropriate educational environments for their disabilities.

DETERMINING SEVERE, PROFOUND, AND MILD INTELLECTUAL DISABILITIES

There are three levels of intellectual disabilities: severe, profound, and mild. Specific factors are used to determine whether a disability is severe, profound, or mild. Intellectual levels are measured using cognitive-based and research-based assessments. An **intellectual disability** is defined as having significant cognitive deficits to intellectual functioning, such as reasoning, problem solving, abstract thinking, and comprehension. A **mild to moderate intellectual disability (ID)** is the most common type of intellectual disability. People with mild to moderate ID can generally participate in independent living skills and learn practical life skills and adaptive behavior. People diagnosed with **severe intellectual disabilities** demonstrate major developmental delays. They struggle with simple routines and self-care skills. Additionally, they often understand speech but have trouble with expressive communication. People with **profound ID** cannot live independently and depend heavily on care from other people and resources. They are likely to have congenital disorders that affect their intellectual functioning.

SOCIAL COGNITIVE LEARNING THEORY

Albert Bandura's social cognitive learning theory features four stages or processes of observational learning: attention, retention, production, and motivation. **Observational learning** is based on the idea that a person modifies behavior after being provided with a model for the behavior. Not to be confused with exact imitation of behavior, observational learning occurs when a behavior is witnessed then demonstrated at a later time as a result of witnessing the behavior. For example, a child learns how to hold eating utensils by watching an adult hold the utensils. **Attention** refers to a person paying attention to what is happening in the environment. In the **retention** stage, a person not only observes the behavior, but stores it in memory to perform later. **Production** requires the person to be physically and mentally able to reproduce the behavior. The **motivation** stage means the person must be motivated or have an incentive to reproduce the behavior. Students with disabilities may struggle with one or more of the observational stages as a characteristic of their disabilities. Limitations, such as attention difficulties, present barriers to appropriately moving through the observational learning processes.

EDUCATIONAL IMPLICATIONS OF A DIAGNOSIS OF AN IMPAIRMENT

Speech or Language Impairment and **Visual Impairment or Blindness** adversely affect a student's educational performance. Students with Speech or Language Impairments and Visual Impairments or Blindness are provided with accommodations, modifications, and related services specific to their disabilities. Students with these impairments may be educated alongside peers and provided with related services outside of the general education classroom. Similar to these disabilities, the educational performances of students with **Deafness or Hearing Impairments** are also affected by their disabilities. Accommodations, modifications, and related services are provided based on the severity of the disability.

An **OI** severely impairs mobility or motor activity. Accommodations, modifications, and related services in the classroom environments may be appropriate for students with Orthopedic Impairments. Students with **ID**, such as students with Down Syndrome, often need supports in place for communication, self-care, and social skills. The educational implications of a student with **TBI** are unique to the individual and are therefore treated on a case by case basis. Students with **MD** have needs that cannot be met in any one program. Sometimes their needs are so great that they must be educated in partial inclusion or self-contained settings.

AUTISM SPECTRUM DISORDER VS. SPECIFIC LEARNING DISABILITIES

Autism Spectrum Disorder (**ASD**) and learning disabilities can exist concurrently. Students with ASD may also have a lot in common with students with learning disabilities. However, ASD is a spectrum disorder that affects children in different ways. ASD is often confused with learning and attention issues, but students with ASD can have IQs ranging from significantly delayed to above average or gifted. Students with **learning disabilities** often have consistently lower IQs. Students with **attention issues** like Attention Deficit Hyperactivity Disorder also have varying needs, depending on if the ADHD exists with a learning disability or ASD. Students with learning disabilities and students with ASD may both have difficulties recognizing and reading nonverbal cues, staying organized, problem solving, and expressing themselves. They may also have issues with desiring or rejecting sensory input. These disabilities are different because ASD involves struggles with social understanding and communication, along with repetitive routines or behaviors. These struggles are not associated with students with learning disabilities.

ROLE OF CULTURAL COMPETENCE IN SCHOOLS AND SPECIAL EDUCATION

Schools have a duty to abide by cultural competence in order to ensure avoidance of **cultural and linguistic bias**. Schools that demonstrate **cultural competence** have an appreciation of families and their unique backgrounds. Cultural competence is important because it assists with incorporating knowledge and appreciation of other cultures into daily practices and teaching. This helps increase the quality and effectiveness of how students with unique cultural and linguistic backgrounds are provided with services. It also helps produce better outcomes for these students. In special education, being culturally competent means being aware of cultural and linguistic differences, especially when considering children for the identification process. Adapting to the **diversity and cultural contexts** of the surrounding communities allows teachers to better understand flags for referrals. Teachers that continually assess their awareness of the cultures and diversity of the communities where they teach demonstrate cultural competence. In order for schools and teachers to be described as culturally competent, they should have a process for recognizing diversity. They should also learn about and incorporate knowledge of cultural diversity into their classrooms.

CULTURAL AND LINGUISTIC DIFFERENCES VS. LEARNING DIFFICULTIES

Many schools are enriched with cultural diversity. It is important for special educators to identify if a suspected learning disability may instead be a **cultural or linguistic difference** in a student. Teachers and schools must increase awareness of cultural and linguistic differences in order to avoid overidentification of this population as having learning difficulties. Some ways a child's behavior may represent cultural or linguistic differences are demonstrated in the **interactions** between teachers and students. In some cultures, children are asked to make eye contact to ensure they are listening, whereas in other cultures, children are taught to look down or away when being spoken to by an adult. Certain facial expressions and behaviors may be interpreted differently by students due to their cultural backgrounds. Additionally, teaching methods that are comfortable and effective for some students may be ineffective for others due to differing cultural backgrounds. Cultural values and characteristics may vary between teachers and students and contribute to the students' school performances. It is important for teachers to be **self-aware** and constantly **assess** whether ineffective teaching methods are due to learning difficulties or differences in cultural and linguistic diversity.

INSTRUCTIONAL STRATEGIES FOR TEACHING ESL STUDENTS AND STUDENTS WITH DISABILITIES

English as a Second Language (ESL) students are often at risk for being **referred** for special education services. This is frequently a result of **inadequate planning** for the needs of English language learners rather than skill deficits. To ensure that the needs of ESL students are met and discrimination is avoided, educators can implement strategies for **targeting their learning processes**. Strategies similar to those utilized in inclusive special education settings are helpful, such as using visuals to supplement instruction. This type of nonlinguistic representation helps convey meaning to ESL students. Working in groups with peers helps students with disabilities and ESL students demonstrate communication and social skills while working toward common goals.

Allowing students to write and speak in their first languages until they feel comfortable speaking in English is a scaffolding strategy that can also be implemented. Sentence frames that demonstrate familiar sentence formats are helpful for all students to practice speaking and writing in structured, formal ways.

TEACHING APPROPRIATE COMMUNICATION SKILLS

Students with disabilities who are also English Language Learners (ELLs) have the additional challenge of **language barriers** affecting their access to learning. These barriers, combined with the disabilities, can also make instruction for these students challenging. For ELL students with disabilities, it is important for teachers to rely on **appropriate instructional strategies** in order to determine what is affecting the students' access to information. Instructional strategies for teaching ELL students are similar to teaching strategies used for nonverbal students. Pairing **visuals** with words helps students make concrete connections between the written words and the pictures. The consistency of seeing the words paired with the visuals increases the likelihood of the students beginning to interpret word meanings. Using **sign language** is another way teachers can facilitate word meaning. When used consistently, students make connections between the visual word meanings and the written words. Teachers can also provide opportunities for ELL students to access language by having all classroom students communicate in a **consistent manner**. The goal of this instructional strategy is for peers to model appropriate verbal communication as it applies to different classroom situations.

BENEFITS THE SOCRATIC METHOD

With the Socratic method of teaching, students are **guided** by their teachers in their own educational discovery learning processes. This involves students intrinsically seeking knowledge or answers to problems. This method can be helpful for facilitating and enhancing the **social and emotional abilities** of students with disabilities, particularly Autism Spectrum Disorder (ASD). The Socratic method requires **dialogue** in order to successfully facilitate the teacher/student guided learning process. This is beneficial for students with autism who generally struggle with appropriate communication and social skills. This method emphasizes **information seeking and communication skills** by engaging students in class discussions, assignment sharing, and group work. Communication for information-seeking purposes is often a deficit of students with ASD. Sharing of ideas is a concept that develops naturally in guided learning and often requires flexibility in the thought process, another skill that students with ASD struggle with. These skills can be taught and reinforced to students with and without disabilities in order to develop skills essential to life-long learning processes.

ERIKSON'S FOUR EARLIEST SOCIAL STAGES OF HUMAN DEVELOPMENT

The stages of human development and behavior are separated into seven human age groups, with the four earliest being **infancy** (birth to 2 years old), **early childhood** (3 to 8 years old), **middle childhood** (9 to 11 years old), and **adolescence** (12 to 18 years old). As children age, they build upon each stage. Growth is unique to each individual. According to Erikson's theory of psychosocial development, each developmental stage is characterized by **crises**. During infancy, babies learn **trust versus mistrust (hope)**. This is when a nurtured and loved infant would develop trust, and a mistreated infant would not. The infancy stage is also formed by **autonomy versus shame (will)**. This stage is characterized by the exertion of will and the seeking of independence by small children. Early childhood is characterized by **learning initiative versus guilt (purpose)**. During this stage, children begin to develop their interpersonal skills. **Industry versus inferiority (competence)** also develops during early childhood. During this stage, teachers begin to play an important role, as school-aged children learn competence in new skills. Throughout middle childhood and adolescence, children learn **identity versus role confusion (fidelity)**. The identity stage is when adolescents seek to form their individual identities.

VALUES OF THE SOCIAL COGNITIVE THEORY

The three values or valuables of the social cognitive theory are **behavioral factors**, **personal factors** (intrinsic), and **environmental factors** (extrinsic). The social cognitive behavior theory suggests that these three variables are connected to each other and therefore promote learning. The basic concepts of the social cognitive theory can become evident in infancy, childhood, and adulthood. These concepts include observational learning, reproduction, self-efficacy, emotional coping, and self-regulatory capability. **Observational learning** is the process by which people learn behavior by observing other behaviors. This is especially influenced by a person's environment. Reproduction occurs when a person repeats modeled behavior. **Reproduction** can be impeded by a person's limited abilities. **Self-efficacy** is when a person puts new knowledge or behavior into action. **Emotional coping** is a learning process where people develop coping skills for dealing with stressful environments and negative influences. The development of good emotional coping skills influences learning processes. **Self-regulatory capability** describes a person's ability to manage choices and behavior even when influenced by negative environments.

GARDNER'S THEORY OF MULTIPLE INTELLIGENCES

Howard Gardner developed the theory of multiple intelligences, which outlines seven different ways he believes people can learn. Gardner's theory was based on the idea that everyone understands the world through different intelligences, and our **individual intelligence strengths** are what make people different. The multiple intelligences are described below.

- **Visual-spatial thinkers** think about things visually. They are very aware of their environments. They are good at activities like completing puzzles, drawing, and reading maps. They learn best through the use of visuals, such as graphs and diagrams.
- **Bodily-kinesthetic thinkers** learn best with a hands-on approach. They process information by doing. They learn best through physical activities.
- **Musical thinkers** are sensitive to music, sound, and rhythm in their environments. They learn best when lesson concepts are turned into musical features like lyrics and songs.
- **Interpersonal thinkers** like to learn by interacting with others. They find learning easy in group environments like seminars and lecture halls.
- **Intrapersonal thinkers** are independent learners. They learn best using introspection.
- **Linguistic thinkers** are efficient and use words to express themselves. They are auditory learners who enjoy reading, word games, and making up stories.
- **Logical-mathematical thinkers** learn best through familiar patterns and relationships. They think conceptually and reasonably.

COGNITIVE BEHAVIORAL THEORY

The cognitive behavioral theory states that people form their own negative or positive concepts that affect their behaviors. The cognitive behavioral theory involves a **cognitive triad** of human thoughts and behaviors. This triad refers to human thoughts about the **self**, the **world and environment**, and the **future**. In times of stress, people's thoughts can become distressed or dysfunctional. Sometimes cognitive behavioral therapy, based on the cognitive behavioral theory model, is used to help people address and manage their thoughts. This process involves people examining their thoughts more closely in order to bring them back to more realistic, grounded ways of thinking. People's thoughts and perceptions can often affect their lives negatively and lead to unhealthy emotions and behaviors. **Cognitive behavioral therapy** helps people to adjust their thinking, learn ways to access healthy thoughts, and learn behaviors incompatible with unhealthy or unsafe behaviors.

SOCIAL AND EMOTIONAL SKILL EXPECTATIONS AND MILESTONES OF TODDLERS AND PRESCHOOLERS

Toddlers **18 months to 2 years old** typically begin to demonstrate their **independence** and show an increasing interest in **communication**. Toddlers exhibit temper tantrums and an increase in defiant behavior. Children in this age group begin to **imitate** the actions of familiar adults and engage in pretend play. They also demonstrate an interest in playing with other children but engage in **side-by-side play** (parallel play) instead of cooperative play. Preschoolers ages **3 and 4** continue to demonstrate independence and build on their communication skills. They may also demonstrate temper tantrums and defiant behavior. Preschoolers are able to verbalize a wider range of **emotions**, especially when they do not get what they want or have trouble communicating what they want. They begin to engage with their peers in **cooperative play** and start to play independently. Preschoolers are still interested in and engage in pretend play. At this age, they begin to recognize adults' moods or feelings. They begin to exhibit moments of helpfulness and kindness.

SOCIAL AND EMOTIONAL SKILL EXPECTATIONS AND MILESTONES OF GRADE SCHOOLERS

Children typically enter kindergarten at ages **5 to 6**. They begin to exert their **independence** and test **boundaries** at home and school. They show a preference to playing with kids their own ages and sometimes their own genders. Their conversational language grows as they interact with other students. At ages **7 to 8**, children start to become aware of what others might think of them. They may be more sensitive to **interpersonal relationships** with their peers. They can aptly express their feelings but get frustrated when they do not have the right words. At ages **9–10**, children begin getting selective with their **peer friendships**. They may prefer a few close friends over getting along with everyone. They begin to demonstrate more **independence** and start attempting to develop their own **identities**. Children in this age group are able to communicate their feelings but can still get frustrated. They demonstrate a wide range of emotions in adult and peer interactions.

PIAGET'S FOUR STAGES OF COGNITIVE DEVELOPMENT

Piaget's four stages of cognitive development are sensorimotor (birth to 18 months), preoperational (18-24 months to age 7), concrete operational (ages 7 to 12), and formal operational (adolescence to adulthood). During the **sensorimotor stage**, newborn infants only have a minute awareness. As they grow, they begin to interact with their environments before developing object permanence at 7–9 months. Another important milestone that develops during this stage is early language development. During the **preoperational stage**, infants grow into young children and their language becomes more meaningful. They develop memory and imagination but cannot yet grasp complex concepts such as cause and effect. The **concrete operational stage** is characterized by concrete reasoning. Children in this stage become more aware of the world around them and are less egocentric. They cannot yet think abstractly or hypothetically. During the **formal operational stage**, adolescents are able to engage in abstract thinking. They are now able to formulate hypotheses and demonstrate logical thought and deductive reasoning.

RIGHTS AND THE ROLES FAMILIES IN THE EDUCATION OF CHILDREN WITH DISABILITIES

Under IDEA, parents and legal guardians of children with disabilities have **procedural safeguards** that protect their rights. The safeguards also provide parents and legal guardians of children with disabilities with the means to resolve any disputes with school systems. Families serve as

advocates for their children with disabilities. **Parents and legal guardians** may underestimate their importance to Individualized Education Program teams. However, they are important members of the Individualized Education Program teams and integral parts of the decision-making processes for their children's educational journeys. Parents and legal guardians often work more closely with their children than other adults. Therefore, as part of the IEP teams, parents and legal guardians often provide insight regarding the children's backgrounds, educational histories, developmental histories, strengths, and weaknesses. Parents and legal guardians are also important decision makers in transition meetings, when students with disabilities move from one level of school to another. Parent and legal guardian input in transition meetings ensures that appropriate services and supports are in place within the next levels of school in order to ensure student success.

Social and Functional Living Skills

TARGETING AND IMPLEMENTING SOCIAL SKILLS INSTRUCTION

Developing good social skills is essential for lifelong student success, and people with disabilities often struggle with these skills. Addressing social skill behavior is most effective when:

- **social skill needs** are specifically identified.
- **social skills instruction** is implemented as a collaborative effort between parents and teachers.

Evaluating **developmental milestones** is helpful in targeting social skills that need to be addressed and taught. If a child with a disability is not demonstrating a milestone, such as back and forth communication, this skill can be evaluated to determine if it should be taught. However, meeting milestones is not a surefire way to measure a student's social skill ability, as some children naturally progress more slowly. Social skill deficits may be acquisition deficits, performance deficits, or fluency deficits. **Acquisition deficits** occur when a student demonstrates an absence of a skill or behavior. **Performance deficits** occur when a student does not implement a social skill consistently. A **fluency deficit** means a student needs assistance with demonstrating a social skill effectively or fluently. Once the student's social skill need is identified, teachers, parents, and other professionals can collaborate to incorporate an established routine or behavior contract or to implement applied behavior analysis.

PURPOSES AND BENEFITS OF SOCIAL SKILLS GROUPS

Social skills groups are useful for helping students with **social skill deficits** learn and practice appropriate skills with their peers. Social skills groups are primarily composed of similar-aged peers with and without disabilities. An adult typically leads the group and teaches students skills needed for making friends, succeeding in school and life, and sometimes obtaining and maintaining a job. Other professionals, such as school psychologists or speech language pathologists, may also lead social skills groups. Social skills groups work by facilitating **conversation** and focusing on **skill deficits**, such as reading facial cues. Social skills groups have many benefits. They can help students learn to appropriately greet others, begin conversations, respond appropriately, maintain conversations, engage in turn-taking, and request help when needed.

RECEIVING SPECIAL EDUCATION SERVICES IN THE LEAST RESTRICTIVE ENVIRONMENT

The Individuals with Disabilities Education Act (IDEA) requires a free and appropriate public education (FAPE) to be provided in a student with a disability's **least restrictive environment (LRE)**. This means that a student who qualifies for special education should be educated in a free, appropriate, and public setting and be placed in an instructional setting that meets the LRE principle. IDEA states that LRE means students with disabilities should participate in the general education classroom "to the maximum extent that is appropriate." **Mainstreaming** and **inclusion** are two words that are associated with LRE because these are the two settings where students with disabilities can participate in the general education classroom while receiving appropriate accommodations, modifications, interventions, and/or related services. The amount of time a student spends in an LRE suitable for his or her individual needs is stated in the Individualized Education Program (IEP). The accommodations, modifications, interventions, and/or related services the student should receive are also outlined in the IEP. Students who need special education services for more than 50% of the day may be placed in instructional settings that meet their LRE needs, such as resource rooms or self-contained classrooms.

CONTINUUM OF SPECIAL EDUCATION SERVICES

IDEA mandates that school systems must educate students with disabilities with students who do not have disabilities to the maximum extent that is appropriate. IDEA also mandates that schools may not take students out of regular education classes unless the classes are not benefitting the students. Supplementary aids and support services must be in place before students can be considered for removal. Schools must offer a **continuum of special education services** that offer a restrictive to least restrictive range. In a typical continuum of services, regular education classrooms offer the **least restrictive access** to students with disabilities. After regular education classrooms, students can be educated in resource rooms, then special classes that target specific deficits. Special schools, homebound services, and hospitals and institutions are the last three least restrictive educational options for children with disabilities. The number of students in these continuum settings decreases as restriction increases. Fewer students benefit from being educated in hospitals or institutions than in resource rooms.

EVIDENCE-BASED METHODS FOR PROMOTING SELF-DETERMINATION

Students with disabilities often need to be taught skills for promoting **self-determination** and **self-advocacy**. These skills may not come easily to students with specific disorders like autism. Self-determination involves a comprehensive understanding of one's own **strengths and limitations**. Self-determined people are **goal-oriented** and intrinsically motivated to **improve themselves**. Teachers can facilitate the teaching of these skills in a number of ways, starting in early elementary school. In early elementary school, teachers can promote self-determination by teaching choice-making skills and providing clear consequences for these choices. Teacher can also promote problem-solving and self-management skills, like having students evaluate their own work. At the middle school and junior high level, students can be taught to evaluate and analyze their choices. They can also learn academic and personal goal-setting skills and decision-making skills. At the high school level, teachers can promote decision-making skills, involvement in educational planning (i.e. attending their Individualized Education Program meetings), and strategies like self-instruction, self-monitoring, and self-evaluation. Throughout the educational process, teachers should establish and maintain high standards for learning, focus on students' strengths, and create positive learning environments that promote choice and problem-solving skills.

TEACHING SELF-AWARENESS SKILLS

Students engage in private self-awareness and public self-awareness. Some students with disabilities have the additional challenge of needing instruction in **self-awareness skills**. Special educators and other professionals can facilitate the instruction of self-awareness skills by teaching students to be **aware** of their thoughts, feelings, and actions. Self-awareness also means teaching students how their thoughts, feelings, and actions **affect other people**. Students can be taught self-awareness by identifying their own strengths and weaknesses and learning to self-monitor errors in assignments. They can also be taught to identify what materials or steps are needed to complete tasks. Additionally, students can learn to recognize that other people have needs and feelings and recognize how their behaviors affect others. Students can also learn self-awareness by recognizing the limitations of their disabilities and learning to advocate for accommodations or strategies that work for them. Special educators or other professionals should frequently talk with students about their performances and encourage students to discuss their mistakes without criticism.

IMPORTANCE OF LEARNING SELF-ADVOCACY SKILLS

Self-advocacy is an important skill to learn for people entering adulthood. For students with disabilities, **self-advocacy skills** are especially important for success in **post-secondary environments**. Teaching and learning self-advocacy skills should begin when students enter grade school and be reinforced in the upper grade levels. Students with disabilities who have the potential to enter post-secondary education or employment fields need to learn self-advocacy skills in order to **communicate** how their disabilities may affect their educational or job performances. They must also communicate the need for supports and possible accommodations in the educational, training, or employment fields. Students with disabilities who graduate or age out of their Individualized Education Programs do not receive the **educational supports** they received at the grade school level. It is essential for students to advocate for themselves in the absence of teachers or caregivers advocating for them, especially when students independently enter post-secondary employment, training, or educational environments. Many colleges, universities, communities, and work environments offer services to students with disabilities who need them, but it is up to the students to advocate for themselves and seek them out.

PROVIDING INSTRUCTION IN THE AREA OF FUNCTIONAL LIVING SKILLS

Also known as life skills, functional skills are skills students need to know to live independently. Ideally, students leave high school having gained functional skills. For students with special needs, **functional skills instruction** is needed to gain independent living skills. Students with developmental disabilities or cognitive disabilities sometimes need to acquire basic living skills, such as self-feeding or toileting. **Applied behavior analysis** is a process where these skills can be broken down, modeled, and taught. These students must also learn functional math and language arts skills, such as managing money and reading bus schedules. Students may also participate in **community-based instruction** to learn skills while completing independent living tasks in the community. These skills include grocery shopping, reading restaurant menus, and riding public transportation. **Social skills instruction** is also important for these students, as learning appropriate social interactions is necessary to function with community members.

Language Development

HELPING STUDENTS DEVELOP ORAL LANGUAGE ABILITIES

Children pick up oral language skills in their home environments and build upon these skills as they grow. Early language development is a combination of genetic disposition, environment, and individual thinking processes. Children with **oral language acquisition difficulties** often experience difficulties in their **literacy skills**. Engaging students in activities that promote good oral language skills is beneficial to these skills as well as their literacy skills. **Strategies** that help students develop oral language abilities include developing appropriate speaking and listening skills, providing instruction that emphasizes vocabulary development, providing students with opportunities to communicate wants, needs, ideas, and information, creating language learning environments, and promoting auditory memory. Developing appropriate speaking and listening skills includes teaching turn-taking, awareness of social norms, and basic rules for speaking and listening. Emphasizing **vocabulary development** is a strategy that familiarizes early learners with

33

word meanings. Providing students with opportunities to **communicate** is beneficial for developing early social skills. Teachers can create **language learning environments** by promoting literacy in their classrooms with word walls, reading circles, or other strategies that introduce language skills to students. Promoting **auditory memory** means teaching students to listen to, process, and recall information.

COMPONENTS OF ORAL LANGUAGE DEVELOPMENT

Oral language learning begins well before students enter educational environments. It is learned first without formal instruction, with **environmental factors** being a heavy influence. Children tend to develop their own linguistic rules as a result of genetic disposition, their environments, and how their individual thinking processes develop. Components of oral language development include phonological components, semantic components, and syntactic components. **Phonological components** focus on the rules for combining sounds. **Semantic components** focus on the smallest units of sounds, morphemes, and how they combine to make up words. **Syntactic components** focus on how morphemes combine to form sentences. This complex system of phonological, semantic, and syntactic components grows and develops as children grow. **Oral language development** can be nurtured by caregivers and teachers well before children enter educational environments. Caregivers and teachers can promote oral language development by providing environments full of language development opportunities. Additionally, teaching children how conversation works, encouraging interaction among children, and demonstrating good listening and speaking skills are good strategies for nurturing oral language development.

HELPING STUDENTS MONITOR ERRORS IN ORAL LANGUAGE

Oral language is the way people express knowledge, ideas, and feelings. As oral language develops, so do **speaking and listening skills**, which have strong connections to reading comprehension and writing skills. Oral language first develops in infancy and becomes fine-tuned with instruction as students enter grade school. Teachers can monitor **oral language errors** with progress monitoring strategies. Teachers can also help students monitor their own **oral language development** as they progress through the reading curriculum. Students can monitor their oral language by listening to spoken words in their school and home environments, learning and practicing self-correction skills, and participating in reading comprehension and writing activities. Students can also monitor oral language errors by learning oral language rules for phonics, semantics, syntax, and pragmatics. These are rules for learning sounds, words, and meanings in the English language. Learning these oral language rules typically generalizes to developing appropriate oral language skills.

EXPRESSIVE LANGUAGE

Expressive language involves the ability to use vocabulary, sentences, gestures, and writing. **Expressive language skills** mean that people can label objects in their environments, put words in sentences, use appropriate grammar, demonstrate comprehension verbally by retelling stories, and more. This type of language is important because it allows people to express feelings, wants and needs, thoughts and ideas, and individual points of view. Expressive language helps people develop spoken and written language and promotes positive interactions with others. Expressive language goes hand in hand with **receptive language**, which is the understanding of language. Children can learn solid expressive language skills by:

- completing tasks that require attention and focus.
- developing pre-language skills, such as understanding gestures like nodding.
- developing good pragmatics.

34

- developing intrinsic social motivation skills.
- developing fine motor skills, which are required for students who use sign language or gestures to communicate.

RECEPTIVE LANGUAGE

Receptive language refers to a person's ability to understand language. Good receptive language means a person is gathering information from the environment and processing it into meaning. People with good **receptive language skills** perceive visual information, sounds and words, basic cognitive concepts like colors and shapes, and written information (i.e. street signs) well. Receptive language is important for developing appropriate communication skills. **Strategies** to build receptive language skills in children include activities that maintain focus and attention. This requires children to participate in activities that require sustained attention free of distractions in order to improve receptive communication skills. **Pre-language skills** are skills that people use before they learn to communicate with words. Building appropriate pre-language skills is another strategy for building receptive language. Lastly, focusing on **social skills and play skills instruction** encourages opportunities for children to interact with their peers or adults. This fosters receptive language skills or targets deficits in these skills.

STAGES OF LANGUAGE DEVELOPMENT IN INFANTS AND CHILDREN

The first stage of language development and acquisition, the **pre-linguistic stage**, occurs during an infant's first year of life. It is characterized by the development of gestures, making eye contact, and sounds like cooing and crying. The **holophrase**, or one-word sentence stage, develops in infants between 10 and 13 months of age. In this stage, young children use one-word sentences to communicate meaning in language. The **two-word sentence stage** typically develops by the time a child is 18 months old. Each two-word sentence usually contains a verb and a modifier, such as "big balloon" or "green grass." Children in this stage use their two-word sentences to communicate wants and needs. **Multiple-word sentences** form by the time a child is two to two and a half years old. In this stage, children begin forming sentences with subjects and predicates, such as "tree is tall" or "rope is long." Grammatical errors are present, but children in this stage begin demonstrating how to use words in appropriate context. Children ages two and a half to three years old typically begin using more **complex grammatical structures**. They begin to include grammatical structures such as conjunctions and prepositions. For example, they may say, "Throw it, the ball," or "Bring me outside." By the age of five or six, children reach a stage of **adult-like language development**. They begin to use words in appropriate context and can move words around in sentences while maintaining appropriate sentence structure.

STAGES OF LITERACY DEVELOPMENT

The development of literacy in young children is separated into five stages. Names of these stages sometimes vary, but the stage milestones are similar. Stage 1 is the **Emergent Reader stage**. In this stage, young children ages 6 months to 6 years demonstrate skills like pretend reading, recognizing letters of the alphabet, retelling stories, and printing their names. Stage 2 is the **Novice/Early Reader stage** (ages 6–7 years). Children begin to understand the relationships between letters and sounds and written and spoken words, and they read texts containing high-frequency words. Children in this stage should develop orthographic conventions and semantic knowledge. In Stage 3, the **Decoding Reader stage**, children ages 7–9 develop decoding skills in order to read simple stories. They also demonstrate increased fluency. Stage 4 (ages 8–15 years) is called the **Fluent, Comprehending/Transitional Reader stage**. In this stage, fourth to eighth graders read to learn new ideas and information. In Stage 5, the **Expert/Fluent Reader stage**, children ages 16 years and older read more complex information. They also read expository and narrative texts with multiple viewpoints.

IMPLICATIONS OF LITERACY DEVELOPMENT FOR CHILDREN WITH DISABILITIES

Literacy development is broken into five stages. Names of these stages sometimes vary.

- Stage 1 (ages 6 months to 6 years) Emergent Reader Stage
- Stage 2 (ages 6–7 years) Novice/Early Reader Stage
- Stage 3 (ages 7–9 years) Decoding Reader Stage
- Stage 4 (ages 8–15 years) Fluent, Comprehending/Transitional Reader Stage
- Stage 5 (16+ years) Expert/Fluent Reader Stage

Children may not always meet the **literacy stage milestones** during the specified ages. However, this does not always indicate a disability. Children who fall significantly behind in their literacy development, continually struggle with skill acquisition, or do not consistently retain skill instruction may be at higher risk of being identified as having **disabilities**. Furthermore, children with **speech and language disorders** are more likely to experience problems learning to read and write. These issues are typically apparent before children enter grade school but can also become evident during their early grade school years. **Early warning signs** include disinterest in shared book reading, inability to recognize or remember names of letters, difficulty understanding directions, and persistent baby talk.

PROMOTING LITERACY DURING THE EARLY STAGES OF LITERACY DEVELOPMENT

Teachers and parents can implement strategies at different stages of literacy development in order to build **good reading skills** in children with and without disabilities. During the **Emergent Reader stage**, teachers and parents can introduce children to the conventions of reading with picture books. They can model turning the pages, reading from left to right, and other reading conventions. Book reading at this stage helps children begin to identify letters, letter sounds, and simple words. Repetitive reading of familiar texts also helps children begin to make predictions about what they are reading. During the **Novice/Early Reader** and **Decoding Reader stages**, parents and teachers can help children form the building blocks of decoding and fluency skills by reading for meaning and emphasizing letter-sound relationships, visual cues, and language patterns. In these stages, increasing familiarity with sight words is essential. In Stage 4, the **Fluent, Comprehending Reader/Transitional stage**, children should be encouraged to read book series, as the shared characters, settings, and plots help develop their comprehension skills. At this stage, a good reading rate (fluency) is an indicator of comprehension skills. **Expert/Fluent readers** can independently read multiple texts and comprehend their meanings. Teachers and parents can begin exposing children to a variety of fiction and non-fiction texts before this stage in order to promote good fluency skills.

RELATIONSHIP BETWEEN LANGUAGE DEVELOPMENT AND EARLY LITERACY SKILLS

Language development and early literacy skills are interconnected. **Language concepts** begin and develop shortly after birth with infant/parent interactions, cooing, and then babbling. These are the earliest attempts at language acquisition for infants. Young children begin interacting with written and spoken words before they enter their grade school years. Before they enter formal classrooms, children begin to make **connections** between speaking and listening and reading and writing. Children with strong speaking and listening skills demonstrate strong literacy skills in early grade school. The development of **phonological awareness** is connected to early literacy skills. Children with good phonological awareness recognize that words are made up of different speech sounds. For example, children with appropriate phonological awareness can break words (i.e. "bat") into separate speech sounds (i.e. "b-a-t"). Examples of phonological awareness include rhyming (when the ending parts of words have the same or similar sounds) and alliteration (when words all have the same beginning sound). Success with phonological awareness (oral language) activities depends on adequate development of speech and language skills.

IMPORTANCE OF ENFORCING WORD RECOGNITION

Many students with specific learning disabilities demonstrate **deficits in reading abilities**. This includes **word recognition abilities**. Teaching **word identification** is important for these students because developing age-appropriate word recognition skills is one of the essential building blocks for creating efficient readers. Children who do not develop adequate reading skills in elementary school are generally below average readers as they age in school. Most districts and teachers use **basal reading programs** that teach word recognition and phonics. Teachers often supplement basal reading programs with **instructional programs** that can be used at home and at school. These are especially useful for students with disabilities or students who are at risk and struggle with word recognition abilities. Elements of basal and supplementary reading programs include instruction for helping students make connections between letters and sounds, opportunities to become comfortable with reading, alphabetic knowledge, phonemic awareness, letter-sound correlations, word identification strategies, spelling, writing, and reading fluency.

CHARACTERISTICS OF EXPRESSIVE LANGUAGE DISABILITIES

Expressive language refers to a person's ability to express wants and needs. Children with **expressive language disabilities** may have trouble conversing with peers and adults and have trouble with self-expression. Answers to questions may be vague or repetitive. They may not demonstrate age-appropriate social skills with peers and adults. Children with expressive language disabilities have a limited vocabulary range and rely on familiar vocabulary words in their expressive language. They can be very quiet and seclude themselves from classroom activities due to difficulties expressing their thoughts and feelings. They may not be able to accurately express what they understand because children with expressive language difficulties have trouble speaking in sentences. Expressive language disabilities indicate issues with **language processing centers** in the brain. Children with this disability can sometimes understand language but have trouble **expressing** it. Children with traumatic brain injury, dyslexia, autism, or learning disabilities demonstrate issues with expressive language.

Planning and Managing the Learning Environments

Planning and Delivering Instruction

TEACHING STRATEGIES FOR STUDENTS LEARNING AT DIFFERENT EDUCATIONAL LEVELS

Learning styles of students differ, regardless of whether or not the students have disabilities. When addressing groups of students in inclusion settings, it is important for teachers to organize and implement teaching strategies that address learning at **different educational levels**. Students generally fall into one or more learning modes. Some are visual learners, some are auditory learners, some are kinesthetic or tactile learners, and some learn best using a combination of these approaches. Teachers can address students' educational levels by creating lessons that allow learning to take place visually, auditorily, and kinesthetically. **Visual learners** have preferences for seeing information that has been visually organized, such as seeing information presented in graphic organizers or diagrams. **Auditory learners** prefer information presented in spoken words. Lessons that target auditory learners provide opportunities for students to engage in conversations and/or question material. **Kinesthetic learners** prefer a hands-on approach to learning. These learners prefer to try out new tasks and learn as they go. Lessons that include opportunities for these three types of learning to occur can successfully target different educational levels.

COMPONENTS OF A DIFFERENTIATED CURRICULUM

Differentiated instruction is different from individualized instruction. It targets the strengths of classroom students and can work well in both special education and general education settings. **Differentiated instruction** is also useful for targeting the needs of students with **learning and attention deficits**. With differentiated instruction, teachers adjust their instructional processes to meet the needs of the individual students. Teaching strategies and classroom management skills are based largely on each particular class of students instead of using methods that may have been successful in the past. Teachers can differentiate content, classroom activities, student projects, and the learning environments. For example, students may be encouraged to choose topics of personal interest to focus on for projects. Students are held to the same standards but have many choices in terms of project topics. **Differentiated content** means teachers provide access to a variety of resources to encourage student choice over what and how they learn. **Differentiated learning environments** are flexible to meet the ever-changing needs of the students.

DIFFERENTIATED INSTRUCTION

Differentiated instruction is effective in general education settings, team-teaching settings, and special education settings because it targets the **strengths** of classroom students. Differentiated instruction is used to target the different ways that students learn instead of taking a one-size-fits-all approach. Differentiated instruction is used in lieu of individualized instruction because it uses a variety of instructional approaches and allows students access to a variety of materials to help them access the curriculum. **Effective differentiated instruction** includes small group work, reciprocal learning, and continual assessment.

Small group work allows for the individual learning styles and/or needs of students to be addressed. In small groups, students receive instruction by rotating through different sized groups. In **reciprocal learning**, students play the role of the teacher, instructing the class by sharing what they know and asking content questions of their peers. Teachers who practice **continual**

38

assessment can determine if their differentiated instructional methods are effective or if they need to be changed. Assessments can determine what needs to be changed in order for students to participate in effective classroom environments.

TEACHING COMMUNICATION TO STUDENTS WHO ARE NONVERBAL

Nonverbal students have extra challenges in addition to learning content. These students may need extra instruction in academic areas as well as specialized instruction in the area of communication skills. Students with **nonverbal disabilities** may also need social skills instruction, struggle with abstract concepts, and dislike changes to their routines. Teachers can **facilitate learning** for nonverbal students by making changes to their classroom environments, teaching strategies for comprehending concepts, and providing materials to accommodate their needs. Teachers can also provide accommodations and/or modifications to classwork and tests to make the content accessible to nonverbal students. Additionally, teachers can assist nonverbal students by taking measures to prevent undesirable behaviors from occurring. Using visuals to represent actions, words, or concepts is a helpful instructional strategy for teaching nonverbal students, especially when teaching new material.

CO-TEACHING MODELS

Co-teaching models are utilized in collaborative, inclusive teaching settings that include students with and without disabilities. General educators teach alongside special educators and hold all students to the same educational standards. In successful co-teaching settings, these models are used interchangeably. In the **One Teach/One Support model**, one instructor teaches a lesson while the other instructor supports students who have questions or need assistance. A **Parallel Teaching model** involves a class being split into two groups, with one instructor teaching each group. The **Alternative Teaching model** may be appropriate in situations where it is necessary to instruct small groups of students. In this model, one instructor teaches a large group of students while the other provides instruction to a smaller group of students. In **Station Teaching**, students are split into small groups and work in several teaching centers while both instructors provide support. Teachers participating in **Team-Teaching** collaboratively plan, implement lesson content, facilitate classroom discussions, and manage discipline. These models all take place in the inclusive classroom setting and are intended to meet the needs of diverse groups of learners.

INTERVENTION STRATEGIES FOR THE INSTRUCTION OF STUDENTS WITH MULTIPLE DISABILITIES

Working with students with multiple disabilities can be challenging to manage. However, strategies used in other special education settings can be implemented to promote the success of students with multiple disabilities. Effective strategies include:

- setting **long-term goals**, which may last for a few years depending on how long students are in the same classrooms.
- working **collaboratively** with team members, like paraprofessionals and related services professionals, to ensure that the students' educational objectives are carried out consistently between all adults.
- developing and maintaining **group goals** that the adults and students in the classrooms can strive to achieve together.
- working with students and paraprofessionals and consulting paraprofessionals frequently for **feedback**.
- demonstrating **patience** when waiting for children to respond or complete tasks.
- learning about how students **communicate**, which may involve gestures, a Picture Exchange Communication System, or other methods.

39

- driving instructional and educational goals based on how students **learn best**.
- considering how students will **respond** when designing lessons, including accounting for response time during instruction.

REMEDIAL INSTRUCTION VS. SPECIAL EDUCATION

Though the terms are sometimes used interchangeably, receiving remedial instruction does not always equal special education. The difference between remedial instruction and special education has a lot to do with the intellectual levels of the students. In **remedial instruction**, a student has average or better than average intellectual abilities but may struggle with **skills** in one or more content areas. When schools or teachers offer remedial instructional programs or opportunities in the classroom, they offer one-on-one instruction to students who are falling behind. Remedial programs are often mainstreamed into general education classrooms to address the varying learning abilities of classroom students. Remedial instruction can be delivered by general education teachers. **Special education** programs address the needs of students who may have lower intellectual abilities that require individualized instruction. Students in special education have **disabilities** that are eligible according to the Individuals with Disabilities Education Act and use Individualized Education Programs. Unlike remedial instruction, special education requires qualified and credentialed special educators to decide how to best provide interventions in classroom settings for students with disabilities.

TEACHING SOCIAL INTERACTIONS TO STUDENTS WHO ARE NONVERBAL

Students who are nonverbal may have access to **communication systems** implemented by trained professionals. Teachers, caretakers, and other professionals work with the students to use the communication systems effectively. The goal of a communication system is to teach a nonverbal student how to "talk" and engage in **age-appropriate social skills**. In order for nonverbal students to learn appropriate social interactions, they must spend time learning communication skills, just as they learn academic content. Communication skills can be taught in isolation or occur within students' daily activities. Giving nonverbal students opportunities to foster communication skills in **familiar environments** ensures that they learn how to socially interact appropriately. Teachers, caregivers, and other professionals must demonstrate how to use communication systems to engage in conversations, make requests, and answer questions. Most importantly, nonverbal students must be instructed to **access** their "words" (communication systems) at all times throughout the school and home environments.

REMEDIAL INSTRUCTION VS. COMPENSATORY APPROACHES TO INTERVENTION

Compensatory interventions can be offered in the form of programs or services that help children with special needs or children who are at risk. The compensatory approach is different from remedial instruction because remedial instruction involves the breaking of concepts or tasks into smaller chunks and reteaching information. The **remedial approach** focuses on repetition and developing or reinforcing certain skills. The **compensatory approach** is implemented when a remedial approach is not working. It focuses on building upon children's strengths and working with or around their weaknesses. Tools such as audiobooks, text-to-speech software, speech recognition software, and other types of assistive technology are compensatory accommodations that provide free and appropriate educations for children with disabilities who might otherwise continue to demonstrate skill deficits without these tools. Compensatory approaches and remedial instruction can and should be delivered at the same time to ensure that children with disabilities are meeting their potential.

LEVELS OF BLOOM'S TAXONOMY OF LEARNING DOMAINS

Bloom's Taxonomy of Learning Domains is a tool that can be used for instructional planning, curriculum planning, and assessment. It is used to promote and elicit higher levels of thinking instead of relying on rote memorization. Bloom's Taxonomy can enhance instructional experiences for students by helping them to extend their **thinking skills**. This taxonomy is a useful tool for teachers wanting to improve students' thinking abilities. The taxonomy includes a list of **cognitive skills** ranking from lower-order thinking to higher-order thinking. **Remembering** is the lowest level on the taxonomy. This involves simply remembering or recalling information. **Comprehending** is the next level, which involves thinking about and understanding information. When students demonstrate **application**, the next level, they show that they can use information and apply it to real-life interactions. In the **analyzing** level, students are able to categorize, compare, and contrast information. Students demonstrate the second to last level, **evaluating**, by making decisions and demonstrating judgement. **Creating** is the last level, which involves using prior knowledge and generalizing it to new concepts.

MAPPING

Concept maps are visual organizers that help students with understanding and comprehension. They are generally easy to create and implement. Concept maps should be used before approaching new learning concepts. The purpose of a concept map is to help students organize new information and make connections between other content, thoughts, and ideas. Concept maps can be constructed as part of **teacher-led instruction**, which is a strategy that may be beneficial for younger grades. They can also be constructed independently or in small groups and then discussed as a class, which is a strategy more beneficial for children in higher grades. Concept mapping starts with **identifying major concepts** from reading selections or texts. Then the major ideas are sorted into **categories**, which can be adjusted as the process continues. Arrows or other visuals can be used to demonstrate how the ideas are connected. The last integral part of the concept mapping process is the **sharing piece**, when students reflect and talk about the processes and concept maps.

CULTURALLY RESPONSIVE TEACHING AND INSTRUCTION

Culturally responsive teaching (**CRT**) involves teachers implementing instruction in a variety of culturally diverse ways in order to target all students. CRT teachers respect their own cultures and the cultures of others by taking the applicable cultures into consideration during planning and instruction. CRT instruction is student centered, considers students' unique abilities and strengths, and helps build and maintain student confidence in their specific cultures. CRT instruction is about reflecting cultural pride, learning styles, and tools. Successful CRT instruction allows all students to **engage** more and **comprehend** content that applies to them. Games created to address learning objectives require attention and processing and can teach skills that emphasize use of cultural tools to solve problems. Social learning helps students become responsible for their own learning processes and develop cultural skills. Benefits of CRT include establishing inclusive classroom environments, encouraging individual development and decision-making, assisting with overall comprehension, and putting a greater emphasis on the value of learning.

VOICE RECOGNITION SOFTWARE

Voice recognition software and communication software can assist students who struggle with speaking or communicating. **Voice recognition software** works through computers and allows people to speak commands into microphones instead of using keyboards. This feature creates a **least restrictive environment** for a student with a disability because it removes the sometimes challenging aspect of using a keyboard while working on a computer. Voice recognition software allows users to carry out commands such as opening documents, saving documents, and moving the mouse cursor. It also allows users to "write" sentences and paragraphs by speaking into the microphones in word processing programs. In order for voice recognition software to be effective, the user must learn to dictate words separately into a microphone. This ensures that the correct word is heard and dictated by the voice-to-text software. Some programs collect information and familiarize themselves with people's particular voice qualities. Over time, the systems learn to adapt to people's voices, and the systems become more efficient.

EFFECTIVELY INSTRUCTING STUDENTS USING ASSISTIVE TECHNOLOGY

Assistive technology (**AT**) refers to tools effective for teaching students with learning disabilities, as they address a number of potential special needs. The purpose of AT is to level the playing field for students with **learning disabilities**, particularly when they are participating in general education classrooms. AT can address learning difficulties in math, listening, organization, memory, reading, and writing. **AT for listening** can assist students who have difficulties processing language. For example, a personal listening device can help a student hear a teacher' voice more clearly. **AT for organization and memory** can help students with self-management tasks, such as keeping assignment calendars or retrieving information using hand-held devices. **AT for reading** often include text-to-speech devices that assist with students' reading fluency, decoding, comprehension, and other skill deficits. **AT for writing** assists students who struggle with handwriting or writing development. Some AT writing devices help with actual handwriting, while others assist with spelling, punctuation, grammar, word usage, or text organization.

TYPES OF ASSISTIVE TECHNOLOGY TOOLS

Assistive technology (**AT**) tools can be separate objects and devices or tools readily available on the Internet to assist in the learning of students with disabilities. The purpose of AT tools is to provide students with disabilities **equal access to the curriculum** by accommodating their individual needs to promote positive outcomes. **Personal listening devices (PLDs)**, sometimes called FM systems, are devices that clarify teachers' words. With a PLD, a teacher speaks into a small microphone, and the words transmit clearly into a student's headphone or earpiece. **Sound field systems** amplify teachers' voices to eliminate sound issues in the classroom environments. **Noise-cancelling headphones** are useful for students who need to work independently and limit distractions or behavioral triggers. **Audio recorders** allow students to record lectures or lessons and refer back to the recordings at their own pace. Some note-taking applications will transcribe audio into written words. Captioning is available to pair visual words with spoken words. **Text-to-speech (TTS) software** lets students see and hear words at the same time. TTS and audiobook technology can help students with fluency, decoding, and comprehension skills.

INSTRUCTING NONVERBAL STUDENTS ON THE USE OF AUGMENTATIVE AND ALTERNATIVE COMMUNICATION SYSTEMS

Students with communication disorders may often require the use of augmentative or alternative communication systems. Communication systems are used to help the students effectively demonstrate **expressive and receptive language** and engage in **social skills**. Teaching appropriate communication skills is a collaborative effort between the students' caretakers, teachers, and other professionals. Typically, **speech services** are written into students' Individualized Education Programs (IEPs), and the services are delivered by **speech language pathologists (SLPs)**. Depending on how it is written in the IEPs, the SLPs may work one-on-one with students or work with the teachers to incorporate speech and language skills throughout students' school days. In order for communication systems to work for nonverbal students, measures must be taken to ensure that the particular systems are appropriate for what the students need. It is important for the caretakers, teachers, other professionals, and even classmates to model using the devices so the students can learn how to "talk" appropriately. Students must also

have constant access to the systems and receive consistent opportunities to communicate with the systems at home and at school.

USE OF VISUAL REPRESENTATION SYSTEMS WITH STUDENTS WITH AUTISM

Assistive technology (AT) helps increase learning opportunities for students with autism by eliminating educational barriers to learning. AT can help improve students' expressive communication skills, attention skills, motivational skills, academic skills, and more. **Visual representation systems** in the form of objects, photographs, drawings, or written words provide concrete representations of words for students with autism. Visual representations, such as simple pictures paired with words, can be used to create visual schedules for students with autism. Photographs can be used to help students learn the names of people, places, or vocabulary words. Written words should be paired with the visual representations in order to create links between the concrete objects and the actual words. The goal is for the students to eventually recognize the words without the pictures. Visual representation systems can also help facilitate easier transitions between activities or places, which can be difficult for students with autism.

BENEFITS OF VOCATIONAL/CAREER EDUCATION

Students with disabilities often participate in vocational or career and technical education in order to gain **independent living skills**. Often, schools and communities offer services for vocational or career and technical education that provide vocational or career training for people with disabilities. These programs offer students **job-specific skills training** and opportunities to earn certifications, diplomas, or certificates. They often involve **hands-on learning experiences** focused on building skills specific to certain occupations. These programs are beneficial to students with disabilities, as they tend to struggle with grasping abstract concepts learned in typical classroom environments. Hands-on training in vocational or career education programs can be a meaningful way for students with disabilities to both learn academic concepts and gain living skills needed to function in post-graduate life. Vocational and technical education opportunities also offer alternatives for students with disabilities who might otherwise drop out of high school. These programs also serve as a viable option for younger students to work towards, as most vocational or career education programs are offered to students in upper grade levels.

SUPPORTING CLASSROOM TRANSITIONS

Transitioning to life after high school can be a difficult process, particularly for students with disabilities. It is important for teachers to facilitate and support these **transitions** before students exit their special education programs. **Structured learning environments** that include independent workstations and learning centers provide opportunities for independent learning to occur. **Independent workstations** give students chances to practice previously introduced concepts or perform previously introduced tasks. **Learning centers** provide small group settings where new skills can be taught. Students can also rotate through different learning centers that offer art lessons, focus on academic skills, or provide breaks or leisure activities. **Classroom layout** also plays an important role. Teachers should plan their classroom layouts based on individual student needs in order to create comfortable, predictable environments for students with disabilities. **Visual schedules** help students transition between centers by providing them with concrete schedule references.

VOCATIONAL SKILLS NEEDED TO BE SUCCESSFUL IN WORK ENVIRONMENTS

Informal vocational training often begins before students even get to high school. Teachers include informal vocational training skills in their classrooms by teaching academic and communication skills. **Academic skills** can both spark and strengthen students' career interests and provide learning platforms to build upon. **Communication skills** generalize to work

43

environments when students learn appropriate communication skills, like how to give and follow instructions and process information. **Social and interpersonal skills**, like problem-solving abilities and learning how to participate in phone conversations, are important for teaching students how to perform in workplaces. Students also need to learn important **vocational and occupational skills** required by most jobs, such as how to interact appropriately with coworkers and keep track of worked hours. Students also need formal or informal training in completing resumes, cover letters, and tax forms. Training may also include interviewing practice and job search guidance.

RESOURCES TO PROMOTE SUCCESSFUL TRANSITIONS TO LIFE AFTER HIGH SCHOOL

In some states, **statements of transition** should be included on Individualized Education Programs (IEPs) at age 14 for students with disabilities. In most states, the Individuals with Disabilities Education Act mandates that transition plans be put in place for students on IEPs at age 16 and every year thereafter. Some schools and communities have programs and/or resources available to facilitate students' successful transitions to life after high school. Throughout the transition process, it is important that students and their caregivers participate in any decision-making processes. **Vocational education courses**, sometimes called career and technical education (CTE) courses, offer academic course alternatives. The courses usually specialize in specific trades or occupations. They can serve to spark or maintain students' interests in vocational fields. Some schools offer **post-secondary enrollment options (PSEO)**, where students can participate in college courses, earning both high school and college credits. **Career assessments**, including interest inventories and formal and informal vocational assessments, serve to gauge students' career interests. These can be worked into students' transitional goals on their IEPs and should be conducted frequently as students' interests change.

COMPONENTS OF A TRANSITION PLAN

Per federal law, transition plans are required to be part of a student's Individualized Education Program during the year the student turns 16 years old. The **transition plan components** include postsecondary goals and transition services. The purpose of the goals is to state what a student wants to achieve after high school. The four goal areas are vocational training, post-secondary education, employment, and independent living. **Transition goals** must be results oriented and measurable. Goals can be general, but the transition activities need to be quantified to reflect what the student can complete in the IEP year. It is common for interests to change from year to year. Therefore, goals and plans may change as well. **Transition services** are determined once the goals are established. Transition services include types of instruction the student will receive in school, related services, community experiences, career or college counseling, and help with adaptive behavior skills. Goals and transition services must be reviewed and updated each year. Academic goals in the IEP can also support transition goals. For example, academic math goals can focus on money management skills as part of a transition plan.

PURPOSE AND IMPLICATIONS OF A TRANSITION PLAN ON THE IEP

In most states, a transition plan should be included on the Individualized Education Program (IEP) for a student with a disability the year the student turns 16 years old. As mandated by the Individuals with Disabilities Education Act, a transition plan should include **goals and services** specific to the student's individual needs. The purpose of a transition plan on a student's IEP is to help guide and prepare the student for post-secondary employment, education, and independent living. A transition plan is driven by the student's **interests**, which can be gathered via formal and informal career assessments, such as interest inventories. A transition plan includes **goals** specific to a student's expressed interests, which can or will be achieved within the IEP year. Successful goals are objective, measurable, and specifically related to a student's expressed interests. These

44

goals can include goals for post-secondary employment, education, and/or independent living, depending on the needs and interests of the specific student. Transition goals can also include student goals for vocational training.

FACTORS THAT INFLUENCE SUCCESSFUL TRANSITIONS TO POST-SECONDARY LIFE

Students, parents or legal guardians, teachers, school professionals, and sometimes community members are key **factors** in successful transitions to post-secondary life for students with disabilities. Factors that influence students' successful transitions include participation in standards-based education, work preparation and career-based learning experiences, and experience with leadership skills. Other factors that influence successful transitions include access to and experience with **community services**, such as mental health and transportation services. Lastly, **family involvement and support** are key factors in facilitating successful transitions for students with disabilities. Standards-based education ensures that students receive consistent and clear expectations with curriculum that is aligned to the Universal Design for Learning standards. Exposure to work preparation and career-based learning experiences ensures that students receive opportunities to discover potential career interests and/or hobbies. Connections and experiences with community activities provide students with essential post-secondary independent living skills. Family involvement and support ensure that students have advocates for their needs and interests. Families can also help students connect with school and community-based supports that facilitate their career interests.

INCLUDING MEASURABLE AND CHALLENGING OBJECTIVES IN LESSON PLANS

Lesson objectives should be **SMART**, meaning they should be specific, measurable, attainable, relevant, and time based. When teachers plan lessons, SMART objectives provide the framework to effectively execute the lesson plans. Specific objectives describe exactly what will be taught within the time frame of the lesson. Specific objectives answer **"W" questions**, such as the questions listed below.

- **What** do I want to accomplish?
- **Why** is this goal important?
- **Who** is involved?
- **Where** is it located?
- **Which** resources are available?

Measurable objectives are important for staying on task and tracking progress. **Attainable** objectives are created with students' strengths and needs in mind. Attainable objectives should keep in mind what students can realistically accomplish within the lesson time frame. Achievable objectives spell out how the goals will be accomplished. A good attainable objective is challenging but realistically achievable based on students' abilities. **Relevant** objectives should build upon prior knowledge and matter to the teacher and the students. Relevant objectives promote student interest and engagement. **Time-bound** objectives set deadlines and help prioritize objectives.

Planning and Managing the Learning Environment

CHARACTERISTICS OF EFFECTIVE STRUCTURED LEARNING ENVIRONMENTS

A structured learning environment is an important component of good **classroom management**. Teachers that create environments that are conducive for teaching and learning create environments where students feel safe. In **effective structured learning environments**, teachers create solid relationships with students by getting to know them and their interests. Often, this information can be used to implement learning activities based on students' interests. Another way to promote effective structured learning environments is to consistently follow implemented rules and maintain **consistency** in procedures in order to communicate what to expect to students. Transitioning students appropriately between activities increases time spent learning. Additionally, teachers that spend time designing effective lesson plans that anticipate student behaviors create solid environments for their students. Teachers can also establish good learning environments by promoting target behaviors. This means promoting standards of behavior and clear consequences for breaking rules. Students that have clear expectations learn in effective structured learning environments.

CURRICULUM AND ASSIGNMENT MODIFICATIONS IN THE CLASSROOM FOR STUDENTS WITH DISABILITIES

Modifications are changes to what students are taught or expected to learn. Students with disabilities can receive **curriculum modifications** as determined by their specific needs and as written out in their Individualized Education Programs. Curriculum modifications allow students to learn material that is different from what their general education peers learn. For example, students with classroom modifications may receive assignments with fewer math problems or with reading samples appropriate for their reading levels. Students with curriculum modifications may receive different grading tiers than their peers. The ways teachers grade their assignments may be different from how the teachers grade their peers' assignments. Students may also be excused from particular projects or given project guidelines that are different and better suited to their individual needs. **Assignment modifications** include completing fewer or different homework problems than peers, writing shorter papers, answering fewer questions on classwork and tests, and creating alternate projects or assignments.

PURPOSE OF NON-TRADITIONAL CLASSROOM SEATING ARRANGEMENTS

Seating arrangements are part of good classroom management strategies, especially for students with disabilities. Special education settings and inclusion settings often require flexibility with instruction and versatility with **seating arrangements**. The traditional setting includes rows of desks facing the area where the teacher conducts instruction. More **student-centered arrangements** include a horseshoe seating arrangement, a group pod arrangement, or a paired arrangement. A **horseshoe seating arrangement** is conducive to student-centered instruction because it allows the students to face each other and the instructor to move around the classroom easily. This setup facilitates classroom discussions and encourages interactions between instructors and students and among peers. The **group pod** or **paired-pod arrangement** is useful for student-centered instruction like small group work. This arrangement is also helpful when students need to rotate through lesson stages or work in small groups on projects. Effective teachers do not use one seating arrangement for the entire year. Best practices indicate that seating arrangements should change and be tied to the intent of lesson objectives.

DETERMINING THE SPECIAL EDUCATION SETTING PLACEMENT

Special education setting placement is determined in a student's Individualized Education Program (IEP), as specified by the Individuals with Disabilities Education Act (IDEA). IDEA requires that students be placed in **general education classrooms** to the maximum extent possible. Students should be placed in environments that are most appropriate for them, known as the **least restrictive environment**. If students can be educated in general education classrooms (**inclusion**) when provided with appropriate accommodations, they can be placed in general education classrooms. When students with disabilities need modifications to curriculum that are significantly below grade level or different than their peers, the students may be placed in **resource rooms** for remedial instruction. However, the students may also participate in the general education curriculum with modified work that meets their current abilities. For example, a student who

46

struggles in math can use a calculator accommodation in the inclusion setting. A student whose math skills are two grade levels below the skills of same-aged peers may be placed in an inclusion setting with modifications or receive instruction in a resource room.

FUNCTION OF A MULTIDISCIPLINARY TEAM-TEACHING MODEL

The three disciplinary team models include a multidisciplinary team, an interdisciplinary team, and a transdisciplinary team. The **multidisciplinary team** is usually composed of the special educator, general education teacher, parents, paraprofessionals, principal, and school psychologist. As a whole, this team presents a comprehensive group of expertise, qualifications, and skills. In the multidisciplinary team model, these professionals do not collaborate, but instead work alongside each other to pursue a **common goal** for the individual student with special needs. The multidisciplinary team model is effective for evaluating a student for referral for special education, completing pre-referral testing, and completing an Individualized Education Program or Evaluation Team Report. Sometimes this team is referred to as the child study team or student support team. In this model, professionals usually pull out students to work with them individually. Parents and legal guardians are a part of this process. Professionals working with the student should openly communicate their processes and the results of any evaluations or informal observations.

INTERDISCIPLINARY TEAM MODEL

An interdisciplinary team model features the **general education teacher** providing all curriculum and accommodations for a student with an Individualized Education Program. In this model, the special educator and other professionals relevant to the education of the student collaborate to ensure that the curriculum meets the needs of the student and the accommodations are appropriate. This model is not a team-teaching model. Advantages of this model include the collaboration of all IEP team members towards a common goal and the student's needs being addressed by one teacher instead of several different teachers or professionals. The disadvantages of this model include difficulties with collaboration between professionals and issues with delivering related services to students who need them. Related service provision sometimes includes one-on-one instruction, which requires the student to be pulled out for a certain amount of time during general education instruction. This model may also not be appropriate for students with intense needs, as they often require **individualized education** in order to meet IEP goals. They may also require specific accommodations and modifications not suitable for the general education classroom.

TRANSDISCIPLINARY TEAM-TEACHING MODEL

In this model, professionals working with the student work together collaboratively to ensure the individual needs of the student are met. The **special educator** may teach in the general education classroom, delivering instruction to both students with and without disabilities. This model features a team-teaching experience for classroom students, where the special educator and general educator may take turns teaching. The presence of the special educator in the general education setting means the special educator can offer advice for **accommodating** the students with special needs in the classroom. Additionally, this model provides opportunities for teachers and other professionals to communicate consistently about students' progress, share ideas, and work collaboratively to solve any issues that arise. The effectiveness of this model relies heavily on the collaboration of the special educator and the general educator addressing the major features of this team-teaching model.

ADVANTAGES AND DISADVANTAGES OF TEAM-TEACHING MODELS

Students with and without disabilities present a variety of **learning abilities** in the general education classroom. One advantage of team-teaching models in this setting is being able to target the unique abilities, learning methods, and skills that each student brings to the classroom. Another advantage is effective classroom management. In an **effective team-teaching model**, one teacher provides the instruction, while the other practices classroom management skills to minimize disruptions and promote a safe learning environment. This model encourages class participation, facilitates group activities, and provides multiple means of engagement for learning content. One disadvantage is there may be an offset between the teachers sharing a class. When one teacher is not open to multiple methods of delivering instruction, the team-teaching approach is ineffective. Planning and making group decisions regarding curriculum can be time consuming and stressful in a team-teaching environment.

LIFTING GUIDELINES FOR STUDENTS WHO REQUIRE PHYSICAL LIFTING

Teachers and paraprofessionals may encounter students with physical disabilities who require **assisted transfers**. In some circumstances, students must be **lift-assisted** from their wheelchairs in order to participate in physical therapy or floor activities. While this practice is more common in low-incidence classrooms and not always a job requirement, it is important to know school guidelines for **lifting techniques** to keep staff and students safe. Knowing school guidelines for lifting can also help prevent back injuries from occurring. Physical therapists working with the students should be consulted before attempting student lifts. They are trained professionals who know specific procedures for lifting students in order to keep the students and staff members safe. Every school district has policies for lift-assisted student transfers. Each student should be evaluated to determine if a one-person lift or two-person lift is needed. Two-person lifts are for heavier students, and some school districts do not allow two-person lifts for safety reasons.

HOW COOPERATIVE LEARNING WORKS

Cooperative learning is an interpersonal group learning process where students learn concepts by working together in **small groups**. Cooperative learning involves collaboration among small groups to achieve common goals. With **formal cooperative learning**, an instructor oversees the learning of lesson material or completion of assignments for students in these small groups. With **informal cooperative learning**, the instructor supervises group activities by keeping students cognitively active but does not guide instruction or assignments. For example, a teacher might use a class period to show a movie but provide a list of questions for students to complete during the movie. In the special education classroom, cooperative learning is helpful when students need specific skills targeted or remediated. It is also helpful for separating students who are learning different content at different levels. For example, a cooperative learning activity may involve multiple groups of students with differing levels of mathematic abilities. Group work also promotes development of interpersonal skills as students interact with one another.

BENEFIT OF MULTIPLE MODALITY INSTRUCTION AND ACTIVITIES

The purpose of multiple modality instruction is to engage students by offering different ways to learn the same material. **Multiple modality teaching** also addresses students' unique learning styles. Learning modalities are generally separated into four categories: **visual** (seeing), **auditory** (hearing), **kinesthetic** (moving), and **tactile** (touch) modalities. This way of teaching targets students who may have deficits in one or more modalities. It is also helpful for students who struggle in one or more of the learning categories. If a student struggles with understanding content that is presented visually, a lesson that includes auditory, kinesthetic, and tactile components may engage learning. Additionally, presenting lesson material and activities in a multi-modal approach helps improve student memory and retention by solidifying concepts through multiple means of engagement. This approach is also useful for students with **attention disorders** who may struggle in environments where one mode of teaching is used. The multiple modality approach ensures that activities, such as kinesthetic or tactile activities, keep more than one sense involved with the learning process.

COMPONENTS OF A SUCCESSFUL TEAM-TEACHING MODEL

A successful team-teaching model is one where the teachers involved set clear, effective, specific **goals** for performance. These goals must demonstrate clarity. All team-teaching members must be clear on the components of the goals and their potential outcomes. Clear goals allow team members and students to know what they are working towards as a classroom. Goals should be specific and measurable. **Goal criteria** should be qualified in percentages or quantities. This provides hard evidence for how effectively the team-teaching classroom is meeting the goals. Challenging goals set high expectations for what the team needs to work towards. Challenging goals ensure that team members and classroom students are working to achieve goals right outside their ability levels. Goals that are too challenging can be frustrating for all team members and students. A successful team-teaching model also reflects **commitment** from team members and any other professionals involved in the classroom.

CLASSROOM TIMING, SCHEDULE, AND ORGANIZATION ACCOMMODATIONS

Timing, schedule, and organizational accommodations change the ways students with disabilities have access to classrooms with the fewest barriers to learning. Students who need these accommodations receive them as written statements in their Individualized Education Programs, 504 Plans, or as teachers see fit during classroom time. **Timing accommodations** allow students more time to complete tasks or tests and/or process instructions. They also allow students to access frequent breaks during assignments or tests. **Schedule accommodations** include taking tests in chunks over periods of time or several days, taking test sections in different orders, and/or taking tests during specific times of day. **Organizational skill accommodations** include assistance with time management, marking texts with highlighters, maintaining daily assignment or work schedules, and/or receiving study skills instruction. When accommodations are written in a student's IEP, the student has access to them for state standardized tests. When and how accommodations are put into place is left to the discretion of the teacher unless specifically written in the student's IEP or 504 Plan.

CREATING INCLUSIVE LEARNING ENVIRONMENTS THAT ADDRESS UNIQUE NEEDS

Effective inclusive environments abide by the **Universal Design for Learning framework**. Special educators and general educators can work together to create learning environments that are accessible to the unique needs of students with language or physical needs. This can be done by providing **multiple ways** for students to access lesson concepts, express learned concepts, and engage in the learning process. For students with language barriers, signs, symbols, pictures, and learning concepts may have different meanings than they do for students without language barriers. Keeping this in mind, teachers can address UDL guidelines for students with **language barriers** by providing diverse ways to activate prior knowledge, emphasizing key learning elements, and using visuals to guide the learning process. For students with **physical barriers**, teachers can level the learning process by making their physical classroom environments accessible and providing different ways for students to express what they have learned. In general, teachers abiding by UDL framework would have these supports in place in order to ensure that the needs of diverse learners are met.

FOSTERING POSITIVE AND INCLUSIVE LEARNING ENVIRONMENTS ADDRESSING STUDENTS WITH LEARNING OR COGNITIVE NEEDS

Whether in the general education classroom or special education classroom, the Universal Design for Learning model should foster **positive and inclusive learning environments**. General education and special education teachers can take measures to ensure the UDL concept is implemented to address the unique needs of students with **cognitive or behavioral needs**. Since each student presents different needs, a one-size-fits-all approach to learning is not suitable or UDL compliant for these students. Special educators and general educators should openly communicate about the unique learning needs of the students with learning or cognitive needs. General strategies include receiving regular **input from special educators** on how to best meet the needs of the students in the classroom. This includes sharing information with any **paraprofessionals and aides** regarding how to assist the students in the general education classroom. UDL base strategies include the general educators providing multiple means by which students can complete the assignments. Students with cognitive disabilities may also benefit from the use of concrete examples and instruction, especially when addressing abstract concepts.

FOSTERING POSITIVE AND INCLUSIVE LEARNING ENVIRONMENTS ADDRESSING STUDENTS WITH BEHAVIORAL NEEDS

The **Universal Design for Learning (UDL) concepts** can be implemented to reduce challenging behavior in the classroom. They can also be used to help students with behavioral needs find success in the general education classroom. **Lack of student engagement** is compatible with the presentation of **challenging behaviors**. When UDL concepts are demonstrated appropriately, engagement can improve. Providing **multiple means of representation** is one UDL strategy for improving engagement and challenging behavior. This means the classroom teacher provides multiple ways of presenting the teaching material in order to engage as many students as possible. Teachers that provide multiple means of representation look to activate prior knowledge and help students make sense of the current content. UDL compliant strategies also include providing **multiple means of expression**. Teachers applying UDL principles recognize that differentiating activities and assignments addresses a variety of abilities and learning styles. UDL compliant teachers should also provide **multiple means of engagement**. Successful engagement in learning can often offset challenging behaviors by helping students focus on lesson material. Offering both challenging and simplistic work options and making engaging, solid connections to past and/or future lesson content can minimize the possibility of problems arising in the classroom.

Instruction

Promoting Student Learning and Development

TEACHING STRATEGIES AND ACCOMMODATIONS FOR STUDENTS WITH WORKING MEMORY DEFICITS

Working memory is critical for remembering letters and numbers, listening to short instructions, reading and understanding content, completing homework independently, and understanding social cues. When **working memory skills** are absent or slow to develop, learning may be difficult. This may get worse for children over time. As they fail to develop or retain working memory capabilities, their overall **cognitive abilities** begin to suffer. Working memory deficits differ from person to person with disabilities, but accommodations can be made to make up for missing or developing skills. Educators can implement **strategies** like reducing the children's workload, providing visual cues, being aware of when children might be reaching memory overload, providing positive feedback, providing testing alternatives, and providing extra time. **Accommodations** on an Individualized Education Program for a student with working memory deficits might include frequent breaks, small group instruction, and extended time for tests and assignments.

CLASSROOM ACCOMMODATIONS THAT ALLOW STUDENTS WITH DISABILITIES TO BE SUCCESSFUL

Accommodations are flexible classroom tools because they can be used to provide **interventions** without time or location boundaries. They remove **barriers** to learning for students with disabilities, and they change how students learn. Accommodations do not change what the students are learning or expected to know. Classroom accommodations may be outlined in students' Individualized Education Programs or 504 Plans, or simply provided on the spot by the special educators or general educators. Accommodations are put into place to ensure that the students with disabilities are accessing the learning process with the fewest barriers, putting them on the same levels as their peers without disabilities. **Presentation accommodations** include allowing students to listen to instructions orally, providing written lists of instructions, and allowing students to use readers to assist with comprehension. **Response accommodations** include allowing students to provide oral responses, capture responses via audio recording, and/or use spelling dictionaries or spell checkers when writing. **Accommodations to setting** include special seating (wherever the students learn best), use of sensory tools, and/or use of special lighting.

EFFECT OF HOME LIFE FACTORS ON LEARNING AND DEVELOPMENT

Students' home lives are interconnected with their school lives. **Home and life factors**, especially negative ones, are difficult for students to avoid generalizing to the school environment. **Home stressors** can often develop into dysfunction at school for children with disabilities. Factors that affect the learning and development of students with disabilities include academic factors, environmental factors, intellectual factors, language factors, medical factors, perceptual factors, and psychological factors. **Academic factors** include developmental delays in core content areas, lack of basic skills, and apparent inconsistency of learning in certain stages of development. **Environmental factors** occur when children are exposed to home life trauma, such as divorce, drug abuse, alcoholism, parental fighting, or family illness. **Intellectual factors** include limited intellectual abilities or unnoticed gifted abilities. **Language factors** include issues with language barriers or language acquisition, such as aphasia, bilingualism, expressive language disorder, or pragmatic language disorder. **Medical factors** include Attention Deficit Hyperactivity Disorder, muscular problems, or hearing problems. **Perceptual factors** include any factors that affect or slow

down students' processing of information. **Psychological factors** include depression, anxiety, or conduct disorders.

SOCIAL SKILL DEFICITS THAT OCCUR IN STUDENTS WITH DISABILITIES

Social skills are a concept that needs to be taught to some students with disabilities, such as students with autism. **Social skills instruction** involves the teaching of basic communication skills, empathy and rapport skills, interpersonal skills, problem-solving skills, and accountability. **Basic communication skills** include listening skills, following directions, and avoiding speaking out of turn. **Empathy and rapport skills** involve teaching students how to demonstrate empathy and build rapport. **Interpersonal skills** must be learned by teaching students to demonstrate skills like sharing, joining activities, and participating in turn taking. **Problem-solving skills** sometimes need to be taught as well. These include teaching students to ask for help, apologize to others, make decisions, and accept consequences. **Accountability** must be taught to students so they can learn to follow through on promises and accept criticisms appropriately. These are skills that do not come naturally to students with social skill deficits.

OBTAINING ACCOMMODATIONS IN THE CLASSROOM SETTING

When parents or legal guardians of children with disabilities believe that **accommodations** may help their children, they can arrange to speak with the teachers about informal supports. **Informal supports** are strategies the teachers can put into place to assist the students with their learning processes. These changes do not require paperwork and can be provided during classroom instruction. Teachers can experiment with informal supports to determine what will be most helpful for removing the barriers to learning the students might be experiencing. If it is determined that students need bigger changes to how they learn, **formal evaluations** can take place. If the students are not already on Individualized Education Programs or 504 Plans, these needs may lead to initial evaluations to collect data on the students' needs. For students with IEPs or 504 Plans, accommodations that help the students can be included on their next IEPs or 504 Plans. The IEPs or 504 Plans can also be **amended** if the need for the accommodations is immediate, such as if they need to be put in place before standardized testing time. In both situations, **data** supporting the need for the accommodations must be provided and listed in the comprehensive initial evaluations, initial IEPs or 504 Plans, or the students' amended IEPs or 504 Plans.

INFORMAL SUPPORTS VS. FORMAL ACCOMMODATIONS

Informal supports are generally easier to implement in the classroom setting. They do not necessarily have to be implemented only for students on Individualized Education Programs or students with disabilities. Students who have not been evaluated for special education services can receive **informal supports** to ensure classroom success. When teachers see students struggling with the ways they are learning, the teachers may use informal supports to help the students. They may demonstrate that the students are able to learn with the accommodations in place. Informal supports are often the first step to indicating that students are in need of **special education services**. **Formal accommodations** come into place when students become eligible for IEPs or 504 Plans. Formal supports are written into the IEPs or 504 Plans and then required by law to be provided. Examples of informal supports include frequent breaks, special seating, quiet areas for test taking or studying, teacher cues, and help with basic organizational skills. These informal supports may eventually turn into formal supports if and when students become eligible for special education services.

INCLUSION CLASSROOM SETTING

The Individuals with Disabilities Education Act does not expressly define a **least restrictive environment** for each specific disability. Typically, it is up to the Individualized Education Program

52

team of professionals, including the student's parent or legal guardian, to determine the best case **LRE setting** possible for an individual student. Mainstreaming is a term that is often used interchangeably with inclusion. A **mainstreaming or inclusion setting** means the student with a disability is included in the general education setting the entire school day. The student may receive supports and services like an aide, related services, assistive technology, accommodations, or modifications that are appropriate for the individual student. These supports and services seek to help the student with a disability gain access to the general education curriculum with the fewest barriers. This model essentially seeks to level the playing field for the student with a disability so that he or she may learn alongside general education peers. For these students, the LRE setting must be justified in the Individualized Education Program.

SELF-CONTAINED CLASSROOM SETTING

The Individuals with Disabilities Education Act states that according to least restrictive environment standards, students in an LRE are ideally spending as much time as possible with their non-disabled peers in the **general education setting**. IDEA states that LRE means a student should receive general education "to the maximum extent that is appropriate," and that special classes, special schools, or removal from the general education classroom should only happen when a child's needs are greater than what can be provided by supplementary aids and services. A **self-contained classroom setting** can be a separate class of students within a school or a separate school that specifically addresses the needs of children with disabilities. In both settings, the needs of the students are greater than what can be offered in the general education classroom, even with educational supports. Settings like these may be specialized in instruction and support for students with similar needs. For these children, their placements in self-contained classrooms must be justified on their Individualized Education Programs.

PARTIAL MAINSTREAM/INCLUSION CLASSROOM SETTING

It is generally up to the Individualized Education Program team of professionals and the student's parent or legal guardian to determine a least restrictive environment that best suits the needs of the student. In a **partial mainstream/inclusion classroom setting**, a student spends part of the day in the **general education classroom**. The student receives part of his or her education in a separate, **special education classroom**. This type of LRE is determined when a student's needs are greater than what services can be provided in the general education classroom, even with educational supports or services in place. For example, a student with severe deficits in mathematical skills may be placed in a classroom outside the general education classroom that targets specific needs and skills. The student may also get pulled out of the general education classroom to receive one-on-one instruction or small group instruction. For these children, their placements in partial mainstream/inclusion classrooms must be justified on their Individualized Education Programs.

SPECIALIZED EDUCATIONAL SETTINGS

School districts sometimes offer specialized educational settings for students with disabilities, such as **special preschools**. Preschools for children with disabilities typically focus on children ages 3–5. They are important resources for teaching early learning, communication, and social skills that are essential for children with disabilities. **Life skills settings** are where students with disabilities can receive specialized instruction in academic, social, behavioral, or daily living skills. **Social behavior skills settings** are sometimes called applied behavior skills or behavior skills. In this type of setting, the primary focus is on social and decision-making skills. **Transition settings** are available for students making the transition from high school to life after high school. Students with Individualized Education Programs can stay in high school until the age of 21 or 22, depending on the calendar month they turn 22. Transition settings assist students with work experiences, post-secondary education experiences, and independent living skills.

PARENTS/LEGAL GUARDIANS ENSURING ACCOMMODATIONS ARE BEING PROVIDED

Accommodations are changes to the ways children with disabilities learn, not changes to what the children are learning. Parents can ensure that accommodations are being provided in a number of ways. Unless specifically stated on the students' Individualized Education Programs or 504 Plans, parents and legal guardians may only receive **formal updates** on how accommodations are being provided or helping the students during specified reporting times. However, parents and legal guardians can ask for **reports** on goal progress or accommodations for their students at any time. Parents and legal guardians can ensure that accommodations are successfully implemented by using the schools' progress reports and by asking the right questions. Parents and legal guardians can **advocate** for their students' accommodations by making sure the accommodations are being implemented on a regular basis. Parents and legal guardians also have the right to ask if students are using the accommodations on a **regular basis**. If they are being used on a regular basis, parents and legal guardians can explore options that might also help the students. Parents and legal guardians can work with the special education teachers and/or the IEP teams to ensure that their students' accommodations are being received and are effective.

EVALUATING, MODIFYING, AND ADAPTING THE CLASSROOM SETTING USING THE UDL

The **Universal Design for Learning (UDL) model** is most successful when the classroom teacher prepares a classroom setting that encourages the success of students with and without disabilities. Knowledge of the **characteristics** of students with different disabilities, as well as the unique **learning needs** of these students, ensures that the classroom teacher is aware of and addresses these needs in the classroom setting. Setting clear short and/or long-term goals for students to achieve is one way to meet the UDL standards. A traditional classroom may offer one assignment for all students to complete, but a UDL compliant classroom may offer **different assignments** or **different ways** for students to complete the assignment. UDL compliant classrooms also offer **flexible workspaces** for the students to complete their classwork. Students may have access to quiet spaces for individual work or group tables for group work. Students in a UDL compliant classroom also receive regular **feedback** throughout their classwork rather than receiving one grade upon assignment completion. UDL compliant teachers recognize that students access information differently and provide different ways for students to gain **access**, such as audio text.

EVALUATING, MODIFYING, AND ADAPTING THE CLASSROOM CURRICULUM USING THE UDL

In order for a **Universal Design for Learning (UDL) model classroom** to be successful, the classroom teacher must evaluate, modify, and adapt the classroom **curriculum** to best suit the needs of the individual students. UDL contrasts with a one-size-fits-all concept of curriculum planning, where lesson plans are developed and implemented strictly based on how teachers expect students to learn. Instead, a successful UDL model addresses the many **specific needs** of a classroom of students. These needs may vary depending on the unique abilities each classroom of students presents. UDL compliant teachers can evaluate the success of lessons by checking the achievement of students using **formal and informal assessments**. UDL compliant teachers utilize these assessments throughout the lessons, instead of upon lesson completion. These teachers use the results of the evaluations to modify and/or adapt classroom instruction to best meet the needs of the students. Evaluation methods given informally can provide a lot of information about whether or not students are grasping the concepts. UDL compliant teachers use evaluation results to reflect upon lessons and determine how to move forward with future lessons.

EVALUATING, MODIFYING, AND ADAPTING THE CLASSROOM MATERIALS AND EQUIPMENT USING THE UDL

In order for a **Universal Design for Learning (UDL) classroom** to be successful, the classroom teacher must evaluate, modify, and adapt the classroom **materials and equipment** to best suit the needs of the individual students. When teachers are **UDL compliant**, they are observing the needs of the students and making necessary changes to materials and/or equipment to ensure student success. A way for teachers to determine the success of classroom materials or equipment is through **formal and informal assessments**. Informal assessments in particular are helpful for receiving immediate feedback as to whether materials are appropriate for student learning. A UDL compliant teacher may offer multiple ways for students to present what they learned, instead of completing pencil and paper assignments. **Multiple assignment completion options** ensure that the unique abilities of students are being targeted, instead of just targeting one or two specific skills. **Equipment** such as audio or digital text, when paired with words, can assist students who have issues with listening or comprehension. A UDL compliant teacher may choose to pair audio output and text during a reading assignment for all students in order to target students with listening or comprehension difficulties.

PRINCIPLES OF THE UNIVERSAL DESIGN FOR LEARNING MODEL

The UDL model contains three principles that aim to level the playing field for all learners. **Principle I** of the Universal Design for Learning model primarily focuses on what **representation or version** of information is being taught. This principle aims to target an audience of diverse learners. By providing multiple ways for students to approach content, teachers can ensure that the unique needs of all learners in their classrooms are met. **Principle II** examines the how of learning. This principle focuses on the concept that students learn best when provided with **multiple ways** to demonstrate what they have learned. In Principle II compliant classrooms, students are given more than one option for expressing themselves. **Principle III** maintains a focus on providing multiple ways for students to engage in the learning process. Principle III compliant teachers provide options for keeping content **interesting and relevant** to all types of learners. In effective UDL model classrooms, these principles are generally met by providing multiple ways to learn the content, express what was learned, and engage in lesson content.

IMPLEMENTING MODIFICATIONS AND ACCOMMODATIONS IN AN INCLUSIVE CLASSROOM SETTING

General educators can work with special educators to create an effective **co-teaching model**. In an effective co-teaching model, both the general educator and special educator demonstrate the **Universal Design for Learning Framework**. This ensures that the needs of the diverse group of learners are being met. For students using Individualized Education Programs, modifications such as reduced work would be expressly written in their IEPs. In a co-teaching model, student modifications would be communicated to the **general educator**. The **special educator** can work with the general educator to provide the modifications in the inclusive classroom setting. Students using IEPs may have accommodations expressly written in their IEPs. These accommodations may or may not be used in an **inclusive setting**, depending on the relevancy of the accommodation. For example, the accommodation of using a calculator would be utilized in a math class but not a social studies class. In addition to expressly written accommodations, special educators and general educators can work together in the setting to provide appropriate **accommodations** during the learning process. These types of accommodations may be part of informal assessments used to adjust instruction.

ROLE OF PARAEDUCATORS

Paraeducators, sometimes referred to as aides or paraprofessionals, are part of students' educational teams. **Paraeducators** work under the supervision of special educators or principals and are key contributors to the learning process for certain students. Their primary role, especially if their positions are funded by the Individuals with Disabilities Education Act, is to provide **educational support** for students. For students using Individualized Education Programs, the use of paraeducators is typically included in the IEPs. Paraeducators can facilitate the learning process for students by removing learning barriers, keeping track of goal progress, or organizing goal-tracking activities. Paraeducators cannot introduce new concepts or take over the role of highly qualified teachers. Paraeducators cannot make changes to what students are learning, unless specific modifications are listed in the students' IEPs. They cannot provide accommodations unless the accommodations are appropriate for what is written in the students' IEPs. The paraeducators may also be instructed by supervising teachers or principals to facilitate and monitor accommodations or modifications for students and reinforce learned concepts.

BENEFITS OF COLLABORATIVE TEACHING AND THE CO-TEACHING MODEL

If determined by an Individualized Education Program (IEP), a student with a disability may participate in an **inclusive setting**. In some classrooms, students participate in **co-taught settings**. In this **collaborative teaching environment**, the general educator and special educator work together to meet the goals of the students with disabilities in the regular education classroom. Students in this setting are all taught to the same educational standards. However, accommodations and modifications may be implemented for students with disabilities. In a successful collaborative teaching model, the special educator and general educator may cooperatively implement the accommodations and modifications for these students. A two-teacher setting also gives students more opportunities to receive individualized instruction, work in small groups, or receive one-on-one attention. Collaborative teaching in the co-taught setting can facilitate differentiated instruction, help the teachers meet the Universal Design for Learning framework, and provide individualized learning opportunities.

FOSTERING THE COMMUNICATION DEVELOPMENT OF STUDENTS WITH ASD

Students with **Autism Spectrum Disorder** (ASD) vary in their need for communication and social skill assistance and instruction. Some students with ASD may demonstrate slight to extreme delays in language, difficulty sustaining conversations, and the inability to understand body language, tone of voice, and facial expressions. Since ASD is a **spectrum disorder**, there typically is no single instructional strategy or technique that works for all students with the disorder. Some **evidence-based strategies** are effective for teaching appropriate communication skills to students with ASD. **Applied behavioral analysis (ABA)** is an evidence-based strategy that involves providing an intervention and analyzing its effectiveness for a student with ASD. **Discrete trial training (DTT)** is a teaching strategy that is more structured than ABA. It focuses on teaching and reinforcing skills in smaller increments. **Pivotal response treatment (PRT)** is an ABA-derived approach that focuses more on meaningful reinforcement when general behaviors occur. PRT targets progress in areas of development rather than focusing on decreasing specific behaviors.

MANAGING DISTRACTIONS THAT MAY AFFECT LEARNING AND DEVELOPMENT

Managing distractions is a part of good teaching practices. Special educators demonstrate good **classroom management strategies** when they:

- create positive learning environments by getting to know students' individual emotional, intellectual, social, and physical needs.
- remove or accommodate environmental triggers specific to students.

- remove or accommodate behavioral triggers.
- encourage students to help with classroom jobs and small tasks.
- create preemptive lesson plans for anticipated behaviors.
- attempt verbal de-escalation first when behavioral issues arise.
- set clear, consistent rules.
- set and follow through with consequences for breaking the rules.
- take time to get to know students and their triggers.
- create seating arrangements that minimize distractions.
- teach social skills, thinking skills, test-taking skills, problem-solving skills, and self-regulation skills alongside academic content.
- use visual aids in lessons.
- utilize peer-instructional opportunities.
- provide opportunities for breaks.
- incorporate computer-based programs, which can hold the attention of students with disabilities like autism.

STRATEGIES FOR PLANNING, IMPLEMENTING, AND FACILITATING INTRINSIC MOTIVATION

Intrinsic motivation is a person's inner drive to engage in an activity or behavior. Students with special needs often struggle with intrinsic motivation as a skill. This requires special educators and other professionals to promote and/or teach students to be intrinsically motivated. Teachers can **promote intrinsic motivation** by giving students opportunities to demonstrate **achievement**. This can be done by challenging students with intellectual risks and helping them focus on challenging classwork or tasks. Teachers should also build upon students' strengths by providing daily opportunities in the classroom for students to demonstrate their **strengths** instead of focusing on their weaknesses. Offering choices throughout the day provides students with ownership of their decision-making and communicates that they have choices in the classroom environment. Teachers should also allow students to **fail without criticism** and instead promote self-reflection in order to build students' confidence. Teachers should also instruct students on how to **break down tasks** and promote other self-management skills and organizational skills.

INSTRUCTIONAL METHODS FOR TEACHING STUDENTS WITH SOCIAL SKILLS DEFICITS

Students with social skills deficits often need instruction in social skill areas. These deficits can be addressed in inclusive settings and may not necessarily require explicit social skills instruction. **Social skills instruction** can be delivered to entire classes or individual students, depending on the needs of the students. Students will sometimes also receive **one-on-one** or **small group social skills instruction** from professionals like speech-language pathologists, especially when this is written in students' Individualized Education Programs (IEPs). In these situations, the idea is for the students to generalize learned concepts to their school and home environments. In both settings, it is important to model appropriate manners, hold students responsible for their actions, and have clear and concise rules and consequences. This solidifies educational environments that are both predictable and safe. Social situations that produce undesired outcomes can be remediated by **role-playing** the situations and teaching students positive responses. **Social stories** are another way to foster social skills growth. Often, these social stories demonstrate how people should respond to specific social situations appropriately.

PROMOTING LEARNING AND DEVELOPMENT

Educators that practice effective strategies for **promoting learning and development** create successful learning environments and help struggling learners. Teachers should take the time to know the **strengths and weaknesses** of individual students in order to plan and implement

57

instructional matches, including curriculum that challenges students without frustrating them. **Scaffolding** is a strategy that breaks larger concepts into smaller chunks. This process helps students learn new concepts and apply prior knowledge. Instruction should be broken up into step-by-step strategies in order to allow students to follow steps or remediate certain concepts. **Modeling and demonstrating** tasks or lessons is useful for demonstrating problem-solving abilities. Students mastering new content should also receive consistent, positive **feedback** for their achievements. Additionally, students should be given opportunities to **talk through their processes** with peers or in teacher-led groups when learning new concepts.

SELECTING DEVELOPMENTALLY APPROPRIATE CURRICULUM

Choosing a developmentally appropriate curriculum is challenging for educators. Special educators have the additional challenge of finding a curriculum that meets the needs of the **individual students with disabilities**. The end result is not usually a one-size-fits-all curriculum because that goes against the intentions of individualized education programs that meet the needs of students with special needs. Instead, special educators often pick and choose curriculum components that best meet the needs of differing abilities in the classroom. When selecting appropriate curriculum, special educators should consider:

- standards and goals that are appropriate to the needs of the classroom students.
- best practices that have been found effective for classroom students.
- curriculum that is engaging and challenging.
- instruction and activities that are multi-modal.
- Individualized Education Program (IEP) goals.
- real-world experiences.
- different ways of learning that help teachers understand students' learning processes.
- collaboration with co-teachers to deliver appropriate instruction.

In some special education settings, the curriculum is already chosen. In these settings, teachers can collaborate with co-teachers to find ways to provide instruction that meets standards and the individual needs of the classroom students.

ACCESSIBILITY COMPONENTS OF A PICTURE EXCHANGE COMMUNICATION SYSTEM

A Picture Exchange Communication System (**PECS**) is a communication system for people with little or no **communicative abilities**. This system is a way for the students to access their environments using a unique communication system. PECS is a way for people with limited communicative abilities to use **picture symbols** to communicate meaning, wants, and needs. Children can learn a PECS system by using pictures to request and receive items. For example, a child may point to a picture symbol to request a book. PECS is a way for students with communication disorders to develop their **verbal communication** without actually speaking. It eliminates frustration and problem behaviors by providing students with an avenue to express what they want to say. It is commonly used for students with Autism Spectrum disorder in the form of augmentative communication devices. It can also be used for students with other impairments whose communicative abilities are affected. PECS focuses on **functional communication skills** and can be practiced in the home, school, and community environments.

USING VISUAL SUPPORTS TO FACILITATE INSTRUCTION AND SELF-MONITORING STRATEGIES

Many students learn best when provided with instruction and activities that appeal to multiple senses. A **multi-modal approach** is especially important for students with developmental disabilities who may need supports that meet their individual ways of learning. **Visual supports** are concrete representations of information used to convey meaning. Visual supports can be used by teachers of students with developmental disabilities to help them understand what is being taught and communicated to them. Visual supports can help students with understanding classroom rules, making decisions, communicating with others, staying organized, and reducing frustrations. **Visual schedules** show students visual representations of their daily schedules. This assists with transitions between activities, which can sometimes be difficult for students with disabilities. Visuals can be used to help students share information about themselves or their school days with their peers and parents. Visual supports can also be used with checklists to help facilitate independence, and behavior checklists can be used to help students self-monitor their behaviors.

USING INSTRUCTIONAL METHODS TO ADDRESS INDEPENDENT LIVING SKILLS

When applicable, goals for independent living skills are included in the **transition section** of students' Individualized Education Plans. However, **independent living skills education** should begin well before students reach high school, regardless of whether or not these skills are addressed in their IEP goals. **Functional skills instruction** is necessary to teach students skills needed to gain independence. Instructional methods used to address independent living skills for students with disabilities include making life skills instruction part of the daily curriculum. An appropriate **task analysis** can be used to determine what skills need to be taught. **Functional academic skills**, especially in the areas of math and language arts, should also be included in the curriculum. Basic skills like telling time, balancing a bank account, and recognizing signs and symbols are just some examples of skills that students can generalize outside of the classroom environment. The goal of **community-based instruction** is to help students develop skills needed to succeed in the community, such as skills needed when riding a bus or shopping. This type of instruction may be harder to implement than basic social skills training, which should take place in the daily curriculum.

Learning Across the Curriculum

PROMOTING CRITICAL THINKING SKILLS

Critical thinking is a self-directed thinking process that helps people make logical, reasonable judgements. This is an especially challenging skill for students with **developmental disabilities**, who often demonstrate deficits in logical thinking and reasoning abilities. In order to teach these students **critical thinking skills**, the focus should be on encouraging critical thinking across **home and school environments** and providing opportunities for students to practice this type of thinking. Teachers and parents can encourage critical thinking by implementing teaching strategies focused on fostering **creativity** in students. Instead of providing outlines or templates for lesson concepts, students can use their prior knowledge to figure out the boundaries of the lessons independently and explore new concepts. Parents and teachers should not always be quick to jump in and help students who are struggling. Sometimes the best way to help is by facilitating ways for students to solve problems without doing things for them. Opportunities for brainstorming, classifying and categorizing information, comparing and contrasting information, and making connections between topics are teaching strategies that also facilitate critical thinking skills.

METACOGNITIVE APPROACH TO TEACHING

Metacognition refers to people's awareness and understanding of their own thinking processes. The **metacognitive approach** to teaching helps students think about their thinking processes and make sense of the world around them. Increasing their levels of **self-awareness** allows students to gain an understanding of how they feel, think, and act. This helps them optimize their educational performances because by learning more about how they feel, think, and act, they begin to understand more about how they learn. Teachers can engage students in metacognitive thinking by teaching them how to think **reflectively**. Teachers should also encourage students to recognize what they do not understand. This allows them to be comfortable with a lack of understanding and learn how to work through it. Instructors can also provide time for students to keep learning journals that note their learning progress throughout the year. Reflecting on projects and assignments, monitoring their own skills, and providing tests that target **higher level thinking objectives**, like essay tests, also promote metacognitive thinking in students.

TEACHING PARTICIPATION IN CAREER-BASED EDUCATION

During their schooling years, students with disabilities have the additional challenge of determining possible **career options** for life after high school. Fortunately, instruction can be provided during the school day or within after-school programs that address career-based skills. Effective **career-based programs** for students with disabilities should work collaboratively with community and school resources. Students should receive information on career options, be exposed to a range of experiences, and learn how to self-advocate. Information regarding career options can be gathered via **career assessments** that explore students' possible career interests. Students should receive exposure to **post-secondary education** to determine if it is an option that aligns with their career interests. They should also learn about basic job requirements, such as what it means to earn a living wage and entry requirements for different types of jobs. Students should be given opportunities for job training, job shadowing, and community service. It is helpful to provide students with opportunities to learn and practice **work and occupational skills** that pertain to specific job interests. Students need to learn **self-advocacy skills**, such as communicating the implications of their disabilities to employers, in order to maintain success in post-secondary work environments.

PRIOR KNOWLEDGE

By the time children enter school, their life experiences have shaped their understandings about how the world around them works. Activating **prior knowledge** is a way to build upon and develop children's prior knowledge and apply it to new concepts. Prior knowledge can be a useful instructional tool for addressing concepts that might otherwise be especially challenging. Prior knowledge is a combination of children's **beliefs and academic experiences** that affect how students learn. Therefore, it is important for educators to gauge this knowledge in order to plan lessons accordingly. **Know, Want to Know, and Learned charts (KWL)** are useful tools to use before lessons begin. Students explore what they know and want to know about concepts. At the conclusion of the lessons, students examine what they have learned about the concepts. The **Known and Unknown chart strategy** works similarly. Teachers can ask what students know about concepts and write responses down in the known column. What students want to learn more about or do not know goes into the unknown column. Both strategies can be implemented as individual or group activities to introduce lessons.

GUIDED LEARNING

Guided learning is practice or instruction completed by the teacher and students together. The goal of **guided learning** is to help students engage in the learning process in order to learn more about how they think and acquire new information. **Guided practice** occurs when the teacher and students complete practice activities together. The advantage of guided practice is that students can learn ways to approach concepts they have just learned. It allows students to understand and ask questions about lesson-related activities before working independently. Guided practice is useful in classrooms for students with and without disabilities because it helps teachers gauge how students learn and what instructional methods work best for them. Additionally, guided practice allows teachers to understand how students are learning the material. It also allows teachers to revisit concepts that are unclear or fine tune any missed lesson objectives.

DIAGNOSTIC PRESCRIPTIVE METHOD

The diagnostic prescriptive approach to teaching is based on the fact that all students are unique learners. The **diagnostic prescriptive approach** examines factors that impede student learning and how to remedy specific issues. A successful approach begins with a **diagnosis** of what students are bringing to the classroom. This can be completed through careful observations and assessments. Once the skill deficits are clear, **prescriptive teaching** can be put into effect. In this process, teachers examine what will help students the most. It may be switching materials, changing to group settings, or recognizing the need for specialized interventions due to disabilities. In order to address multiple needs in the classroom, lesson plans should be **multi-modal**. Developing strategies in advance to address students' needs is also a highlight of this method. Another important part of this method is evaluating results to determine what was effective or ineffective for entire classes and individual students.

DEVELOPMENTALLY APPROPRIATE MATH SKILLS FOR YOUNG CHILDREN

Starting in pre-kindergarten and first grade, children should be able to count to 100, learn how to write numbers, and demonstrate basic addition and subtraction skills. Older students can demonstrate skills associated with counting money and telling time, and they can also understand decimal, place value, and word problem concepts. Students with disabilities may or may not develop what are considered to be **developmentally appropriate mathematics skills** by certain ages or grades. In inclusive special education settings, the needs of these students can be addressed with a number of strategies. **Scaffolding** is the process of breaking down concepts into chunks. Scaffolding addresses the issues that arise when some students are well behind others by allowing students to work at their own pace and helping them connect prior knowledge to new information. This ensures that students have solidified knowledge of concepts before moving on to new concepts.

TEACHING MATHEMATICS

Students whose disabilities affect their performances in mathematics require specialized instruction. Eligible students will have Individualized Education Program goals to address their specific needs but are also expected to learn content connected to **state standards**. Additionally, **accommodations and modifications** are available for qualifying students to assist with mathematics instruction. Strategies that can be effective for math instruction for students with disabilities include:

- using the same instructional strategies in all settings, including the home environment and all school environments.
- using concrete objects to teach math concepts, such as using manipulatives to count out number values.
- providing assistive materials, such as calculators and scrap paper.
- explaining and modeling objectives clearly.
- allowing time for students to check their work.
- activating prior knowledge to assist students with learning new concepts.
- providing opportunities for extra tutoring or one-on-one instruction.
- assisting students with self-monitoring their progress.
- encouraging math games to engage learning and interest in math concepts.

COMPONENTS OF DIRECT READING INSTRUCTION

The purpose of direct learning instruction is to specifically target the needs of students with learning disabilities. **Direct learning instruction** can be provided in many educational settings. Direct instruction breaks concept learning into specific tasks and processes, with focus on mastering one skill before moving onto another skill. With **direct reading instruction**, the key components are teaching phonemic awareness, phonics, fluency, vocabulary development, and comprehension. Effective reading programs address all five areas of reading instruction. **Phonemic awareness** focuses on breaking words into sound units (phonemes). **Phonics** focuses on connecting these sound units with letters (graphemes). Phonics instruction allows students to approach decoding by sounding words out instead of attempting to read the whole words. **Fluency** instruction focuses on teaching students to read unfamiliar words and texts quickly and accurately. **Vocabulary development** helps increase familiarity with frequently occurring words in texts. **Comprehension** instruction focuses on helping students to understand what they have read. In comprehension instruction, learners connect prior knowledge to the texts.

BENEFITS OF THE DIRECT READING PROCESS

Direct reading instruction is an approach to teaching reading which focuses on specific skill development for early readers. Students frequently enter their schooling years with deficits in reading skills, especially when they are identified as having disabilities. Effective **direct reading programs** include the teaching of phonemic awareness, phonics, fluency, vocabulary development, and comprehension. Teachers are generally trained to implement direct reading programs instead of creating direct instruction curriculum. Specific programs ensure that teachers use the same curriculum and methods in order to effectively implement direct reading instruction. Direct reading instruction and programs are especially helpful for **skill remediation** for at-risk students. Efficient direct reading instruction communicates high standards for learning, is replicable or able to be implemented across a variety of settings, and offers support materials, professional development, and implementation guidance. Direct reading instruction is also proven to be effective for the improvement of reading abilities in at-risk students.

TEACHING SOCIAL STUDIES

Depending on their special education classroom placements, students with **disabilities** receive varying degrees of instruction in other core content areas like social studies and science. Students with mild disabilities, such as learning disabilities, likely participate in inclusive classroom settings or general education classroom settings. Depending on a student's grade level, the student may attend a classroom setting with one or two teachers or switch classes and attend settings with many different teachers. Across all settings, students with mild disabilities receive any **accommodations or modifications** explicitly written in their Individualized Education Programs. Students with mild to moderate disabilities may receive instruction in special education classrooms for part or most of the day. In these instances, general education social studies or science classes may not be the most appropriate educational settings. Special educators then teach the content in the special education classrooms, sometimes connecting it with related tasks or skills. Students with moderate disabilities may receive **indirect instruction** in these content areas that is loosely based on content standards and more appropriate for the ways they acquire knowledge.

TEACHING SPECIAL EDUCATION

Special education classrooms, whether inclusive, self-contained, or resource room settings, often need to deliver instruction in **multiple subject areas**. Students in these settings also represent many **levels of learning**. Therefore, one instructional strategy is not always the most effective way to teach students in these settings. In order to provide quality instruction, special educators can place students with similar skill levels into **small groups** during instruction in the content areas. This way, small groups of students can be working on skills that cater to their specific needs. **Classroom centers** are another way to group students. Classroom centers often feature self-guided instruction in skill or content areas where students can work at their own pace. **Rotating centers** allows teachers to instruct groups of students while the other groups work independently on previously learned skills. **Thematic instruction** is a teaching strategy where multiple subject areas are connected and taught within one lesson unit. Themes are effective in special education classrooms because they tie multiple content areas together. Special educators should also provide **multiple levels of materials and books** for student learning to target different learning levels.

MODIFYING THE STAGES OF WRITING TO ASSIST STUDENTS WITH LEARNING DISABILITIES

The **writing process** can be especially challenging for new learners but especially for students with disabilities. The writing process can be facilitated by special educators and general educators in order to build adequate writing skills. Teachers must first address the needs of their classes before engaging in the pre-writing stage. Getting to know students provides insight into their prior knowledge and abilities. In the **pre-writing (brainstorming) stage**, teachers help students prepare for the writing process by establishing good content or thinking of things that interest them to write about. In the **writing stage**, students should be taught to write their content using graphic organizers or diagrams that assist with using appropriate formatting, grammar, and punctuation. The **rewriting/revising stage** can be facilitated by providing checklists of errors and having students self-check and revise their own work. In the **editing/proofreading stage**, students can self-check their work or exchange their final written projects with other students or their teachers. This can also be facilitated using formatting checklists and/or grammar and punctuation checklists to monitor the writing process.

IMPLICATIONS OF A MATHEMATICS DISABILITY

Disabilities like **dyscalculia** are specific learning disabilities associated with mathematics. Students that have specific learning disabilities in mathematics have trouble with number-related concepts and using symbols or functions. Symptoms of **math disorders** include difficulties with counting numbers, solving math word problems, sequencing events or information, recognizing patterns when adding, subtracting, multiplying or dividing, and understanding concepts associated with time, like days, weeks, seasons, etc. Recalling math facts is also difficult for students with math disabilities. The severity of the disability is impacted when it **coexists** with dyslexia, Attention Deficit Hyperactivity Disorder, anxiety, or other disabilities. Special educators, math tutors, or other professionals can help students with math deficits by providing multi-modal instruction to engage multiple senses and enhance the chances of the students learning the concepts. They may also receive supports according to 504 Plans or Individualized Education Programs that level the educational playing field, such as use of a calculator. Use of concrete examples, visual aids, graph paper, or scratch paper can also assist students with math disabilities.

TEACHING COMPREHENSION WITH RESEARCH-BASED READING INTERVENTION STRATEGIES

Comprehension refers to a person's understanding of something. As it pertains to reading, **comprehension** is the understanding of content that has been read. Students with disabilities often struggle with comprehension, which makes teaching **comprehension strategies** essential to their learning. Special educators should teach students to **monitor** their comprehension by being aware of what they have read, identifying what they do not understand, and implementing problem-solving strategies to address what they do not understand. Special educators can also teach students to demonstrate **metacognitive strategies**, such as identifying specifically what they do not understand in texts (i.e. identifying the page numbers or chapters where they are struggling), looking back through the texts to find answers to comprehension questions, rereading sentences or sections they do not understand, and putting sentences they do not understand into their own words. **Graphic organizers**, like story maps and Venn diagrams, also allow students to map out the information they have read by laying out important concepts.

EFFECTS OF DEFICITS IN LANGUAGE DEVELOPMENT ON THE LEARNING PROCESSES

Without interventions, children with deficits in language development will likely have issues with overall academic success. **Academic success** is inextricably linked with good language development. **Good language development skills** include the ability to understand spoken and written words, as well as literacy skills. When a core knowledge of language is developed in young children, it can be built upon as the children grow and develop during their grade school years. Reading and writing are language-based skills. **Phonological awareness** is an essential skill and key building block for language development. Phonological awareness is a term that refers to students' awareness of sounds, syllables, and words. Students that develop strong phonological skills typically develop good literacy skills. Students with deficits in reading, writing, or math may have difficulties with phonological awareness and miss some building blocks essential for academic success. These deficits generalize to core subject areas as students are required to demonstrate grade-level appropriate skills.

HELPING STUDENTS WITH DISABILITIES BECOME SOLID EMERGENT READERS

Emergent reading refers to the reading and writing abilities of young readers. They precede **conventional literacy**, which refers to older children's reading and writing behaviors, such as decoding, reading comprehension, oral reading fluency, spelling, and writing. Children with learning disabilities may demonstrate discrepancies between emergent literacy behaviors and conventional literacy behaviors. They may flip-flop between the two stages, showing progress one moment or day and then seeming to forget the next. Educators can foster skills in emergent and conventional reading by teaching **phonological awareness** and **written letter/sound recognition**. These are both baseline skills that affect students' future phonological awareness development. Additionally, educators can provide engaging, age-appropriate activities that facilitate connections between emergent literacy and conventional literacy skills. Activities that promote students' print awareness and knowledge of book conventions also help build solid emergent reader skills.

Assessment

Assessment

TYPES OF DEVELOPMENTAL ASSESSMENTS

Developmental assessments measure the development of infants, toddlers, and preschoolers. These **norm-referenced tests** measure fine and gross motor skills, communication and language, and social, cognitive, and self-help milestones that young children should achieve at certain ages. When a child is suspected of having a **developmental delay**, a developmental assessment is useful in identifying the child's strengths and weaknesses. Developmental assessments map out the **progress** of a child compared to the progress of similar-aged children. Developmental assessments are also useful in identifying if the delay is significant or can be overcome with time. These assessments can be used to determine what **educational placement** is most appropriate for a child with a developmental delay. Developmental assessments are administered via observations and questionnaires. Parents, legal guardians, caregivers, and instructors who are most familiar with the child provide the most insight on developmental strengths and weaknesses.

SCREENING TESTS FOR IDENTIFYING STUDENTS

When determining if a child needs special education, **screening tests** are the first step. The Individuals with Disabilities Education Act (IDEA) offers guidance for schools to implement screening tests. Districts and schools often have school-wide processes in place for screening students for **special education**. Screening tests can also be used to identify students who are falling behind in class. The advantage of screening tests is that they are easily administered. They require few materials and little time and planning in order to administer. Additionally, they can be used to quickly assess students' strengths and weaknesses. They do not have to be administered one-on-one and can be used class wide. Screening tests can be as simple as paper and pencil quizzes assessing what students know. Screening tests are used for measuring visual acuity, auditory skills, physical health, development, basic academic skills, behavioral problems, children at risk for behavioral problems, language skills, and verbal and nonverbal intelligence.

INDIVIDUAL INTELLIGENCE TESTS VS. INDIVIDUAL ACADEMIC ACHIEVEMENT TESTS

Intelligence tests measure a student's capacity for abstract thinking, mental reasoning, judgment, and decision-making. These **norm-referenced tests** help determine a student's **overall intelligence**, which correlates with **potential academic performance**. Intelligence tests can be used to determine if a student's deficits are due to intellectual disabilities or related to specific learning disabilities or emotional disorders. Intelligence tests are also known as **intelligence quotient tests (IQ tests)**. IQ tests should be administered by trained professionals in order to ensure the tests are administered accurately. Intelligence tests can also measure verbal skills, motor performance, and visual reasoning. Unlike intelligence tests, individual academic tests measure a student's strengths and weaknesses in individual skills. They are also norm referenced and used to determine if a student needs **special education services**. Results from individual academic tests help determine areas of concern or possible deficits for an individual student. Unlike intelligence tests, individual academic tests can be administered by teachers.

ADAPTIVE BEHAVIOR SCALE ASSESSMENTS

Adaptive behavior scales are useful for diagnosing a student with an **intellectual disability** that affects the development or progression of adaptive behavior. They are used in preschools and for determining eligibility for **special education** in grade schools. They are also used in planning

65

curriculum for students with intellectual disabilities. Adaptive behavior scales are standardized but not always norm referenced because of difficulties comparing expectations for some adaptive and maladaptive skills exhibited by similar-aged peers. In terms of curriculum planning, these assessments can determine what type and how much assistance a student may need. Adaptive behavior scale assessments identify a student's level of **independence**. Adaptive behavior scales can be used to determine **skill abilities** associated with daily living, community functioning, social skills, communication, motor functions, and basic academic skills. Teachers and other professionals can administer adaptive behavior scales to students with intellectual disabilities to determine starting points for improving their adaptive behavior deficits.

CURRICULUM BASED MEASUREMENT FOR MEASURING STUDENT ACADEMIC PROGRESS

Curriculum Based Measurement (**CBM**) is a way for teachers to track how students are **progressing** in mathematics, language arts, social studies, science, and other skills. CBM is useful for addressing how students with special needs are progressing on their Individualized Education Program (IEP) goals. It is also useful for communicating progress to parents or legal guardians. CBM results can determine whether or not current **instructional strategies** are effective for particular students. In the same respect, CBM can determine if students are meeting the **standards** laid out in their IEP goals. If instructional strategies are not effective or their goals are not being met, CBM progress (or lack of progress) signals that the teachers should change instructional strategies. CBM can be revisited to determine whether or not the newly implemented strategies are effective. Progress can sometimes be charted to present a visual for how a student is progressing in a particular content area or with a specific skill.

WOODCOCK JOHNSON ACHIEVEMENT TESTS

HIGH-INCIDENCE DISABILITIES — Norm Referenced

Woodcock Johnson achievement tests can be used as diagnostic tools for identifying children with **high-incidence disabilities**. The Woodcock Johnson Tests of Achievement and the Woodcock Johnson Tests of Cognitive Abilities are comprehensively useful for assessing children's:

- intellectual abilities.
- cognitive abilities.
- aptitude.
- oral language.
- academic achievements.

These norm-referenced tests are valuable in understanding children's strengths and weaknesses and how they compare to cohorts of normally progressing, similar-aged peers. For example, Woodcock Johnson Tests (**WJ tests**) are useful in identifying children with language disorders because children with language disorders typically score lower on the Listening Comprehension and Fluid Reasoning test sections. The WJ tests are useful diagnostic tools for identifying children with Attention Deficit Hyperactivity Disorder (ADHD) as well. While children with ADHD may perform similarly to children with learning disabilities, their key deficits are in the Cognitive Efficiency, Processing Speed, Academic Fluency, Short-Term Memory, and Long-Term Retrieval test sections.

LEARNING DISABILITIES IN READING AND MATHEMATICS

The Woodcock Johnson achievement tests (**WJ tests**) include a test of **achievement** and a test of **cognitive abilities**. Together, these assessments are useful in the diagnostic process of identifying a student with a **disability**. Additionally, they are helpful for identifying specific **deficits** in a student's reading or math skills. WJ tests are norm referenced and compare the results of a child's performance to that of a cohort of children of similar chronological age and average intellectual abilities. These assessments provide information about a child's **reading disorder**, such as dyslexia, because they measure phonological awareness, rapid automatized naming, processing speed, and working memory. WJ tests report on a child's cognitive functioning in these test areas. These assessments also provide useful information for students with learning deficits in **mathematics**. Performances on the Math Calculation Skills and Math Reasoning test sections provide information on specific deficits in general comprehension, fluid reasoning, and processing speed. Children that have deficits in these areas demonstrate relationships to learning disabilities in mathematics.

EVALUATING STUDENTS WITH SPECIAL NEEDS USING THE WESCHLER INTELLIGENCE SCALE

The Weschler Intelligence Scale is an assessment that measures the cognitive abilities of children and adults. The **Weschler Intelligence Scale for Children (WISC)** measures a child's **verbal intelligence** (including comprehension and vocabulary) and **performance intelligence** (including reasoning and picture completion). The WISC is an intelligence quotient test that is useful for helping diagnose a student with a **cognitive disability**. A score below 100 indicates below-average intelligence. WISC results are useful tools for evaluating a student with a disability. Tests results can be used to measure and report on a student's general intelligence and provide insight into the student's cognitive abilities in order to determine an appropriate educational pathway. Results can be reported in a student's Evaluation Team Report and Individualized Education Program in order to justify special education services or have a starting point for Individualized Education Program goals. WISC results are especially important in an Evaluation Team Report, generally completed every 3 years or less, because they contribute to describing the **overall performance profile** of a student with a disability.

KAUFMAN ASSESSMENT BATTERY FOR CHILDREN

The Kaufman Assessment Battery for Children (**K-ABC**) is a unique standardized test because it is used to evaluate preschoolers, minority groups, and children with learning disabilities. The K-ABC can be used to assess children ages 2–18 and is meant to be used with children who are nonverbal, bilingual, or English speaking. However, it is especially useful in assessing the abilities of students who are **nonverbal**. The K-ABC can be used to help determine students' educational placements and assist with their educational planning. This assessment has four components that measure students' abilities, which are described below.

- The **sequential processing scale** assesses short-term memory and problem-solving skills when putting things in sequential order.
- The **simultaneous processing scale** assesses problem-solving skills for completing multiple processes simultaneously, such as identifying objects and reproducing design shapes using manipulatives.
- The **achievement component** measures expressive vocabulary, mathematics skills, and reading and decoding skills.
- The **mental processing component** assesses the abilities a student demonstrates on the sequential and simultaneous processing scales.

The K-ABC is also unique because it includes a **nonverbal scale** that can be administered to children with hearing or speech impairments and children who do not speak English.

VINELAND ADAPTIVE BEHAVIOR SCALE

The Vineland Adaptive Behavior Scale (**VABS**) assesses the personal and social skills of children and adults. **Adaptive behavior** refers to the skills needed for day-to-day activities and independent living. Children with disabilities sometimes have deficits in adaptive behavior, and the VABS is useful for planning their **educational pathways**. It is an especially useful tool for developing **transition plans and goals** for students of appropriate ages on Individualized Education Programs. The VABS is a process that involves people who know the students best, like parents and/or teachers. The teacher version and parent version of this assessment can be delivered via interview or survey. The parent version focuses on a student's adaptive behavior at home, while the teacher version focuses on adaptive behavior in the school setting. Version II of the VABS assesses four **domains**: communication, daily living skills, socialization, and social skills. A student's comprehensive score from both the teacher and parent version are used to report abilities in the four domains.

TYPES OF COGNITIVE ASSESSMENTS

Cognitive tests assess the **cognitive functioning abilities** of children and adults. They are useful tools for diagnosing and/or identifying children with disabilities who are eligible for **special education services** under the Individuals with Disabilities Education Act. Examples of cognitive tests used in diagnosing or identifying children with disabilities include aptitude tests and intelligence quotient (IQ) tests. There are also cognitive assessments that measure verbal reasoning, numerical reasoning, abstract reasoning, spatial ability, verbal ability, and more. Children's cognitive abilities are related to how quickly they **process** information. Assessment results can be good measurements of how quickly children may learn new information or tasks. Cognitive assessments provide specific information about children's cognitive functioning by providing measurements of their intelligence, attention, concentration, processing speed, language and communication, visual-spatial abilities, and short and long-term memory capabilities. Individual assessment results can be used to evaluate a child's need for special education services. Results can also be used on a child's Evaluation Team Report or for developing goals on the Individualized Education Program.

PRENATAL, PERINATAL, AND NEONATAL DISABILITIES

Prenatal, perinatal, and neonatal risk factors can be genetic or environmental. These risk factors put infants at risk for developing **intellectual disabilities** that affect their day-to-day lives. An intellectual disability (**ID**) is a disability that significantly limits a child's overall cognitive abilities. **Prenatal risk factors** include genetic syndromes (i.e. Down Syndrome), brain malformation, maternal diseases, and environmental influences. Drugs, alcohol, or poison exposure can all affect an unborn child. **Perinatal (during delivery) risk factors** include labor and delivery trauma or anoxia at birth. **Neonatal (post-birth) risk factors** include hypoxic ischemic injury (brain injury), traumatic brain injury, infections, seizure disorders, and toxic metabolic syndromes. Early screening and applicable assessments are tools used to identify young children with intellectual disabilities. Early screening and assessments can assist with providing a child with ID with special education services under the Individuals with Disabilities Education Act. These tools can also help assess the severity of need, deficit areas, and need for special services, such as occupational therapy.

ADVANTAGES AND DISADVANTAGES OF CURRICULUM-BASED ASSESSMENTS

Curriculum-based assessments (**CBAs**) are assessments that determine if students are making adequate progress through the curriculum. They can be administered by a teacher, special educator, or school psychologist. CBAs have advantages over norm-referenced assessments, like developmental assessments, because they are not used to compare performances between students. Other types of assessments measure a student's cumulative abilities across multiple skills instead of assessing individual skills. CBAs measure student progress in more **individualized** ways. They are especially useful for measuring Individualized Education Program (IEP) goal progress.

Since CBAs are **teacher-created assessments**, they provide opportunities to assess students informally and formally on IEP goals. For example, a teacher may verbally quiz a student on ten addition problems to determine if the student is making progress on math IEP goals. CBAs are also used in the Response to Intervention process to identify students with special needs by measuring the effectiveness of interventions provided to them.

ADVANTAGES AND DISADVANTAGES OF USING FORMAL ASSESSMENTS

Formal assessments measure whether or not students are learning what they are supposed to be learning. Formal assessments help teachers determine what their students know. They typically measure how students are **performing** compared to their similar-aged peers. Examples of formal assessments include quizzes, tests, standardized tests, achievement tests, aptitude tests, and norm-referenced tests.

Formal assessments have the same set of expectations for all students and are graded using the same criteria. However, students with disabilities do not always learn or retain previously taught content in the same ways as their similar-aged peers. Using **universal criteria** to assess what students have learned is one disadvantage to formal assessments for students with disabilities. An advantage of formal assessments is that they allow teachers to collect **baseline data** on students' educational performances by comparing their performances to age or grade-based performance criteria. Additionally, students with disabilities can receive **accommodations and modifications** on these types of assessments. Accommodations and modifications are implemented based on needs specific to each student. The goal is to level the playing field for these students on formal assessments, like standardized state tests.

USES, ADVANTAGES, AND DISADVANTAGES OF USING INFORMAL ASSESSMENTS

Informal assessments can provide teachers with a lot of information about students' educational **strengths and weaknesses**. Informal assessments are also used to guide teachers' daily instruction by providing constant and immediate **feedback** about students' learning processes. Examples of informal assessments include observations and rating scales, checks of daily work, homework, group projects, checklists, and rubrics.

Informal assessments offer some advantages. They are often easy to implement and allow teachers to gather useful data. Informal assessments may naturally be less stressful for students because they do not realize they are being tested. When test stress factors are removed, results from informal assessments may provide the best reflections of students' **abilities**.

Disadvantages of informal assessments include **hidden bias or stereotypes** within the person administering the assessment. Teachers implementing informal assessments must be conscious of and avoid bias in order to receive accurate information about students' educational performances. Another disadvantage is that students may also feel more pressure to perform well on formal assessments versus informal assessments, affecting their performances on the informal assessments.

HOW FORMATIVE ASSESSMENTS WORK

The goals of formative assessments are to provide ongoing feedback and monitor students' learning. These assessments are a process of informal assessment strategies that help educators gather information about student learning. Formative assessments help **differentiate instruction** and are considered part of the **student learning process**. Formative assessments communicate what the students are learning and also check for understanding. They provide information needed to adjust teaching and learning while it is happening.

Formative assessments also provide opportunities for students to receive **feedback** on their individual performances and engage in their paths to success. Teachers can use formative assessments to allow students to participate in the learning process, outside of sitting and listening to lectures. **Discussions** are examples of formative assessments, where teachers can initiate discussions about topics and gauge students' understanding. **Exit slips** are written questions posed by teachers at the ends of their classes, intended to determine what the students have learned. The **think, pair, share method** requires students to work together to solve problems. Students are asked to brainstorm answers to questions posed by the teachers, then they are paired with other students before sharing their thinking with their partners.

HOW SUMMATIVE ASSESSMENTS WORK

Summative assessments are less flexible than formative assessments due to how performance data is collected. The goal of summative assessment is to evaluate what a student has learned at the **end of an instructional section or unit**. Summative assessments often measure the mastery of learning standards.

Summative assessments use standards or benchmarks to measure student success at certain **checkpoints** during the learning process. They are almost always high stakes, heavily weighted (unlike formative assessments), and formally graded. Information from summative assessments can be used to report on student progress. Teachers can use a variety of summative assessments to determine where students are in the learning process. These types of assessments also play a role in identifying benchmarked progress and the educational needs of students with disabilities.

These types of assessments feature a narrower range of question types, such as multiple choice, short answer, and essay questions. Examples of summative assessments include state tests, end of unit or chapter tests, end of semester exams, and assessments that formally measure the mastery of a particular benchmark.

ALTERNATE ASSESSMENTS

Students with and without disabilities are typically expected to take the same standardized tests, sometimes with accommodations and/or modifications. Some students with disabilities take **alternate assessments**, which are forms of the standardized tests that other students take. Students that participate in alternate assessments are unable to participate in state standardized tests even with accommodations. Less than 1% of students in public school districts participate in alternate assessments. They are mostly intended for students with **intellectual disabilities** or **severe cognitive delays**. Alternate assessments are based on **Alternate Achievement Standards (AAS)**, which are modified versions of state achievement standards. Alternate assessments are a way for students' progress to be assessed with standards that are more appropriate for their skills. Teachers, parents, and students work collaboratively to demonstrate that the achievement standards are met. For example, a state standard for math may not be appropriate for a student with an intellectual disability. Instead, the student may have the alternative standard of demonstrating the ability to count money to make a purchase.

ROLE FORMAL ASSESSMENTS PLAY IN THE EDUCATION OF A STUDENT WITH DISABILITIES

Formal assessments measure how well a student has mastered learning material and are useful in detecting if a student is **falling behind** in general or at the end of a taught unit. Formal test results can be used to compare the performance of a student with disabilities against other students of similar demographics. **Developmental assessments** are norm-referenced tests that are designed to assess the development of small children. Developmental assessments are used to identify the strengths and weaknesses of a child suspected of having a disability. **Intelligence tests** are another type of norm-referenced test that can determine a student's potential to learn academic skills. Intelligence tests, sometimes called IQ tests, also indicate a student's specific level of intelligence. This is helpful in knowing if a student's learning problems are associated with sub-average intellectual abilities or other factors, such as an emotional disturbance. A student with an emotional disturbance or specific learning disability would have an average or above-average intelligence score, whereas a student with intellectual disabilities would have a sub-average score. **Curriculum-based assessments** are also helpful in determining where, specifically, a student needs the most help within a content area.

INTEREST INVENTORIES

Interest inventories are tools for measuring people's interests or preferences in activities. They are useful for gathering information about a student's likes and dislikes. In special education, interest inventories are sometimes used to help develop the **transition portion** of an Individualized Education Plan (IEP). A student's interests as determined by an interest inventory can be used to drive the entire IEP. For an older student with a driving interest in mind, interest inventories can also be reflected in the annual IEP goals. Interest inventories can come in the form of observations, ability tests, or self-reporting inventories. They can also work as age-appropriate **transition assessments** used in the transition statement section of the IEP. An advantage of interest inventories is they help students get to know their strengths and interests. They are also useful in guiding students with disabilities into thinking about post-secondary careers, education, or independent living.

ROLE INFORMAL ASSESSMENTS PLAY IN THE EDUCATION OF A STUDENT WITH DISABILITIES

Informal assessments are a little more flexible for teachers, particularly in the ways they can be administered in the classroom. In special education, informal assessments play an important role in **adjusting instruction** to meet the specific needs of the student. Using informal assessment outcomes to drive instruction ensures that academic or behavioral student needs are met. Informal assessments are also helpful in adjusting instruction to meet **specific goals or objectives** on a student's Individualized Education Program. Checklists, running records, observations, and work samples are all informal assessments from which data for IEP goals can be collected. **Checklists** can include a list of behaviors or academic skills the student is meant to achieve. Checklists enable the teacher to check off skills that a student can do. **Running records** help provide insight into student behavior over time by focusing on a sequence of events. **Work samples** are helpful in providing a concrete snapshot of a student's academic capabilities.

Individualized Programs and Modifications

DEVELOPING AND WRITING MEASURABLE IEP GOALS

According to the Individuals with Disabilities Education Act (IDEA), Individualized Education Program goals must contain specific **components** for students eligible for special education and placed on IEPs. Components of a **measurable IEP goal** include condition, performance, criteria, assessment, and standard. **Condition** refers to when, where, and how the disability will be addressed. For example, an IEP goal may state, "By the end of this IEP, Jacob will use appropriate skills to communicate his needs in 4/5 trials." "By the end of this IEP" is the condition of the goal. **Performance** is what the student is expected to accomplish during the condition of the goal. "Jacob will use appropriate skills to communicate his needs" is a performance example in the goal above. The last part of the goal stating "in 4/5 trials" is the **criteria** that outlines how well the goal will be performed. Measurable goals also include how skill mastery will be **assessed**, such as through observations or work samples. Goals should also be **standards-based**, and goals must be connected to state standards.

DETERMINING THE PLACEMENT OF A STUDENT WITH A DISABILITY

With every student, the goal is placement in the **general education classroom** as much as possible, while still meeting the student's educational needs and ensuring a successful educational experience. IDEA does not require that students be placed in the regular education classroom. However, this is the first option that should be considered by a student's IEP team. Ultimately, the IEP determines what **environment** best suits the student based on the student's specific needs. The IEP is responsible for determining what educational environment would provide the student with the maximum appropriate educational benefit. While justification for removing a student from the regular education classroom is common and appropriate, as occurs when a student is placed in a resource room, the IEP team must explain the reasoning on the student's IEP. **Justification** must specifically list why the student cannot be educated with accommodations and services in the regular education classroom during any part of the school day. Justification for removal cannot be due to perceived instructional limitations of the regular education teacher or concerns over extra instructional time needed to educate a student with a disability.

ROLES/RESPONSIBILITIES OF THE SPECIAL EDUCATION INSTRUCTOR IN FULL/PARTIAL INCLUSION SETTING VS. A SELF-CONTAINED CLASSROOM

Students with mild to moderate disabilities are often placed in **inclusion** or **partial inclusion classrooms**. The responsibilities of the special educator include assisting and collaborating with the general education teacher to create a curriculum with **modifications** that meets the learning styles and needs of the students with disabilities. The special educator may circulate during lessons or classwork to help students when needed and provide modifications to the general education curriculum to best meet the individual needs of each student.

The role of a special educator in a **self-contained classroom** is much different. Students in a self-contained classroom typically have disabilities that severely limit their abilities to receive quality education in inclusion or partial inclusion settings. Students with moderate disabilities in self-contained classrooms receive **modified instruction** with accommodations. The special educator is usually assisted by teaching assistants or paraprofessionals who help the educator meet the needs of individual students.

Special educators in inclusion, partial inclusion, and self-contained classrooms share some similar **responsibilities**. These responsibilities include monitoring IEP data on annual goals for each student, giving standardized pretests and posttests, facilitating parent-teacher conferences, completing annual IEP reviews, and developing curriculum.

SPECIALLY DESIGNED INSTRUCTION

Specially Designed Instruction (**SDI**) in special education refers to the teaching methods and strategies used by special educators to teach students with learning disabilities and other learning disorders. SDI is used to meet the specific needs of learners who may not be successful learning in the same ways as their similar-aged peers. SDI should be adapted to the **unique learning needs** of students, address the learning issues specific to a child's disability, and ensure student access to the general education classroom. In SDI, the teaching methodology should be changed without sacrificing content aligned with the state standards.

UNIVERSAL DESIGN FOR LEARNING

The universal design for learning is a flexible approach to learning that keeps students' individual needs in mind. Teachers that utilize **UDL** offer different ways for students to access material and engage in content. This approach is helpful for many students, but particularly those with learning and attention issues. The three main principles of UDL are **representation**, **action and expression**, and **engagement**. Through these principles, UDL ensures multiple means of representation, multiple ways for students to interact with the material, and multiple ways to motivate students.

ROLE OF LOCAL EDUCATION AGENCY MEMBERS IN THE IEP MEETINGS

Local education agency (**LEA**) representatives represent local educational agencies and are knowledgeable about special education curriculum, general education curriculum, and community resources. An LEA member is also referred to as a **district representative**. An LEA member is a member of the school district where any special education meetings take place. In an **Individualized Education Program (IEP) meeting**, LEAs are members of the school district that referred the student for special education services. LEAs contribute their knowledge during the IEP meeting. An LEA member must be a licensed professional who knows the student and is familiar with the IEP process. The role of LEA members in IEP meetings is to make sure the information presented is compliant with the Individuals with Disabilities Education Act (IDEA) standards. LEAs are also responsible for ensuring that the school district is **compliant** with procedural components of IDEA and that eligible students are receiving free and appropriate public educations (FAPEs).

INVOLVEMENT OF STUDENTS ON IEPs IN THE TRANSITION PROCESS IN HIGH SCHOOL

Most states require **transition statements** to be made when students reach age 14 during the Individualized Education Program (IEP) year. Federal law requires students 16 years of age or older to have transition statements, post-secondary goals for independent living, employment, and education, and summaries of performance that include the results of the most recent transition assessments. Per federal law, students of transition age must be invited to their **IEP meetings**. It is important for students on IEPs to **participate** in the transition process because it helps them figure out what they want to do after they graduate from high school. Participation in the process gets them thinking about living independently, post-secondary education options, and employment options. Students usually have opportunities to participate in formal and informal assessments like interest inventories that help them narrow their interests. Transition goals for independent living, employment, and education should be based on the results of these assessments and any other interests the students have expressed. The students participate in the **implementation** of the transition goals by completing activities associated with their indicated interests.

ROLE OF THE SUPPORT TEAM IN THE EDUCATION OF A CHILD WITH A DISABILITY

A **student support team (SST)** assists with identifying and supporting a student needing special education services. In this support team model, a group of educators works to identify and provide early intervention services for any student exhibiting academic or behavioral problems. Most schools have a system by which the interventions for the student are implemented. The purpose of this SST is to offer different supports, such as monitoring student progress, developing intervention plans, and referring students for intervention services. While the primary goal of this SST is to provide support for students **struggling with school**, it can also shift focus to supporting students at risk of **dropping out of school**.

A support team can also be a team of **professionals** in charge of the implementation of an IEP for a student with a disability. A student-based support team is created for any student with an IEP. The purpose of this SST is to enhance a student's learning process and development. Members of this type of SST include the child, parent or legal guardian, special educator, a general educator, and a representative of the school system. The SST may also include relevant service professionals, student or parent advocates, school psychologists, or any others with knowledge or expertise about the student.

AMENDMENTS TO AN INDIVIDUALIZED EDUCATION PROGRAM

A student's Individualized Education Program (**IEP**) is in effect for one year. Academic goals, objectives, benchmarks, transition goals, and any accommodations and modifications are to be in place for the student for the duration of the IEP. An **amendment** can be made when a change needs to be made to the IEP before the year is over. An amendment is an agreement between the student, parents or legal guardians, and the IEP team. IEP meetings for amendments can be requested at any time. IEP amendments can be requested if a student is not making adequate progress toward the goals, if the goals become inappropriate in some way for the student, or when the student has met all IEP goals and requires new ones. If new information about the student becomes available, the IEP can be amended. Students who need accommodations and modifications added or removed can also request amendment meetings.

HOW NEEDS OF STUDENTS WITH IEPS ARE MET IN THE SCHOOL ENVIRONMENT

IEPs communicate what **services** are to be provided for children with disabilities in the school setting, the children's **present levels of performance (PLOPs)**, and how their disabilities affect **academic performance**. IEPs also specify **annual goals** appropriate to the students' specific needs and any accommodations or modifications that need to be provided. Schools and teachers working with students with disabilities have the responsibility to implement these IEP components when working with the students. Additionally, schools and teachers working with students with disabilities must ensure that the students' individualized annual goals are met within a year of the students' IEP effective dates. It is up to the IEP teams to determine what classroom settings would most benefit the students, while also appropriately meeting their IEP goals with the fewest barriers. Special educators must determine how data is collected, then record and obtain data on how the students are meeting their IEP goals. Special educators are responsible for providing intervention services based on the data results. They must also ensure that any accommodations or modifications listed on the IEPs are implemented in both general education and self-contained classrooms.

ACCOMMODATION VS. MODIFICATION IN IEPS

Formal accommodations and modifications for a student with a disability are listed on the Individualized Education Program. **Accommodations** change *how* a student learns the material, while a **modification** changes *what* a student is taught or expected to learn. In classroom instruction, accommodations level the playing field for students with disabilities by helping them learn the same material and have the same expectations as their classmates. For example, a student with a reading difficulty might receive the accommodation of being able to listen to the text being read. Modifications are for students who are academically far behind their peers. An example of a classroom instructional modification would be a student receiving a shorter reading assignment or an assignment catered to the student's reading level.

Accommodations for tests look a little different because the tests are assessing what the students learned. An appropriate example of a **test accommodation** is giving the student extra time to complete the test. **Classroom test modifications** may involve giving the students less to learn and including less material on the tests. For state standardized tests, accommodations like extra time and frequent breaks can be provided. Students that need modifications to state tests may complete alternate assessments that may not cover the same material as the standard exams.

ENSURING A SMART ANNUAL GOAL IN AN IEP

A good IEP goal describes how far the student is expected to **progress** toward the IEP goal by the next IEP. Since IEPs should be revised once a year, a good annual IEP goal should describe what the student is capable of doing in a one-year time frame. Creating **SMART** IEP goals can help the student determine realistic expectations for what can be achieved in a year. SMART IEP goals are specific, measurable, attainable, results oriented, and timebound. Goals are **specific** when they list the targeted result of the skill or subject area. Goals should also be specific to the student's needs. Goals that are **measurable** state the way a student's progress will be measured. Measurable goals list how accurately a student should meet the goal. **Attainable** goals mean the goal is realistic for the student to achieve in one year. **Results-oriented** goals outline what a student needs to do to accomplish the goal. For example, a SMART goal may state, "During the school week, Robert will use his device to communicate greetings 80% of the time in 4/5 trials." **Time-bound** goals include a timeframe for the student to achieve the goal. They also list when and how often progress will be measured.

ROLE AN INITIAL EVALUATION ASSESSMENT PLAYS IN QUALIFYING A STUDENT FOR SPECIAL EDUCATION

When a student is determined to need special education, it means the student has a disability or disabilities adversely affecting educational performance. It may also mean the student's needs cannot be addressed in the general education classroom with or without accommodations, and **specially designed instruction (SDI)** is required. An **initial evaluation** of the student is required for special education eligibility. The evaluation is comprehensive and includes existing data collected on the student and additional assessments needed to determine eligibility. Individual school districts decide what assessments should be completed for the student's initial evaluation. Each district is responsible for and should provide assessments that measure functional, developmental, and academic information. The student's parents or legal guardians are responsible for providing outside information relevant to the student's education, such as medical needs assessed outside of the school district by qualified providers.

PURPOSE OF AN IEP FOR AN INDIVIDUAL STUDENT

The purpose of an Individualized Education Program is to guide the learning of a student with a **disability** in the educational environment. An Individualized Education Program is a written statement for a student eligible for **special education**. An initial IEP is **implemented** once the child has been evaluated and determined as needing special education. After the initial IEP, **IEP meetings** are conducted annually (or more) in order to update the plan to meet the needs of the student. IEPs are created, reviewed, and revised according to individual state and federal laws. These plans include the amount of time the student will spend in the special education classroom based on the level of need. They also include any related services the student might need, such as speech-language therapy, and academic and behavioral goals for the year. As the student learns and changes, performance levels and goals change as well. A student's present levels of performance are included and updated yearly, as are the academic and behavioral goals.

MEMBERS OF AN INDIVIDUALIZED EDUCATION PROGRAM TEAM

Individualized Education Programs are conducted **annually**, following the initial IEP. IEP team members meet at least once a year to discuss a student's progress and make changes to the IEP. The required members of a student's IEP team include the student's parents or legal guardians, one of the student's general education teachers, the special education teacher, a school representative, an individual who can interpret the instructional implications of evaluation results, anyone else who has knowledge or expertise about the student, and, if appropriate, the student. **Parents and legal**

guardians contribute unique expertise about the student, typically having the benefit of knowing the child well. **General education teachers** can speak on behalf of how the student is performing in the general education classroom. The **special education teacher** can report on progress made toward academic and behavioral goals and present levels of performance. A **school representative** must be qualified to provide or supervise specially designed instruction, be knowledgeable of the general education curriculum, and be knowledgeable about school resources. The **individual who can interpret evaluation results** can be an existing team member or someone else who is qualified to report on evaluation results. **Advocates**, such as counselors or therapists who see the student outside the school day, can also attend the meeting to speak on the student's behalf.

LEGAL RIGHTS FOR PARENTS OR LEGAL GUARDIANS

Individualized Education Program (IEP) meetings occur annually for each student. However, it is a **parent or legal guardian's right** to request a meeting at any point during the school year. The student's school is responsible for identifying and evaluating the child, developing, reviewing, and/or revising the IEP, and determining what placement setting best suits the needs of the student. It is within the parent or legal guardian's rights to have **input** in all processes related to the student. Under the Individuals with Disabilities Education Act (IDEA), parents have the right to participate in IEP meetings, have an independent evaluation outside the one the school provides, give or deny consent for the IEP, contest a school's decision, and obtain private education paid for by the public school. In specific circumstances, if the student is determined to need services that the public school cannot provide, the public school district may need to pay for the student's tuition at a private school where the student's needs can be met.

COLLABORATIVE CONSULTATION BETWEEN EDUCATIONAL PROFESSIONALS

Collaborative consultation refers to the special educator or other professional providing advice to the general education teacher about the student on the Individualized Education Program. Special educators and other IEP team members, such as school psychologists and related service professionals, serve as the **experts** and have knowledge about how individual students learn and behave. This is especially important when students with IEPs are included in the general education classroom. Special educators and general education teachers must work collaboratively to ensure that students are reaching their potential in the general education setting. Examples of **collaborative consultation** include the special educator serving as a consultant to the general education teacher by providing advice on a student's IEP, accommodations, modifications, skill techniques, and IEP goal tracking. Another way the special educator or other professional can assist the general educator is by providing skill and strategy instruction to students on IEPs outside the general education classroom. The idea behind this method is for students to generalize these skills and strategies to the general education classroom.

PUBLIC SCHOOL RESPONSIBILITIES TO PARENTS AND LEGAL GUARDIANS OF STUDENTS ON IEPs

The school must invite the parents or legal guardians to any **IEP meetings** and provide advance notice of the meetings. Each meeting notice is required to include the purpose of the meeting, its time and location, and who will attend. The location of the meeting is likely the student's school, but legally it must be held at a mutually agreed upon place and time. If the parent or legal guardian cannot attend the IEP meeting, the school must ensure participation in another way, such as video or telephone conference. The meeting can be conducted without the parent or legal guardian if the school district cannot get the parent or legal guardian to attend. A parent or legal guardian can request a meeting, and the school can refuse or deny the request. If denied, the school must provide a **Prior Written Notice** explaining their refusal. A Prior Written Notice is a document outlining important school district decisions about a student on an IEP.

ENVIRONMENTAL MODIFICATIONS FOR STUDENTS WITH DISABILITIES IN THE CLASSROOM

Students with disabilities may need environmental modifications in order to be successful in their classrooms, homes, and communities. **Environmental modifications** are adaptations that allow people with disabilities to maneuver through their environments with as little resistance as possible. They allow for more **independent living experiences**, especially for those with limited mobility. Environmental modifications ensure the health, safety, and welfare of the people who need them. Examples of environmental modifications in the home, community, or school include ramps, hydraulic lifts, widened doorways and hallways, automatic doors, handrails, and grab bars. Roll-in showers, water faucet controls, worktable or work surface adaptations, and cabinet and shelving adaptations are also environmental modifications that can be provided if necessary. Other adaptations include heating and cooling adaptations and electrical adaptations to accommodate devices or equipment. Environmental modifications in the home are typically provided by qualified agencies or providers. The Americans with Disabilities Act ensures that environmental modifications are provided in the **community** to avoid the discrimination of a person with a disability.

Foundations and Professional Responsibilities

Foundations and Professional Responsibilities

INDIVIDUALS WITH DISABILITIES EDUCATION ACT

The Individuals with Disabilities Education Act (**IDEA**) includes six major principles that focus on students' rights and the responsibilities public schools have for educating children with **disabilities**. One of the main principles of the IDEA law is to provide a **free and appropriate public education (FAPE)** suited to the individual needs of a child with a disability. This requires schools to provide special education and related services to students identified as having disabilities. Another purpose of IDEA is to require schools to provide an appropriate **evaluation** of a child with a suspected disability and an **Individualized Education Program (IEP)** for a child with a disability who qualifies under IDEA. Students with IEPs are guaranteed **least restrictive environment (LRE)**, or a guarantee that they are educated in the general education classroom as much as possible. IDEA also ensures **parent participation**, providing a role for parents as equal participants and decision makers. Lastly, **procedural safeguards** also serve to protect parents' rights to advocate for their children with disabilities.

PEOPLE PROTECTED BY PARTS B AND C OF IDEA LAW

Early intervention services are provided to children with special needs from birth to age three under **IDEA Part C**. Children from birth to age 3 who are identified as having disabilities and qualify under IDEA receive **Individualized Family Service Plans (IFSPs)**.

Special education and related services are provided to children with disabilities from ages 3 to 21 under **IDEA Part B**. Children ages 3 to 21 who are identified as having disabilities and qualify under IDEA receive educational documents, called **Individualized Education Programs (IEPs)**.

INDIVIDUALIZED EDUCATION PROGRAMS VS. INDIVIDUALIZED FAMILY SERVICE PLANS

IFSPs and IEPs are both educational documents provided under IDEA to service the rights of children with disabilities and their families. The major differences between IEPs and IFSPs, aside from the ages they service, is that **IFSPs** cover **broader services** for children with disabilities and their families. IFSP services are often provided in the children's homes. **IEPs** focus on special education and related services within the children's **school settings**.

PURPOSE OF IEPS AND FUNCTION OF THE PLOPS

An IEP is a written statement for a child with a disability. Its primary purposes are to establish **measurable annual goals** and to list the **services** needed to help the child with a disability meet the annual goals.

The IDEA law mandates that a statement of the child's academic achievement and functional performance be included within the IEP. This statement is called **Present Levels of Performance (PLOPs)**. It provides a snapshot of the student's current performance in school. Present Levels of Performance should also report how a student's disability is affecting, or not affecting, progress in school.

The IDEA law mandates that an **Annual Goals section** be provided within the IEP. Annual goals lay out what a student is expected to learn within a 12-month period. These goals are influenced by the student's PLOPs and are developed using objective, measurable data based on the student's previous academic performance.

CHILD FIND LAW

Child Find is part of the Individuals with Disabilities Education Act (IDEA) and states that schools are legally required to find children who have **disabilities** and need **special education** or other services. According to the **Child Find law**, all school districts must have processes for identifying students who need special education and related services. Children with disabilities from birth to age 21, children who are homeschooled, and children in private schools are all covered by the Child Find law. Infants and toddlers can be identified and provided with services so that parents have the right tools in place to meet their children's needs before they enter grade school. The Child Find law does not mean that public schools need to agree to evaluate students when evaluations are requested. Schools may still refuse evaluation if school professionals do not suspect the children of having disabilities.

STEPS TO IMPLEMENTING IEPs

The five most important steps in the **Individualized Education Program (IEP)** process are the identification via "Child Find" or the referral for special education services, evaluation, determination of eligibility, the first IEP meeting at which the IEP is written, and the ongoing provision of services during which progress is measured and reported. The referral can be initiated by a teacher, a special team in the school district, the student's parent, or another professional. The evaluation provides a snapshot of a student's background history, strengths, weaknesses, and academic, behavioral, or social needs. An IEP team of professionals as well as the student's parent(s)/guardian(s) uses the evaluation and any other reports regarding a student's progress to determine if the student is eligible for special education services. Once a student has been found eligible for special education, the first IEP meeting is held during which an IEP is written by a special education teacher or other specialist familiar with the student. The IEP meeting, either initial or annual, is held before the new IEP is implemented. Once the IEP meeting has occurred, services will be provided as detailed in the written IEP, during which the student's progress will continually be measured and reported. The IEP team includes the student, parent(s)/guardian(s), special education teacher, general education teacher, school psychologist, school administrator, appropriate related service professionals, and any other professionals or members that can comment on the student's strengths.

MANIFESTATION DETERMINATION

Manifestation determination is a process defined by the Individuals with Disabilities Education Act (IDEA). The **manifestation determination process** is put into effect when a student receiving special education needs to be removed from the educational setting due to a suspension, expulsion or alternative placement. Manifestation determination is the process that determines if the **disciplinary action** resulted from a **manifestation of the student's disability**. This is important because if the action was a manifestation of the disability, the outcome of the disciplinary action may change. During the initial part of this process, relevant data is collected about the student and the circumstances of the offending behavior. The student's Individualized Education Program team determines whether or not the student's behavior was related to the disability. If they determine that the behavior was not related to the disability, the disciplinary action is carried out. If the behavior is determined to be related to the disability, the student is placed back into the original educational setting.

PROVISION OF TITLE III OF THE AMERICANS WITH DISABILITIES ACT

Title III of ADA prohibits the discrimination of people with disabilities in **public accommodations**. Title III seeks to level the playing field of access for people with disabilities participating in public activities. Businesses open to the public, such as schools, restaurants, movie theaters, day care facilities, recreation facilities, doctor's offices, and restaurants, are required to comply with **ADA standards**. Additionally, commercial facilities, such as privately-owned businesses, factories, warehouses, and office buildings, are required to provide access per ADA standards. Title III of ADA outlines the general requirements of the **reasonable modifications** that businesses must provide. Title III also provides detailed, specific requirements for reasonable modifications within businesses and requires new construction and building alterations to abide by ADA regulations. Title III also outlines rules regarding **enforcement of ADA regulations**, such as the consequences for a person or persons participating in discrimination of a person with a disability. Title III provides for **certification of state laws or local building codes**. This means that a state's Assistant Attorney General may issue certification to a place of public accommodation or commercial facility that meets or exceeds the minimum requirements of Title III.

LARRY P. V. RILES

The *Larry P. v. Riles* (1977) court case examined possible **cultural discrimination** of African-American students. The court case questioned whether an intelligence quotient (IQ) test was an accurate measurement of a student's true intelligence. The case argued that there was a disproportionate number of African-American students identified as needing special education services (EMR program services). The court plaintiff Larry P. argued that IQ tests were **biased** against African-American students, which resulted in their placements in limiting educational settings. The defendant Riles argued that the prevalence of African-American students in the EMR classes was due to genetics and social and environmental factors. The court ultimately ruled that the IQ tests were discriminatory and resulted in the disproportionate placement of African-American students in the EMR setting. It was determined that these particular assessments were **culturally biased**, and the students' performances would be more accurately measured using adaptive behavior assessments, diagnostic tests, observations, and other assessments.

DIANA V. STATE BOARD OF EDUCATION

Diana v. State Board of Education (1970) is a court case that examined the case of a student who was placed in special education after results of the Stanford Binet Intelligence test indicated she had a mild case of "mental retardation." This class-action lawsuit was developed on behalf of nine **Mexican-American children**, arguing that IQ scores were not an adequate measurement to determine special education placement in the EMR setting. The case argued that Mexican-American children might be at a disadvantage because the IQ tests were written and administered in English. This might possibly constitute **discrimination**. The plaintiffs in the case argued that IQ scores were not a valid measurement because the children might have been unable to comprehend the test written in English. In the conclusive results of this case, the court ordered children to be tested in their primary language, if it was not English. As a result of this case, IQ tests were no longer used as the sole assessments for determining **special education placement**. There was also increased focus on **cultural and linguistic diversity** in students.

WINKELMAN V. PARMA CITY BOARD OF EDUCATION

This court case began as an argument against a **free and appropriate public education** as required by the Individuals with Disabilities Education Act (IDEA). The parents of Jacob Winkelman believed their son was not provided with a FAPE in his special education setting in Parma City Schools. The disagreement became about whether or not children can be **represented by their**

parents per IDEA law in federal court. The U.S Court of Appeals for the Sixth Circuit argued that IDEA protected the rights of the children and not the parents. In the end, the District Court ruled that parents could represent their children within disputes over a free and appropriate public education as constituted by IDEA. Ultimately, this settled the question of whether or not **parents have rights under IDEA**, in addition to their children. The court case determined that parents play a significant role in the education of their children on Individualized Education Programs (IEPs) and are IEP team members. Therefore, parents are entitled to litigate *pro se* for their children.

HONIG V. DOE

Honig v. Doe (1998) was a Supreme Court case examining the violation of the **Education for All Handicapped Children Act** (EAHCA, an earlier version of the Individuals with Disabilities Education Act) against the California School Board. The offense occurred when a child was suspended for a violent behavior outburst that was related to his disability. The court case centered on two plaintiffs. Both were diagnosed with an Emotional Disturbance and qualified for special education under EAHCA. Following the violent incident, the school suspended the students and recommended them for expulsion. The plaintiff's case argued that the suspension/expulsion went against the **stay-put provision of EAHCA**, which states that children with disabilities must remain in their current educational placements during review proceedings unless otherwise agreed upon by both parents and educational representatives. The defendant argued that the violence of the situation marked an exception to the law. The court determined that schools are able to justify the placement removal of a student when maintaining a **safe learning environment** outweighs a student's right to a free and appropriate public education.

PENNSYLVANIA ASSOCIATION FOR RETARDED CHILDREN V. COMMONWEALTH OF PENNSYLVANIA

The Commonwealth of Pennsylvania was accused by the Pennsylvania Association for Retarded Children (PARC 1971), now known as the Arc of Pennsylvania, of denying a **free and appropriate public education** to students with disabilities. The Commonwealth of Pennsylvania was accused of refusing to educate students who had not met the "mental age of 5." The groups argued before the District Court of the Eastern District of Pennsylvania. This case was significant because PARC was one of the first institutions in the country to challenge the **placement of students with special needs**. The plaintiffs argued that all children should and would benefit from some sort of educational instruction and training. Ultimately, this was the beginning of instituting the state requirement of a free and appropriate public education (**FAPE**) for all children in public education from ages 6–21. The Commonwealth of Pennsylvania was tasked with providing a FAPE and sufficient education and training for all eligible children receiving special education. They could no longer deny students based on their mental ages. This triggered other state institutions to make similar decisions and led to the creation of similar federal policies in the **Education for All Handicapped Children Act** (1974).

1990 AMENDMENTS TO THE IDEA

The **Individuals with Disabilities Education Act (IDEA)** replaced the Education for All Handicapped Children Act in 1990. IDEA amendments changed the **age range** for children to receive special education services to ages 3–21. IDEA also changed the language of the law, changing the focus onto the **individuals with disabilities** rather than the **handicapped children**. Therefore, the focus shifted from the conditions or disabilities to the individual children and their needs. IDEA amendments also **categorized** different disabilities. IDEA 1997 increased the emphasis on the individualized education plans for students with disabilities and increased parents' roles in the educational decision-making processes for their children with disabilities. Part B of the 1997 amendment provided services to children ages 3–5, mandating that their learning needs be outlined in **Individualized Education Programs** or **Individualized Family Service Plans**. Part C of IDEA provided **financial assistance** to the families of infants and toddlers with disabilities. Part C states that educational agencies must provide **early intervention services** that focus on children's developmental and medical needs, as well as the needs of their families. Part C also gives states the option to provide services to children who are at risk for developmental disabilities.

EFFECT OF THE INDIVIDUALS WITH DISABILITIES EDUCATION IMPROVEMENT ACT OF 2004 ON IDEA

In 2004, the Individuals with Disabilities Education Act implemented the **Individuals with Disabilities Education Improvement Act**. IDEA was reauthorized to better meet the needs of children in special education programs and children with special needs. As a result of these changes:

- Special educators are required to achieve Highly Qualified Teacher status and be certified in special education.
- Individualized Education Programs must contain measurable **annual goals** and descriptions of how progress toward the goals will be **measured and reported**.
- Schools or agencies must provide science or research-based **interventions** as part of the evaluation process to determine if children have specific learning disabilities. This may be done in addition to assessments that measure achievement or intelligence.

The changes made to require science or research-based interventions resulted in many districts implementing **Response to Intervention procedures**. These procedures meet the IDEA 2004 requirement of providing interventions in addition to achievement reports or intelligence tests on the Individualized Education Programs for children with disabilities.

DEVELOPMENT OF EDUCATIONAL LAWS LIKE GOALS 2000 AND NO CHILD LEFT BEHIND

President Bill Clinton signed the **National Educational Goals Act**, also known as Goals 2000, into effect in the 1990s to trigger standardized educational reform. The act focused on **outcomes-based education** and was intended to be completed by the year 2000. The goals of this act included ensuring that children are ready to learn by the time they start school, increasing high school graduation rates, demonstration of competency by students in grades 4, 8, and 12 in core content areas, and positioning the United States as first in the world in mathematics and science achievement. Goals 2000 was withdrawn when President George W. Bush implemented the **No Child Left Behind Act (NCLB)** in 2001. NCLB also supported standards-based reform, and it mandated that states develop more **skills-based assessments**. The act emphasized state testing, annual academic progress, report cards, and increased teacher qualification standards. It also outlined changes in state funding. NCLB required schools to meet **Adequate Yearly Progress (AYP)**. AYP was measured by results of achievement tests taken by students in each school district, and consequences were implemented for school districts that missed AYP during consecutive years.

EVERY STUDENT SUCCEEDS ACT OF 2015

NCLB was replaced in 2015 by the Every Student Succeeds Act (**ESSA**). ESSA built upon the foundations of NCLB and emphasized **equal opportunity** for students. ESSA currently serves as the main K–12 educational law in the United States. ESSA affects students in public education, including students with disabilities. The purpose of ESSA is to provide a **quality education** for all students. It also aims to address the achievement of **disadvantaged students**, including students living in poverty, minority groups, students receiving special education services, and students with limited English language skills. ESSA determined that states may decide educational plans as long as they follow the government's framework. ESSA also allows states to develop their own educational standards and mandates that the curriculum focus on preparing students for post-secondary educations or careers. The act requires students to be tested annually in math and reading during grades 3–8 and once in high school. Students must also be tested in science once in elementary school, middle school, and high school. **School accountability** was also mandated by ESSA. The act requires states to have plans in place for any schools that are underperforming.

ESL Rights for Students and Parents

As public schools experience an influx of English as a Second Language (ESL) students, knowledge of their **rights** becomes increasingly important. The **Every Student Succeeds Act (ESSA)** of 2015 addresses funding discrepancies for ESL students and families. ESSA allocates funds to schools and districts where low-income families comprise 40% or more of the enrollment. This is intended to assist with ESL students who are underperforming or at risk for underperforming. ESSA also provides funding for ESL students to become English proficient and find academic success. However, in order for schools and districts to receive this funding, they must avoid discrimination, track ESL student progress, assess ESL student English proficiency, and notify parents of their children's ESL status. Avoiding discrimination includes preventing the over-identification of ESL students for special education services. The referral and evaluation process must be carried out with caution to ensure that students' perceived disabilities are actual deficits and not related to their English language learning abilities.

Rehabilitation Act of 1973

The Rehabilitation Act of 1973 was the law that preceded IDEA 1975. The Rehab Act serves to protect the rights of people with disabilities in several ways.

- It protects people with disabilities against discrimination relating to **employment**.
- It provides students with disabilities equal access to the **general education curriculum** (Section 504).

Americans with Disabilities Act of 1990 (ADA)

The Americans with Disabilities Act (1990) also protects the rights of people with disabilities.

- The ADA provides **equal employment** for people with disabilities. This means employers must provide reasonable accommodations for people with disabilities in their job and work environments.
- It provides **access** for people with disabilities to both public and private places open to the public (i.e. access ramps and automatic doors).
- It provides **telecommunications access** to people with disabilities. This ensures people with hearing and speech disabilities can communicate over the telephone and Internet.

Elementary and Secondary Education Act (ESEA)

The Elementary and Secondary Education Act (ESEA) also protects the rights of people with disabilities.

- Passed by President Johnson in 1965, ESEA was part of the president's "War on Poverty." The law sought to allow **equal access to a quality education**.
- ESEA extended more funding to secondary and primary schools and emphasized high **standards and accountability**.
- This law was authorized as **No Child Left Behind** (2001) under President Bush, then reauthorized as the **Every Student Succeeds Act** (ESSA) under President Obama.

Section 504

A Section 504 Plan comes from the civil rights law, Section 504 of the Rehabilitation Act of 1973, and protects the rights of individuals with disabilities. A 504 Plan is a formal plan or blueprint for how the school will provide services to a student with a disability. This essentially removes barriers for individuals with disabilities by ensuring that **appropriate services** are provided to meet their special needs. A 504 Plan includes:

- **Accommodations**: A 504 Plan includes accommodations a student with a disability may need to be successful in a regular education classroom. For example, a student with ADHD may need to sit near the front of the room to limit distractions.
- **Related Services**: A 504 Plan includes related services, such as speech therapy or occupational therapy, a student may need to be successful in the general education classroom.
- **Modifications**: Although it is rare for a 504 Plan to include modifications, sometimes they are included. Modifications change what the student is expected to do, such as being given fewer homework assignments.

504 Plans vs. Individualized Education Programs

- A 504 Plan and an Individualized Education Program are similar in that they serve as a blueprint for a student with a disability. However, a 504 Plan serves as a blueprint for how the student will have **access to school**, whereas the IEP serves as a blueprint for a student's **special education experience**.
- A 504 Plan helps level the playing field for a student with a disability by providing services and changes to the **learning environment**. An IEP provides individualized special education and related services to meet the **unique needs of a student with a disability**. Both IEPs and 504 Plans are provided at no cost to parents.
- The 504 Plan was established under the **Rehabilitation Act of 1973** as a civil rights law. The Individualized Education Program was established under the **Individuals with Disabilities Education Act** (1975 and amended in 2004).
- Unlike an IEP, a 504 Plan does **not** have to be a planned, written document. An IEP is a **planned, written document** that includes unique annual learning goals and describes related services for the student with a disability.

Informed Parental Consent

The Individuals with Disabilities Education Act (IDEA) requires that parents be **informed** before a student is evaluated for special education services. IDEA mandates that a school district receive **parental consent** to initiate an evaluation of a student for special education services. Consent means the school district has fully informed the parent of their intentions or potential reasons for evaluation of the student. Legally, the request must be written in the parent's native language. This consent does not mean the parent gives consent for a student's placement in special education. In order for a student to be initially placed in special education or receive special education services, parental consent must be given for this issue separately. At any time, parents can withdraw consent for special education placement or special education services. Schools are able to file **due process** if they disagree with the parental withdrawal of consent. Parents also have a right to consent to parts of a student's Individualized Education Program (IEP), but not necessarily all of the IEP. Once parental consent is granted for all parts of the IEP, it can be implemented.

TIERS OF THE RESPONSE TO INTERVENTION MODEL

- **Tier 1: High Quality Classroom Instruction, Screening, and Group Interventions**: In Tier 1, all students are screened using universal screening and/or the results of statewide assessments. Students identified as at risk receive supplemental instruction. Students who make adequate progress are returned to their regular instruction. Students who do not make adequate progress move to Tier 2.
- **Tier 2: Targeted Interventions**: These interventions are designed to improve the progress of the students who did not make adequate progress in Tier 1. Targeted instruction is usually in the areas of reading and math and does not last longer than one grading period.
- **Tier 3: Intensive Interventions and Comprehensive Evaluation**: Students who are not successful in Tier 2 move on to Tier 3. They receive intensive interventions that target their specific deficits. Students who do not meet progress goals during intensive interventions are referred to receive comprehensive evaluations and are considered to be eligible for special education under IDEA.

STAKEHOLDERS IN SPECIAL EDUCATION

Stakeholders that play roles in educating students with disabilities include the students, parents, general educators, administrators, and community members. Students should receive an educational **curriculum** based on strict standards, such as the Common Core Content Standards. This ensures that they receive good educational foundations from which to grow and expand upon during their school careers. Parents, legal guardians, and sometimes agencies act in the best interests of their children. If they do not think the Individualized Education Programs suit the needs of their children, they can request **due process hearings** in court. FAPE and LRE ensure that students are educated alongside peers in general education classrooms by general educators. General educators collaborate with special educators to create **successful inclusion classrooms**. When inclusion is done successfully, the students with disabilities meet their IEP goals.

INFORMATION TO BE EVALUATED DURING MULTI-FACTORED EVALUATIONS OR EVALUATION TEAM REPORTS

Multi-Factored Evaluations are processes required by the Individuals with Disabilities Education Act to determine if a student is eligible for special education. When a student is suspected of having a disability, the parent or school district can initiate the evaluation process. **Student information** that is evaluated in a Multi-Factored Evaluation includes background information, health information, vision testing, hearing testing, social and emotional development, general intelligence, past and current academic performance, communication needs, gross and fine motor abilities, results of aptitude or achievement tests, academic skills, and current progress toward Individualized Education Program (IEP) goals. Progress reporting on IEP goals is only appropriate during an annual MFE when a student has already qualified for special education services. The purpose of an MFE is to provide **comprehensive information** about a student for professionals working with the student. An MFE also helps determine what academic or behavioral **goals** or related services might be appropriate for a student with disabilities.

FREE AND APPROPRIATE PUBLIC EDUCATION COMPONENTS

The Individuals with Disabilities Education Act (IDEA) defines free and appropriate public education (FAPE) as an educational right for children with disabilities in the United States. FAPE stands for:

- **Free**: All students found eligible for special education services must receive free services, expensed to the public instead of the parents.
- **Appropriate**: Students are eligible for educations that are appropriate for their specific needs, as stated in their Individualized Education Programs (IEPs).
- **Public**: Students with disabilities have the right to be educated in public schools.
- **Education**: An education must be provided to any school-aged child with a disability. Education and services are defined in a student's IEP.

Ideally, FAPE components are put in place in order to guarantee the best education possible that also suits the individual needs of a student with a disability. FAPE should take place in the least restrictive environment, or the environment with the fewest barriers to learning for the individual student with a disability.

MULTI-FACTORED EVALUATION OR EVALUATION TEAM REPORT

A Multi-Factored Evaluation (**MFE**), sometimes referred to as an Evaluation Team Report (**ETR**), serves as a snapshot of a child's abilities, strengths, and weaknesses. An MFE is conducted to determine a student's eligibility for special education. Once a student with a disability qualifies for special education, an MFE is conducted at least every three years after the initial MFE date. MFEs are conducted for students ages 3 to 21 who are on IEPs. The purpose of the MFE is to influence a student's **Individualized Education Program**. An MFE reports on a student's **current abilities** and how the disability may affect **educational performance**. MFEs can also determine if a student qualifies for related services, such as occupational therapy or speech-language therapy. An MFE can be requested by a parent or school district when a child is suspected of having a disability. The school district typically has 30 days or less to respond to a parental request to evaluate a student, giving consent or refusal for an evaluation. While initial MFEs are conducted as a means to determine special education qualification, annual MFEs are conducted to address any changes in the needs or services of a student already receiving special education services.

LEAST RESTRICTIVE ENVIRONMENTS TO DELIVER SPECIAL EDUCATION SERVICES

Special education services are delivered to students that qualify with a **disability** defined by the Individuals with Disabilities Education Act (IDEA). IDEA law also requires that students who qualify for special education must receive special education services in **least restrictive environments** that provide the fewest barriers to their learning. A student's most appropriate instructional setting is written out in the **Individualized Education Program (IEP)**. Some special education instructional settings include:

- no instructional setting
- mainstream setting
- resource room
- self-contained classroom
- homebound instruction

With **no instructional setting**, students participate in the general education curriculum but may receive related services, such as speech-language therapy or occupational therapy. In the **mainstream setting**, students are instructed in the general education classroom for most or part of the day and provided with special education supports, accommodations, modifications, and related services. A **resource room** is an environment where students receive remedial instruction when they cannot participate in the general curriculum for one or more subject areas. A **self-contained classroom** is a setting for students who need special education and related services for more than 50% of the day. **Homebound instruction** is for students who are homebound or hospital bound for more than four consecutive weeks.

PURPOSE OF SPECIAL EDUCATION

Special education is specially designed instruction delivered to meet the individual needs of children with disabilities. Special education includes a free and appropriate education in the least restrictive environment. In the past, a special education model might consist of a self-contained classroom of students with special needs whose needs were addressed in that setting. Today, students who qualify for special education must receive instruction in **free and appropriate settings**. This means they receive special education services in settings that provide the **fewest barriers** to their learning. The most appropriate setting varies, depending on the student and the disability. The purpose of special education is to ensure that the unique needs of children with disabilities are addressed. In the public school setting, the Individuals with Disabilities Education Act mandates that students with disabilities receive free and appropriate public educations. The goal of special education is to create **fair environments** for students with special needs to learn. Ideally, the settings should enable students to learn to their fullest potential.

DUE PROCESS RIGHTS AVAILABLE TO PARENTS AND LEGAL GUARDIANS

When parents or legal guardians and school districts cannot agree on components of a student with a disability's Individualized Education Program (IEP), parents and legal guardians have a right to **due process**. Due process is a legal right under the Individuals with Disabilities Education Act (IDEA) that usually involves the school district violating a legal rule. Examples of these violations include a school district not running an IEP meeting, failing to conduct a tri-annual evaluation, or failing to implement a student's IEP. Disputes often involve a student's instructional placement, appropriate accommodations or modifications, related services, or changes to IEPs. School districts' due process policies vary depending on the district. IDEA, however, mandates that a **due process legal form** be completed by the parent or legal guardian in order to move forward. This form must be completed within two years of a dispute. **Mediation**, or the process of coming to an agreement before filing due process, can be a solution to the dispute. IEP meetings, even when it is not time for an annual review, are also appropriate options for resolving a dispute before filing due process.

PURPOSE OF MEDIATION IN LIEU OF A PARENT OR LEGAL GUARDIAN FILING FOR DUE PROCESS

Mediation is a process used to address a dispute prior to a parent or legal guardian filing for due process. The purpose of mediation is to **resolve a dispute** between the parent or legal guardian of a student with a disability and the school district. Disputes occur when the parent or legal guardian does not agree with an IEP component, such as what related services are provided or the way a student's IEP is being implemented. Mediation is not a parent or legal guardian's legal right, but school districts often support mediation to offset a **due process filing**. Mediation involves the attempt to resolve a dispute and includes a meeting between the parent or legal guardian, school district member, and a neutral third party, such as a mediator provided by the state. States have lists of **mediators** available for these situations. Agreements that come out of the mediation process are put into writing and, if appropriate, put into a student's IEP. Disagreements can continue to be mediated, or the decision may be made to file due process. Prior to mediation, parents or legal guardians and school districts have the option of holding IEP meetings (outside of annual meetings) to resolve disputes.

CONFIDENTIALITY AND PRIVACY OF STUDENT RECORDS

Health Insurance Portability and Accountability Act of 1966 (HIPAA), **FERPA** is a law privacy. However, FERPA is specific to the privacy of students. The FERPA law applies ol or agency that receives funds from the U.S. Department of Education. This ensures that is or agencies cannot share any confidential information about a student without a parent or student's written consent. **Student educational records** can be defined as records, files, documents, or other materials which contain a student's personal information. Individualized **Education Programs** and **Evaluation Team Reports (ETRs)** are examples of private documents under the FERPA law. The responsibility of a school covered by FERPA is to maintain confidentiality and privacy. The members of an IEP team, such as special educators, related service professionals, general educators, or other professionals, cannot share any identifying, private information about a student. Information addressing the needs of individual students found on an IEP, Evaluation Team Report, or other identifying document must remain confidential unless express written consent is given by the parent or legal guardian.

PRE-REFERRAL/REFERRAL PROCESS FOR IDENTIFYING AND PLACING A STUDENT WITH A DISABILITY

The purpose of a pre-referral process for a child with a suspected disability is to attempt **reasonable modifications and accommodations** before the child is referred for special education services. Schools often have **pre-referral teams** whose purpose is to identify the strengths and needs of a child, put reasonable strategies into action, and evaluate the results of this pre-referral intervention. If the results do not show any change, another intervention can be attempted, or the student can be referred for a special education evaluation.

If a child is suspected of having a disability and did not succeed with pre-referral interventions, the school or parent can request an **evaluation**. During the evaluation process, the school compiles information to see if the student needs special education or related services. This information is used to determine if the student's disability is affecting school performance and if the student qualifies for special education. The evaluation lists and examines the student's strengths, weaknesses, and development and determines what supports the student needs in order to learn. An evaluation must be completed before special education services can be provided.

ROLE OF A SCHOOL PSYCHOLOGIST IN THE SPECIAL EDUCATION

School psychologists are certified members of school teams that **support the needs of students and teachers**. They help students with overall academic, social, behavioral, and emotional success. School psychologists are trained in data collection and analysis, assessments, progress monitoring, risk factors, consultation and collaboration, and special education services. In special education, school psychologists may work directly with students and collaborate with teachers, administrators, parents, and other professionals working with particular students. They may also be involved in counseling students' parents, the Response to Intervention process, and performing initial evaluations of students who are referred for special education services. School psychologists also work to improve academic achievement, promote positive behavior and health by implementing school-wide programs, support learning needs of diverse learners, maintain safe school environments, and strengthen and maintain good school-parent relationships.

OVERREPRESENTATION OF STUDENTS FROM DIVERSE BACKGROUNDS

Disproportionate representation occurs when there is not an equal representation of students from different **cultural and linguistic backgrounds** identified for special education services. Students from different cultural and linguistic groups should be identified for special education services in similar proportions. This ensures that no one group is **overrepresented** and

overidentified as having special needs due to their cultural or linguistic differences. Disproportionality can occur based on a child's sex, language proficiency, receipt of free and reduced lunch, or race and ethnicity. Historically, most disproportionality has been a civil rights issue and due to a child's cultural or linguistic background. Recently, the focus has been on the disproportional number of students who spend time in special education classrooms instead of being educated alongside regularly educated peers.

The referral process, **Response to Intervention (RTI)**, provides safeguards against disproportionality. The RTI process requires instruction and intervention catered to the unique, specific needs of the individual student. The purpose of RTI is not the identification of a disability or entitlement to services. Instead, it focuses on data used to make educational decisions about individuals, classrooms, schools, or districts. Models like RTI address disproportionate representation, but they are not perfect.

Collaborating with the Learning Community

COLLABORATING WITH IEP TEAM MEMBERS

It is important for Individualized Education Program (IEP) team members to **collaborate** with each other in order to certify that students are receiving educational plans that are suitable to their needs in the least restrictive environments. **IEP team members** include special education teachers, general education teachers, parents or legal guardians, students, school district representatives, and others knowledgeable about the students' performances. Each member brings a valuable piece of information about the students for instructional planning and IEP planning meetings. It is important for special educators to establish good relationships and collaborate with the students and parents or legal guardians in order to gauge the students' strengths and weaknesses. Collaboration is essential between the general and special educators in order to ensure that students' IEP goals and needs are being met in the appropriate settings. Collaboration with district team members or others like school psychologists is helpful for gaining insight on special education procedures or assessment results.

COMMUNICATING WITH RELATED SERVICE MEMBERS ACROSS ALL SPECIAL EDUCATION SETTINGS

In order to provide the best educations possible for students with disabilities, it is important for special educators and related service members to **communicate** effectively. Communication is important due to the degree of collaboration required between the special educators and the related service members. Related service members are often Individualized Education Program (IEP) team members and help students meet their IEP goals and objectives. **Related service members**, like speech pathologists and occupational therapists, also work on a consultation basis with special educators. They may also consult with general education teachers to ensure that students receive required related services in the general education or inclusive classroom settings. Special educators and related service members must collaborate in order to ensure the needs of the students are met, especially when IEP goals or objectives are out of the scope of the special educators' knowledge bases. For example, a speech pathologist might help a teacher address a student's fluency goal.

COMMUNICATING WITH PARENTS OF STUDENTS WITH DISABILITIES

It is good practice to communicate with parents outside of progress reporting times and Individualized Education Program meetings. This is especially important for students with **communication deficits** who may not be able to communicate with their parents or legal guardians. Communication also helps prevent potential crises or problem behaviors and alerts parents or legal guardians before any major issues arise. Special educators should find methods of communication that work best for parents or legal guardians, such as phone calls, emails, or writing in daily communication logs. Email is beneficial for creating paper trails, especially for any discussions about educating students. However, email lacks tone and body language and can sometimes be misunderstood. Phone calls fulfill an immediate need to speak with a parent or legal guardian. However, there are no paper trails with phone calls, and they can also lead to misunderstanding. Phone calls may be time consuming, but they can be conducted on special occasions or when behavioral issues need to be discussed. Written communication logs are useful for writing brief summaries about students' days. With any mode of communication, it is essential to **document** what is communicated between the parents or legal guardians and the educators.

ROLES OF PARENTS/LEGAL GUARDIANS AND THE SCHOOL DISTRICT DURING EVALUATION

If parents or legal guardians suspect their children have disabilities, they can request that the school districts **evaluate** the children for special education. A parent or legal guardian can send a **written evaluation request** to the child's school, principal, and the school district's director or director of special education services. In some states, parents and legal guardians may be required to sign a school district form requesting the evaluation. Parents should follow up on the request and/or set a timeframe for the school district to respond. The school district may choose to implement the **Response to Intervention (RTI) pre-referral process**. RTI is a process by which the school gives the student special academic support before determining whether or not to move forward with the evaluation process. Not all states or school districts have the same method for applying RTI. Under IDEA, the timeframe for completion of RTI is 60 days. However, some states can set their own timelines. RTI should not be the only means by which the school district collects data on the student and should be part of a comprehensive evaluation conducted by the student's school.

SPEECH LANGUAGE PATHOLOGIST

Speech language pathologists (**SLP**) provide interventions for children with communication disorders. They can assist, evaluate, prevent, and diagnose a variety of **speech issues**, from fluency to voice disorders. Before children reach grade school age, it is important that they receive early interventions for suspected communication disorders. SLPs are helpful with targeting speech or language issues, identifying at-risk students, or providing interventions for children and adults. SLPs also play a role in helping children develop good reading and writing skills, especially when deficits are evident. SLPs work collaboratively with special educators to deliver **interventions** to children with speech and language disorders in grade school. In schools, SLPs play a role in prevention, assessment, intervention, program design, data collection and analysis, and Individualized Education Program compliance. SLPs work with special educators, parents, students, reading specialists, occupational therapists, school psychologists, and others in order to provide effective services to students who require them.

OCCUPATIONAL THERAPIST

Students with special needs may need **occupational therapy services**. The amount of services students receive is defined on their Individualized Education Programs (IEPs). **Occupational therapists (OTs)** may help students on IEPs refine their fine motor skills, improve sensory processing deficits, improve visual skills, and improve self-care skills. OTs can also assist with behavior management, social skills, and improving attention and focus. When a student is identified as possibly needing OT services, the OT spends time observing the student in a variety of settings where the skill or skill deficit will be demonstrated. Prior to the student's IEP meeting, the OT typically meets with the student's teachers, parents, and other professionals in order to discuss observations, assessment results, and determinations. **Determinations** are then put into the IEP and implemented as related services. Fine motor skill instruction begins with the OT instructing the student on a particular skill. OTs can set up regimens for teachers and parents to generalize using the fine motor skills in the classroom and home environments.

REASONABLE ACCOMMODATIONS FOR STUDENTS

According to the Americans with Disabilities Act, a **reasonable accommodation** is a change to workplace conditions, equipment, or environment that allow an individual to effectively perform a job. Title I under ADA requires businesses with more than 15 employees to abide by certain regulations, ensuring that their needs are reasonably met. Any change to the work environment or the way a job is performed that gives a person with a disability access to **equal employment** is considered a reasonable accommodation. Reasonable accommodations fall into **three categories**: changes to a job application process, changes to the work environment or to the way a job is usually done, and changes that enable employee access to equal benefits and privileges that employees without disabilities receive. These effectively level the playing field for people with disabilities to receive the same benefits as their peers. It also allows for the fewest barriers to success in the workplace. Many communities have resources available to help people with disabilities find jobs. They also have resources that help employers make their workplaces accessible for people with disabilities.

PARAPROFESSIONAL

The U.S. Department of Education requires **paraprofessionals** to have high school diplomas or equivalent under Title 1 law. Paraprofessionals (paras), sometimes called **paraeducators**, assist classroom teachers with classroom activities and help students with special needs. In a special education setting, a para works with a certified teacher to help deliver **instruction** and help students meet **Individualized Education Program goals and objectives**. Paras are not responsible for teaching new skills or introducing new goals and objectives to students. In this respect, special educators generally work alongside the paras and students to introduce new skills, goals, or objectives. At times, paras may be responsible for helping students maintain behavior plans, working with students who may be aggressive or violent, and providing physical assistance if necessary. Training is usually provided by the school district for situations when physical assistance is a possible necessity. Paras can also help take notes on students' progress toward meeting their goals or objectives. They can also discuss how students are progressing with behavior plans.

Behavioral and Crisis Support

BEHAVIOR ISSUES OF STUDENTS AND INTERVENTION STRATEGIES

Behavior issues occur with students with and without disabilities. However, they may occur more frequently or to a higher degree for some students with disabilities. Behavior issues are often a **manifestation** of a child's disability. For example, students with Attention Deficit Hyperactivity Disorder may present with attention and focus issues and impulsivity. **Common behavior issues** include:

- emotional outbursts
- inattention and inability to focus
- impulsivity
- aggression
- abusive language
- oppositional defiance

- lying or stealing
- threatening adults or peers

Other behavior issues may include inappropriate sexual behavior, inability to control sexual behavior, self-harm, or self-harm attempts. Behavior issues can be **avoided** or **remediated** with classroom management skills, like setting clear and consistent classroom goals, setting time limits, and providing visuals to assist with transitions or concepts. When a student is in an aggressive state, it is important for the teacher to remain calm, provide choices for the student, and restate the consequences of any aggressive outbursts.

MANAGING STUDENTS WITH EMOTIONAL DISTURBANCES

Managing a classroom of students with emotional disorders can be challenging and unpredictable. Students with emotional disorders have Individualized Education Program goals that focus on **controlling** or **monitoring** their daily behavior choices. However, this does not always mean they will engage in meeting these goals. It is important for educators to know how to **manage** issues students with emotional disorders may bring to the classroom. When creating resources and lesson plans, an educator should:

- establish a **safety plan**, which includes knowing how to implement a **crisis prevention plan**.
- maintain an environment that reduces **stimulation** and provides **visual cues** for expected behavior.
- implement **intervention-based strategies** for managing student behavior.
- collect and use **data** to identify triggers, track behaviors, and recognize successful strategies that produced positive outcomes.
- practice open **communication** about classroom expectations to students, parents, and other teachers.

Special education teachers can be good resources for many of these components, especially when students with emotional disorders are in inclusive settings.

CONCEPT OF ANTECEDENTS, BEHAVIOR, AND CONSEQUENCES AS STIMULI USED IN BEHAVIOR ANALYSIS

Antecedents and consequences play a role in behavioral analysis, which is important for evaluating the behaviors of students. The purpose of behavior analysis is to gather information about a specific behavior demonstrated by a student. **Antecedents** refer to the actions or events that occur before the behavior occurs. It is important to recognize antecedents for behaviors to better understand under what circumstances the behavior is occurring. The **behavior** is the undesirable action that occurs as a result of the antecedent. **Consequences** are what happens immediately after the behavior occurs. These can be natural or enforced. A certain consequence might be what the student desires by doing the behavior. Understanding the antecedents, behavior, and consequences and the relationships between them for a particular behavior allows a professional to determine how to minimize or eliminate the behavior. In some circumstances, antecedents can be manipulated, changed, or removed in order to avoid the undesired behavior. Consequences can be manipulated, changed, or removed in order to avoid reinforcing the undesired behavior.

BEHAVIOR RATING SCALE ASSESSMENTS

Behavior rating scales address the needs of students with emotional disorders who are referred to special education. Problems with behavior are often the reason a student has been referred for special education. Behavior rating scales are used in determining a student's **eligibility** for special education. Behavior rating scales are also useful in addressing **undesirable behaviors** demonstrated by students with other disorders in special education. They are similar to adaptive behavior scales because teachers or other professionals can administer the scales with little training as long as they are familiar with the students. Behavior rating scales help rate the frequency and intensity of the behaviors for a particular student. Behavior frequency and intensity are often rated with numbered rating scales. They serve as starting points for learning more about a student's behavior so that behavior interventions and management can take place. These scales are **norm-referenced**, so the outcomes of the behavior rating scales are compared to the behaviors of others.

NEGATIVE AND POSITIVE REINFORCEMENT RELATED TO APPLIED BEHAVIOR ANALYSIS

Part of applied behavior analysis is applying negative and positive reinforcement strategies. **Reinforcement** is a process that involves increasing the possibility of a desired behavior occurring. The goal of reinforcement is for the desired behavior to continue occurring in the future. **Positive reinforcement** works by providing a desired **reward** for a desired behavior. By reinforcing the desired behavior when it is exhibited, it increases the likelihood that the behavior will occur in the future. For example, parents may give a child an allowance for doing chores, and the allowance is the positive reinforcement for the behavior (the chores). In contrast, **negative reinforcement** is when a stimulus, usually an **aversive stimulus**, is removed to enforce a desired behavior. Negative reinforcement should not be seen as a punishment because a punishment is given to decrease a behavior. With negative reinforcement, the goal is for behaviors to increase by stopping, removing, or avoiding negative outcomes. An example of negative reinforcement is making a child finish dinner before receiving a popsicle. The popsicle is the reward for demonstrating the expected behavior.

DEVELOPING POSITIVE BEHAVIORAL INTERVENTIONS AND SUPPORTS

Positive behavioral intervention and support (**PBIS**) plans can be implemented in classrooms or schoolwide to encourage specific, positive outcomes in groups of students with and without disabilities. A PBIS plan, such as an anti-bullying campaign, is put in place to encourage **good behavior** and/or **school safety**. The goal of a PBIS plan is to teach students appropriate behavior, just as they would learn any other academic subject. PBIS plans are put in place to teach students positive behavior or safety procedures that are incompatible with undesirable behaviors. Appropriate PBIS plans should be based on the results of data collected on targeted, large-scale behaviors. They should also be research based and proven effective. As with any behavioral plans, PBIS plans are most successful when student progress is monitored. An effective PBIS plan removes **environmental triggers** for behavior, reducing the chances of the behavior occurring in the first place. PBIS plans should change if they do not work or stop working.

DEVELOPING FUNCTIONAL BEHAVIOR ASSESSMENT

A functional behavior assessment (**FBA**) is a formal process used to examine student behavior. The goal of an FBA is to identify what is causing a specific behavior and evaluate how the behavior is affecting the student's educational performance. Once these factors are determined, the FBA is useful in implementing **interventions** for the specific behavior. When an FBA is developed, a student's behavior must be specifically defined. Then the teacher or other professional devises a plan for collecting data on the behavior. This is helpful in determining what may be causing the behavior, such as environmental triggers. Collected data is analyzed to determine the big picture for what may be causing the behavior. The analyzed data is used to formulate a hypothesis about what is causing the behavior, so the teacher or other professional can then implement the most appropriate plan for addressing the student's specific behavior. Often, this means implementing a **behavior intervention plan**, which includes introducing the student to actions or processes that

93

are incompatible with the problem behavior. It is important to monitor the plan to ensure effectiveness or remediate certain steps.

IMPLEMENTING CRISIS PREVENTION PLANS

Students with disabilities sometimes display symptoms of their particular disorders that require trained adults to implement **crisis prevention plans**. Some organizations, such as the Crisis Prevention Institute, specialize in crisis prevention and intervention training for professionals. Crisis prevention plans are put in place to help the students **avoid** the behaviors before they occur. The goal is to keep the students functioning appropriately in their environments by removing or being aware of possible **behavioral triggers**. Crisis prevention plans are important to have in place for when students' behaviors become safety concerns. It is helpful to recognize warning signs that crises may be starting, and this can be done by providing interventions when people exhibit behaviors that are typical for them. Clear structure and expectations allow students to understand direct consequences for undesired choices, prior to crisis mode. When students enter crisis mode, the crisis prevention plans provide clear processes that professionals can use to de-escalate the situations.

DEVELOPING BEHAVIOR INTERVENTION PLANS

A behavior intervention plan is based on a **functional behavior assessment (FBA)**. A **behavior intervention plan (BIP)** is a formal plan that follows the results of an FBA. The purpose of the BIP is to teach the student actions, behaviors, or processes that are incompatible with the problem behavior. The BIP may be included on an Individualized Education Program or 504 Plan, or components of the BIP may be written out as IEP goals. Once an FBA is conducted, a BIP is put in place that describes the behavior, lists factors that trigger the target behavior, and lists any interventions that help the student avoid the behavior. The target behavior is the behavior that needs to be changed. The interventions determined by the FBA and listed in the BIP focus on the problem behavior. The interventions include problem-solving skills for the student to use instead of demonstrating the target behavior. When the interventions fail to target the problem behavior and/or are no longer effective for targeting the behavior, an FBA must be revisited and a new BIP should be developed.

POSITIVE CLASSROOM DISCIPLINE STRATEGIES

Promoting positive classroom discipline is part of effective classroom management. This involves holding students accountable for their actions, and it starts with establishing clear and consistent **consequences** when poor choices are demonstrated. Students learn to predict consequences and self-correct their behaviors. It is helpful to give **reminders** before immediately resorting to consequences. Reminders help students remember the consequences for breaking rules regarding behavior. **Pre-reminders** are one way to enforce and remind students of expectations before diving into lessons. **Nonverbal reminders**, such as looks, touches, silence, or removal, are possible ways to distract students from engaging in poor choices. Removal involves tasks like sending students to throw things away. **Spoken reminders** can be used to further encourage self-management skills and should be used as precursors for reminding students about expectations instead of delivering immediate consequences.

PROMOTING APPROPRIATE BEHAVIOR IN INCLUSIVE LEARNING ENVIRONMENTS

Effective classrooms have good management strategies in place that promote good learning environments and minimize disruptions. When it comes to students with disabilities, planning classroom management strategies presents different challenges. In **inclusive learning environments**, it is important for teachers to keep all students on track with their learning. General educators and special educators can demonstrate effective classroom management strategies by figuring out what is causing students to act out or misbehave. Effective teachers understand how students' special needs come into play with expected classroom behaviors. They also promote positive classroom experiences, establish clear expectations for behavior, and reinforce positive behaviors. Teachers with effective classroom management strategies demonstrate good leadership and organizational skills. They collaborate with other professionals and students' parents to ensure the success of students with special needs in their classrooms. Lastly, effective classroom management includes setting goals for inclusive classrooms to achieve. Clear goals help establish good rapport with students with special needs because they know what is expected of them.

SUPPORTING MENTAL HEALTH ISSUES

Students with disabilities present mental health issues in some circumstances and in some educational settings. These students may not necessarily be diagnosed with emotional disturbances, as mental health issues can occur concurrently with other disabilities. General and special educators across all special education settings can **support** these students by learning how to **recognize mental health issues** in schools. Students' mental health symptoms may fluctuate on an hourly, daily, or weekly basis. Teachers can use observations and other research-based strategies for identifying any issues. They may also already be aware of such issues or work in settings where mental health issues are predominant. Intervention techniques and supports rely on the individual needs of each specific student. Training in managing students with certain mental health disorders may also be useful. Occasionally, training in crisis prevention plans is required of teachers working with students who may become aggressive due to their disorders.

WORKING WITH STUDENTS WITH PHYSICAL DISABILITIES

Students with physical disabilities may be included in **general education classrooms** with accommodations if their disabilities do not coexist with other disabilities, such as learning disabilities. They may also be placed in inclusive settings or partially inclusive settings with Individualized Education Program goals, depending on their least restrictive environments. In these settings, it is essential for educators to practice **instructional strategies** that facilitate the learning processes and accommodate the needs of students with physical disabilities. Classrooms should be arranged so they can be **navigated** easily by everyone. This includes giving students using wheelchairs adequate aisle space and work space. **Partner work** is helpful for students with physical disabilities, who may struggle with handwriting or using keyboards. Partners can assist the students with skills like note taking, which may be difficult for students with physical disabilities. Additionally, assignments can include **accommodations** or **modifications** to meet the specific needs of students with physical disabilities. For example, text-to-speech software can be provided for students who struggle with using regular keyboards.

Praxis Practice Test

1. The U.S. Department of Education's definition of emotional disturbance includes a criterion that learning is impeded, but not by:

- a. IQ score levels.
- b. Health problems.
- c. Sensory impairments.
- d. Any of the above (among others).

2. The definition of emotional disturbance under IDEA includes which of the following criteria?

- a. A child cannot form or maintain satisfying interpersonal relations.
- b. A child has behaviors or feelings not appropriate to circumstances.
- c. A child exhibits a., b., or both long-term, which affects education.
- d. Neither a. nor b. are mentioned as criteria in the definition.

3. Which of the following criteria is NOT included in the federal definition of emotional disturbance?

- a. Generally depressive affect
- b. A generally euphoric affect
- c. Somatic/phobic symptoms
- d. All of the above are included.

4. Which of the following is NOT true of minority children and special education in the USA?

- a. Fewer minority children get special services in proportion to their prevalence in the population.
- b. Schools with more white teachers and students put more minority students in special services than white students.
- c. Black children have higher rates of being identified as having intellectual disabilities and emotional disturbances than white children.
- d. Black children represent more of the population of disabled children than they do the general population of children.

5. Federal law states that in awarding grants, etc., the secretary may give priority to projects that address needs of "children whose behavior interferes with their learning and socialization":

- a. Ahead of projects addressing disabilities.
- b. After projects addressing content areas.
- c. After projects addressing gifted children.
- d. Neither ahead of nor after any of these projects.

6. Legally, if a child's behavior interferes with the child's and/or other children's education, the child's IEP team must first consider:

- a. Positive behavioral supports.
- b. Assigning a different teacher.
- c. A more restrictive placement.
- d. All of the above alternatives.

96

7. Which of the following is NOT an example of a maladaptive behavioral characteristic?

    a. Self-injury
    b. Aggression
    c. Depression
    d. Delinquency

8. Susan seems to worry about anything and everything. She worries the school bus will crash, that something bad will happen to her parents or baby brother, that the house will burn down, that there will be a bomb in the school, etc. She has not had any recent experiences that could be contributing to her worries. Susan's most likely DSM-5 diagnosis is:

    a. Obsessive-compulsive disorder.
    b. A generalized anxiety disorder.
    c. Post-traumatic stress disorder.
    d. None of the above.

9. Lana has just turned 13. She has periods when she seems excited and happy, but also irritable. She will speak rapidly and almost continuously, stay up all night, and make highly questionable decisions. At other times, her buoyancy seems to deflate. She withdraws socially, cries easily, and may sleep all day. Lana's most likely DSM-5 diagnosis is:

    a. Bipolar disorder.
    b. Schizophrenia.
    c. Attention deficit disorder.
    d. Conduct disorder.

10. Jimmy, age 11, loses his temper daily, gets into fights, constantly argues with his parents and teachers, openly flouts rules, blames others for his problems, does things to others out of spite, and seeks revenge for real or imagined insults. What is the most likely provisional DSM-5 diagnosis for Jimmy?

    a. Antisocial personality disorder
    b. Obsessive-compulsive disorder
    c. Oppositional defiant disorder
    d. Histrionic personality disorder

11. Chris is in elementary school. Recently, his schoolwork has deteriorated. He seems to have trouble bathing and brushing his teeth. He shows little interest in his friends or social activities. At times, he says things that don't make sense. Lately his affect is flattened. When he does show feelings, they are inappropriate to the situation – laughing in church and crying during a party his parents had, for instance. He reports hearing voices and seeing people or things that are not there. These symptoms have developed gradually. Which of the following is the most likely DSM diagnosis for Chris?

    a. Major depressive episode
    b. Childhood schizophrenia
    c. Oppositional defiant disorder
    d. None of the above

12. Alice runs to wash her hands every time she touches anything. She habitually counts objects. She worries about catching germs, even though she rarely gets sick. She asks her mother for sterile medical gloves to use at school because of all the germs there. Before sitting down to dinner with the family, she always twirls in a circle three times, replying to her parents' queries that she "has to" do this. What is Alice's most likely DSM diagnosis?
- a. Avoidant personality disorder
- b. Dependent personality disorder
- c. Obsessive-compulsive disorder
- d. Narcissistic personality disorder

13. Allene lived in an area hit by a major hurricane. Her family's house was destroyed, but the family somehow managed to survive. Though time has passed, Allene still has nightmares that wake her up. She also has episodes wherein she relives the events of the disaster, feeling that she is actually experiencing them. Allene probably has:
- a. Some version of panic disorder.
- b. Post-traumatic stress disorder.
- c. A generalized anxiety disorder.
- d. Obsessive-compulsive disorder.

14. You have a student who seems depressed and refer him for evaluation. How can a psychologist make a differential diagnosis of either bipolar disorder or depression?
- a. There is really no way to do this.
- b. It will last longer if it is bipolar disorder.
- c. Depression is more serious than bipolar disorder.
- d. There are no manic symptoms with depression.

15. Cathy refuses to go to school, not out of defiance but fear. She will go other places and still likes to see her friends. She most likely has:
- a. Social phobia.
- b. Agoraphobia.
- c. School phobia.
- d. Simple shyness.

16. Nina exercises excessively and rigidly controls her diet, alternatively fasting and eating only tiny amounts. Her weight was normal when she began this behavior and she is now underweight. She strongly believes, however, that she is fat. She is obsessed with losing more weight. Nina is likely subject to:
- a. Anorexia nervosa.
- b. Bulimia nervosa.
- c. Obsessive-compulsive disorder.
- d. None of the above.

17. Warren is overweight and overeats. He also bites his nails, and when not eating he is usually chewing on something. One psychologist feels Warren's behaviors indicate oral fixation. This psychologist's approach is most likely:
- a. A behavioral one.
- b. A sociological one.
- c. A psychodynamic one.
- d. A cognitive one.

18. A teacher sees signs of suspected physical abuse in one of her students. The administrator at her school has advised teachers to report suspected abuse to him before contacting Child Protective Services. Which of the following is NOT true with respect to this situation?

    a. The teacher should report it to the administrator and let him decide.
    b. Federal and state laws require educators to report suspected abuse.
    c. It is illegal to have a school administrator decide whether to report this.
    d. Educators should report suspicions, not decide whether or not abuse exists.

19. Which of the following is more likely to engage in excessive physical activity?

    a. A child with ADD
    b. A child with ADHD
    c. Either a. or b.
    d. Neither a. nor b.

20. A teacher tells the class that if every student makes it through an entire 50-minute language arts class without getting out of his/her seat, the entire class will get 10 minutes of free time. This is an example of a(n):

    a. Interdependent group contingency.
    b. Independent group contingency.
    c. Dependent group contingency.
    d. None of the above.

21. Mr. Wilson tells his students that each time Scott finishes his in-class assignment on time the whole class can skip one day's homework. This is an example of a(n):

    a. Independent group contingency.
    b. Interdependent group contingency.
    c. Individual student contingency.
    d. Dependent group contingency.

22. Ms. Mott informs her pupils that whoever requests permission to speak 100% of the time in today's reading group and does not talk out of turn will receive a food treat. This is an example of which kind of contingency?

    a. An interdependent group contingency
    b. A dependent group contingency
    c. An independent group contingency
    d. An individual student contingency

23. A student is referred for evaluation by a behavior specialist for a behavior disorder. Which of the following is NOT a component of the evaluation process?

    a. What type of intervention is expected
    b. When the behavior in question began
    c. Who referred the pupil for evaluation
    d. Where the behavior at issue occurred

24. An assistant principal has observed a student's disruptive and even destructive behavior in school and is recommending that he be expelled. This student is diagnosed with a behavior disorder. What are the legal ramifications of this recommendation?

    a. Expelling a student for property destruction is legal.
    b. Expelling the student without due process is illegal.
    c. There is no provision for this in federal or state law.
    d. Expulsion is not legally viewed as placement change.

25. A school has received some additional funds to hire teachers' aides. Which of the following would be best for a teacher's aide to do in a class of students with emotional/behavioral disorders (EBD) during a period of independent seatwork?

    a. Only help students who are stuck and cannot continue.
    b. Work 1 on 1 with as many individual students as possible.
    c. Give running commentary so students have feedback.
    d. Give frequent verbal prompts to work independently.

26. Clyde has EBD and has been newly placed in a regular class. In his first three days in this class, he refuses to complete the science worksheet that the teacher gives all students. He is not refusing other activities. What should the teacher do first?

    a. Tell Clyde to take the worksheet home and do it as homework instead.
    b. Offer Clyde a system of reinforcements for doing the worksheet in class.
    c. Assign a student who excels in science to help Clyde with the worksheet.
    d. Talk with Clyde to ascertain if these worksheets are appropriate for him.

27. A few EBD students become overexcited during special recreational events at school, and their behavior becomes disruptive. The classroom teacher wants the special education teacher to remove them from these events. What is the best solution to this situation?

    a. The special education teacher should remove the disruptive students from these events as the classroom teacher requested.
    b. The special education teacher should help the classroom teacher write behavioral contracts for each of the disruptive students.
    c. The special education teacher should provide a separate alternative activity for the students who have disruptive behaviors.
    d. The special education teacher should excuse the disruptive students from these events, letting them stay home at these times.

28. Audrey secretly gorges on large quantities of food and then induces vomiting. Her weight is normal. Which of the following is likely the most accurate diagnosis for her?

    a. Anorexia nervosa
    b. Eating disorder NOS
    c. Bulimia nervosa
    d. None of the above

29. Charlie was diagnosed with separation anxiety as a child, and entering his teens he is heading toward agoraphobia. A psychologist recommends a program of systematic desensitization via successive approximations toward his goal of being able to leave home for school and social activities without panic or avoidance. This psychologist most likely follows which approach?

    a. Psychodynamic
    b. Behaviorist
    c. Sociological
    d. Cognitive

30. An eclectic approach to behavior management uses:

    a. Electric stimulation.
    b. Offbeat techniques.
    c. Elective procedures.
    d. Various approaches.

31. The federal definition of serious emotional disturbance:

    a. Excludes children with schizophrenia.
    b. Includes children with schizophrenia.
    c. Does not address child schizophrenia.
    d. Only includes some schizophrenia symptoms.

32. How does IDEA address social maladjustment in children in terms of its definition of serious emotional disturbance (SED)?

    a. It includes social maladjustment within this definition.
    b. It excludes social maladjustment from the definition.
    c. It excludes social maladjustment unless SED co-exists with it.
    d. It does not address social maladjustment with SED.

33. Achenbach classifies general patterns of disordered behavior. Which of the following is NOT one of these?

    a. Rationalizers
    b. Externalizers
    c. Internalizers
    d. All of the above are patterns of disordered behavior.

34. Quay describes several dimensions of disordered behavior. One of these is personality disorders, which include symptoms of anxiety, withdrawal, and physiological complaints. Which of the following is NOT one of the other dimensions of disordered behavior?

    a. Immaturity
    b. Conduct disorders
    c. Socialized delinquency
    d. All of the above are dimensions of disordered behavior.

35. Systematically evaluating and teaching social skills to students with SED is LEAST likely to involve the use of which of the following?
   a. Modeling
   b. Discussion
   c. Extinction
   d. Rehearsal

36. Which of the following would NOT be part of therapies used to support SED programs?
   a. b., c., and d. would all be part of such therapies.
   b. Music/art
   c. Exercising
   d. Relaxation

37. Which of these might be used in programs for SED students?
   a. Individual counseling
   b. Group counseling
   c. Affective education
   d. All of the above might be used.

38. Response to Intervention (RTI) has been successfully used on individuals with learning disabilities and is now being applied to emotional/behavioral disorders (E/BD). One element of RTI is delivering support to students as soon as possible. Which of the following is NOT another element of RTI?
   a. Progressive levels of support's intensity
   b. Referral of students to special education
   c. Interventions based upon valid research
   d. Monitoring to assess students' progress

39. Using Response to Intervention (RTI) programs for students with E/BD poses some challenges. One is that an RTI program requires sufficient personnel to implement it. Which additional elements are needed?
   a. Sufficient funding for plans
   b. Professional development
   c. a., b., and d. are all elements needed.
   d. Additional research into RTI

40. In the most popular model of RTI containing three tiers of support, which of the following does tier 1 NOT include?
   a. Individualized support
   b. Including all students
   c. Screenings for tier 2
   d. All of the above are included in tier 1.

41. In the three-tier model of RTI, which of the following is NOT included in tier 2 interventions?
   a. Students for whom tier 1 did not work are targeted.
   b. Students found from tier 1 screenings are targeted.
   c. Interventions in this tier often employ small groups.
   d. These are all included in tier 2 intervention services.

42. In the three-tier model of RTI, which of the following is LEAST likely to be included in tier 3 behavioral interventions?

    a. Individualized support
    b. Psychiatric evaluation
    c. Wrap-around services
    d. All of the above are included.

Answer Key and Explanations

Answer Key

Question	Answer	Question	Answer	Question	Answer
1	D	15	C	29	B
2	C	16	A	30	D
3	B	17	C	31	B
4	A	18	A	32	C
5	D	19	B	33	A
6	A	20	A	34	D
7	C	21	D	35	C
8	B	22	C	36	A
9	A	23	A	37	D
10	C	24	B	38	B
11	B	25	A	39	C
12	C	26	D	40	A
13	B	27	B	41	D
14	D	28	C	42	B

1. D: The federal definition of emotional disturbance includes a criterion that learning is impeded, but not by a., b., or c., among others, making d. the correct answer. The definition states that a child must meet one or more of five criteria "...over a long period of time and to a marked degree that adversely affects a child's educational performance..." The first of these criteria is that the child is unable to learn, but this inability cannot be explained by "intellectual, sensory, or health factors." IQ score levels a. represent intellectual factors. Health problems b. represent health factors. Sensory impairments c. represent sensory factors.

2. C: Under IDEA, a child may exhibit a., b., or both over a long time and to such an extent that it has a negative impact on the child's education, making c. the correct answer. In addition to an inability to learn that is not caused by intellectual, sensory, or health factors, other criteria in the federal definition include being unable to develop or continue good interpersonal relationships a. with peers or teachers and/or exhibiting behaviors or feelings that are not appropriate to the circumstances b.. Since these are two of five criteria, d. is incorrect.

3. B: The federal definition of emotional disturbance does not include a generally euphoric affect b., which would mean the child is typically in a good mood or experiences feelings of great happiness or wellbeing. (Euphoric affect alone does not indicate mania.) Having a generally depressive affect a. or a pervasive mood of unhappiness is one of the criteria in the definition. Another criterion is having somatic (physical) symptoms or phobic (specific fear) symptoms c. related to personal issues or problems in school. Since b. is not included, answer d. is incorrect.

4. A: It is not true that fewer minority children get special education services in proportion to their prevalence in the population a.. The reverse is true: Minority children are over-represented among those receiving special education services in proportion to their numbers in the general population. Researchers have found that schools with mainly white teachers and students place more minority students into special education services than white students b.. This can be attributed to racial and cultural biases in educators. Additionally, most assessment instruments are created by white authors and can be biased. It is true that black children have higher rates of being identified as

104

having intellectual disabilities and emotional disturbances than white children c.. It is also true that black children represent more of the population of disabled children than they do the general population of children d.. For example, in the school year 1998-1999, black children made up 14.8% of those aged 6-21 years in the population, yet they represented 20.2% of all children with disabilities.

5. D: Federal law states the secretary may give priority to projects addressing the needs of children whose behavior interferes with their learning and socialization neither ahead of nor behind any of the projects listed in the answer choices d.. The law gives a list of 23 types of projects, all addressing various needs or designed for various purposes, to which the secretary may give priority. They are equally eligible to receive priority, and are not ranked in order of importance. A few of these include projects addressing disabilities a.; projects addressing content areas b. such as reading, math, or history; and projects addressing the needs of gifted or talented children c..

6. A: IDEA states that if a child's behavior interferes with the child's and/or other children's education, the child's IEP team must first consider positive behavioral supports a. and interventions "....and other strategies, to address that behavior." Assigning a different teacher b. is not a provision of this law. This would also be inappropriate. In most cases, the teacher must either know or be able to learn how to use positive behavioral intervention and support strategies. A more restrictive placement c. goes against IDEA's concept of least restrictive environment (LRE). Placements into more restrictive learning environments are only made if all other, less restrictive interventions have failed. Since only a. is correct, d. is incorrect.

7. C: Depression c. is not an example of a maladaptive behavioral characteristic. Depression is an example of a psychological characteristic. Other examples of psychological characteristics include anxiety, neurosis, and psychosis. Maladaptive behavioral characteristics include self-injury a., such as gouging one's own eyes, slapping one's own face, head banging, etc.; aggression b., such as physically attacking others, hitting, slapping, shoving, etc.; relational aggression, such as verbally or socially maligning others; and delinquency d., such as truancy, tardiness, vandalism, theft, and other criminal acts.

8. B: Based on the information given, Susan most likely has a generalized anxiety disorder b.. Children with this diagnosis exhibit overall patterns of being overly and unrealistically anxious. They are likely to worry about anything and everything. Obsessive-compulsive disorder a. does not fit the description. OCD is also an anxiety disorder, but differs from GAD in its symptoms. OCD is characterized by obsessive (i.e. repetitive) thoughts and compulsive actions, such as repeated hand-washing; and by having to perform bizarre rituals before doing routine activities, such as constantly checking if doors are locked, appliances are turned off, etc. Susan does not have post-traumatic stress disorder c. because the question states that she has not had any recent experiences that could contribute to her anxiety. PTSD occurs in reaction to traumatic events, and is characterized by flashbacks, nightmares, and panic attacks. Because b. is correct, answer d. is incorrect.

9. A: Lana's most likely diagnosis is bipolar disorder a.. This is evidenced by her extreme mood swings, from an excessively elevated mood wherein she is overly talkative, goes without sleep, and exhibits poor judgment (the manic phase) to an excessively depressed mood wherein she is withdrawn, feels so unhappy she cries easily, and shows exhaustion, apathy, and withdrawal by sleeping all day (the depressive phase). Many adults with bipolar disorder have their first episodes around Lana's age. Schizophrenia b. is not characterized by clear mood swings between mania and depression, but includes other symptoms such as disordered thinking and speech, loss of contact with reality, delusions, hallucinations, and other symptoms depending on the specific type of schizophrenia. Attention deficit disorder c. is characterized by a short attention span and an inability to focus on one activity. Conduct disorders d. are characterized by hostility, hypersensitivity or "touchiness," anger, aggression, antisocial behavior, lack of concern for others, and delinquent or criminal acts.

10. C: Jimmy's most likely provisional diagnosis is oppositional defiant disorder c.. Children and teens with this disorder have short tempers, are aggressive, are prone to arguing very easily, consistently defy rules, blame others for their behavior or mistakes, are easily annoyed, often overreact, and display spiteful and vengeful behaviors. The description of Jimmy fits the DSM criteria for this disorder. Antisocial personality disorder a. is similar, but is not a good provisional diagnosis for Jimmy because he is 11 years old. ASPD is diagnosed in adults, but not children. Obsessive-compulsive disorder b. does not fit with Jimmy's behavior. OCD is characterized by obsessive thinking and compulsive doing (i.e. being unable to stop dwelling on certain thoughts and engaging in repetitive, ritualistic actions). OCD falls under the category of personality disorders characterized by anxiety, while ODD falls under the category of personality disorders characterized by counter-social behaviors. Histrionic personality disorder d. belongs to the same group as ODD, and its symptoms include dramatic or erratic behaviors that are counter-social. One symptom of HPD is blaming others, but other symptoms include extremely dramatic behavior, rapid emotional changes, overly seductive behavior, constant need for approval, being overly concerned with one's looks, being overly sensitive to criticism, and being easily influenced by others. These symptoms do not fit the description of ODD.

11. B: The most likely diagnosis for Chris's symptoms is childhood schizophrenia b.. All of his symptoms are symptoms of this illness. It causes: difficulties with academic activities because it interferes with normal thinking and cognition, difficulties with self-care due to disorientation and lack of motivation, social withdrawal, illogical thinking and speech, lack of emotion, emotions inappropriate to the situation, and hallucinations. The onset is gradual and usually occurs in younger (elementary age) children. The description does not fit a major depressive episode a. as well. This condition would be of finite duration. It could include social withdrawal and deterioration in self-care and schoolwork, but not the other symptoms described. These symptoms are not ones associated with oppositional defiant disorder c.. Symptoms include anger, aggression, argumentativeness, irritability, and defiance of rules or laws, but do not include hallucinations, illogical thought and speech, lack of emotion, or deterioration in self-care. Because b. is the correct answer, d. is incorrect.

12. C: Alice's most likely diagnosis is obsessive-compulsive disorder c.. Children as well as adults have been diagnosed with this disorder. Symptoms include compulsively repeating actions, such as hand-washing; counting things; preoccupation (obsession) with subjects of anxiety, such as germ phobias; worry over unlikely/unrealistic negative outcomes; and compulsively engaging in ritualistic behaviors. Patients often feel they must complete these rituals or something dire will happen. Alice's symptoms do not fit with avoidant personality disorder a., wherein patients are timid and extremely shy socially, which results in social isolation; have feelings of inadequacy; and are hypersensitive to criticism and rejection. They tend to avoid all situations they find stressful. Alice's symptoms are not consistent with dependent personality disorder b.. People with this disorder depend on others too much, are submissive, need to always be in a relationship, and want to be taken care of to the point that they will tolerate abuse or poor treatment. Alice does not have symptoms of a narcissistic personality disorder d.. Persons with this disorder have an inflated sense of their own importance and superiority, a sense of entitlement, and difficulty seeing others' needs or points of view. They tend to be arrogant and self-centered.

13. B: Allene probably has post-traumatic stress disorder b.. This disorder occurs in reaction to one or more traumatic events that cause sufficient psychological damage that the person does not simply get over it with time. Symptoms include nightmares and flashbacks, both of which Allene has. A panic disorder a. is not consistent with her symptoms. This disorder is associated with panic attacks, which strike suddenly and unexpectedly. Symptoms include physical ones such as a pounding heart, a feeling of asphyxiation, dizziness, cold extremities, and cold sweats. While PTSD can include panic attacks, panic disorder is not caused by traumatic events, and does not generally involve nightmares and flashbacks. Allene does not have a generalized anxiety disorder c., wherein patients worry about almost everything. Additionally, a generalized anxiety disorder is not caused by traumatic life events, and does not involve flashbacks and nightmares. She does not have symptoms of obsessive-compulsive disorder d., such as obsessive thoughts and compulsive actions. OCD does not involve flashbacks and nightmares, and is not caused by traumatic experiences.

14. D: Differential diagnosis with depressive symptoms would rule out bipolar disorder if there are no manic symptoms, as these are not part of depression d.. In bipolar disorder, the patient has symptoms of depression (sadness, feelings of hopelessness, loss of interest in activities, loss of motivation, and, in extreme cases, suicidal thoughts) at some times and symptoms of mania (elevated mood, hyperactivity, irritability, and poor judgment) at other times. It is not true that there is no way to determine the difference between bipolar disorder and depression a.. Bipolar disorder does not necessarily last longer than depression b.. While bipolar disorder is a lifelong condition once manifested, medication may control it, and some patients experience remission of their symptoms with or without medication. While a major depressive episode is time-limited according to the DSM-5, depressive disorder and other conditions involving depression may continue indefinitely. It is not true that depression is more serious than bipolar disorder c., or vice versa. The severity of both conditions ranges from mild to profound, and both can be equally serious.

15. C: Cathy most likely has school phobia c.. Phobias in general are conditions which may start with a traumatic experience related to one aspect of something, but then generalize to an entire group of things, events, or situations. Professionals may refer to school phobia as school refusal. Cathy does not likely have agoraphobia b., which is fear and avoidance of anxiety-provoking situations such as unfamiliar places. This phobia is particularly associated with a fear of leaving one's house. Cathy is afraid to go to school, but will go other places. She does not have social phobia a. as she still likes to socialize with her friends outside of school. Simple shyness d. is not an explanation for her fear of going to school. In fact, Cathy was a shy person to begin with, but did not always fear going to school. This fear is not normal among shy people.

16. A: Nina is likely subject to anorexia nervosa a., an eating disorder. Children with this disorder have distorted body images, seeing themselves as fat even when they are not. In extreme cases, their appearance can be skeletal to others, yet they still see fat when they look in the mirror. Anorexics fast and rigidly limit their diets, often exercising to excess as well. Nina does not have bulimia nervosa b., another eating disorder wherein patients alternately binge eat and induce vomiting to keep from gaining weight as a result of the binge eating. Some anorexics may also induce vomiting and/or purge using laxatives, but they do not overeat or binge. Nina does not have obsessive-compulsive disorder c.. Though she is obsessed with losing weight, this is a symptom of an eating disorder. OCD is a type of anxiety disorder that does not manifest in eating or dieting behaviors, but rather in obsessive worrying about a variety of things and compulsive doing of a variety of repetitious, ritualistic behaviors. Since a. is the correct answer, d. is incorrect.

17. C: This psychologist most likely uses a psychodynamic approach c.. Oral fixation is a Freudian term describing fixation in the first, or oral, stage of psychosexual development. Freudian/psychoanalytic/psychodynamic theorists believe that unsatisfactory resolution of each stage can result in fixation in that stage in later life. A behavioral psychologist a. would not use the term oral fixation. Behaviorists do not explore inner states or attribute behaviors to early childhood relationships. They would seek to modify the presenting behaviors by manipulating their consequences, to decrease target behaviors, and to increase other behaviors. A sociological approach b. would not involve attributing Warren's behaviors to oral fixation or thinking in terms of unresolved psychosexual conflicts. Instead, it would involve thinking in terms of social interactions and attributing his behaviors to social factors. A psychologist with a cognitive approach d. would not attribute behavior to psychosexual stages or fixations in them, but to irrational beliefs and negative "self-talk." He or she would seek to change these, reframing the way Warren sees himself and his actions to effect behavioral changes.

18. A: It is not true that the teacher should report her suspicions to the administrator and let him decide a.. Even though some schools use this policy, the fact is that federal and state laws require educators to report suspected abuse b.. If the administrator in this case simply wanted the responsibility of reporting to CPS (possibly to protect teachers) and would do so, the teacher could report her suspicions to him. However, it is against the law to let the administrator decide whether to report the teacher's suspicions c. because school administrators are not trained child abuse investigators. Thus, all educators who suspect child abuse should report their suspicions rather than trying to decide if they are correct d..

19. B: A child with ADHD b. is more likely to engage in excessive physical activity. ADHD is Attention Deficit Hyperactivity Disorder. Children with hyperactivity are overly active physically to the point that it interferes with their education as they cannot sit still or stay in their seats and are constantly moving around. A child with ADD a. has Attention Deficit Disorder. What ADD and ADHD have in common are symptoms of attentional deficits, such as being unable to focus on one task, being unable to sustain attention for sufficient periods of time, and being unable to attend to the task at hand because they are so easily distracted. A child with ADD is less likely to be hyperactive than a child with ADHD. The diagnosis of ADHD was added to address the fact that some children with ADD are also hyperactive, while others are not. Since b. is the correct answer, c. and d. are incorrect.

20. A: This is an example of an interdependent group contingency a.. Behavioral contingencies can apply to a whole group, to individuals, or to a combination of both. In an interdependent group contingency, every student must meet a behavioral objective for the entire class to receive a reward. With an independent group contingency b., each student would receive the same reward for meeting the same behavioral objective individually. With a dependent group contingency c., if an individual student meets the stated behavioral objective, the whole group receives the designated reward. Since a. is correct, answer d. is incorrect.

21. D: This is an example of a dependent group contingency d.. The whole class receiving the specified reward is dependent on Scott's meeting the stated behavioral objective. An independent group contingency a. would offer the same reinforcement individually to each student in the class who met the stated objective. An interdependent group contingency b. would give the reinforcement to the whole class if every student in the class met the objective. An individual student contingency c. would give a specified reward to an individual student for meeting a stated objective.

22. C: This is an example of an independent group contingency c.. Each member of the group can earn reinforcement individually for meeting the stated objective. An interdependent group contingency a. would reward the entire group for every member meeting the objective. A dependent group contingency b. would reward the entire group for one member meeting the objective. An individual student contingency d. would reward one student for individually meeting a stated objective apart from or in addition to any group contingencies.

23. A: The type of intervention that is expected a. is not a component of the evaluation process. Determining this during the evaluation process would be premature. The results of the evaluation process will help school staff determine which types of interventions will be most effective. Determining when the behavior began b. is a component of the evaluation process. Knowing the age of onset can help professionals arrive at a diagnosis. Finding out who referred the pupil for evaluation c. is part of the evaluation process. The teacher or other personnel who made the referral should be known so the behavior specialist can ask for further information about the behavior from the person who has witnessed it the most if such information is needed. Finding out where the behavior occurred d. is a component of the evaluation process as it can help the behavior specialist determine antecedents and consequences of the behavior and whether it is situation-specific. It can also help them make a diagnosis.

24. B: It is illegal under IDEA to expel a student without due process b. if the behavior causing the issue is related to the student's disability. Therefore, it is incorrect that it is legal to expel a student for property destruction a. in this case, as the student has a diagnosed behavior disorder and his behavior is related to his disability. It is incorrect that federal or state law does not have provisions addressing this issue c., as federal law states that expulsion for disability-related behavior without due process is unlawful. Most state laws follow the federal laws under IDEA. It is also incorrect that expulsion is not legally viewed as a placement change d.. U.S. courts of law regard expulsion as an unplanned change of placement, which is not educationally best for students.

25. A: It would be best for the aide to only help students who cannot proceed without some assistance a.. The purpose of independent seatwork is for students to improve their problem solving and time management skills. They will need help at times, but too much help will foster dependence rather than independence. The aide should not work 1 on 1 with as many individual students as possible b., as this would provide students with too much help and encourage dependence. Also, the aide will likely not have time to get to all students during the period, meaning they would receive unequal treatment. Moreover, the aide might not get to students who need assistance because he or she is spending time with others who don't need it as much. Giving a running commentary to provide feedback c. is excessive. Not only will it not promote independence, but it could also interfere with the students' ability to concentrate. Giving frequent verbal prompts to work independently d. is not consistent with the purpose of independent work. The aide should only give occasional verbal prompts to individual students if they are off-task.

26. D: The teacher should first talk with Clyde to find out more information from him and ascertain whether the worksheets are appropriate for him d.. He is not refusing other activities in the new class, so the problem may just be with the science worksheets. Assigning the worksheets as homework instead a. might be indicated if the teacher had already found out from Clyde that, for example, he did not have the same kinds of time limits or schedule in his previous class and felt pressured to do the science worksheets in class. This, however, is not the case. The teacher does not have any such information yet. Offering Clyde a reinforcement system b. would only be indicated if the teacher had already established that Clyde did not get any intrinsic reward for doing the worksheets, or if he needed reinforcements in general to complete any task. Again, this is not the case. Assigning another student to help Clyde c. is also premature. If these worksheets will not be effective for Clyde and he could learn the same material in a different format, it would waste the time and energy of both students if the other student were to help Clyde with an activity that is not appropriate for him. The first thing the teacher should do is find out if this is the case.

27. B: The best solution is for the special education teacher to help the classroom teacher write behavioral contracts for each of the disruptive students b.. Each contract should specify what behavior is expected of the student, the criteria (e.g. what percentage of the time, for how long, how many times, etc.), the conditions for the expected behavior, and what reinforcement will be given for compliance. Contracts are an effective behavioral technique to help EBD students learn to control their behavior because they constitute a clear agreement, specify what is expected, and reinforce the targeted good behaviors. Removing the students a., providing a separate alternative activity for them c., or excusing them from school during such events d. are all violations of the inclusion policy mandated by IDEA because they exclude the students from certain events. The law states that these students have the right to be included in educational activities regardless of their disability, which in this case causes disruptive behavior. Both teachers rather than just one are responsible for collaborating to help the students succeed.

28. C: Audrey's most accurate diagnosis is bulimia nervosa c.. In this eating disorder, individuals binge eat, usually privately or secretly, and then purge by inducing vomiting before they can digest the food and gain weight. They may also purge by taking laxatives. People with diagnoses of anorexia nervosa a., another eating disorder, do not binge eat. They starve themselves, and may purge by vomiting and/or using laxatives to lose even more weight. However, they do not eat large amounts. The diagnosis of eating disorder NOS b., or Not Otherwise Specified, is not the most accurate diagnosis because Audrey's behavior fits the symptoms of bulimia nervosa. "NOS" is a category used in the DSM when the symptoms of a disorder do not fit the criteria for any other related disorder. Because b. is correct, answer d. is incorrect.

29. B: This psychologist most likely follows a behaviorist b. approach. Behaviorism involves making an operational definition of the behavior by measuring what happens with the person and then modifying that behavior through operant conditioning, which manipulates the consequences of behaviors. Phobias can be treated by systematic desensitization, a process wherein successive approximations, or small increments toward the goal, are reinforced. Aversive reactions to certain stimuli or situations can gradually be reduced or eliminated in this way. A psychologist with a psychodynamic a. approach would not use behavioral techniques. S/he would want to explore the person's past experiences and delve into the person's unconscious using free association and dream analysis, would likely attribute the problem to early childhood relationships, and would seek to remediate it by supplying whatever is deemed missing from childhood development. A sociological c. approach would look at social systems and try to change social interactions to remediate the problem. A cognitive d. approach would help change the person's view of himself by identifying irrational beliefs, negative "self-talk," etc., and then reframing the person's attitudes.

30. D: An eclectic approach means that the practitioner uses various approaches d.. Such practitioners take techniques and strategies from a variety of orientations, selecting and using whichever ones they find to be most effective in each individual case. Eclectic is not a synonym for electric a.. It is not a synonym for offbeat b.. It is also not a synonym for elective c., which refers to something that is voluntary and not required to maintain a person's life or health.

31. B: IDEA's definition of serious emotional disturbance (SED) includes children with schizophrenia b.. It does not exclude them a.. It is not true that the federal definition does not address this illness c.. The definition does not just include certain symptoms of the illness d., but rather includes the actual diagnosis of schizophrenia. The law's inclusion of schizophrenia is very justified because this illness causes severe problems with educational performance. Students who develop schizophrenia typically lose academic abilities they developed previously. Proficiency in math, writing, art, and every other subject is often lost as cognitive skills deteriorate.

32. C: IDEA excludes children with social maladjustment "unless it is determined that they are seriously emotionally disturbed" c. In other words, the law does not classify social maladjustment itself as a serious emotional disturbance. Therefore, it is incorrect that IDEA includes social maladjustment in the definition of SED a.. It is incorrect to state simply that the definition excludes social maladjustment b. because exclusion of socially maladjusted children with the proviso "unless they are found to be SED" c. is more accurate. It is also incorrect to state that the definition of SED does not address social maladjustment with SED d..

33. A: "Rationalizers" a. is not one of Achenbach's categories. The act of rationalizing is justifying, defending, explaining, or excusing something by making it seem rational or reasonable. Achenbach divides disordered behavior patterns into "externalizers" b., which include those who act out, are disruptive, or are aggressive; and "internalizers" c., which include those who are depressed, anxious, or withdrawn. Since a. is the correct answer, d. is incorrect.

34. D: Choices a., b., and c. are all dimensions of disordered behavior described by Quay, making d. the correct answer. Immaturity a. is characterized by behaving in a passive manner, displaying inadequate coping skills, and preferring to play with younger children. Conduct disorders b. are characterized by disobedience, irritability, and aggression. Socialized delinquency c. is characterized by involvement in gangs and the subcultures they create.

35. C: Extinction c. is least likely to be used to evaluate or teach positive social skills to SED students. Extinction is a behavioral technique that involves ignoring a behavior that is reinforced when the student receives attention for engaging in that behavior. When the motivation for repeating a behavior is attention, the behavior will eventually cease due to the continued absence of this reinforcement. Modeling a. provides students with examples of positive social behaviors which they can learn by imitating them. Discussion b. helps students understand social interactions by getting feedback on their own and others' behavior. They can then change their social behaviors in response to the insights they gain. Rehearsal d. allows students to practice new behaviors in a safe environment, giving them a better chance of behaving appropriately in real life situations. These techniques are often used to teach social skills.

36. A: Choices b., c., and d. would all be part of therapies used to support SED programs, making a. the correct answer. Music and art b. therapy can be very beneficial to emotionally disturbed students. They afford alternative modes of self-expression, and can also be soothing. Students whose emotional disabilities interfere with their social interactions find a welcome respite in these activities as they do not require such interactions. Additionally, their higher level of success with such individual activities can increase self-esteem and self-efficacy. Exercising c. helps to expend excess energy in students with hyperactivity, allowing more calmness and focus. Physical activity also helps students by giving them a different mode of expression than academic and verbal interactions. Additionally, exercise is known to release endorphins, improving overall mood, which is very beneficial to students with anxiety, depression, and anger. Relaxation d. exercises teach students to concentrate, to release muscle tension, to control their thoughts and reactions, to relieve stress, and to use imagery, which are all valuable coping skills.

37. D: Choices a., b., and c. might all be used in programs for SED students, making d. the correct answer. Some students benefit most from individual counseling a. wherein they receive 1 on 1 attention. Group counseling b. can teach social skills to students with deficits in this area. It also allows students to share their experiences, find others with whom they have things in common, exchange ideas for coping, and receive group support. Some students will benefit from attending both individual and group counseling sessions. Affective education c. helps students learn how their behavior is perceived by others, learn how others are affected by their behavior and why they react as they do, and learn skills for negotiating social interactions more successfully.

38. B: Referral of students to special education b. is not an element of RTI. RTI, similar to school-wide positive behavior supports (SWPBS), seeks to avoid immediate referrals of students to special education by first implementing RTI programs to support socially acceptable behavior. RTI programs do feature tiers, or levels, which get progressively more intense in their degrees of support a. according to need. These programs do base their interventions on valid, up-to-date research in the field c.. These programs also monitor students to assess their level of progress d..

39. C: Choices a., b., and d. are all elements needed to design and implement RTI programs for E/BD students, making c. the correct answer. Sufficient funding for schools to develop these plans a. is required. In addition to having enough staff, professional development b. is required to train teachers, therapists, aides, and other staff in the techniques that will be used. Moreover, scientists in the field are calling for more research into RTI d.. Their chief areas of concern are research into higher-level (e.g. tier 2 and 3 as opposed to tier 1) interventions and research into whether or not RTI enhances the identification of students with E/BD, which is lacking.

40. A: Individualized support a. is not included in tier 1 of the 3-tier model of RTI. All students are instructed in behavioral expectations, and socially appropriate behavior is encouraged and reinforced in all students b.. Tier 1 also includes screenings of students who may have needs for tier 2 interventions c.. Because a. is the correct answer, d. is incorrect.

41. D: Choices a., b., and c. are all included in tier 2 intervention services, making d. the correct answer. Students with whom tier 1 interventions were ineffective receive interventions targeting them a.. Students whose need for greater support was discovered via screenings conducted as part of tier 1 services are also targeted for increased intervention b.. Interventions designed at the tier 2 level often make use of small groups c., which facilitates their implementation.

42. B: Psychiatric evaluation b. is least likely to be included in tier 3 behavioral interventions in an RTI program. This would only be done if a student was specifically referred to a psychiatrist by an educator or team who suspected a psychiatric disorder. Even when such a referral is made, it is not necessarily considered a part of RTI interventions. Every student in tier 3 of RTI receives individualized support a.. This may include such things as a comprehensive functional behavior analysis and an individualized behavioral support plan. Wrap-around services c. are included if they are needed in tier 3 behavioral interventions. These include such things as family support and community support in addition to school support. Since b. is correct, d. is incorrect.

How to Overcome Test Anxiety

Just the thought of taking a test is enough to make most people a little nervous. A test is an important event that can have a long-term impact on your future, so it's important to take it seriously and it's natural to feel anxious about performing well. But just because anxiety is normal, that doesn't mean that it's helpful in test taking, or that you should simply accept it as part of your life. Anxiety can have a variety of effects. These effects can be mild, like making you feel slightly nervous, or severe, like blocking your ability to focus or remember even a simple detail.

If you experience test anxiety—whether severe or mild—it's important to know how to beat it. To discover this, first you need to understand what causes test anxiety.

Causes of Test Anxiety

While we often think of anxiety as an uncontrollable emotional state, it can actually be caused by simple, practical things. One of the most common causes of test anxiety is that a person does not feel adequately prepared for their test. This feeling can be the result of many different issues such as poor study habits or lack of organization, but the most common culprit is time management. Starting to study too late, failing to organize your study time to cover all of the material, or being distracted while you study will mean that you're not well prepared for the test. This may lead to cramming the night before, which will cause you to be physically and mentally exhausted for the test. Poor time management also contributes to feelings of stress, fear, and hopelessness as you realize you are not well prepared but don't know what to do about it.

Other times, test anxiety is not related to your preparation for the test but comes from unresolved fear. This may be a past failure on a test, or poor performance on tests in general. It may come from comparing yourself to others who seem to be performing better or from the stress of living up to expectations. Anxiety may be driven by fears of the future—how failure on this test would affect your educational and career goals. These fears are often completely irrational, but they can still negatively impact your test performance.

> **Review Video: 3 Reasons You Have Test Anxiety**
> Visit mometrix.com/academy and enter code: 428468

Elements of Test Anxiety

As mentioned earlier, test anxiety is considered to be an emotional state, but it has physical and mental components as well. Sometimes you may not even realize that you are suffering from test anxiety until you notice the physical symptoms. These can include trembling hands, rapid heartbeat, sweating, nausea, and tense muscles. Extreme anxiety may lead to fainting or vomiting. Obviously, any of these symptoms can have a negative impact on testing. It is important to recognize them as soon as they begin to occur so that you can address the problem before it damages your performance.

> **Review Video: 3 Ways to Tell You Have Test Anxiety**
> Visit mometrix.com/academy and enter code: 927847

The mental components of test anxiety include trouble focusing and inability to remember learned information. During a test, your mind is on high alert, which can help you recall information and stay focused for an extended period of time. However, anxiety interferes with your mind's natural processes, causing you to blank out, even on the questions you know well. The strain of testing during anxiety makes it difficult to stay focused, especially on a test that may take several hours. Extreme anxiety can take a huge mental toll, making it difficult not only to recall test information but even to understand the test questions or pull your thoughts together.

> **Review Video: How Test Anxiety Affects Memory**
> Visit mometrix.com/academy and enter code: 609003

Effects of Test Anxiety

Test anxiety is like a disease—if left untreated, it will get progressively worse. Anxiety leads to poor performance, and this reinforces the feelings of fear and failure, which in turn lead to poor performances on subsequent tests. It can grow from a mild nervousness to a crippling condition. If allowed to progress, test anxiety can have a big impact on your schooling, and consequently on your future.

Test anxiety can spread to other parts of your life. Anxiety on tests can become anxiety in any stressful situation, and blanking on a test can turn into panicking in a job situation. But fortunately, you don't have to let anxiety rule your testing and determine your grades. There are a number of relatively simple steps you can take to move past anxiety and function normally on a test and in the rest of life.

> **Review Video: How Test Anxiety Impacts Your Grades**
> Visit mometrix.com/academy and enter code: 939819

Physical Steps for Beating Test Anxiety

While test anxiety is a serious problem, the good news is that it can be overcome. It doesn't have to control your ability to think and remember information. While it may take time, you can begin taking steps today to beat anxiety.

Just as your first hint that you may be struggling with anxiety comes from the physical symptoms, the first step to treating it is also physical. Rest is crucial for having a clear, strong mind. If you are tired, it is much easier to give in to anxiety. But if you establish good sleep habits, your body and mind will be ready to perform optimally, without the strain of exhaustion. Additionally, sleeping well helps you to retain information better, so you're more likely to recall the answers when you see the test questions.

Getting good sleep means more than going to bed on time. It's important to allow your brain time to relax. Take study breaks from time to time so it doesn't get overworked, and don't study right before bed. Take time to rest your mind before trying to rest your body, or you may find it difficult to fall asleep.

> **Review Video: <u>The Importance of Sleep for Your Brain</u>**
> Visit mometrix.com/academy and enter code: 319338

Along with sleep, other aspects of physical health are important in preparing for a test. Good nutrition is vital for good brain function. Sugary foods and drinks may give a burst of energy but this burst is followed by a crash, both physically and emotionally. Instead, fuel your body with protein and vitamin-rich foods.

Also, drink plenty of water. Dehydration can lead to headaches and exhaustion, especially if your brain is already under stress from the rigors of the test. Particularly if your test is a long one, drink water during the breaks. And if possible, take an energy-boosting snack to eat between sections.

> **Review Video: <u>How Diet Can Affect your Mood</u>**
> Visit mometrix.com/academy and enter code: 624317

Along with sleep and diet, a third important part of physical health is exercise. Maintaining a steady workout schedule is helpful, but even taking 5-minute study breaks to walk can help get your blood pumping faster and clear your head. Exercise also releases endorphins, which contribute to a positive feeling and can help combat test anxiety.

When you nurture your physical health, you are also contributing to your mental health. If your body is healthy, your mind is much more likely to be healthy as well. So take time to rest, nourish your body with healthy food and water, and get moving as much as possible. Taking these physical steps will make you stronger and more able to take the mental steps necessary to overcome test anxiety.

> **Review Video: <u>How to Stay Healthy and Prevent Test Anxiety</u>**
> Visit mometrix.com/academy and enter code: 877894

Mental Steps for Beating Test Anxiety

Working on the mental side of test anxiety can be more challenging, but as with the physical side, there are clear steps you can take to overcome it. As mentioned earlier, test anxiety often stems from lack of preparation, so the obvious solution is to prepare for the test. Effective studying may be the most important weapon you have for beating test anxiety, but you can and should employ several other mental tools to combat fear.

First, boost your confidence by reminding yourself of past success—tests or projects that you aced. If you're putting as much effort into preparing for this test as you did for those, there's no reason you should expect to fail here. Work hard to prepare; then trust your preparation.

Second, surround yourself with encouraging people. It can be helpful to find a study group, but be sure that the people you're around will encourage a positive attitude. If you spend time with others who are anxious or cynical, this will only contribute to your own anxiety. Look for others who are motivated to study hard from a desire to succeed, not from a fear of failure.

Third, reward yourself. A test is physically and mentally tiring, even without anxiety, and it can be helpful to have something to look forward to. Plan an activity following the test, regardless of the outcome, such as going to a movie or getting ice cream.

When you are taking the test, if you find yourself beginning to feel anxious, remind yourself that you know the material. Visualize successfully completing the test. Then take a few deep, relaxing breaths and return to it. Work through the questions carefully but with confidence, knowing that you are capable of succeeding.

Developing a healthy mental approach to test taking will also aid in other areas of life. Test anxiety affects more than just the actual test—it can be damaging to your mental health and even contribute to depression. It's important to beat test anxiety before it becomes a problem for more than testing.

> **Review Video: <u>Test Anxiety and Depression</u>**
> Visit mometrix.com/academy and enter code: 904704

Study Strategy

Being prepared for the test is necessary to combat anxiety, but what does being prepared look like? You may study for hours on end and still not feel prepared. What you need is a strategy for test prep. The next few pages outline our recommended steps to help you plan out and conquer the challenge of preparation.

STEP 1: SCOPE OUT THE TEST

Learn everything you can about the format (multiple choice, essay, etc.) and what will be on the test. Gather any study materials, course outlines, or sample exams that may be available. Not only will this help you to prepare, but knowing what to expect can help to alleviate test anxiety.

STEP 2: MAP OUT THE MATERIAL

Look through the textbook or study guide and make note of how many chapters or sections it has. Then divide these over the time you have. For example, if a book has 15 chapters and you have five days to study, you need to cover three chapters each day. Even better, if you have the time, leave an extra day at the end for overall review after you have gone through the material in depth.

If time is limited, you may need to prioritize the material. Look through it and make note of which sections you think you already have a good grasp on, and which need review. While you are studying, skim quickly through the familiar sections and take more time on the challenging parts. Write out your plan so you don't get lost as you go. Having a written plan also helps you feel more in control of the study, so anxiety is less likely to arise from feeling overwhelmed at the amount to cover.

STEP 3: GATHER YOUR TOOLS

Decide what study method works best for you. Do you prefer to highlight in the book as you study and then go back over the highlighted portions? Or do you type out notes of the important information? Or is it helpful to make flashcards that you can carry with you? Assemble the pens, index cards, highlighters, post-it notes, and any other materials you may need so you won't be distracted by getting up to find things while you study.

If you're having a hard time retaining the information or organizing your notes, experiment with different methods. For example, try color-coding by subject with colored pens, highlighters, or post-it notes. If you learn better by hearing, try recording yourself reading your notes so you can listen while in the car, working out, or simply sitting at your desk. Ask a friend to quiz you from your flashcards, or try teaching someone the material to solidify it in your mind.

STEP 4: CREATE YOUR ENVIRONMENT

It's important to avoid distractions while you study. This includes both the obvious distractions like visitors and the subtle distractions like an uncomfortable chair (or a too-comfortable couch that makes you want to fall asleep). Set up the best study environment possible: good lighting and a comfortable work area. If background music helps you focus, you may want to turn it on, but otherwise keep the room quiet. If you are using a computer to take notes, be sure you don't have any other windows open, especially applications like social media, games, or anything else that could distract you. Silence your phone and turn off notifications. Be sure to keep water close by so you stay hydrated while you study (but avoid unhealthy drinks and snacks).

Also, take into account the best time of day to study. Are you freshest first thing in the morning? Try to set aside some time then to work through the material. Is your mind clearer in the afternoon or evening? Schedule your study session then. Another method is to study at the same time of day that you will take the test, so that your brain gets used to working on the material at that time and will be ready to focus at test time.

STEP 5: STUDY!

Once you have done all the study preparation, it's time to settle into the actual studying. Sit down, take a few moments to settle your mind so you can focus, and begin to follow your study plan. Don't give in to distractions or let yourself procrastinate. This is your time to prepare so you'll be ready to fearlessly approach the test. Make the most of the time and stay focused.

Of course, you don't want to burn out. If you study too long you may find that you're not retaining the information very well. Take regular study breaks. For example, taking five minutes out of every hour to walk briskly, breathing deeply and swinging your arms, can help your mind stay fresh.

As you get to the end of each chapter or section, it's a good idea to do a quick review. Remind yourself of what you learned and work on any difficult parts. When you feel that you've mastered the material, move on to the next part. At the end of your study session, briefly skim through your notes again.

But while review is helpful, cramming last minute is NOT. If at all possible, work ahead so that you won't need to fit all your study into the last day. Cramming overloads your brain with more information than it can process and retain, and your tired mind may struggle to recall even previously learned information when it is overwhelmed with last-minute study. Also, the urgent nature of cramming and the stress placed on your brain contribute to anxiety. You'll be more likely to go to the test feeling unprepared and having trouble thinking clearly.

So don't cram, and don't stay up late before the test, even just to review your notes at a leisurely pace. Your brain needs rest more than it needs to go over the information again. In fact, plan to finish your studies by noon or early afternoon the day before the test. Give your brain the rest of the day to relax or focus on other things, and get a good night's sleep. Then you will be fresh for the test and better able to recall what you've studied.

STEP 6: TAKE A PRACTICE TEST

Many courses offer sample tests, either online or in the study materials. This is an excellent resource to check whether you have mastered the material, as well as to prepare for the test format and environment.

Check the test format ahead of time: the number of questions, the type (multiple choice, free response, etc.), and the time limit. Then create a plan for working through them. For example, if you have 30 minutes to take a 60-question test, your limit is 30 seconds per question. Spend less time on the questions you know well so that you can take more time on the difficult ones.

If you have time to take several practice tests, take the first one open book, with no time limit. Work through the questions at your own pace and make sure you fully understand them. Gradually work up to taking a test under test conditions: sit at a desk with all study materials put away and set a timer. Pace yourself to make sure you finish the test with time to spare and go back to check your answers if you have time.

After each test, check your answers. On the questions you missed, be sure you understand why you missed them. Did you misread the question (tests can use tricky wording)? Did you forget the information? Or was it something you hadn't learned? Go back and study any shaky areas that the practice tests reveal.

Taking these tests not only helps with your grade, but also aids in combating test anxiety. If you're already used to the test conditions, you're less likely to worry about it, and working through tests until you're scoring well gives you a confidence boost. Go through the practice tests until you feel comfortable, and then you can go into the test knowing that you're ready for it.

Test Tips

On test day, you should be confident, knowing that you've prepared well and are ready to answer the questions. But aside from preparation, there are several test day strategies you can employ to maximize your performance

First, as stated before, get a good night's sleep the night before the test (and for several nights before that, if possible). Go into the test with a fresh, alert mind rather than staying up late to study.

Try not to change too much about your normal routine on the day of the test. It's important to eat a nutritious breakfast, but if you normally don't eat breakfast at all, consider eating just a protein bar. If you're a coffee drinker, go ahead and have your normal coffee. Just make sure you time it so that the caffeine doesn't wear off right in the middle of your test. Avoid sugary beverages, and drink enough water to stay hydrated but not so much that you need a restroom break 10 minutes into the test. If your test isn't first thing in the morning, consider going for a walk or doing a light workout before the test to get your blood flowing.

Allow yourself enough time to get ready, and leave for the test with plenty of time to spare so you won't have the anxiety of scrambling to arrive in time. Another reason to be early is to select a good seat. It's helpful to sit away from doors and windows, which can be distracting. Find a good seat, get out your supplies, and settle your mind before the test begins.

When the test begins, start by going over the instructions carefully, even if you already know what to expect. Make sure you avoid any careless mistakes by following the directions.

Then begin working through the questions, pacing yourself as you've practiced. If you're not sure on an answer, don't spend too much time on it, and don't let it shake your confidence. Either skip it and come back later, or eliminate as many wrong answers as possible and guess among the remaining ones. Don't dwell on these questions as you continue—put them out of your mind and focus on what lies ahead.

Be sure to read all of the answer choices, even if you're sure the first one is the right answer. Sometimes you'll find a better one if you keep reading. But don't second-guess yourself if you do immediately know the answer. Your gut instinct is usually right. Don't let test anxiety rob you of the information you know.

If you have time at the end of the test (and if the test format allows), go back and review your answers. Be cautious about changing any, since your first instinct tends to be correct, but make sure you didn't misread any of the questions or accidentally mark the wrong answer choice. Look over any you skipped and make an educated guess.

At the end, leave the test feeling confident. You've done your best, so don't waste time worrying about your performance or wishing you could change anything. Instead, celebrate the successful completion of this test. And finally, use this test to learn how to deal with anxiety even better next time.

Review Video: 5 Tips to Beat Test Anxiety
Visit mometrix.com/academy and enter code: 570656

Important Qualification

Not all anxiety is created equal. If your test anxiety is causing major issues in your life beyond the classroom or testing center, or if you are experiencing troubling physical symptoms related to your anxiety, it may be a sign of a serious physiological or psychological condition. If this sounds like your situation, we strongly encourage you to seek professional help.

Thank You

We at Mometrix would like to extend our heartfelt thanks to you, our friend and patron, for allowing us to play a part in your journey. It is a privilege to serve people from all walks of life who are unified in their commitment to building the best future they can for themselves.

The preparation you devote to these important testing milestones may be the most valuable educational opportunity you have for making a real difference in your life. We encourage you to put your heart into it—that feeling of succeeding, overcoming, and yes, conquering will be well worth the hours you've invested.

We want to hear your story, your struggles and your successes, and if you see any opportunities for us to improve our materials so we can help others even more effectively in the future, please share that with us as well. **The team at Mometrix would be absolutely thrilled to hear from you!** So please, send us an email (support@mometrix.com) and let's stay in touch.

> **If you'd like some additional help, check out these other resources we offer for your exam:**
> **http://MometrixFlashcards.com/PraxisII**

Additional Bonus Material

Due to our efforts to try to keep this book to a manageable length, we've created a link that will give you access to all of your additional bonus material.

> **Please visit**
> **http://www.mometrix.com/bonus948/priispedtsbded** to
> **access the information.**

FINE FASHION JEWELRY FROM

Sarah Coventry

Schiffer Publishing Ltd

4880 Lower Valley Road, Atglen, PA 19310 USA

To Karen Pohlman, Lynn Melnick, Shawn Quill, Kristin Sedlak, Julianne Cockenour, Heather McGlaughlin, and Virginette Centeno—each of you are priceless to me.

Top: Silvertone openwork frames of alternating textured and polished curves with pearl centers, 1" dia. NP (no price).

Bottom: "Gracious Lady." Oval pendant showing profile of a women sketched in black, on ivory background, cameo-like, 24" chain. NP.

Design by Blair Loughrey
Pages 110-122 Layout by Bonnie M. Hensley
Type set in Nevison/Korinna/Zurich
1 2 3 4

ISBN: 0-7643-1142-5
Printed in China

Published by Schiffer Publishing Ltd.
4880 Lower Valley Road
Atglen, PA 19310
Phone: (610) 593-1777; Fax: (610) 593-2002
E-mail: Schifferbk@aol.com
Please visit our web site catalog at
www.schifferbooks.com
We are always looking for people to write books on new and related subjects. If you have an idea for a book, please contact us at the above address.

This book may be purchased from the publisher.
Include $3.95 for shipping.
Please try your bookstore first.
You may write for a free catalog.

In Europe, Schiffer books are distributed by:
Bushwood Books
6 Marksbury Ave.
Kew Gardens
Surrey TW9 4JF England
Phone: 44 (0)208 392-8585; Fax: 44 (0)208 392-9876
E-mail: Bushwd@aol.com
Free postage in the UK. Europe: air mail at cost.

Contents

Acknowledgments

It is through the willing assistance, generosity, creativity, and expertise of many that I am able to present to you this most intriguing and dazzling collection of jewelry, advertisements, brochures, and catalogs, exclusively from Sarah Coventry®. I hope that this book will prove to be a valuable, and most enjoyable, resource for the collectors, dealers, and admirers of costume jewelry for years to come.

A project such as this could never be accomplished solely by the efforts of one individual; thus, I owe a multitude of thanks to all who had a hand in its production, especially—Marjorie Wiley, Aileen Van Tyle, and Mr. Joyce, for their willingness to lend their collections to be photographed, their valuable time, warm hospitality, and countless other contributions; Betty L. Donley, also for the loan of her collection; Robyn Stoltzfus, for gathering the collection together, photographing the original catalogs and advertisements, and for her readiness to help and good nature; jewelry expert and dealer Roseann Ettinger, for her hours of hard work and efforts in the pricing; Blair Loughrey, for his creative eye, photography, and superb design; Anne Davidsen for her able assistance and photography contributions; Nancy Schiffer, for her editorial support, and costume jewelry expertise; Tammy Ward for her time and helpfulness; and all others who helped to make this project a possibility and a success.

Above all, I wish to acknowledge and thank the collectors, dealers, and admirers of costume jewelry, whose passion for Sarah Coventry I hope may be enriched and incited by this beautiful book.

Preface

Upon examination of original company catalogs and other literature distributed by Sarah Coventry, Inc., the words "goldentone" and "silvertone" were used in the descriptions of their jewelry items. Therefore, in keeping with these guidelines, descriptions of jewelry items herein also utilize these words. These, and other terms often associated with the material composition of jewelry (e.g., copper, platinum), are in no way meant as an indication of an item's material composition. Likewise, terminology often associated with types of precious stones/gems, or other material substances (e.g., ivory, turquoise, ruby, sapphire, tiger eye) are intended only as a description of color and *not* an indication of the material used in the item's composition.

Examination of original company literature reveals that the majority of jewelry items and sets were assigned individual names for identification purposes. To aid the reader, these item and set names are included, when known, in the caption description and are placed in quotations marks. Item and set names gave buyers and sellers familiarity with Sarah Coventry's numerous designs, enabling them to recognize the jewelry on a "first name" basis. They proved especially helpful given the similarities between many of Sarah Coventry's jewelry designs, and the vast number of accessories they distributed over their 30+ years in the costume jewelry business. All references to Sarah Coventry jewelry names have been gathered from the available promotional advertisements, catalogs, brochures, and other original materials from the company. A compilation of these original materials is reprinted and included throughout this book to encourage further research by those inspired to learn more about Sarah Coventry—their jewelry designs, advertising/campaigning strategies, company operations, and much more (see Campaign Advertising, and Company Catalogs).

Additional terms pertaining to the costume jewelry field, or whose usage may be unfamiliar or uncommon are following the Preface. Descriptions for these have been gathered from resources provided by experts in the costume jewelry field. A complete listing of these individuals and their sources of information is found in the bibliography section at the back of this book.

bangle: a type of ornamental bracelet of a rigid circular shape, often made of metal, glass, or plastic, and formed to slip over the hand or clasped on.

baroque: natural pearl or cultured pearl of irregular shape.

cabochon: opaque stones in which the top is rounded (or dome-shaped), and the bottom is flat, no facets; appear in various shapes and sizes, though oval or circular cabochons are most prevalent.

costume jewelry: jewelry and accessories made using an array of non-precious (occasionally semi-precious) materials; available at low-cost and mass-produced; most designs intended for short-term use, because fashion trends are constantly influx; valued as decoration.

cuff bracelet: a type of wide, rigid bangle that resembles a cuff.

filigree: fine plain, twisted, or plaited wire, used to form delicate and intricate designs.

marquise: (or **navette**) a cabochon or rhinestone that is elliptical in shape and pointed at both ends.

openwork: a style of decoration in which open areas—those void of decoration—become part of the decoration or design pattern inherent in the item; can exist in the form of filigree or pierced designs.

pavé: closely matched or evenly set stones, placed so no metal is visible to give the appearance of paving; in fashion jewelry pavé is usually glued.

prong-set: the use of several pointed prongs to secure a stone in a jewelry setting.

rhinestones: cut glass made to resemble precious gemstones or jewels; faceted, and usually backed with a foil or tin to further enhance their ability to capture and reflect light; elegant, but inexpensive, these may appear clear or colored.

stickpin: a straight pin usually with ornamentation at the top, meant to be worn vertically.

variegated: coloring that contains more than one hue or intensity.

PRICING

Individual jewelry items and sets are priced giving a range, e.g., $48-65. These values represent items priced in mint condition, taking into consideration fluctuations due to market, availability/rarity of item, desirability, intricacy of design, materials involved, and geographical location. They are not meant to set firm prices, but instead to give collectors and dealers a range of prices that they might expect to pay for a particular item, and give an indication of those items that are more valuable or rare. Value ranges were compiled by an outside source and are not the result of the author's nor the collectors' calculations. Neither the author nor the publisher accepts responsibility for any outcomes resulting from using this guide.

Introduction

COMPANY HISTORY

Sarah Coventry jewelry was designed for a new style of consumer that emerged in America after World War II. Sarah Coventry, Inc., began in 1949, as an off-shoot of the parent company C.H. Stuart, Inc., a privately established "direct-to-the-consumer marketing" company, with headquarters located in Newark, New York. "Founded on the principles of small-town, small-business America" and devoted to "hard work, quality products, complete customer satisfaction, and concern for others," (1978 company brochure, form no. 89, rev. 6/78), Sarah Coventry, Inc. became the world's largest direct seller of costume jewelry, and an acknowledged fashion leader in contemporary jewelry, during the 1950s, '60s, '70s, and early '80s (*Annual Review*, 1965).

Welcome to Sarah Coventry!

From 1978 company brochure, form no. 89, rev. 6/78.

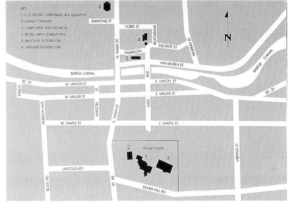

Map showing C. H. Stuart Corporate Headquarters—parent company to Sarah Coventry and Sarah Coventry International, as well as other retail corporations. Stuart Park, Newark, New York, not dated.

Above: Corporate Headquarters, Newark, New York. According to company brochure, circa 1978, more than 350 office employees and several thousands of sales managers and Fashion Show Directors (F.S.D.s) comprised "The Sarah Coventry Family." From 1978 company brochure, form no. 89, rev. 6/78.

Right: From 1978 company brochure, form no. 89, rev. 6/78.

America: Where Dreams Come True

Sarah Coventry is a Company built on a dream - a dream that is being realized. Generally acknowledged to be the country's leading distributor of quality, fashion jewelry, our product is available through in-home Fashion Shows.

The idea of a company built on the direct selling method originated with C.W. "Bill" Stuart, Sarah Coventry's founder and board chairman. It all began in 1949 and today Sarah is the largest and most visible of more than eight companies whose parent is C.H. Stuart Inc., a privately held concern founded in Newark, New York in 1852. We believe that attitudes are stronger than facts, and Sarah Coventry's exciting growth affirms this.

Since the first Fashion Show in 1949, Sarah Coventry has blossomed into an elaborate and sophisticated International operation with subsidiaries in Canada, The United Kingdom and Australia.

As with other C.H. Stuart enterprises, we were founded on the principles of small-town, small-business America; hard work, quality products, complete customer satisfaction, and concern for others. The key to Sarah Coventry's success is that despite our size, we retain these ideals - caring and sharing.

Our best sellers.

Sarah Coventry is jewelry, yet some of our best sellers are people. Like the handful of people pictured above. They're our top Field Sales Managers and we applaud their success.

Most of them began their careers as Fashion Show Directors, which is easy and fun. We'll teach you everything you need to know and we'll provide you with all the jewelry you need to start. Then all you do is arrange Shows in friends' homes where you display the jewelry and take orders. Best of all, you work

where you want, when you want. If you'd like to know more about the inviting world of Sarah Coventry just RSVP 800-448-7000 (in New York RSVP 800-962-9711) or write: Sarah Coventry, Newark 21, New York State 14593. Who knows? You might just become a best seller, too.

Our best sellers, left to right, front row are: Kathy Luther, Betty Gordon, Vicki Neufeld; second row, left to right: Jeanette Wientjes, Shirley Krieger, Sarah Hoyt, Virginia Brocker, Janice Benys, Lynne Griffith.

©1980 Sarah Coventry U.S.A.

sarah coventry®

1980 promotional ad, seen in Spring 1980 contemporary women's magazines, form no. 277.

1972 promotional ad, proclaiming the great opportunities extended to Sarah Coventry's network of employees, as seen in *Vogue*, form 205.

Many joined the Sarah Coventry Family. Promotional ad touting Sarah Coventry's many successes nationwide, not dated.

From 1949 to 1984, Sarah Coventry attained success worldwide by offering a wide array of fine fashion jewelry lines sold exclusively through in-home fashion shows, also known as the party plan method of direct selling. In 1949, their first year in business, they held the first in-home jewelry party, which proved a huge success, and the first teenage fashion show in the United States.

Over their 30+ years in costume jewelry distribution, Sarah Coventry, Inc. became the most successful and visible of the eight companies under C. H. Stuart, Inc. (which included Aquasport, Inc., a manufacturer of fiberglass boats; Artcraft Concepts, Inc., a designer, manufacturer, and distributor of craft products; Caroline Emmons, also a direct seller of costume jewelry through the party plan method; Gateway Home Decorators, a developer of interior decorating ideas for the home; and others). Outside of the United States, Sarah Coventry International, also a division of C.H. Stuart, Inc., directed jewelry distribution—with subsidiaries in the United Kingdom, Canada, Australian, and Belgium. According to Coventry's *Annual Review* (1965), jewelry sales in 1964 totaled $24 million, with an estimate of 65 million pieces of jewelry sold, and an average of 35,000 pieces *sold* on any given workday.

> *Success for Sarah Coventry came through "a mixture of the orthodox and the off-beat in selling and promotional methods and by capitalizing on the fact that hardly a housewife breathes who isn't interested in swelling the family's financial coffers."*
> —Annual Review, 1965

Sarah Coventry, Inc. grew as a company firmly committed to "quality, ethics, service, opportunity, and progress" (1978 company brochure, form 89, rev. 6/78). Women accounted for 90% of the company's workforce—working as Fashion Show Directors (F.D.S.s); Unit Directors; Branch, Region, and Area Managers; and even company Vice Presidents. To promote sales, Sarah Coventry, Inc. used the concept of social gatherings and get-togethers. F.S.D.s hosted in-home jewelry fashion shows, where they encouraged customers to try on and purchase jewelry in the comfort, privacy, and relaxed, unhurried atmosphere of the home. All were encouraged to join the "Sarah Coventry Family."

Sarah Coventry

SPARKLES AS...

Bonnie

GIVES A FASHION SHOW
IN NEW YORK

Brochure showing that even top models were inspired to become Sarah Coventry Fashion Show Directors, not dated.

Sarah says: "You, too, can enjoy extra income as a Fashion Show Director!"

curiously enough...

Bonnie Jones,

America's favorite cover girl,

opened her home to a group of top fashion models... and *Sarah Coventry,*

"Fashion Show selling

is fun!" they said.

In Sequoit,
New York,
by happy
coincidence,
(neither knew it),
Bonnie's sister,
Mrs. Robert Miller,
was giving a fashion
show at the same
time ... with the
very same special
guest ...
Sarah Coventry Jewelry!

Sarah Coventry Fashion Show Directors and other employees were motivated through a series of friendly competitions, incentives, and rewards, given to those who achieved the highest volume of sales. Gift certificates, bonus cruises, free and discounted jewelry ensembles, the opportunity to be apart of Sarah's Jewelry Selection Committee, and much more were rewarded to employees for good salesmanship.

Through exclusive in-home jewelry fashion shows, using the party plan method of direct selling, Sarah Coventry extended many bonuses and incentives to its hostesses, sales managers, directors, and other employees. From 1961 company brochure, form no. 110.

SARAH'S
FOUR STAR
HOSTESS PLAN

As a hostess you get $1.00 credit for each guest at your show who buys Sarah Coventry jewelry.

As a hostess you get $1.00 credit for each show booked at your show.

As a hostess you get $2.00 credit when your show is held within two weeks from the day you were booked.

Plus all that, as a hostess you may buy as many as three jewelry items at half the regular price after you have selected your free hostess gift.

Sarah Coventry INC.
NEWARK, NEW YORK STATE

Sarah Coventry, Inc. Copyright 1961, Form No. 110¹

AN INVITATION FOR YOU
TO ATTEND *Sarah Coventry's*
JANUARY JEWELRY SELECTION MEETING
AS THE TOP UNIT DIRECTOR
IN YOUR ZONE AND HELP
SELECT OUR AUGUST ISSUE
OF FASHION JEWELRY

All of Sarah's Unit Directors are eligible to compete for this exciting honor to come to Newark and look at hundreds of fresh designs and help us select an exciting issue of jewelry for August 1966.

THE RULES FOR WINNING THIS HONOR ARE:

1. Have a Unit that averages SIX or MORE Fashion Show Directors from October 7, 1965 to December 23, 1965 (IBM Dates).

2. Have the highest Personal Sales in your Zone from October 7, 1965 to December 23, 1965 (IBM dates).

3. Maintain a minimum average of at least 50 per cent Activity in your Unit (on IBM) from October 7, 1965 to December 23, 1965.

Some had the opportunity to help select Sarah Coventry's exclusive jewelry lines and be a part of Sarah Coventry's Jewelry Selection Committee. Two company brochures outlining competition rules, calendar of events, and prize opportunities, c. mid-to-late 1960s.

AN
INVITATION
FOR YOU
TO ATTEND

Sarah Coventry's

JEWELRY SELECTION
MEETING
in
January 1967
As the top U.D. in your Zone

WINNER'S SCHEDULE

JANUARY 11

Brunch at the Newark Country Club with top office personnel, followed by a red carpet tour of the Sarah Offices and factory. Then dinner with the Selection Committee at the famous Caruso's Restaurant in Canandaigua, well known for its excellent cuisine.

JANUARY 12

Attend Sarah's Selection Meeting and help select the August 1967 issue of jewelry. Lunch at the well-known Garlock House in Palmyra. Afternoon free to shop. President's Dinner at the Depot Restaurant in Rochester, famous for its steaks and old-time railroad atmosphere.

JANUARY 13

Review of jewelry selections followed by an informative jewelry clinic with the Selection Committee in Newark.

All of Sarah's Unit Directors are eligible to compete for this most exciting honor of coming to Newark and helping the Selection Committee select the August 1967 issue of jewelry...an experience you'll never forget.

EMPLOYEES TAKE THE SPOTLIGHT

Left: Leaflet from the Sales Executive Club of New York gathering, where Sarah Coventry was seated as the guests of honor. Featuring photographs of Sarah Coventry's President Rex Wood, Exec. VP John Joyce, VP of Sales Promotion, Advertising, and Public Relations Al Winfrey, and Fashion Coordinator Aileen Van Tyle. Not dated.

Below: Aileen Van Tyle. October 22, 1959.

(I)
Here's REX WOOD, president of Sarah Coventry, chatting with ALLAN KELLER, internationally famous columnist of the New York World Telegram.
(II) Stuart Clarkson, shown here with REX, is Conference Director of the National Conference Board. After hearing REX, Mr. Clarkson invited him to speak at an important Board Meeting.
(III) JOHN JOYCE, exec. VP of Sarah Coventry, tells an attentive audience of the great sales power of Sarah Coventry.
(IV) AL WINFREY, Sarah's VP in charge of Sales Promotion, advertising and public relations, makes the first award to a lucky winner of a jewelry treasure chest.
(V) REX has just dramatized his point of the "unexpected opportunities in direct selling" by advising audience to look under their chairs for lucky gifts.
(VI) AILEEN VANTYLE, Fashion Coordinator for Sarah, starts the Fashion Show held before an overflow audience of 650.
(VII) Three lovely models demonstrate the versatility of Sarah Coventry jewelry. They're wearing SUMMER MAGIC.
(VIII) To the strain's of "Around the World in Eighty Days" model shows WORLD'S FAIR.

Sarah Coventry's Signet
Aileen Van Tyle
Sarah's ... onsultant
Window ... th Avenue
(se...) October 22, 1959

11

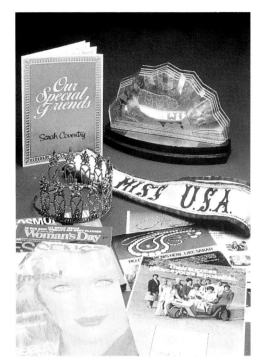

From 1978 company brochure, form no. 89, rev. 6/78.

CAMPAIGN ADVERTISING

"Sarah Coventry's national advertising appears in the most widely read magazines, on network television on the ever popular TV Game Shows. More than 90% of the American population knows the name Sarah Coventry means quality jewelry sold in the home . . . by invitation only!"

1978 company brochure, form no. 89, rev. 6/78

MAGAZINES

Success during the 1950s, '60s, '70s, and early '80s came for Sarah Coventry, Inc. due in part to their development of effective and impressive magazine and television ad campaigning. Ads for Sarah Coventry's exclusive jewelry lines ran throughout a number of the country's most popular and widely circulated magazines, such as *Vogue, Cosmopolitan, Good Housekeeping, Mademoiselle, McCall's, Woman's Day, Ladies Home Journal, Essence, Glamour, Self, Ebony,* and *Harper's Bazaar.* In spring 1980 alone, fourteen popular women's magazines with a total estimated circulation of over 45 million nationwide carried ads for Sarah Coventry's jewelry collections.

Sarah Coventry's National Magazine Advertising Schedule March '80 · June '80

Month	Magazine	Jewelry
March '80	Cosmopolitan Living	Regency Necklace
April	Mademoiselle	Orchid Choker
	Glamour	Regency Necklace
	Working Woman	Regency Necklace
	Self	Our Best Sellers
May	Cosmopolitan	Karat Gold
	Essence	Regency Necklace
	McCall's	Orchid Choker
	Good Housekeeping	Karat Gold
	New Woman (May/June)	Karat Gold
	Working Mother	Orchid Choker
June	Cosmopolitan	Orchid Choker
	Mademoiselle	Karat Gold
	Redbook	Regency Necklace
	Ladies' Home Journal	Orchid Choker
	Good Housekeeping	Regency Choker
	Self	Orchid Choker
	Woman's Day	Regency Necklace
	Working Woman	Karat Gold

These reprints of advertisements which appear in several women's magazines are available to you in quantities of five, and can be ordered on your Manager Literature Supply Form #6.

Form Number	Reprint
276	Karat Gold
277	Our Best Sellers/Orchid Choker
278	Regency Necklace

Above: Schedule showing Sarah Coventry's rigorous advertising campaign for spring of 1980. Boosting sales and brand name recognition, a number of the country's most popular women's magazines ran ads for Sarah Coventry's exclusive jewelry lines.

Right: As seen in *Essence* and *Good Housekeeping,* 1980, form no. 281.

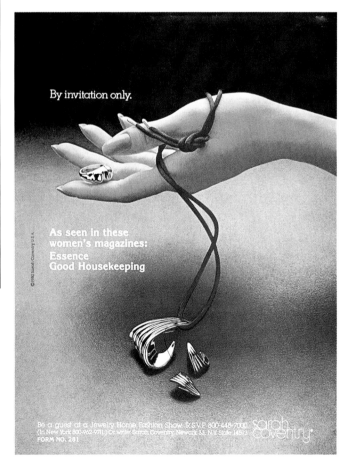

By invitation only.

As seen in these women's magazines:
Glamour
Ladies' Home Journal

Be a guest at a Jewelry Home Fashion Show. R.S.V.P. 800-448-7000.
(In New York 800-962-9711.) Or write: Sarah Coventry, Newark 32, N.Y. State 14593.
FORM NO. 281

Left: As seen in *Glamour* and *Ladies' Home Journal*, 1980, form no. 281.

Below: As seen in contemporary women's magazines for fall 1978, form 268.

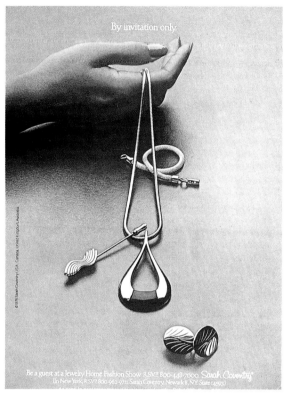

By invitation only.

Be a guest at a Jewelry Home Fashion Show. R.S.V.P. 800-448-7000.
(In New York, R.S.V.P. 800-962-9711. Sarah Coventry, Newark 8, N.Y. State 14593.

Right: As seen in contemporary women's magazines for fall 1978, form 268.

Far right: As seen in spring 1980 contemporary women's magazines, form no. 277.

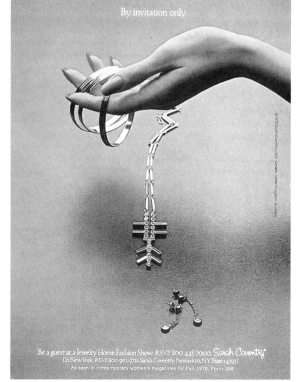

By invitation only.

Be a guest at a Jewelry Home Fashion Show. R.S.V.P. 800-448-7000.
(In New York, R.S.V.P. 800-962-9711. Or write: Sarah Coventry, Newark 10, N.Y. State 14593.
As seen in contemporary women's magazines for Fall 1978. Form 268.

By invitation only.

Be a guest at a Jewelry Home Fashion Show. R.S.V.P. 800-448-7000.
(In New York 800-962-9711. Or write: Sarah Coventry, Newark 22, N.Y. State 14593.
Seen in Spring 1980 contemporary women's magazines.   Form No. 277.

THE NECK HOOP WITH KNOW-HOW

A glossy, golden hoop with a look-of-marble teardrop pendant. Set it off with chains, a wristful of wavy bangles and our latest tapered hoop earrings. The total look is bound to raise your fashion I.Q. 20 points.

Try them on at a Sarah Coventry Jewelry Home Fashion Show soon. For full details: call 800-448-7000 toll free (except New York State, Hawaii and Alaska) or write: Sarah Coventry Inc., Newark 300, New York State 14593.

Sarah Coventry
The jewelry with know-how

As seen in *Glamour*, 1976, form 240.

NO ONE KNOWS HOW...LIKE SARAH

Sarah's quality jewelry knows how to sparkle up your wardrobe in a very special way with this exclusive hammered silvertone Scandia Collection, priced in the U.S.A. from $5.00 to $13.00.

Sarah Coventry
The jewelry with know-how

Sarah's know-how is all yours at a Sarah Coventry Jewelry Home Fashion Show. For when and where, call 800-448-7000 toll-free (in New York State, 800-962-9711), or write: Sarah Coventry, Inc., Newark 314, New York State 14593.

As seen in *Essence* and *Ebony Fashion Fair*, 1977, form 255.

as seen in

COSMOPOLITAN

❋ Sarah Coventry holds a "Fashion Show in the Clouds" to introduce its newest style creation... *Jet Flight*

Sarah Coventry INC.
NEWARK, NEW YORK STATE

THE EXCITING NAME IN FASHION JEWELRY

As seen in *Cosmopolitan*, 1961, form no. 110.

HIGH FASHION AT 32,000 FEET!

Sarah Coventry holds a "Fashion Show in the Clouds" to introduce its newest style creation... *Jet Flight*

High above the clouds in an American Airlines 707 Jet Flagship, Sarah Coventry's newest jewelry creation recently made its dramatic bow.

A dynamic swirl of silver and black capturing the beauty of jets in motion, JET FLIGHT scored an instant hit with the plane's modern-minded passengers. To quote one entranced onlooker, "I never dreamed fashion jewelry so inexpensive could be so beautiful."

Would you like to attend a pleasant, informal Sarah Coventry Fashion Show in the company of your own friends and neighbors? If so, drop us a line today. See how easy and economical it can be — with the help of Sarah's gift bonus plan — to complete a fabulous collection, all your own, of the world famous fashion jewelry.

Write Sarah Coventry, Inc., Dept. C-51, Newark, New York State.

Sarah Coventry
As featured on QUEEN FOR A DAY - TV

14

In the 1970s, J.J. Kinnersely, appointed company spokeswoman, and Lee Meriwether, star of the entertainment world, furthered sales and company/employee recruitment through their involvement in Sarah Coventry's television and magazine ad campaigns.

Sarah Coventry even developed a song to sing the praises of the "warmth," "fun," "fellowship," and "success" of their in-home fashion shows. Company brochure/song sheet, *Sarah's Song*, printed 8/76, form no. 158.

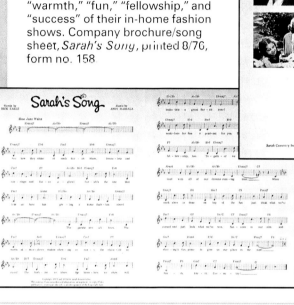

Two company brochures announcing actress-model J.J. Kinnersley's (cover girl for *McCall's* and *Ladies' Home Journal*) television appearance to help recruit Fashion Show Directors and "[tell] women all over America how to wear Sarah Coventry jewelry and how to make Sarah's 'know how' theirs!" c.1976, and form 185.

Lee Meriwether, lovely star of the entertainment world, models Sarah's latest jewelry fashion, 1972 promotional ad.

Added fame came to Sarah Coventry through the award of Sarah Coventry jewelry to the participants and winners of beauty pageants held nationally and worldwide. In 1975, Sarah Coventry jewelry crowned the head of Miss Universe.

Queen of the Lakes, August 20, 1959. Inside, this promotional brochure also reveals the prizes for the winner of the "Miss Ozone" pageant, held in Baton Rouge, Louisiana, which includes a "three-piece gold and rhinestone ensemble" from Sarah Coventry.

Fall/Winter 1976 Jewelry Collection

Miss Universe 1975 wearing the official crown created for her by Sarah Coventry.

TELEVISION

In television, Sarah Coventry jewelry designs captured the limelight, through commercials airing on the major TV networks of ABC, NBC, and CBS. Promotional ads and campaigning were targeted to a mostly female audience, and TV shows promoting Sarah Coventry jewelry lines, in 1975, aired over 554 million times in homes across America (1975 promotional ad, form 162). As a result, brand name recognition for Sarah Coventry surged. In fact, in one year's time, Sarah Coventry achieved 90% name recognition among women between the ages of 20 and 45, ranking it closely with companies such as Coca-Cola and Kodak.

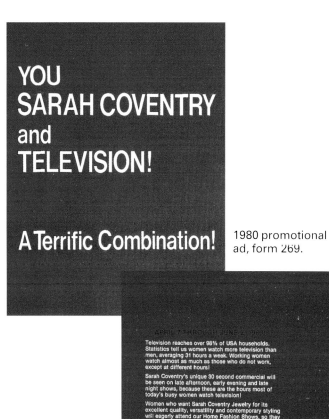

YOU
SARAH COVENTRY
and
TELEVISION!

A Terrific Combination!

1980 promotional ad, form 269.

Television reaches over 98% of USA households. Statistics tell us women watch more television than men, averaging 31 hours a week. Working women watch almost as much as those who do not work, except at different hours!

Sarah Coventry's unique 30 second commercial will be seen on late afternoon, early evening and late night shows, because these are the hours most of today's busy women watch television!

Women who want Sarah Coventry Jewelry for its excellent quality, versatility and contemporary styling will eagerly attend our Home Fashion Shows, so they can see more of Sarah Coventry's fabulous Jewelry!

You — Sarah Coventry and Television are a terrific combination — but only because you make it work!

© 1980 Sarah Coventry, Newark, New York State 14593 Printed in U.S.A. Form 269

Sarah Coventry
The jewelry with know-how

is on all three big national networks
CBS. . . NBC . . . ABC

MARY TYLER MOORE   DICK CLARK   ANGIE DICKINSON   WALTER CRONKITE   CAROL BURNETT

Here's the kind of talent that will be backing you up on TV this Fall!

1976 promotional folder, form 186.

PRIME TIME AND LATE NIGHT SHOWS LIKE THESE...

TUNE TODAY'S WOMAN IN TO SENSATIONAL SARAH COVENTRY JEWELRY!

Little House on the Prairie

THE Big Event...

Between April 7 and June 2, 1980 Sarah Coventry's new Spring commercial will be seen by millions of today's women across the country who appreciate the opportunity to touch, feel, try on and buy our exciting, contemporary jewelry!

Today's discriminating customer demands well designed, high quality jewelry so she looks to Sarah Coventry for all her jewelry needs. We have fantastic fashion jewelry as well as superbly crafted karat gold jewelry!

A Sarah Coventry Jewelry Home Fashion Show — by invitation only — is the easy, convenient way to shop. It's the answer for the active woman who enjoys a friendly, relaxed atmosphere, where trying on jewelry is the smartest way to choose. It also means tips on fashion trends and accessorizing for that up-to-date, confident fashion look!

If you would enjoy a career in fashion, try the opportunity of a lifetime as a Sarah Coventry Jewelry Fashion Show Director, full or part-time! You'll love the flexible hours! It's easy, and we'll teach you all you need to know about it! Talk to your Fashion Show Director, or for more information look for Sarah Coventry under Jewelers in the yellow pages of your telephone directory and call toll free!

Now we welcome you to sit back and enjoy today's Fashion Show — as our commercial explains, Sarah Coventry has jewelry for the neck — the fingers — the ears — the wrist and the lapel — and it's yours to see at a Sarah Coventry Jewelry Home Fashion Show!

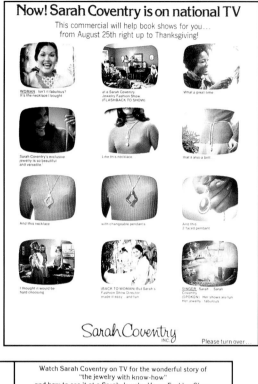

Right: 1974 promotional ad, form no. 169.

Far right: 1975 promotional ad, form 162.

Center row: 1976 promotional ad, form 185.

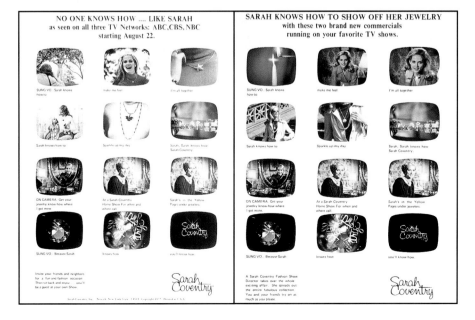

Aileen on "TO TELL THE TRUTH"

M. C. BUD COLLIER POSES WITH AILEEN FOLLOWING THE SHOW.

THE PANEL HAS CAST THEIR VOTES

Sarah's own employees took on top active roles promoting all aspects of the Sarah Coventry name and their exclusive jewelry lines—including televised guest appearances on *To Tell the Truth*, a gameshow of the 1950s and '60s.

Promotional ad, not dated.

Shows such as *Days of Our Lives*, *Walter Cronkite, Evening News*, *Carol Burnet Show*, '*Tonight*,' *Johnny Carson*, *Barnaby Jones*, and many more joined in to spread the Sarah Coventry name. Employees of Sarah Coventry made special guest appearances on shows such as *To Tell the Truth*. Also jewelry designs were offered as merchandise and contestant prizes on the top TV gameshows, including *Hollywood Squares*, *Family Feud*, *Wheel of Fortune*, and *The Price is Right*. *Queen for a Day* proved one of the company's most successful televised campaigns.

Despite the many successes Sarah Coventry saw in costume jewelry distribution and sales from the 1950s through the early '80s, the decade of the '80s also saw the down-plight of costume jewelry fashions and Sarah Coventry. During the late '70s and early '80s, demographics shifted, and women (Sarah's target employee and consumer) sought other avenues in the work place. No longer was Sarah's party plan method for jewelry sales as successful as it had been in previous years. Sales for Sarah Coventry dropped as a result, and eventually their rather large inventory became too difficult to maintain. The fashion craze for costume jewelry slowly began to fade. In 1984, Sarah Coventry was purchased by a Canadian firm. Today, Sarah Coventry jewelry remains a success on the collectors' market . . . . .

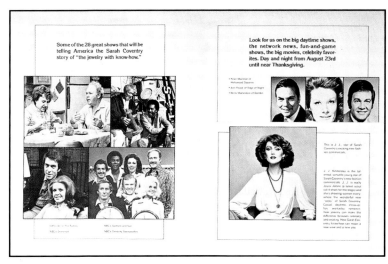

Queen for a Day

Division Manager, Dock McDonald of California and members of the Sarah family, were guests of "Queen For A Day", and welcomed by genial Jack Bailey and Fashion Commentator Jean Cagney.

One of Sarah Coventry's most successful televised campaigns. From 1959 company brochure.

Sarah Coventry®

Above: As seen in *Ladies' Home Journal*, 1976, form 243.

Right: Promotional ad showcasing Sarah Coventry jewelry's versatility and adaptability. As seen in *Good Housekeeping*, 1975, form 232.

Sarah Coventry's fashion jewelry lines were "created for the many sides of your life—the fashionable, the casual, [and] the practical" (Fall/Winter 1976 catalog, p. 2). Jewelry items were created to be versatile, and to accessorize a variety of new clothing styles and fashionable looks. Necklaces could be worn also as belts, or looped several times to be worn as a bracelet. Pendants came off their chains to be worn as pins, and were reversible with a different design on the front and back.

Numerous ideas for accenting a particular outfit or look were featured throughout company advertisements and jewelry packaging. Hostesses and Fashion Show Directors offered personal demonstrations of the alternative ways the jewelry pieces could be worn and adapted to suit any wardrobe or occasion.

Many Sarah Coventry jewelry items were made to be interchangeable and reversible. This pendant necklace and ring, for example, came with interchangeable pieces. Pendant necklace with black and white interchangeable loops, 2" h., on 24" chain; ring with black, green, and white tops. $40-50.

As seen in *Good House-keeping*, 1975, form 232.

Jewelry packaging and advertisements often offered various ways an item could be worn to accessorize. Large and small leaf pins with center pearl, shown as a set, connected by chain. "Chit-Chat" 6771, SarahGlo. Shown on original display card and box, dated 1961. (For matching earrings, see pg. 78). $45-55.

Reverse side of display card gives a variety of ideas for how accessories can be worn (shown with back of original box).

To ensure high quality and keep jewelry lines current and "versatile," a team of product developers closely followed and predicted the latest trends in jewelry fashion, design, and sales. According to a company advertisement, stones for their pieces were "glazed, re-glazed, and then glazed again for sparkle and durability" (*Good Housekeeping*, 1975, form 232). Pieces also included a smooth finish on both the front and the back. With an emphasis on fashion versatility, the jewelry was made to be worn in multiples, mixed and matched, and layered.

Price wise, Sarah Coventry offered inexpensive fashion jewelry, priced to appeal to the average, everyday consumer. Individual pieces typically went for under $10 dollars, while ensembles, including matching and/or coordinating rings, pins, earrings, necklaces, and bracelets, cost from $30 to $40, for a three- to five-piece set. Sarah's motto—"the priceless look of beauty is seldom a matter of price"— held true even for the elegant and most expensive of their jewelry lines, e.g., those replete with rhinestones and colorful faux stones.

To identify jewelry designs, look for Sarah Coventry's exclusive signature jewelry tags, often marked "Sar Cov," "Sarah Cov," "Coventry," or "Sarah." (Note: some jewelry designs may not bear the Sarah Coventry name or tag.)

Examples of original Sarah Coventry jewelry packaging.

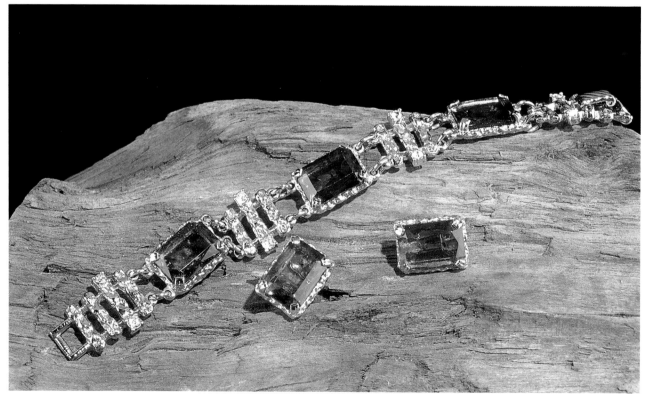

Link bracelet (7.5") and matching clip-on earrings (.75"), baguette cut
amethyst centers set in embellished goldentone frames, with openwork and
clear rhinestones accents. (For matching necklace, see pg. 49). $70-85 set.

Pendants

"Man in a natural state is surrounded by an abundance of flora and fauna in an infinite range of splendid colors and shapes. Just think how many different flowers there are! And think too of the adornment and colorful plumage displayed in the animal kingdom."
"The Meaning of Adornment," by Daniel Swaroski,
in *Jewels of Fantasy: Costume Jewelry of the 20th Century*

"Rajah." Goldentone elephant pendant (1.125" h.), on 25" strand of amber colored beads. $50-75.

BIRDS

Above: Openwork swan pendant (2.125" dia.), silvertone with clear rhinestones and blue eye, 25" chain. $40-50.

Right: Pendant resembling peacock's tail feathers, goldentone ribbed frame with three red and black oval shapes (1.65" dia.), on 22" chain. $38-42.

Three-part goldentone owl pendant, with open-work head and body, black bead eyes, and solid bottom tail feathers (4" h.), on 24" chain. $35-45.

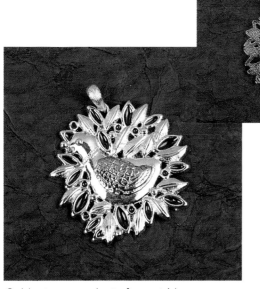

Left: Reverse side of pendant—"Sarah Coventry Christmas 1978."

Below: Silvertone and enamel circular pendant of bird resting on a branch (1.5" dia.), on 25" chain. $38-42.

Goldentone pendant of a partridge in a pear tree, with red and green leaves and berries, 2" dia. $30-38.

BUTTERFLIES

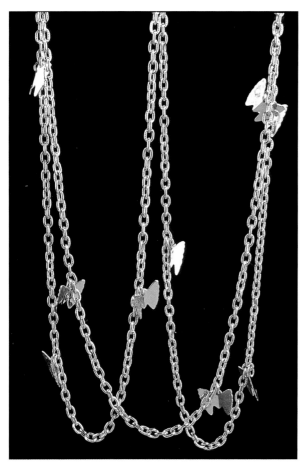

Left: "Pandora." Goldentone butterfly pendant, on 16" chain. $20-25.

Below: Top left: R2-D2 pendant, goldentone on 16" chain. $20-25.
Top right: "Butterfly Duo." Goldentone lapel pin of two butterflies with connecting chain (each with own backing). 18-25.
Bottom: "Words of Love." Openwork goldentone necklace: "Amor, Liebe, Love, Amore, Amour," 17.5". Possibly children's pieces. $30-40.

"Silvery Flutter Byes." Goldentone necklace with butterfly charms, 52" (meant to be draped several times). $28-35.

Goldentone sand dollar pendant (1.85" dia.), on 24" chain. $25-30.

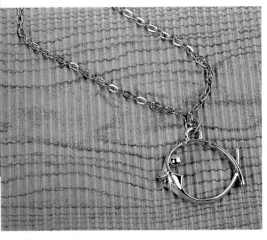

"Hawaiian Fantasy." Pendant of three fish, goldentone with red rhinestone eyes, on 16.5" chain. $30-40.

"Splash." Openwork fish pendant, silvertone, on 24" chain. $22-25.

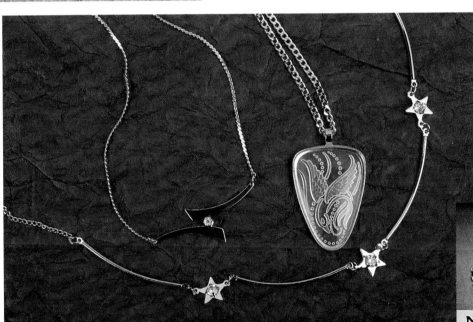

Outer: "Enchantment Choker." Necklace of goldentone stars with clear rhinestone centers, 15". $25-30.
Inner left: "Starlite." Goldentone necklace of two curved extensions fastened by single clear rhinestone, 15". $20-25.
Inner right: Etched glass pendant set in goldentone frame depicting bird or aquatic design, on 24" chain. $38-45.

NO ONE KNOWS HOW...LIKE SARAH

From "Sea Star" jewelry collection. Goldentone hoop necklace with starfish pendant. $22-28.

Promotional ad, as seen in *Good Housekeeping*, 1977, form 253.

PLANTS & FLOWERS

Left: Small globe pendant, goldentone with green enamel Christmas tree, topped by clear rhinestone star, .75" dia. $22-28.

Center: Reverse side of pendant— "Limited Edition 1979, Sarah Coventry."

Right: Goldentone filigree acorn pendant, on 24" chain. $20-25.

"The Big Apple." Openwork apple pendant (1.125" h.), silvertone, on 18" chain. $22-25.

Leaf shaped pendant with center marquise shaped clear rhinestone (1.5" h.), on 19" chain. (For matching earrings, see pg. 79). $38-48.

Detail of reverse side of pendant.

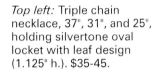

Top left: Triple chain necklace, 37", 31", and 25", holding silvertone oval locket with leaf design (1.125" h.). $35-45.

Top right: "New Seasons." Goldentone link necklace with eight leaf "charms," 24". $28-35.

Left: Goldentone open-work pendant, teardrop shaped with leaf-like designs, 4" h. $28-35.

Right: "Rose-Marie." Oval pendant of pink and red rose on white background set in goldentone frame (1.75" h.), on 24" chain. $35-45.

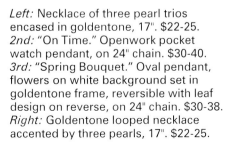

Left: Necklace of three pearl trios encased in goldentone, 17". $22-25.
2nd: "On Time." Openwork pocket watch pendant, on 24" chain. $30-40.
3rd: "Spring Bouquet." Oval pendant, flowers on white background set in goldentone frame, reversible with leaf design on reverse, on 24" chain. $30-38.
Right: Goldentone looped necklace accented by three pearls, 17". $22-25.

CROSSES, HEARTS, & STARS

Left: "Marriage Cross." Traditional goldentone cross pendant, on 24" chain. $20-25.

2nd: "Tiara." Pentagon shaped pendant of goldentone slats, on 24" rope chain. $25-30.

3rd: Oval pendant with goldentone flower on black background, on 24" rope chain. $20-25.

4th: Goldentone link necklace, .75" w., 16.5" l. $35-40.

Right: Openwork ornate goldentone cross with faceted amber colored center stone, on 24" chain. $48-60.

Baroque goldentone cross with center pearl (3.75" h. x 2.25" w.), on 25" chain. $48-55.

Openwork silvertone cross pendant of intertwined loops (3.5" h. x 2.5" w.), on 25" chain. $48-55.

"Serenity Cross." Cross pendants (1.5" h. x 1" w.), available in silvertone and goldentone, on 18" chain. $38-45.

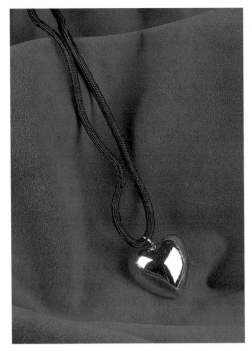

Silvertone heart pendant (three-dimensional), on 29" black cord. $22-27.

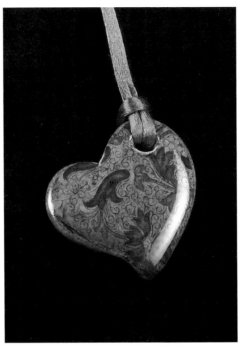

"Batik." Polished cinnamon colored heart pendant with overall floral decoration, on brown cord. $30-38.

"Cupid's Touch." Heart pendant, black with clear rhinestone in goldentone frame and back, on 16" chain. *Courtesy of Betty L. Donley.* $22-28.

Frosted heart pendant (three-dimensional) accented by a clear rhinestone, on 18" chain, marked "Sarah Cov Canada." $20-25.

Left: "Duo Heart." Silvertone looped double heart pendant, variegated blue. $22-28.
Right: "Pizzazz." Variegated blue bar, with silvertone caps, 14". $18-22.

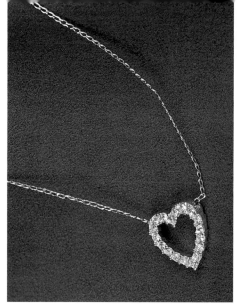

Goldentone necklace with star spangles, 52". $25-35.

"Sweetheart." Heart pendant of silvertone and clear rhinestones, on 16" chain. *Courtesy of Betty L. Donley.* $25-30.

GEOMETRIC

Oval goldentone and enameled pendant, in muted earthtones, on 16" chain. $32-38.

"Front Row." Square goldentone and enameled pendant (1.25" sq.), in black, orange, and yellow, on 17" linked chain. $35-40.

Oval pendant (1") of blue, green, yellow, red, and gray geometric design in goldentone frame, mosaic-like, on 18" chain. $30-38.

Clockwise from top left:

Rectangular silvertone and enameled pendant, in black and red, on 16.5" chain. $28-32.

Unique goldentone and black enameled geometrically shaped emblem pendant, on 18" chain. $22-28.

Triangular goldentone and enamel pendant, red, yellow, blue, and off-white, with clear rhinestone set in goldentone flower-like frame, on 16" chain. $25-32.

Diamond shaped pendant, goldentone with cross-hatched surface and surrounding twisted framed, 2.75" h. $30-40.

Goldentone octagonal pendant of geometric openwork center surrounded by floral openwork perimeter (2" dia.), on 18" chain. $28-35.

Circular silvertone and enamel pendant, teal cross-like design encircled by pale blue halo, with ornate openwork, on 24" chain. $27-35.

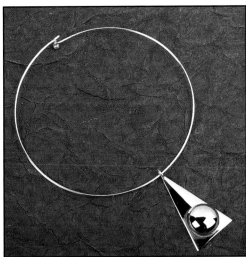

Choker necklace, silvertone hoop with polished geometric pendant (2" h.), modern lines, 5" dia. $40-50.

Openwork arrowhead shaped pendant (3" h.), curved silvertone bars, on 26" chain. $25-35.

"Continental." Pendant of unusual shape with red ovals set in silvertone frame (2.25" h.), on 18" chain of linked bars. $35-40.

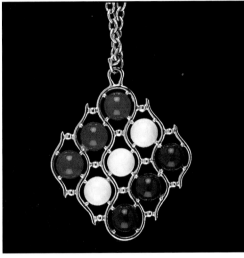

Pendant of red, white, and blue balls held in silvertone openwork frame (3.25" h.), on 27" chain. $38-45.

Pendant of red plastic and silvertone hoop (3.25" dia.), on 24" chain. $25-35.

Silvertone openwork teardrop shaped frame with black triangular loose center charm (3" h.), on 20" chain. $30-40.

Necklace, black centers mounted in seven openwork round and semi-circular, polished and twisted silvertone frames, 18" overall. $50-75.

Right: "Filigree Jet." Pendant with oval black center and silvertone scroll-like filigree frame (1" h.), on 17.5" chain. $35-45.

Below: Pendant with round black center surrounded by filigree-like looped silvertone frame, on silvertone chain. $30-40.

Above: "Jet Set." Choker with black faceted center stone set in modern-looking silvertone frame, 15" link and twisted bar chain. $40-50.

Right: Advertisement for "Jet Set," as seen in *Vogue,* 1976, form 242. Note items retailed for: necklace $12, earrings $13, bracelet $14, and ring $8.

Above: Choker with oval olive center, goldentone frame and scroll-like filigree openwork on, 16" chain. $30-38.

Left: "Evergreen." Oval pendant with modern look, rich olive green oval center in goldentone frame, on 24" chain.

"Broadway." Oversized (2.25") pendant with variegated brown center, in goldentone frame, on 24" brown cord. $32-38.

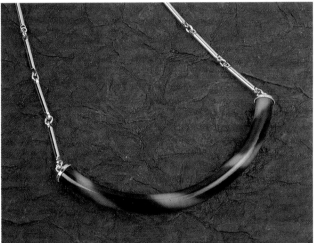

Above: Curved tortoiseshell colored bar, with goldentone caps, on 17" chain. $20-25.

Right: "Trendsetter." Silvertone choker-length necklace with small wooden cube, 16" overall. $18-25.

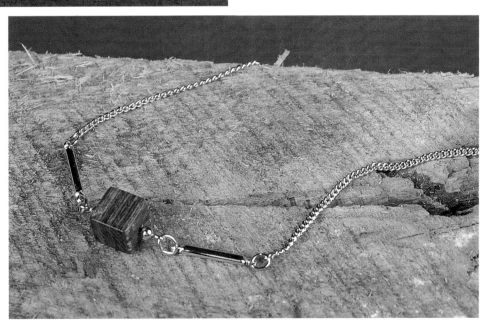

Necklaces

Above: From "Sea Star" jewelry collection. Necklace of twisted bars and round links, 42". $18-22.

Right: "Tailored Accent." Silvertone linked chain necklace, 29". $18-22.

CHAINS

"Slicker Chain." Linked single strand silvertone chain, 24". *Courtesy of Betty L. Donley.* $15-20.

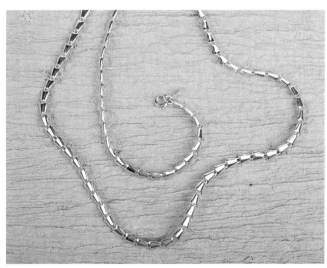

Above: Silvertone reticulated chain, 32". $15-20.

Right: "Sara Lariat." Flat silvertone chain with flowerhead and black prong-set center stone, 18". $20-25.

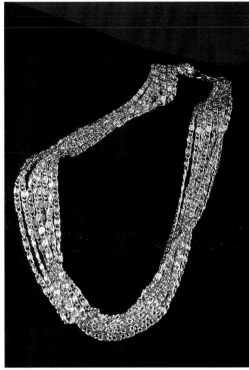

"Silvery Cascade." Eight stranded necklace of chain links in various widths, 16". *Courtesy of Betty L. Donley.* $25-30.

"Serenade." Silvertone link and bar necklace with silvertone chain link tassel, accented with a marquise shaped pink rhinestone, 32.5". $22-30.

Necklace of graduated filigree panels, 17". $50-75.

Four stranded necklace of chain links in various widths, 25.5". $22-28.

Silvertone necklace of leaf-like pendants, 17.75". $45-55.

Silvertone link fringe necklace, 16.5". $55-65.

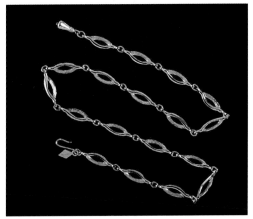

Above: "Delightful." Goldentone chain of eyelet shaped links, 18". $18-22.

Right: Goldentone chain, 38". $18-22.

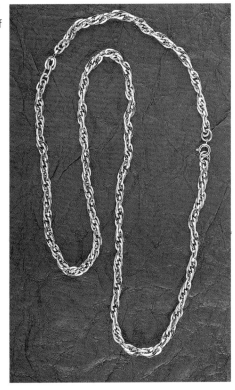

Above: Wide, flat goldentone chain, 19.5" l. x .425" w. $20-25.

Right: Wide, flat goldentone chain, 16". (For matching bracelet, see pg. 86). $20-25.

"Sarah Coventry chains . . . wear three or four or more, all at once! Non stop. Wind one high under your chin. Let another swoop full length. Wrap one around your wrist as a bracelet. Wear chains with tweeds, with prints, day or night" (promotional ad, 1973, form no. 214).

"Golden Braids." Goldentone twisted rope necklace, 17". $15-20.

"Egyptian." Goldentone snake (chain) necklace, 16". $25-30.

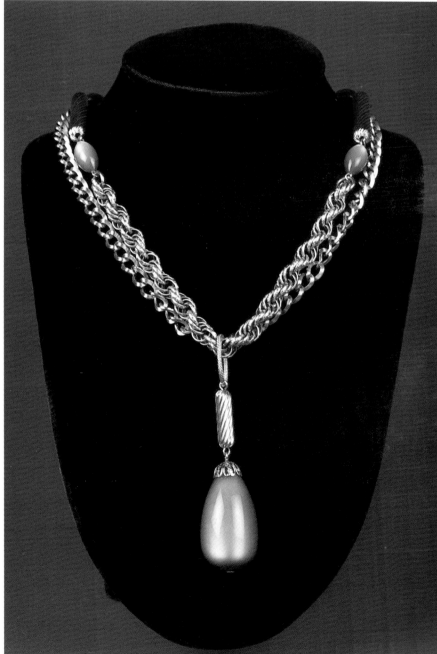

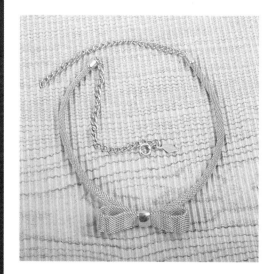

Above: "Bow Tie." Goldentone mesh rope necklace with small bow fastened in the middle, 17". $25-35.

Left: Goldentone double stranded necklace, chain link and twisted rope with olive beads and goldentone "barrels;" oversized olive teardrop shaped pendant (1.5" h.). $35-45.

Above: "Spring Posie." Flat goldentone chain with flower, 16" to 18". $25-32.

Right: Goldentone necklace with filigree openwork and dangling goldentone bars, 19". $48-60.

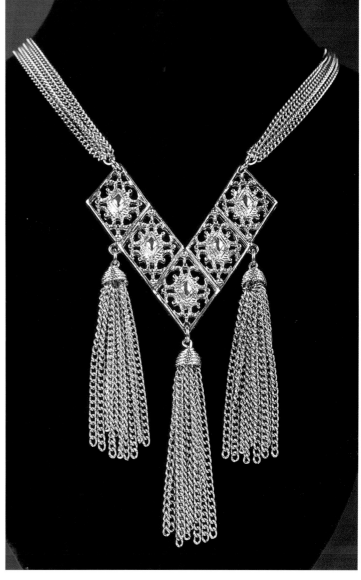

Right: Goldentone necklace of V-shaped filigree openwork pendant with three tassels (tassels: 4.65" l.), on 28" goldentone chain. $50-65.

Below left: "Goddess." Double stranded goldentone link necklace (bib-choker) of bars and round links in diamond pattern, 18". $38-45.

Below right: Detail.

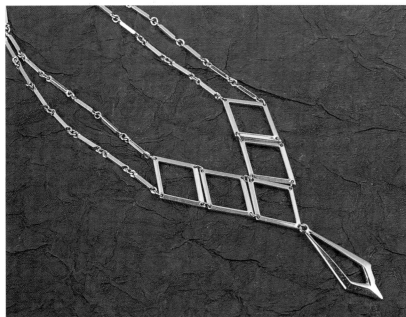

BEADS

"Spinner." Purple and white swirled center bead flanked by two smaller purple beads, on silvertone chain, 16" overall. $18-25.

Doubled goldentone necklace with variegated blue stones of two sizes, 39". $25-35.

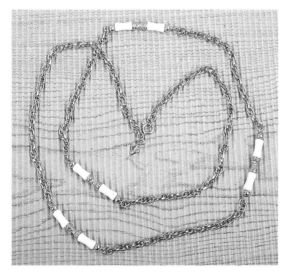

Goldentone necklace with white and goldentone "barrel" accents, 32". $25-35.

"Bittersweet." Goldentone linked necklace with brown, coral, and textured ivory, and yellow beads, 68". $25-35.

"Oriental Lanterns." Goldentone bar and round link necklace with variegated green and goldentone filigree openwork "barrels," 33". $25-32.

Goldentone linked necklace of bars and round links, filigree and openwork diamonds, and elongated white beads, 32". $22-27.

Red and black opaque beaded necklace, 36" l. $20-25.

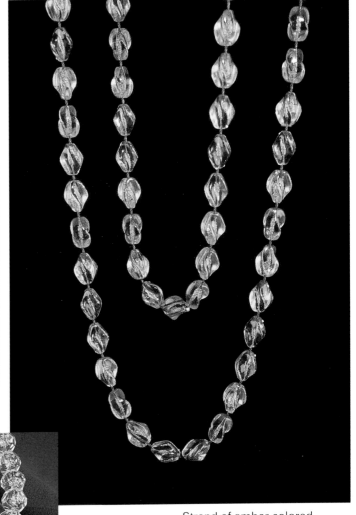

Strand of amber colored beads, 37". $28-35.

Above: "Golden Ice." Triple-stranded necklace of clear beads and a twisted goldentone chain, 20". $35-40.

Right: "Pastel Beads." Pink opaque beaded necklace, with extension that could also be worn as a bracelet, 37". $28-32.

"Sarah knows how to brighten up your summer look with the brilliance of white jewelry. Like all of Sarah's designs, these pieces mix well with each other and add dazzle to your summer fashions." As seen in *Woman's Day*, 1978, form no. 259.

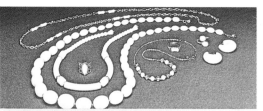

Above: White beaded double-stranded necklace, 30". $22-25.

Right: Necklace of white beads, two oversized "baubles," and goldentone star shaped pendant/clasp with filigree, openwork edging. $30-40.

Right: Promotional ad seen in spring 1980 contemporary women's magazines, form no. 278.

Far right: Assortment of necklaces showing varying types of clasps. Blue opaque, pearl, and variegated coral. $22-30 each.

PEARLS

Two baroque pearl drop pendants with goldentone caps (1.5" h.), on 31" goldentone chain. $30-38.

Double strand silvertone chain and pearl necklace (36" to 37"), with oversized pearl drop pendants (1.5" h.), shown with original box. $38-50.

Five strand graduated pearl necklace, 18" to 23" strands, with four pearl clasp. $30-40.

Above: Triple strand pearl necklace with silvertone clasp accented with pearls, 18". $30-40.

Right: Triple strand pearl necklace with reversible clear rhinestones and pearl clasp, 15". (For matching earrings, see pg. 82). $35-45.

Detail of reverse pearl side of clasp.

Goldentone necklace of bars and round links, accented with round and elongated pearl beads, 22". $28-35.

Goldentone necklace with trio of elongated and round pearls, 17". $20-25.

Necklace of pearls encased in goldentone thread "sacks," 13". $22-27.

Right: Pearl necklace with three large pearl "baubles," 60". $30-40.

Below: Goldentone necklace of bars, round links, and pairs of pearls wound in goldentone, 30". $30-40.

Above: Double strand graduated pearl and goldentone chain link necklace, 54". Also available in goldentone. $30-35.

Right: Silvertone chain link necklace of pairs of round pearls and elongated pearls encased in goldentone spiraled threading, 52". $30-40.

Below left: Silvertone chain accented with round pearls and silvertone filigree elongated beads, 53". $30-40.

Below right: Silvertone chain with ivory, gray, and black pearls, 43". $30-40.

Left: "First Love." Goldentone bar and round link necklace with small seed pearls, 54". $20-26.

Below: Silvertone necklace with pearls tied together by silvertone, glittered threading, 78". $25-30.

Snowflake shaped pendant of four pearls and set in silvertone mounting, accented by clear rhinestones, on 18" chain. $32-38.

Small silvertone locket with center pearl set in embellished silvertone mounting, on 18" chain. $35-40.

Oversized round, baroque pearl with goldentone filigree caps, mounted as a pendant (.75" dia.), on 19" chain. $35-40.

FAUX STONES

Far left: Oval pendant, purple center stone set in frame accented by four pearls (1.125" h.), on 18" chain. (For matching earrings, see pg. 76). $48-58.

Left: Oval tiger eye center stone set in goldentone openwork frame and surrounded by six pearls, 1.25" h. $38-48.

GENUINE
TIGER EYE

Sarah Coventry®

Your GENUINE TIGER EYE Jewelry was hand crafted by skilled European Artisans. Tiger eye is a gem that began as a blue asbestos mineral called crocidolite. Through a process of oxidation, the color transforms into golden browns with rippling rays of light following the natural fibers of the stone. Because tiger eye is one of Nature's genuine gems, the color and surface pattern is completely natural and will vary with each stone, making your Sarah Coventry Jewelry selection exclusively yours.

"Inca Fire." Silvertone ornate openwork pendant with variegated red center cabochon, 1.5" sq. $38-48.

Reverse side of pendant showing ornate metalwork design.

"Roman Holiday." Pendant of variegated blue stone set in decorative silvertone openwork frame (1.25" h.), on 24" chain. $38-48.

Above: Goldentone openwork pendant accented by amber and yellow-green stones set in cross-like pattern. $45-55.

Right: "Omega." Openwork goldentone cross shaped pendant with amber prong-set center stone, on 24" chain. $38-45.

Above: "Safari." Round, Aztec style pendant (1.5" dia.) with burgundy center stone, on chain with variegated round and elongated burgundy beads, 30" l. $38-48.

Right: Pendant of richly colored amber faceted stone, set in goldentone frame. $28-35.

Far right: Triple strand necklace of twisted and chain links, with tourmaline faceted rhinestones set in goldentone frames, 53". (For matching earrings, see pg. 77). $40-55.

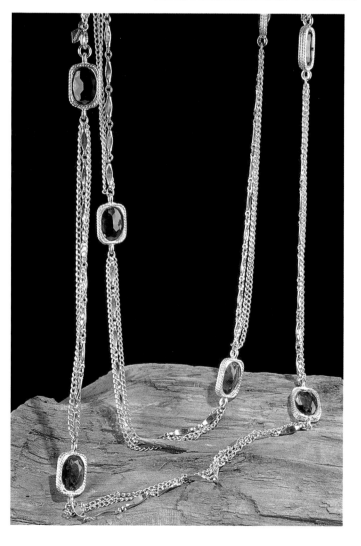

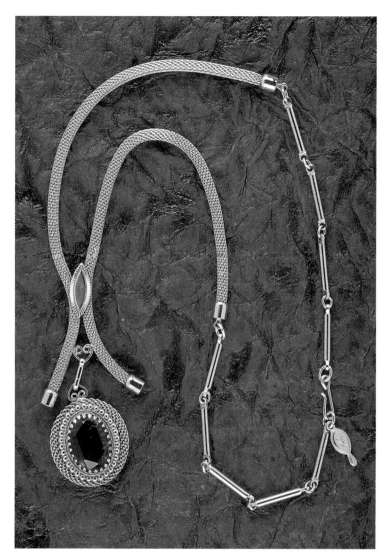

Above: "Golden Rope." Oval pendant of smooth amber stone wrapped in goldentone threads, on 24" chain. $35-45.

Left: "Festive." Oval amber faceted stone prong-set in goldentone frame, rope-like mesh and linked chain, 18" overall. $35-48.

Below: Pendant of large amethyst colored stone prong-set in goldentone frame, accented by clear rhinestones (2.75" h.), on 24" chain. (For matching earrings & bracelet, see pg. 22). $50-75.

Pendant, amethyst faceted center stone prong-set in silvertone modern, geometric frame, 1.5" h. $35-45.

Large charcoal colored faceted stone prong-set in silvertone frame accented by clear and smoky rhinestones. (For matching earrings, see pg. 80, *center pair*; for matching bracelet, see 92). $50-65.

RHINESTONES

"Sarah's quality jewelry knows how to sparkle up your wardrobe in a very special way . . . " (as seen in *Essence Magazine* and *Ebony Fashion Fair* brochure, ©1977, form no. 255).

Six clear rhinestone flower-shaped, backed pendants on 17" chain. $40-45.

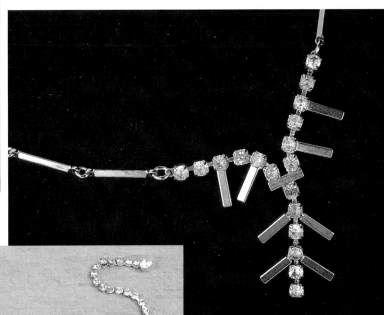

Above: Goldentone bar and round link necklace with clear rhinestones, 18". $38-48.

Left: Necklace of clear and green rhinestones, round and rectangular cuts, set in silvertone frame, 18". (For matching earrings, see pg. 81; for matching bracelet, see pg. 92). $50-75.

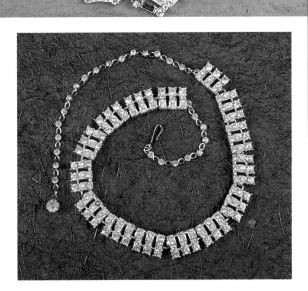

Above: Necklace of clear rhinestones set in leaf-like patterns, silvertone frame, 12.5". (For matching bracelet, see pg. 119). $48-65.

Left: Necklace of clear rhinestones set in silvertone frame, 18" overall. $50-70.

Pins

"This is the year for pins, predicts Sarah Coventry. They take on a host of new roles and positions, perching shoulder high on collarless styles, skipping to the waistline on softly fitted fashions, and dipping to the hip on the new long-jacketed suits."

Annual Review, 1965

LEAVES

Folded leaf of highly goldentone textured surface with clear rhinestones, 3". (For matching earrings, see pg. 77). $30-38.

Two leaves with goldentone textured surfaces and cascading pine needle-like accents, 3" (at longest points). $30-35.

Palm frond with alternating shiny and textured surfaces, 2.25" l. $30-35.

"Autumn Splendor." Pink leaf with goldentone stem and trim, 3" l. $28-32.

Goldentone leaf with veined open-work center and green trimming, 3.5" l. (For matching earrings, see pg. 78). $30-38.

Acorn with textured goldentone cap and leaf and openwork nut, 1.5" h. $25-30.

Pin of goldentone leaves, stem, and petals, with teardrop shaped pearl, 3.625" h. $30-38.

Goldentone textured leaf-like loop with two pearl accents (1"), 3". $25-30.

Left: Leaf-like with white prong-set stone and goldentone beaded and textured blade-like leaves, 4.125" (at longest point). $28-32.

Below: Circular frame of twisted goldentone hoops, garnished by poesy of pearl and jade-colored stone prong-set with goldentone stem and arched leaves, 2" dia. $22-28.

"Pins, again, are the most important accessory, according to Sarah Coventry. They poise on the back shoulder of an open backed dress to spotlight back interest, or are centered in the back on strapless models. Pins add glamour to evening bags, dress up evening gloves, and dramatize pumps. Earrings are long and delicate, with dangles of pearls. Heavy bracelets cover the bare arm."

Annual Review, 1965

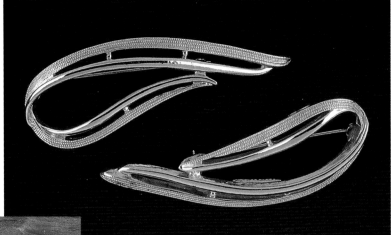

Above: Two silvertone leaf-like loops, 2.625" l. (For matching earrings, see pg. 78). $18-22 each.

Right: Leaf, silvertone stem and frame with ribbed outer edges, 2.25" x 2.75". $22-28.

Below right: Two grape leaves with curled edges, white enamel over goldentone, with grape-like bunches of pale blue cabochons, 2.25" w. $30-35.

Silvertone leaves with jagged edges and openwork centers, 3.25". $22-27.

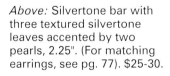

Above: Silvertone bar with three textured silvertone leaves accented by two pearls, 2.25". (For matching earrings, see pg. 77). $25-30.

Right: Two leaves folded and curved with textured surface and small and medium size pearls, 3" l. (For matching earrings, see pg. 77). $28-35.

FLOWERS

Daisy-like flower with pearl center, silvertone stem, textured leaves, and openwork, ribbed petals tipped by clear rhinestones, 2.25" h. (For matching earrings, see pg. 80). $32-40.

Goldentone hoop surrounding flower of openwork looped petals, pearl center, and solid goldentone leaves, 1.5" dia. $18-24.

Flower, openwork leaves and petals of beaded and polished silvertone with solid silvertone stem and faceted black center. (For matching bracelet and earrings, see pg. 109). $32-38.

Above: Flower of white enamel petals and center ball, silvertone textured leaves, and polished stem and stamens, 2.75" h. $30-35.

Right: Flower with white enamel petals, goldentone beaded center, polished stem, and green, veined leaves, 2.75"h. $32-38.

Flower pin with white enamel, textured goldentone center and leaves, and polished stem, 3.75" h. $32-38.

Left: Flowerhead with jagged openwork petals and aurora borealis center stones (3.5" h.). $32-38. *Top:* variegated green cabochons and pearls prong-set in goldentone bouquet with leaves and ribbons (2" dia.). $35-38. *Bottom:* goldentone leaf of textured surface with stem, red bug with raised, painted black spots, and a yellow and a clear rhinestone (2.25" h.). $30-38. *Right:* oversized baroque pearl prong-set in goldentone looped flower-shaped frame (2" dia.). $30-35.

Named after the Northern Lights, "Aurora Borealis" stones present an array of rainbow-like, iridescent colors in a single stone. During the 1950s, these stones originated, reflecting a new look for costume jewelry that diverged from the traditional glass stones of single colors.

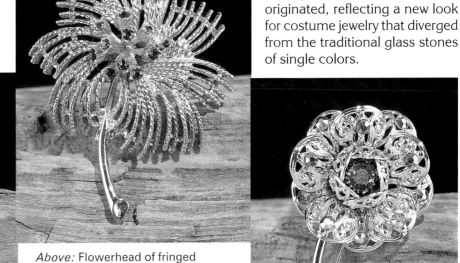

Flower of textured goldentone surface with veined openwork petals, prong-set raspberry center, and surrounding pink and raspberry rhinestones, 3". (For matching earrings, see pg. 80). $30-35.

Above: Flowerhead of fringed twisted goldentone petals, prong-set with red, blue, green, and purple rhinestones, 3" h., 2.25" dia. $38-45.

Right: Filigree flowerhead of openwork goldentone loops accented by aurora borealis stones, with stem and textured goldentone leaves, mounted as pin, 4" h. (For matching earrings, see pg. 80). $45-55.

Flowerhead pin, goldentone textured openwork petals and highly textured, pitted amber center, 2.5" dia. $28-32.

Top left & right: J & K, twig-like design, with leaves. $12-15 each. *Center:* marquise shaped prong-set amber colored rhinestone in flower-like goldentone frame with decorative rows of clear rhinestones and twisted goldentone edging. $40-50. *Bottom left:* poodle, goldentone with painted black eye. $15-22. *Bottom right:* rose flowerhead of goldentone textured petals and leaves. $18-25.

FRUITS

Faceted amber jewel topped by textured goldentone leafy frond, pineapple pin, 2" h. x 1" w. $30-35.

Above: "Touch of Elegance." Three goldentone stem-like loops, with prong-set green faceted "berries," goldentone filigree caps, conjoined by green faceted rhinestone, 3.5" h. $30-35.

Right: Bright pink apple pin with goldentone openwork leaf, stem, and frame, 1.35". $25-38.

Apple pin of interconnected, concentric circles, with textured leaves, and stem, 1.5". Available in silvertone and goldentone. $20-25.

Two cherries pin of textured goldentone with leaves and stem, 2.125" h. Matching earrings also available, but not pictured. $22-30.

Strawberry pin of silvertone textured surface with polished seeds, 2" h. (For matching earrings, see pg. 78). $25-30.

Peach pin of silvertone textured surface, 1.25". $22-28.

BIRDS

Baby birds resting on a branch, variegated blue, coral, and green bodies, textured goldentone heads, wings, and feet, and red rhinestone eyes, .75" h. $15-30 each.

Above right: Owl of textured goldentone with yellow-green eyes, resting on branch, 1.5 h. $22-25.

Right: "Professor." Goldentone owl with red rhinestone eyes and movable glasses, resting on branch, 1.25" h. $22-25.

Left: Owl, textured goldentone frame and body, accented by small seed pearls, and green rhinestone eyes encircled by clear rhinestones, resting on goldentone branch accented by large singular pearl, 1.5" h. $30-38.

BUTTERFLIES

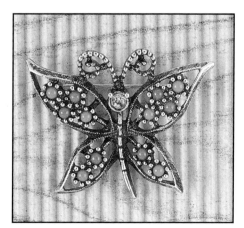

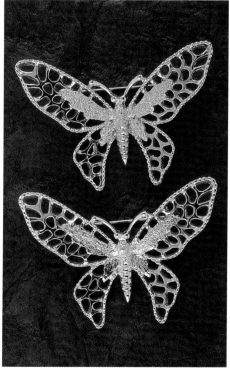

Butterfly pin of goldentone openwork set with green and coral cabochons, 1.5" (wing span). $18-25.

"Madame Butterfly." Openwork butterfly pins of polished and textured goldentone and silvertone surface, 2.5" (wing span). Available in silvertone and goldentone. $18-22 each.

DOGS

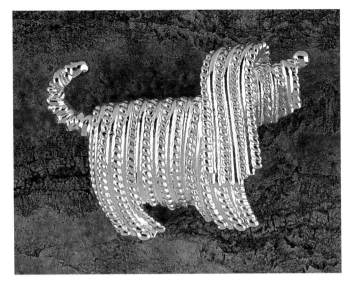

Shaggy dog of twisted silvertone tasseled surface, 1.75" l. $20-25.

Pair of French poodles, textured and polished silvertone surfaces, with faceted blue rhinestone eyes, enameled features (bow, collar, toenails), and heart shaped pendant at neck, 2.25". $30-40 a pair.

OTHER WILDLIFE

Turtle pin, goldentone with brassy amber faceted stone surrounded by frame of twisted goldentone bands, forming turtle's shell; spring clasp enables shell top to open revealing hidden compartment beneath, 1.75". $28-38.

Above:
Top: Goldentone hedgehog with red rhinestone eye. $28-32. *Left:* Angelfish, silvertone frame and faceted purple-iridescent center. $32-38. *Center:* Long-stem rose of goldentone. $18-22. *2nd from right:* Goldentone angel with pearl head and clear rhinestone halo. $20-25. *Right:* Goldentone wishbone holding flower with blue center rhinestone and seed pearls. $20-25. *Bottom left:* Goldentone top hat with clear rhinestones and twisted goldentone cane. $35-40. *Bottom right:* Ladybug, goldentone head, legs, and accents, with red plastic body. $25-30.

Left: Two goldentone openwork zebra pins, 1.25" w. $30-35 a pair.

GEOMETRIC

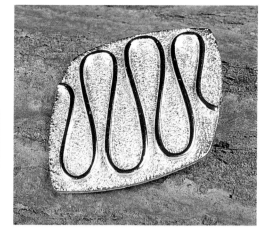

Above: Diamond shaped pin/pendant, silvertone textured surface with raised modern-looking, S-curve design, 2" x 3". *Courtesy of Betty L. Donley.* (For matching earrings & link bracelet, see pg. 114). $25-28.

Left: "Fashion Twist." Silvertone stickpin with wave pendant. $8-12.

Right: Crescent shaped silvertone pin, textured and ribbed openwork, 2.5". $18-24.

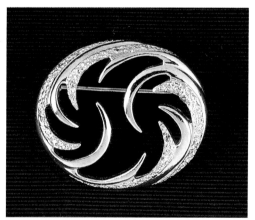

"Carousel." Silvertone oval pin with wave pattern of alternating smooth and textured curves, 1.425" l. $20-25.

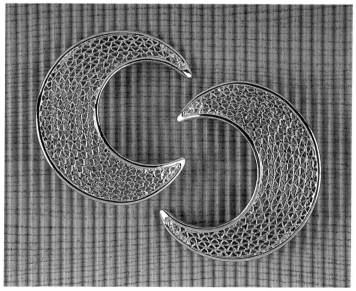

Two identical crescent shaped pins, silvertone with cross-hatched openwork center, 2" h. $15-20 each.

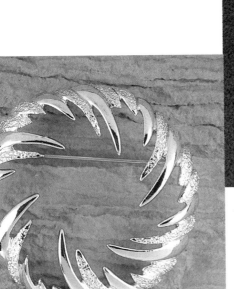

Above: Silvertone circular frame of inter-twined textured and smooth curves, 2.25" dia. $22-27.

Left: Circular frame with wave pattern of alternating polished goldentone and silvertone, textured curves, 1.75" dia. $25-28.

Described in company advertisement, circa 1972, as "spritely . . . treasure from the sea . . . openwork . . . versatile . . go-with-everything."

Silvertone circle pin of filigree scrolls, 1.75" dia. $18-25.

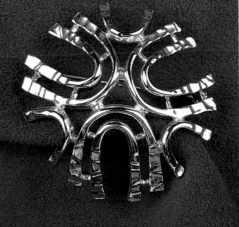

Silvertone circular wreath-like frame of textured roses and leaves, 1" dia. $18-25.

"Sea Sprite." Round openwork goldentone frame of U-shaped curves revolving around an open triangular center, 2" dia. Also available in silvertone, and with matching earrings, not pictured. $18-24.

Flowerhead pin of goldentone and silvertone alternating petal-like waves revolving around a bulbous center, 2" dia. $20-25.

Circular flower-shaped frame of twisted and polished goldentone loops, conjoined by floral and leaf-like embellishments, 1.5" dia. $20-24.

Left: "Antique Scroll Bar." Long, narrow pin with Victorian curved design. $18-25.
Right: "Octagon." Goldentone pin of two interlinking octagonal shapes. $15-22.

Silvertone openwork snowflake pin, 1.5" dia. $18-22.

"Black Magic." Heart shaped pin, goldentone with black center. $12-18.

GEOMETRIC WITH FAUX STONES

"Black Charmer." Triangular pin of silvertone hoops and beaded silvertone circular frames set with black faceted centers, 1.75". $30-35.

Oval silvertone-blue center with rippled surface surrounded by triangular shaped frame of silvertone filigree openwork, 1.75". $35-40.

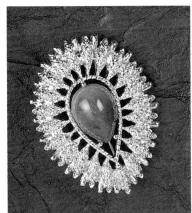

"Granada." Variegated charcoal teardrop shaped center stone prong-set in silvertone fringe-like frame, 2" h. $28-32.

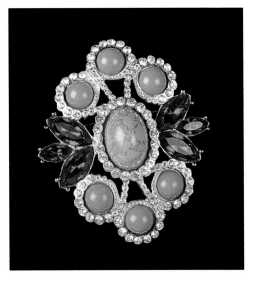

Above: Southwest motif, eyelet shaped turquoise center, seed pearls, and amethyst rhinestones, set in openwork silvertone frame. $30-35.

Left: Goldentone and clear rhinestone circular framework surrounding oversized oval turquoise center cabochon and six round blue cabochons, offset by green marquise shaped rhinestones prong-set in a leaf-like design, 2.5". $40-50.

Square shaped flowerhead pin, petals of intricate silvertone openwork framing blue cabochons, with seed pearl accents, and pearl center mounted in silvertone, 2" sq. $35-40.

Twisted silvertone starfish shaped frame inlaid with various size and shape pale blue rhinestones, 2.25" dia. $35-40.

Geometrically shaped pin of interconnected loops with textured and polished surfaces, and coral center cabochon, 2". (For matching pin & earrings, silvertone with turquoise center, see pg. 111). $22-28.

Criss-cross design of coral cabochons set in goldentone openwork frame, 2.5" l. $22-28.

Pin/pendant of variegated coral center surrounded by goldentone frame, 2" h. $22-30.

Circle pin, wreath-like with five variegated coral cabochons, set in goldentone filigree frames, 1.75". (For matching bracelet, see pg. 91). $25-28.

Left: Circle pin of goldentone interconnected chain links and blue, yellow, orange, and iridescent rhinestones, 1.75" dia. $40-50.

Center left: Round pin of goldentone filigree openwork with center cluster of pearls, pink oval cabochons, and olive marquise shaped rhinestones, 2.75" dia. $32-38.

Center: Openwork circle pin with turquoise opaque and opal faceted cabochons, 1.75" dia. $28-32.

Center right: Round openwork pin of interwoven goldentone vines and textured leaves, inlaid with aurora borealis stones, 2.25" dia. $32-40.

Left: Circle pin, oval olive colored cabochons trimmed by goldentone semi-circular curved framework. $22-25. *Top:* Goldentone openwork wreath-like frame replete with blue cabochons, and pink and blue rhinestones set in a swirling pattern. $30-35. *Bottom:* Goldentone floral frame, highly decorative surrounding amber center stone. $32-38. *Right:* Circle pin, goldentone loop with rose and filigree leaf. $18-22.

Above: Shell shaped pin, oversized (1") pearl with ribbed, arched extensions, 2.75" l. *Courtesy of Betty L. Donley.* (For matching earrings, see pg. 73). $22-27.

Right: "Elegance." Goldentone stickpin with pearl set in beaded goldentone oval frame. $12-18.

RHINESTONES

Circular frame, with a three-leaf or bow-like accent inlaid with clear rhinestones, 1.5" dia. $20-25.

Above: Goldentone snowflake stickpin inlaid with clear rhinestones. $15-20.

Below: Diamond or snowflake shaped pin, clear rhinestones set in silvertone, ornate openwork frame, 2.25" dia. (For matching bracelet, see pg. 92). $35-40.

"Persian Princess." Two diamond-shaped openwork pins, clear rhinestones set in stylized silvertone frames with large center pearl and four seed pearls, 2.5" x 2.75". (For matching earrings, see pg. 80). $32-40 each.

Left: Assorted flowerhead/ snowflake shaped pins lavish with clear rhinestones. 1.75" to 2.75" dia. *Left,* rotating curves of solid goldentone and clear rhinestones. *Center,* faceted green prong-set center stone. *Right,* faceted smoke-colored prong-set center. *Top,* faceted iridescent center rhinestone. L: $28-35; C: 35-45; R: 30-35; T: $30-35; B: 32-38.

Center left: Detail of *center*.

Center: Detail of *right*.

Center right: Detail of *left*.

Left: Daisy-like frame, silvertone leaves and stem iridescent and clear rhinestones. $22-30.
Top: Flower-shaped silvertone frame of stylized arched openwork petals, lavish with small clear rhinestones, gray rhinestone middle accents, and slightly larger clear rhinestone center (for matching earrings, see pg. 80, bottom right). $32-40.
Right: Wreath-shaped circular pin of marquise-shaped rhinestones, interwoven by ribbon-like bands of clear rhinestones (for coordinating earrings, see pg. 81). $35-48.

Clear rhinestones set in silvertone floral openwork bouquet, 2" h. x 1.5" w. $35-40.

Cascade of black marquise shaped stones prong-set with loops and curves, inlaid with clear rhinestones, silvertone frame, 2.75" x 2". (For matching earrings, see pg. 81; for matching bracelet, see pg. 92). $38-48.

Flower shaped pin, silvertone frame of arching petals and dangling leaves set with clear rhinestones, 3.25". $35-48.

Right: Silvertone openwork and clear rhinestone strawberry-shaped pin, topped by silvertone textured leaves, accented by singular pink rhinestone; shown with box and tag. $35-45.

Below left: Silvertone fern-like pin of many leaves inlaid with clear rhinestones, 2.75" l. $28-32.

Below right: Silvertone openwork hummingbird inlaid with iridescent aurora borealis stones, 2.5" l. $32-42.

Earrings

HOOPS

Above: "Showtime." Clip-on wide hoop earrings, classic, tailored look, 1" w. $8-10.

Right: "Trilogy." Two pairs of goldentone pierced earrings, triangle and crescent shaped. $6-8 each.

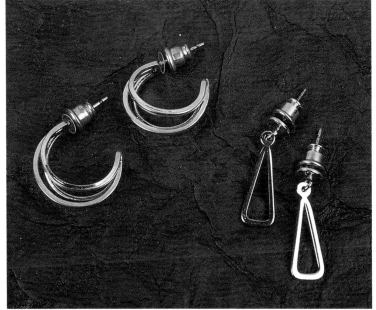

Clip-on many-hooped goldentone earrings, 1" dia. x .25" w. $15-20.

Bright pink and goldentone hoop clip-on earrings with goldentone accents, 2.15" l. $15-20.

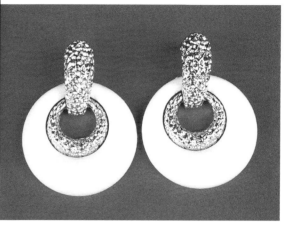

Hoop clip-on earrings of textured silvertone and white plastic hoops. $15-22.

Twisted and plain silvertone hooped pendant clip-on earrings, 1" dia. $12-15.

"Hulabaloo." Goldentone clip-on earrings with circular red, blue, and turquoise spangles, 3" l. Earrings also available with spangles of different colors. $12-16.

DANGLES

"Swing into Summer . . . These striking 'fun 'n fashion' earrings are Sarah's answer to the demand for high-fashion baubles that swing and sway at your ears and give you a feeling of up-to-the-minute fashion" (promotional ad, 1966, form no. 80).

Silvertone pendant clip-on earrings of four intersecting rings, 1.75" (dangling). $15-18.

Goldentone tassel and pearl clip-on earrings, 2" l. $18-22.

"Carnival." Goldentone hoops with dangling red, white, and blue beads. $16-22.

Clip-on silvertone tassel pendant earrings, 2" (dangling). $18-22.

Clip-on silvertone tassel pendant earrings, 2.25" (dangling). $18-22.

Diamond shaped filigree openwork clip-on earrings with goldentone chain-like tassels. $18-22.

Left: Goldentone clip-on earrings of suspended goldentone inter-linked flower. $16-22.

Center: Clip-on earrings, goldentone frame with black center. (For matching ring, see pg. 94). $20-24.

Right: Multicolored mosaic-like oval center surrounded by goldentone frame, clip-on earrings. $16-22.

BUTTON

Above: Goldentone knotted, button clip-on earrings. $8-10.

Below: Round, button clip-on earrings, goldentone framing an orange, yellow, green, and black stitched design. (For matching bracelet, see pg. 84). $12-15.

Round textured clip-on earrings with shooting star design, 1.25" dia. $7-10.

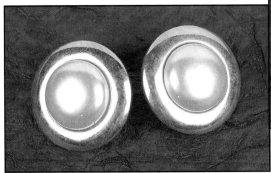

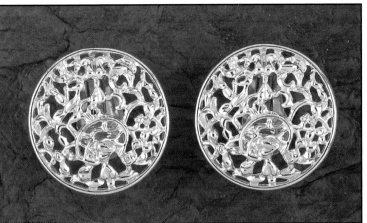

Clip-on button earrings, oversized pearls encircled by goldentone frame. $12-16.

Round silvertone clip-on earrings with intricate openwork designs, 1.25" dia. $18-24.

GEOMETRIC

Crescent shaped goldentone clip-on earrings with center of black enamel, 1". $12-15.

Shell shaped clip-on earrings, oversized pearls mounted in goldentone frame of arched, ribbed extensions. (For matching pin, see pg. 66). $16-22.

Clip-on teardrop shaped earrings, with outer frame and inner surface of textured and polished goldentone with blue, amber, pink, and purple rhinestones, 1". (For matching pendant necklace & coordinating earrings, see pg. 114). $22-28.

Openwork clip-on earrings, goldentone frame with polished and textured intertwining curves, 1.25" h. $25-30.

Filigree layers of goldentone in diamond-like pattern, clip-on earrings, 1.5" h. $20-25.

Clip-on earrings, goldentone frames of polished and textured intertwining loops, 1.5" h. *Courtesy of Betty L. Donley.* (For matching bracelet, see pg. 85). $22-25.

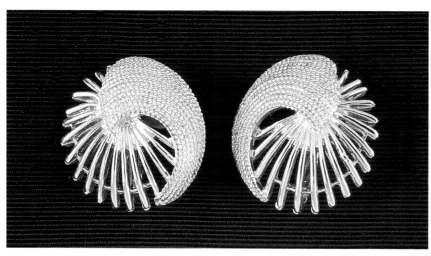

Above: Silvertone clip-on earrings in starburst design, beaded, textured, and ribbed surfaces, 1". $18-24.

Right: Circular, spiraling squares of filigree openwork with center knot, silvertone clip-on earrings, 1.75" dia. $18-24.

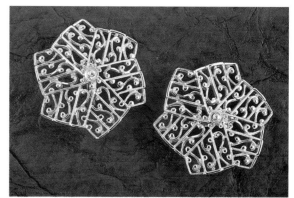

Blue cabochons set in goldentone filigree square frames, clip-on earrings. $18-22.

Above: "Americana." Goldentone embellished frame with red, white and blue cabochons, clip-on earrings. $20-25.

Left: Pierced earrings similar in style and colored cabochons, with slightly different goldentone embellishing. $20-25.

"... inspired by America's own native lore and artistry. Copied after legendary gemstones ... our sun-drenched blue combined with silvertone has an antique, hand-wrought look" (promotional ad, 1973, form no. 215).

Oval variegated turquoise cabochons set in round beaded and textured silvertone clip-on earring frames. (For matching bracelet, see pg. 91). $18-22.

Sarah Coventry jewelry...inspired by America's own native lore and artistry.

Copied after legendary gemstones ... our sun-drenched blue combined with silvertone has an antique, hand-wrought look. Our "Indian Maiden" collection, like all Sarah Coventry jewelry, is available only at Fashion Shows held at home. Private, personal, unhurried. And it's the happiest way to select holiday gifts. If you'd like to attend call your local Sarah representative or send us your name, address, telephone. Sarah Coventry, Inc., Newark 236, New York State 14513.

©1973 Sarah Coventry, Inc.—Canada, Australia, United Kingdom, Belgium • Earrings reg. $7.50, pierced $7; bracelet $10, ring $6, necklace (not shown) $12.

Oval clip-on earrings with purple center jewels mounted in silvertone frames, gothic-like with four pearls. (For matching pendant necklace, see pg. 47). $25-30.

Clip-on earrings of variegated blue cabochons in silvertone frames with leaf-like accents, 1.25". (For matching bracelet, see pg. 91). $20-35.

Baroque pearl center, round tiger eye, rectangular-cut green, and oval variegated pale blue, black, and royal blue cabochons mounted in silvertone frames, 1" dia. $25-30.

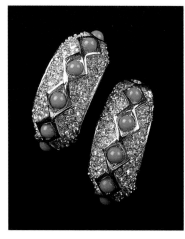

Clip-on hoop earrings, goldentone frame with center row of turquoise cabochons surrounded by clear rhinestones. $38-48.

From top to bottom: Textured goldentone looped frames, leaf-like design. $15-22. Faceted yellow-iridescent jewel center prong-set in twisted goldentone square frames. $25-35. Round goldentone frames with openwork, textured and polished surfaces, and round ball shaped accents. $18-24. Goldentone tea cup (with handle) and saucer design frames with tiger eye jeweled center. $20-25. Opal center stone prong-set in decorative goldentone frames with clear rhinestone accents. $18-24.

Tourmaline faceted rhinestones set in beaded goldentone frame, .75". (For matching necklace, see pg. 48). $30-40.

Pearl, and blue and coral cabochons prong-set in goldentone circular frames with leaf-like embellishments, 1" to 1.5". $25-28.

LEAVES & PLANTS

Clip-on earrings of silvertone leaves and pearls. (For matching pin, see pg. 53). $20-25.

Top: Folded leaf clip-on earrings, goldentone highly textured and clear rhinestones surfaces. (For matching pin, see pg. 51). $22-28. *Bottom:* Two-leaf clip-on earrings, goldentone frames with pearl colored leaf surfaces, 1" to 1.5". $20-25.

Silvertone leaf clip-on earrings, veined, textured leaf surfaces with pearl berries. (For matching pin, see pg. 53). $20-25.

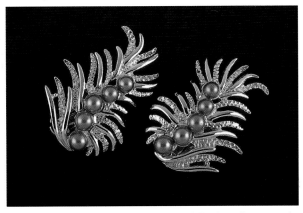

Clip-on earrings, leaf-like, with polished and textured surfaces and five gray center pearls, 1.5" h. $25-30.

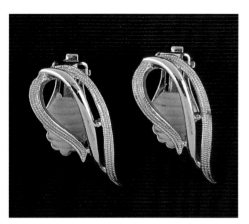

Stylized silvertone leaf-like loops mounted as clip-on earrings, 1". (For matching pin, see pg. 53). $18-22.

Clip-on leaf earrings with prong-set pearl center and veined surface, shown with original box and display card, dated 1960, "Chit-Chat" 7802. Unlike the display card for "Chit-Chat," the back of this card lacks ideas for accessorizing. (For matching pin set with display card, see 21). $22-28.

Leaf shaped clip-on earrings, goldentone with veined surface, goldentone center stalk, and prong-set pearl accent, 1". $22-25.

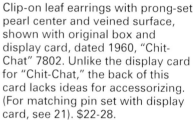

Above: Leaf shaped clip on earrings, goldentone frames with openwork veined centers, and green enamel trimming. (For matching pin, see pg. 51). $22-28.

Left: Strawberry shaped clip-on earrings with textured and polished surfaces, 1". (For matching pin, see pg. 57). $20-27.

Round silvertone clip-on earrings with figural leaf-like openwork, 1.35" dia. $18-24.

Silvertone leaf shaped clip-on earrings prong-set marquise shaped clear rhinestone center, 1" h. (For matching pendant necklace, see pg. 26). $22-28.

FLOWERS

Screw-on pendant earrings, round flowerhead of white cabochons and clear rhinestones centers set in goldentone frame with solid and openwork goldentone leaf embellishments, 1.25" h. $16-22.

Flowerhead clip-on earrings, yellow petals, with goldentone accents and pearl centers. $18-25.

Round clip-on earrings, flower-like, silvertone frames, with opaque black center cabochon. (For matching ring, see pg. 98). $16-22.

Silvertone flowerhead clip-on earrings, with petals of intricate openwork, and smooth, polished center balls, 2" dia. $20-25.

Silvertone openwork frames, flower-shaped, ribbed openwork and clear rhinestone tipped petals, with center pearl. (For matching pin, see pg. 54). $25-30.

Above: Flowerhead frames, filigree openwork with six aurora borealis stones, mounted as clip-on earrings, 1" dia. (For matching pin, see pg. 55). $23-30.

Left: Flower clip-on earrings, with openwork veined petals, raspberry colored center, and surrounding rhinestones, , 1.25" dia. (For matching pin, see pg. 55). $22-28.

RHINESTONES

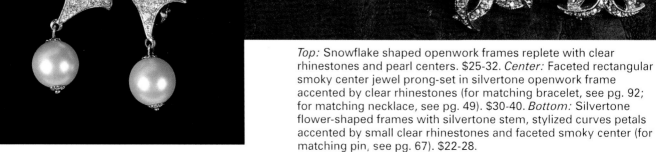

"Persian Princess." Clear rhinestone mounted in silvertone openwork frames with adorning pearls, 2" dangling. (For matching pin, see pg. 66). $25-35.

Top: Snowflake shaped openwork frames replete with clear rhinestones and pearl centers. $25-32. *Center:* Faceted rectangular smoky center jewel prong-set in silvertone openwork frame accented by clear rhinestones (for matching bracelet, see pg. 92; for matching necklace, see pg. 49). $30-40. *Bottom:* Silvertone flower-shaped frames with silvertone stem, stylized curves petals accented by small clear rhinestones and faceted smoky center (for matching pin, see pg. 67). $22-28.

"Midnight Madness." Square smoky, faceted center stone prong-set in black metalwork frame accented by small pink rhinestones, 1.25" x 1". (For matching bracelet & pin, see pg. 118). $40-50.

Winged silvertone frames pave set with aurora borealis rhinestones. $25-30.

Black opaque faceted marquise stones prong-set in silvertone frame, with clear rhinestones in crescent setting. (For matching bracelet, see pg. 92; for matching pin, see pg. 68). $30-40.

Green rectangular and clear rhinestones set in silvertone frames of spiraling geometric shapes, center trio of clear rhinestones. (For matching bracelet, see pg. 92; for matching necklace, see pg. 50). $28-35.

Top: Three round faceted green stones surrounded by clear rhinestones set in heart shaped silvertone frames. $28-32. *Bottom:* Three large marquise clear stones accentuating stylized curved silvertone frames set with clear rhinestones (for coordinating circle pin, see pg. 67, bottom right). $28-35.

Amethyst faceted center jewel surrounded by clear rhinestones set in silvertone frame. $35-45.

Reversible round clip-on earrings, pearls mounted in arched frame, and clear rhinestones set in silvertone frame. (For coordinating strand of pearls with matching reversible clasp, see pg. 43). $30-45.

"Paris." Cascading rows of clear rhinestones, silvertone interconnected and tassel-like frames, 3". $35-42.

Round openwork silvertone hooped frames set with clear rhinestones, in sunburst design, 1.125" dia. $25-28.

Silvertone teardrop frames, diamond-shaped with flower-like openwork, set with clear rhinestones. $22-28.

Iridescent purple faceted stones clutched in silvertone poesy-like frames. $25-32.

Bracelets

CUFFS & BANGLES

Above: Thatched net-like openwork silvertone cuff bracelet, spring clasp, 1" w. $30-38.

Right: Silvertone cuff bracelet with wave designs, spring clasp, 2.75" dia. Available in silvertone and goldentone. $28-38.

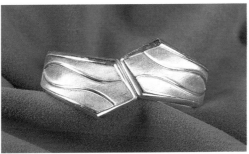

Openwork goldentone cuff bracelet, squiggle patterned design. $25-32.

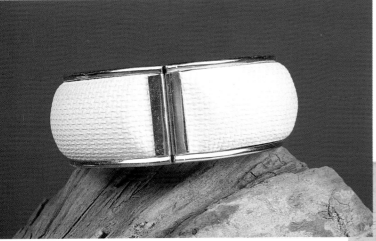

Above: Thick textured white plastic surrounded by goldentone, cuff bracelet with spring clasp. $28-38.

Right: Jade green plastic with center goldentone band, goldentone cuff bracelet with spring clasp. $25-35.

Large cuff bracelet with large faceted green-yellow jewel prong-set in twisted goldentone frame and goldentone band decorated with floral and leaf-like engravings, with two leaf attachments accentuating the center stone. $75-100.

Stitched design of orange, yellow, green, and black threads decorating a goldentone frame bangle. (For matching earrings, see pg. 72). $25-32.

Above: Goldentone cuff bracelet with decorative engraved flourishes, 2.75" dia. $35-45.

Left: Goldentone bangle bracelet of five twisted, beaded, engraved, and smooth hoops banded together, 2.75" dia. $18-25.

Four cuff bracelets: goldentone with engraved floral pattern; silvertone spring clasp with dramatic geometric lines; goldentone with center band of decorative openwork; and silvertone/pewter with triangular goldentone and copper overlaying accents. T: $28-35; L: $20-24; R: $20-28; B: $20-30.

Three cuff bracelets: silvertone bangle with banded etching; opal and garnet-colored stones prong-set in ornate silvertone openwork frame; goldentone banded bangle. Each 2.75" dia. T: $24-28; L: $35-45; R: $24-28.

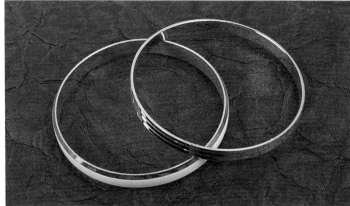

Pair of goldentone bangles: goldentone, and goldentone with center white band, 2.75" dia. $18-25 each.

Trio of three goldentone bangles, each with star engravings. $18-25 each.

LINKS

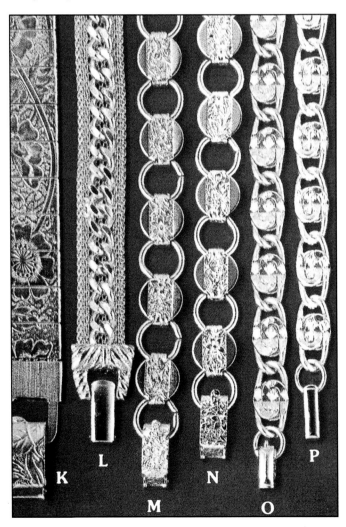

Far left: From Fall/ Winter 1978 company catalog, page 60.

Left: Link bracelet of polished interconnecting leaf-like loops, 7" l. x 2" w. (For matching earrings, see pg. 74). *Courtesy of Betty L. Donley.* $28-35.

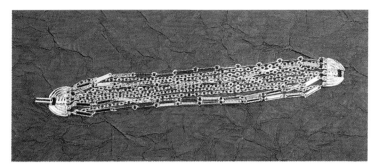

Above: Ten strand goldentone chain link bracelet, 7" l. $22-27.

Right: "Chiffon." Ten strand goldentone chain link bracelet, 7.25". $24-28.

Goldentone link bracelet of the chain link bands and three teardrop shaped spangles, 7.25" l. $22-28.

Wide, flat goldentone bracelet, 7.5" w. (For matching necklace, see pg. 37). $18-22.

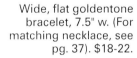

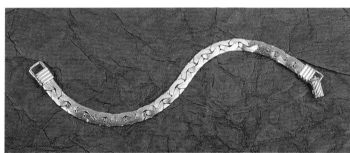

Goldentone bracelet of flat spiral chain links, 7". *Courtesy of Betty L. Donley.* $20-25.

"Young and Gay." Link bracelet of alternating solid and open goldentone loops interconnected by floral etched goldentone bands, 7.5" l. (For matching bracelet & earrings, in silvertone, see pg. 113). $15-22.

Link bracelet of open and solid goldentone loops with raised star design, 7". $28-35.

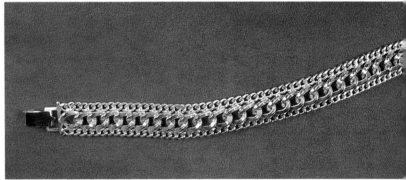

"Classic Elegance." Silvertone chain link bracelet of wide and narrow links, 6.75". $20-25.

From Fall/Winter 1978 company catalog, page 61.

"Counterpoint." Link bracelet of goldentone inter-linking coiled loops, 7.5". $18-22.

Above: Link bracelet of silvertone grape leaves and bunches of grapes, 7.5" l. x 1" w. $28-35.

Left: Link bracelet with grape-vine design, 7.5" l. $25-32.

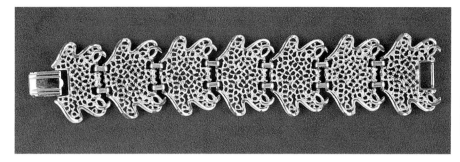

Link bracelet of silvertone openwork leaf-shaped links, 8" l. x 1.5" w. $27-32.

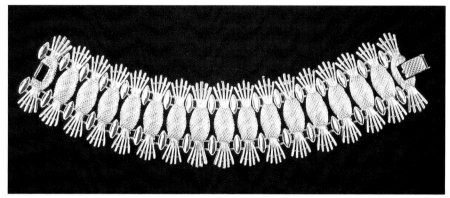

Silvertone link bracelet in pineapple design, 7.5" l. x 1.5" w. $32-38.

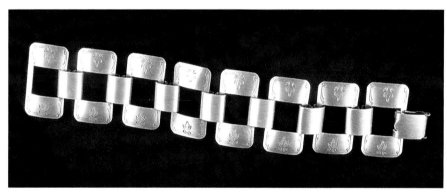

"Melody." Link bracelet of sectioned silvertone rectangles with leaf-like engravings, 1.4" w. x 7.5" l. $30-35.

Silvertone link bracelet of modern, solid and openwork rectangles, 7" l. $32-40.

CHARMS

Silvertone chain link bracelet with silvertone star charm with center turquoise cabochon. $25-30.

Square goldentone calendar charm (1" sq.) accented by rectangular cut red rhinestone, on 7.5" goldentone chain link bracelet. $22-28.

Silvertone chain link bracelet with coin charms, 7". $25-30.

LINKS WITH FAUX STONES

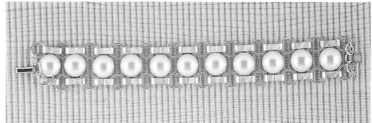

Link bracelet of pearls set in silvertone frame, 7" l. x 1" w. $25-35.

Link bracelet of circular silvertone openwork frames with center of black plastic, 8". $35-40.

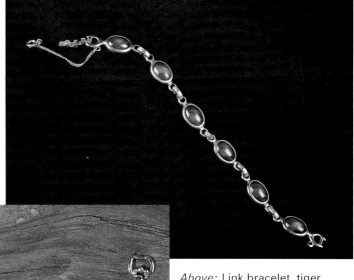

Above: Link bracelet, tiger eye stones in goldentone oval frames, 7.75" l. $20-25.

Left: Link bracelet of opal and iridescent gemstones set in decorative goldentone frames, 7.5" l. $24-32.

Link bracelet of diamond-shaped turquoise, red, green, and black cabochons set silvertone oval frames, 8". $28-32.

Silvertone link bracelet with oval pastel-colored opaque stones in mounted prong settings, 7". $30-40.

Link bracelet of round variegated cabochons of various colors set in swirling beaded silvertone openwork frames, 7" l. x 1.5" w. $32-42.

Above: Large opaque oval stones set in rectangular filigree and openwork silvertone frames, 7.25" . $38-45.

Left: Link bracelet of various colors of variegated cabochons, baroque pearl, and tiger eye stone, in a variety of cuts, set in decorative silvertone openwork and textured frames, 7.5" l. x .75" w. $38-48.

Oval variegated turquoise cabochons set in round beaded and textured silvertone frames, link bracelet, 7". (For matching earrings, see pg. 75). $30-35.

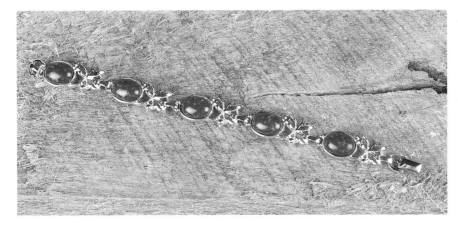

Above: Goldentone link bracelet set with variegated coral cabochons set in goldentone openwork flower-like looped frames, 7". (For matching pin, see pg. 64). $28-35.

Left: Link bracelet of oval variegated blue cabochons set in silvertone frame with leaf-like embellishments, 7" l. (For matching earrings, see pg. 76). $28-38.

Goldentone wide mesh band with goldentone tip, and variegated green oval stone set in beaded goldentone sliding frame, 3" dia. $40-50.

Link bracelets (*top to bottom*): silvertone frame set with pearls and clear rhinestones; goldentone bars and inter-linking loops conjoined by clear rhinestones; brown and orange balls mounted in goldentone curving frame accented by yellow-green rhinestones. 7" l. each. T: $38-45; C: $38-48; B: $32-40.

RHINESTONES

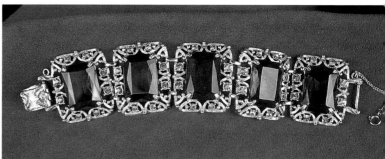

Large faceted rectangular-cut smoky jewels prong-set in silvertone filigree openwork frames replete with clear rhinestones. (For matching earrings, see pg. 80, *center;* for matching necklace, see pg. 49). $40-50.

Clear rhinestones set in silvertone openwork scale shaped linked frame, 7.25" l. (For matching earrings, see pg. 66). $38-48.

Clear rhinestones set in rectangular silvertone frames accented by green rectangular cut gemstones, chain guard, 7". (For matching earrings, see pg. 81; for matching necklace, see pg. 50). $40-50.

Link bracelet, V-shaped silvertone links lined with clear rhinestones. $38-48. Gray rhinestones prong-set in silvertone openwork claw shaped frames. $32-40.

Link bracelet of black marquise shaped stones prong-set in silvertone settings and offset by clear rhinestones set in silvertone crescent shaped frames. (For matching pin, see pg. 68; for matching earrings, see pg. 81). $45-60.

"Night Garden." Silvertone twisted frame with flecked iridescent center stone center, adjustable. $20-25.

Rings

The ring fling. Deliberate lure. From Sarah Coventry.

Wear them in multiples. Bold, beautiful, eye-riveting. The ring thing is all excitement, dramatics and focus on you. Collect them for pure zing. Sarah Coventry is the fine fashion jewelry available only at Fashion Shows held at home. Relaxed, private, time to try on all you wish. If you'd like to attend, call your local Sarah representative or send us your name, address, phone. Sarah Coventry, Inc., Newark 243, New York State 14513.

The ring-fling collection priced $5.00 to $10.00.

Sarah Coventry

Promotional ad, 1973, form no. 213.

Oval shimmery blue center mounted in beaded silvertone frame, adjustable. $20-25.

Silvertone frame with milky faceted center surrounded by filigree openwork trim set with blue rhinestones, adjustable. $22-28.

Sarah Claus

We hate to steal Santa's thunder, but he can't bring you Sarah Coventry jewelry. However, you can play Santa and see beautiful and unusual Christmas gifts for everyone on your list at one of our Jewelry Home Fashion Shows. For information about how to select from our holiday collection send your name, address and phone number to Sarah Coventry Inc., Newark 298, New York State 14593 or call 800-448-7000 toll-free (except in New York, Hawaii & Alaska).

Sarah Coventry
The jewelry with know-how

Promotional ad, as seen in *Women's Day*, 1976, form 245.

Left: "Hidden Rose." Multi-colored, swirled pink center stone mounted in goldentone filigree frame with pearl accents. $25-28.

Below: Iridescent center stone, encircled by goldentone arching trim frame, adjustable. $20-25.

Left: Multicolor center in goldentone frame. $18-25. *2nd:* Black cameo in goldentone frame. $20-25. *3rd:* Goldentone frame, undulating curved surface, with center pearl. $18-22. *Right:* Goldentone frame, flowerhead-like, with prong-set red rhinestones. $20-25.

Cameo ring, black background, ivory profile of a women, and goldentone frame, adjustable. $22-28.

Cameo ring, coral background, ivory profile of women with embellished goldentone frame. $22-28.

Goldentone frame with opaque black center, adjustable. (For matching earrings, see pg. 72). $22-28.

Clockwise from top left:

Goldentone frame with a large white center, encircled by goldentone ring, adjustable. $22-28.

"Seaswept." Green elongated diamond shaped cabochon mounted on triple banded goldentone frame with dramatic lines, adjustable. *Courtesy of Betty L. Donley.* $20-25.

Goldentone beaded frame with variegated green center cabochon, adjustable. $20-25.

Left: Goldentone frame with two concentric, rings, highly textured, encircling two white opaque cabochons. $22-28.
Right: "Genuine Tiger Eye." Tiger eye prong-set in decorative goldentone frame. $20-25.

Goldentone openwork encasement, ruby center, and crowned by clear prong-set rhinestone, adjustable. $22-28.

"Majorca." Goldentone beaded frame with red rhinestone center in prong setting, adjustable. $22-28.

"Tiger's eye, a major jewelry trend of the 1970s."
"The Return of the Ornament: 1965–Present,"
by Vivienne Becker, in *Jewels of Fantasy:
Costume Jewelry of the 20th Century*

Prong-set oval red, tiger eye
like stone, with a goldentone
band. $18-24.

Prong-set oval opal-like stone
in a goldentone band,
adjustable. $20-25.

"Ebb Tide." Silvertone, metallic
colored pearl prong-set in
silvertone filigree, scrolled frame,
adjustable. $22-28.

Silvertone frame with prong-set pale
blue rhinestone, accented by clear
rhinestones, adjustable. $30-40.

"Love Story" birthstone ring. Royal
blue heart shaped rhinestones
mounted in silvertone heart shaped
frames with decorative leaf-like
embellishments, adjustable. $28 35.

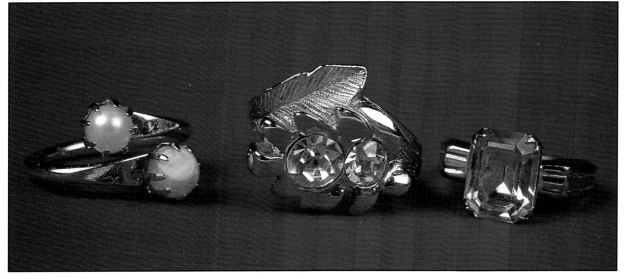

From left: Two pearls prong-set in goldentone frame. $22-25.
Clear rhinestone mounted in goldentone frame with leafy
embellishments. $24-28. Silvertone frame with -prong-set pale
blue square rhinestone. $30-35.

Left: Goldentone frame with embellish looping and prong-set faceted amber stone, adjustable. $25-30.

Center: Silvertone band with pearl in a prong setting. $22-30.

Right: Elongated baroque pearl mounted in embellished beaded goldentone frame, adjustable. $25-30.

Left: Goldentone knotted frame crowned by a single pearl. $24-28.

Center: "Space Age." Wide goldentone band ring topped by large single pearl, adjustable. $24-28.

Right: "Homestead." Pale opaque cabochons mounted goldentone openwork frame of curved design, adjustable. *Courtesy of Betty L. Donley.* $22-28.

From left to right:
"Lovely Lady." Goldentone filigree frame with opaque white oval center. $24-28. "Directions." Goldentone frame with red and green enameled triangular shapes. $20-25. "Annette." Goldentone frame with square-cut tiger eye stone. $22-25. "City Slicker." Goldentone filigree frame with opaque white almond shaped stone. $24-28. Goldentone frame with variegated blue center. $18-22. "Cleopatra." Modern-looking silvertone frame with multicolored center. $25-32.

Turquoise center cabochon mounted in silvertone frame with filigree trim, adjustable. $22-28.

Round, silvertone top in sunburst pattern with opaque black center cabochon, adjustable. (For matching earrings, see pg. 79). $22-28.

"Heritage." Variegated turquoise center mounted in openwork tarnished silvertone filigree frame, adjustable. $22-28.

"My Bouquet." Silvertone ring embellished by flowers, adjustable. $20-25.

Left: Goldentone frame decorated with scroll-like designs, adjustable. $20-25.

Center: Goldentone ring with round face and horizontal parallel design, adjustable. $18-24.

Right: "Silvery Lace." Silvertone filigree band. $20-25.

Left: Goldentone frame decorated with design of inter-linking rings, adjustable. $18-24.

Center: Goldentone basketweave design, adjustable. $20-25.

Right: "Shrimp Design." Goldentone ring with arched top. $18-24.

Left: Prong-set faceted sapphire colored jewel center surrounded by clear prong-set rhinestones, overall flower-like design, with silvertone frame. $28-32.

Center: Faceted sapphire center prong-set and encircled by a wide band of clear prong-set rhinestones, silvertone adjustable band. $30-32.

Right: Silvertone band with smooth sapphire center surrounded by a ring of clear sapphires prong-set in silvertone frame, adjustable. $28-35.

Left: Elegant diamond shaped silvertone frame replete with clear rhinestones. $30-38.

Right: Ring bejeweled by prong-set iridescent and gray rhinestones, silvertone adjustable frame. *Courtesy of Betty L. Donley.* $30-38.

Dazzling Combinations

"Hearts and flowers, either single or in bunches, inspired by reality of stylized, . . . were the favorite subjects of costume jewelry."

"The Luxury of Freedom, the Freedom of Luxury: The United States 1935-1968," by Deanna Farneti Cera, in *Jewels of Fantasy: Costume Jewelry of the 20th Century*

LEAVES & FRUITS

Openwork silvertone leaf pin (3" h.) and matching clip-on earrings (1.5" h.). $45-65 set.

Above & left: Openwork and goldentone textured leaf pin (1.75 h.) with matching clip-on earrings (.75" h.). Also available in silvertone. $48-65 set.

Far left: Maple leaf shaped pin (2.125" h.) with matching clip-on earrings (1" h). $45-65 set.

"Petite." Three-leaf silvertone pin (1.5") and matching clip-on earrings (1"). $35-50 set.

Above: Two-leaf pin with brown, wood-like inlay (2.25") and goldentone accents, and matching clip-on earrings (1.25"). $40-55 set.

Left: Goldentone and silvertone oak leaf pin (2.5" l.) and matching clip-on earrings (1.125"). $48-65 set.

Above: Goldentone and silvertone maple leaf pin (2.75" h.) and matching clip-on earrings (1"). $48-65 set.

Left: Individual jewelry pieces and sets could be worn in a variety of ways and with a variety of fashion ensembles. As seen in *Glamour*, 1963, form no. 93.

Leaf pin (3" l.) of textured surface accented by clear rhinestones, and embellished by amber rhinestones prong-set in goldentone openwork, with matching clip on earrings (1.5" h.). $55-80 set.

...g clip-on earrings (1" h.), with ...set pearls. $40-60 set.

Wreath pin (2" dia.) and matching earrings (1" dia.) of alternating goldentone and silvertone leaves. $40-60 set.

Leaf shaped pin (3.5" l.) and clip-on earrings (1" h.) of textured goldentone cone-shaped leaves. $48-60 set.

In the '70s, "new jewelry design . . . was about freedom and movement, with themes, textures, and shapes that were organic . . . based on nature yet somehow unnatural. [It] began to look like the pocked surface of the moon, like exploding molecular structures, like a bubbling cauldron of molten metal . . . "
"The Return of the Ornament: 1965–Present," by Vivienne Becker, in *Jewels of Fantasy: Costume Jewelry of the 20th Century*

Folded leaf pin of textured surface with coral opaque "berries" (3.5" l.), matching clip-on earrings (1.25" h). $50-65 set.

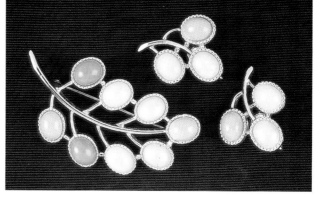

Leaf-like pin (2.5") of goldentone frame with oval pastel cabochon "berries," matching clip-on earrings (1"). $45-58 set.

Above: Link bracelet (7.5" l. x .75" w.) and matching clip-on earrings (1.5") of decorative solid and openwork two-leaf design, silvertone spiral accents. $45-65 set.

Right: Goldentone and silvertone link bracelet (7") and matching clip-on earrings (1") of openwork leaf-like design. $48-68 set.

Bracelet and matching necklace, alternating lengths of leaf-like goldentone extensions with prong-set pearls and clear rhinestones, 17" and 7.5". $150-175 set.

Apple pin/pendant (2.5"), and matching clip-on earrings (1.25"). Available in silvertone and goldentone. $45-60 set.

Pin (2" w.) and matching clip-on earrings (.75" h.), red pitted/modeled centers, and rhinestone accents. $48-65 set.

Apple pin (1.5") and matching clip-on earrings (1.25"), goldentone frames and leaves, with iridescent pearl center. $50-75 set.

Above: Apple pin (1.75" h.) and clip-on earrings (1.25" h.), goldentone frame and leaves with prong-set center baroque pearls. $48-65 set.

Right: Promotional ad, as seen in *Mademoiselle*, 1963, form no. 41.

WILDLIFE

Right: "Woodland Flight." Round silvertone openwork pin with ducks and cattails, and clip-on earrings. $45-65 set.

Far right: Round silvertone openwork pin (2.25" dia.) and matching clip-on earrings (1" dia.), depicting rustic scene of two deer and pine trees. $45-65 set.

FLOWERS

Circle flowerhead goldentone pin (2" dia.) and clip-on earrings (1" dia.). $40-55 set.

Above: Silvertone daisy pin and matching daisy clip-on earrings. $40-55 set.

Right: Floral openwork goldentone pin (1.5" dia.) with matching clip-on earrings (.75" dia.). $45-60 set.

Flowerhead pin (1.25" dia.) and matching clip-on earrings (.75" dia.), decorative goldentone openwork and textured petals. $45-65 set.

Pin/pendant (2.25" dia.) and matching clip-on earrings (.75" dia.), silvertone with pierced floral designs. $40-55 set.

Flower pin (2.75" dia.) with pearl center set in silvertone openwork frames, matching clip-on earrings (1.5" dia.). $45-60 set.

Above: Flowerhead pin (2.25" dia.) and matching clip-on earrings (1" dia.), of alternating white enamel and goldentone petals. $40-55.

Left: Plastic daisy pin (2.25" h.) with goldentone stem and leaves, with matching daisy clip-on earrings (1" dia.). $45-65 set.

Daisy pin (2.5"h.) and matching clip-on earrings (1" dia.), turquoise petals and yellow-green centers set in silvertone frame, pin with silvertone stem and leaves. $50-65 set.

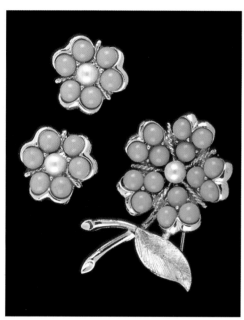

Flower pin (2" h.) and matching clip-on earrings (.5" dia.) with turquoise cabochons and center pearls, goldentone frame and stem with leaf. $50-70 set.

Pink rose clip-on earrings with goldentone backings, matching pin with goldentone stem (2" x 2.25"), pin and earrings have pink center rhinestones. $45-65 set.

Two flower pins (2.75" l.) with matching clip-on earrings (.75" dia.), silvertone frames and petals and turquoise balls/cabochons. $50-68 set.

Flower/leaf shaped openwork pin (2.75" l.) and matching clip-on earrings (.75"), with various colored opaque variegated cabochons, pearl centers, in silvertone frame. $55-70 set.

Flower pin (2.25" h.) and matching clip-on earrings (1" dia.), with green-yellow iridescent center rhinestones and clear rhinestone accented petals, silvertone frame and stem. $65-85 set.

Openwork flowerhead pin (3" h. x 2" dia.) and clip-on earrings (.75" dia.), with pink rhinestones, goldentone frame and stem. $50-75 set.

Right: Link bracelet (7.75" l.) and matching clip-on earrings (1.125"), flowers with black faceted centers and petals of textured silvertone trimmed by openwork loops. (For matching pin, see pg. 54). $45-60 set.

Below: Clip-on earrings and pendant, bud-like with baroque pearls and leafy goldentone petals, on 18" goldentone chain. $48-65 set.

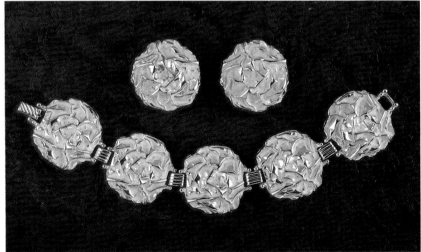

Silvertone link bracelet (7.75" l.) and matching clip-on earrings (1" dia.) of textured, rose-like clusters. $40-60 set.

GEOMETRIC

Circular swirl openwork pin (2.25" dia.) with black center, coordinating earrings (1" h.). $45-60 set.

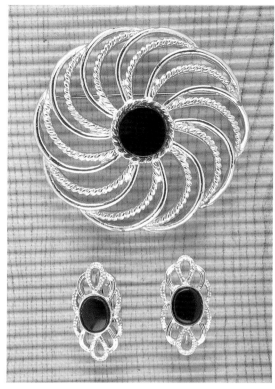

Silvertone openwork pin (2.5" l.) and clip-on earrings (1.5"), shell shaped with textured surface and clear rhinestone center. $48-65 set.

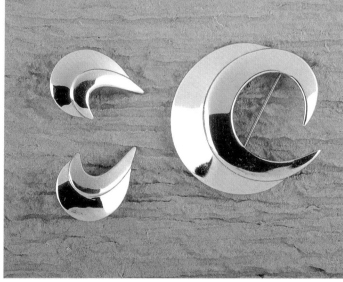

Silvertone crescent shaped pin (1.75" dia.) with matching clip-on earrings (1" dia.). $40-55 set.

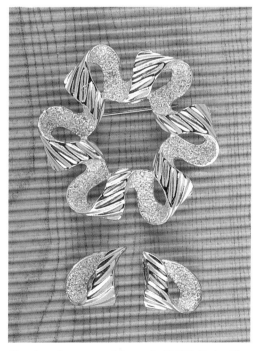

Goldentone and silvertone pin (2" dia.) with matching clip-on earrings (1" dia.) in geometric floral design. $48-68 set.

Circular silvertone ribbon pin (2.25" dia.) with matching clip-on earrings (.75" h.), textured and reticulated surfaces. $45-65 set.

Pin (2") with matching clip-on earrings (1"), silvertone intertwined geometric loops, polished and textured surfaces, with center turquoise cabochon. (For matching pin, goldentone with coral center, see pg. 64). $48-68 set.

Silvertone circle pin (2.75" dia.) and matching clip-on earrings (.75" dia.), flower-like with frame of round loops set with clear rhinestones. $50-70 set.

Round openwork silvertone pin (2" dia.) and matching clip-on earrings (1" dia.), with green, amethyst, magenta, and light blue rhinestones of various sizes and shapes. $60-75 set.

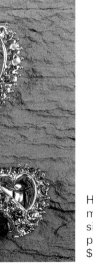

Teardrop shaped pin (2.75" h.) and clip-on earrings (1"), prong-set with marquise and round rhinestones, of iridescent blue, pale blue, and royal blue. $85-100 set.

Heart shaped pin (1.5" h.) and matching clip-on earrings (1" h.), silvertone frame trimmed with prong-set pale blue rhinestones. $45-60 set.

Snowflake shaped pin (1.75" dia.) and clip-on earrings (.75" dia), with center pearls set in goldentone frames with clear rhinestones. $48-65 set.

Circular swirl pin (3" dia.), pearl centers set in silvertone textured frames, and matching clip-on earrings (1" dia.). $42-60 set.

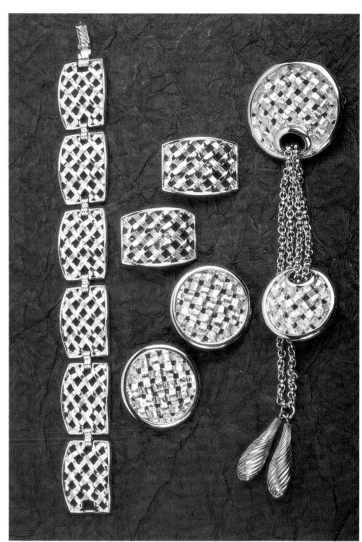

Rectangular thatched openwork goldentone link bracelet (7.25" l.), round and rectangular clip-on earrings (1.25" h.), and pin/necklace set, small- and large-sized pin connected by double stranded goldentone chain accented by two teardrop shaped pendants (1"), chain 12". L: $40-55 set; R: $50-75 set.

This advertisement showcases the variety of fashionable possibilities in which Sarah Coventry's adaptable jewelry sets can be worn. As seen in *Cosmopolitan,* 1963, form no. 80.

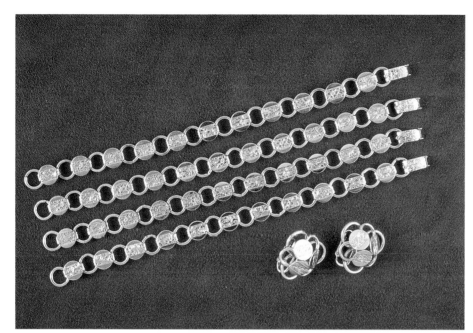

"Young and Gay." Four link bracelets (7.5" l.), with matching button clip-on earrings (1"), of decorative coin-like circles and round loops. Available in goldentone and silvertone. (For matching bracelet, in goldentone, see pg. 86). Bracelets: $15-22 each; earrings: $10-15.

Link bracelet (7.5" l.) and matching clip-on earrings (1" dia.), of conjoining thatched silvertone crescents. $45-65 set.

Link bracelet (7.5" l.), pin (3.5" h.), and clip-on earrings (2.5" h.), silvertone frame set with black cabochons and accented by clear rhinestones, geometric, southwest style. Small silvertone and clear rhinestone "spangles" adorn the pin and earrings. $75-100 set.

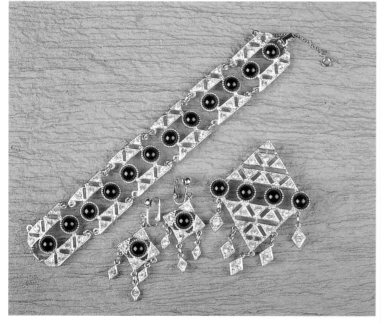

Close-up of pin from set.

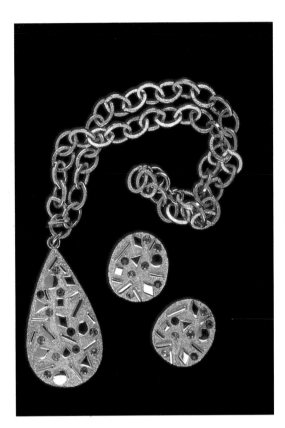

Oversized teardrop shaped pendant (2.5" h.), with coordinating circular clip-on earrings (1" h.), textured and polished goldentone background flecked with blue, amber, pink, and purple rhinestones. (For matching earrings, see pg. 73). $65-85 set.

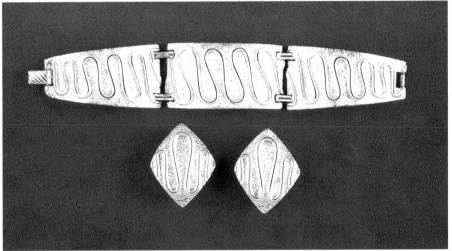

Silvertone link bracelet (7" l. x 1.25" w.) and matching clip-on earrings (1.5" h.) of modern-like S-curve design. (For matching pin, see pg. 60). $50-65 set.

Black and silvertone chain linked necklace (55" l.) and matching clip-on earrings (2.25" l.), tasseled with silvertone caps. $38-58 set.

Mother-of-pearl clip-on spangle earrings, with matching pendant on 18" goldentone cord. $40-60 set.

Highly decorative, beaded silvertone surface embellished by blue cabochons, and clear and amethyst rhinestones, cuff bracelet (2.75" dia.) with fringed clasp, matching adjustable ring (1.15"), hoop earrings, and pin, magic-carpet shape, and trimmed with fringe. $150-200 set.

Link bracelet (7" l.) and matching circular pin (2" dia.), goldentone marquise shaped openwork frame with alternating oval coral and green cabochons prong-set in decorative geometric pattern. $65-85 set.

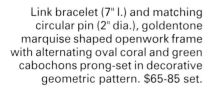

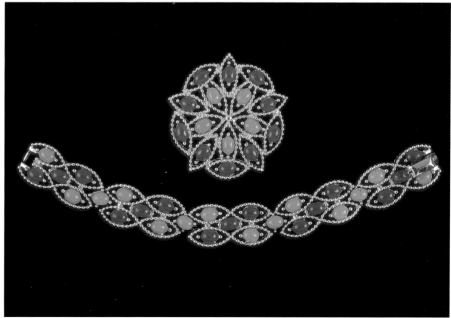

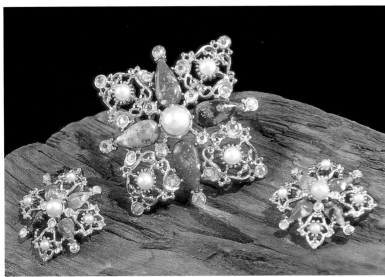

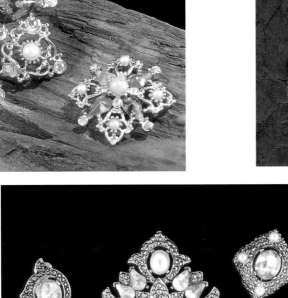

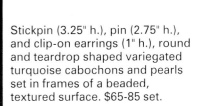

Openwork pendant/pin (2" sq.) and clip-on earrings (1" sq.), teardrop shaped variegated pale and royal blue, green, and coral cabochons, pearl centers, and accenting clear rhinestones set in goldentone frame. $48-65 set.

Pin (2.5" sq.) and matching clip-on earrings (1" sq.), multicolor, olive, and red cabochons set in two-tiered twisted goldentone frames. $48-65 set.

Stickpin (3.25" h.), pin (2.75" h.), and clip-on earrings (1" h.), round and teardrop shaped variegated turquoise cabochons and pearls set in frames of a beaded, textured surface. $65-85 set.

Close-up of earrings from set.

Round pin (1.25" dia.) and matching clip-on earrings (1"), center pearls framed in goldentone, surrounded by inlaid red, and goldentone filigree trimming. $50-70 set.

Pendant (1" h.), and clip-on earrings (1.5" h.), rich ruby colored baguette centers prong-set in twisted goldentone rectangular frames, 19" chain. $50-75 set.

"Carmel Twist." Matching link bracelet (7.5" l.), ring (.75" dia.), and clip-on earrings (.75" dia.), of round iridescent center stones prong-set in twisted silvertone frames. $70-90 set.

Link bracelet, ring (adjustable), pin, and earrings, silvertone decorative and looped frame, center round and variegated turquoise centers, oval shaped with pearl accents (pin with teardrop pendant). $100-150 set.

Blue translucent teardrop shaped pendant (1.25 h.), on 16" to 20" chain, with matching clip-on earrings (1"). $48-68 set.

Clip-on earrings (.75" sq.), link bracelet (7.5" l.), and necklace (18" l.), ivory and gray pearls set in sectioned, openwork rectangle and square goldentone frames. $60-85 set.

Circle pin (2" dia.), link bracelet (7" l.), and clip-on earrings (1.25" h.), silvertone frame with prong-set pearls and blue cabochons, embellished by silvertone, textured leaves. $70-90 set.

"Midnight Madness." Pin (1.75" x 2.5") and matching link bracelet (7.5" l.), antique metalwork, openwork frames with prong-set large faceted smoky center stone and small pink rhinestone accents. (For matching earrings, see pg. 81). $100-135 set.

Rhinestones

Necklace (17.5" l.) and matching bracelet (7.75" l.), conjoining V-shaped silvertone frame with small clear rhinestone accents and prong-set clear rhinestone centers. $100-125 set.

Link bracelet (7.5" l.) and necklace (17" l.), silvertone frame with clear rhinestones in decorative leaf-like designs. (For individual necklace, see pg. 50). $100-135 set.

Necklace and matching link bracelet, faceted smoky rhinestones prong-set in openwork silvertone frame of textured and polished loops and curves. $100-125 set.

Link bracelet (7.5" l.) and matching pin (3.25" h.), silvertone frame in leaf-like pattern inlaid with clear rhinestones, pin flower-like, with large rhinestone center and dangling leafy bough center set in flower/star pattern, with clear rhinestones. $100-120 set.

Dark green faceted center jewel surrounded by clear rhinestone leaves, pin (2" h.), clip-on earrings (1" dia.), and pendant (1.25" h.), on 18" chain. $125-150 set.

Detail of pin.

Necklace (17.5" l.) and matching pin, blue and clear faceted round and marquise shaped rhinestones, with silvertone leaf accents. $95-115 set.

"Glitter Bits." Delicate shell shaped earrings and pendant of bands of clear rhinestones. Note: earrings are marked with R (for right) and L (for left). $50-75 set.

Clip-on flowerhead looped pendant earrings with clear rhinestones (1.25" long), and matching goldentone necklace, 18" l. $85-110 set.

Goldentone necklace and clip-on earrings (1.25" h.) of inter-linking loops and clear rhinestone accents, 18" l. $100-125 set.

Necklace (17") and matching link bracelet (7" l.), silvertone frame with gray oval centers surrounded by clear rhinestones. $85-100 set.

"Peacock." Cuff bracelet (3" dia.) and matching clip-on dangle earrings (2"), alternating bands of blue and green enamel and clear rhinestones. $100-125 set.

Accessories

Watches

Goldentone and silvertone lady's watch with goldentone and silvertone reticulated stretch band, oval face encased by clear rhinestone frame with shell-shaped goldentone and silvertone top and bottom accent. $75-100.

Lady's watch, silvertone stretch band with heart-shaped and scroll-like filigree openwork, oval face encircled by ring of clear rhinestones. $75-100.

Cufflinks

Man's rectangular silvertone cuff links (1") and matching tie clip, textured center band with pale blue center rhinestone encased in diamond-shaped frame (1.5" l.). *Courtesy of Betty L. Donley.* $35-50 set.

Belts

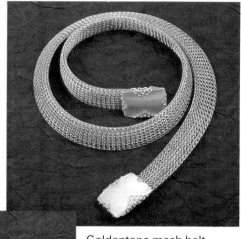

Man's silvertone rectangular cuff links with ribbed end, .75". $15-20.

Goldentone mesh belt (may also double as a purse strap), rectangular mother-of-pearl buckle accents at either end, encased in goldentone filigree meshwork, 38" l. $25-30.

Silvertone meshwork belt, 31.5" l. x 1.5" w. $25-30.

APPENDIX:
Company Catalogs

1976

Fall/Winter 1976 Jewelry Collection

Miss Universe 1975 wearing the official crown created for her by Sarah Coventry.

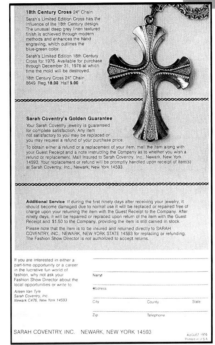

18th Century Cross 24" Chain

Sarah's Limited Edition Cross has the influence of the 18th Century design. The unusual deep grey linen textured finish is achieved through modern methods and enhances the hand engraving, which outlines the blue-green color.

Sarah's Limited Edition 18th Century Cross for 1976. Available for purchase through December 31, 1976 at which time the mold will be destroyed.

18th Century Cross 24" Chain
8649 Reg. **18.00** Half **9.00**

Sarah Coventry's Golden Guarantee

Your Sarah Coventry jewelry is guaranteed for complete satisfaction. Any item not satisfactory to you may be replaced or you may request a refund of your purchase price.

To obtain either a refund or a replacement of your item, mail the item along with your Guest Receipt and a note instructing the Company as to whether you wish a refund or replacement. Mail Insured to Sarah Coventry, Inc., Newark, New York 14593. Your replacement or refund will be promptly handled upon receipt of item(s) at Sarah Coventry, Inc., Newark, New York 14593.

Additional Service If during the first ninety days after receiving your jewelry, it should become damaged due to normal use it will be replaced or repaired free of charge upon your returning the item with the Guest Receipt to the Company. After ninety days, it will be repaired or replaced upon return of the item with the Guest Receipt and $1.50 to the Company, providing the item is still carried in stock.

Please note that the item is to be insured and returned directly to SARAH COVENTRY, INC., NEWARK, NEW YORK STATE 14593 for replacing or refunding. The Fashion Show Director is not authorized to accept returns.

If you are interested in either a part-time opportunity or a career in the lucrative fun world of fashion, why not ask your Fashion Show Director about the local opportunities or write to

Aileen Van Tyle
Sarah Coventry, Inc.
Newark C476, New York 14593

Name

Address

City   County   State

Zip   Telephone

SARAH COVENTRY, INC.   NEWARK, NEW YORK 14593   AUGUST 1976
Printed in U.S.A.

We have chosen the finest designs from our artists' creations to present as our Fall/Winter 1976 Sarah Coventry Collection. All were created for the many sides of your life—the fashionable, the casual, the practical. All bear Sarah's unmistakable touch of quality workmanship. Now, take a few moments to "window shop" through the pages and decide for yourself which pieces will help bring out the best in your wardrobe for the coming season of fashion at its best.

David L. Gibson
President of Sarah Coventry

Sarah's generous hostess plan You receive $1.00 credit* for each guest through nine who buys Sarah Coventry jewelry. You receive $2.00 credit* for the tenth buying guest and for every additional buying guest. You receive an extra $1.00 credit* to help defray cost of money order when your COD order is delivered. You will receive $2.00 credit* for the first booking secured at your show (to be held within 3 weeks). You will receive $3.00 credit* for each additional booking (to be held within 3 weeks). After you have selected your jewelry at full retail you may select 3 items at half the regular price.
*Hostess credit applies to regular priced items.

Hostess bonus plan In addition to your Hostess Credits, you receive a Bonus Point Coupon with your order of $50.00 minimum Star Total. Save these coupons toward Sarah Coventry jewelry or beautiful gift items.

Sarah's 2-and-1 plan You'll save money because for each two items of Sarah Coventry or Lord and Lady Coventry jewelry you purchase at regular price, you may purchase another item at half price.

Single earring replacement If you lose one earring you may purchase a ½ pair for half the current full price, as long as we have the item available. (This cannot be used as full price selection on 2-and-1 plan or any specials.)

Call us toll free For more information about our Hostess Plan call us toll free at (800) 448-7000.

Your Fashion Show Director is authorized to collect full payment.
Copyright Sarah Coventry, Inc. 1976

Newest fashion trends from Sarah

A. 8334
Zulu Choker 16"
Reg. 15.00 Half 7.50

B. 8405
Rajah Necklace 25"
(Removable Drop)
(Handstrung beads imported from Germany)
Reg. 22.00 Half 11.00

Jewelry shown actual size.   3

A. 9416
Triple Bangle Bracelet
(3 Pieces - 1 Goldentone,
1 Silvertone, 1 Copper)
Reg. 10.00 Half 5.00

B. 7423 (Sil.)
Showtime Earrings (Clip)
Reg. 7.50 Half 3.75

C. 7421 (Gol.)
Showtime Earrings (Clip)
Reg. 7.50 Half 3.75

D. 8406
Cinema Pendant 30"
(Removable Drop) Reversible—
Tortoise-Tone/Eggshell
Reg. 17.00 Half 8.50

E. 7401
New Yorker Earrings
Reg. 8.00 Half 4.00

F. 8401
New Yorker Choker 15"
Reg. 12.00 Half 6.00

G. 9369
Atlantis Bracelet
Reg. 10.00 Half 5.00

H. 7369
Atlantis Earrings
Reg. 9.00 Half 4.50

Newest fashion trends from Sarah

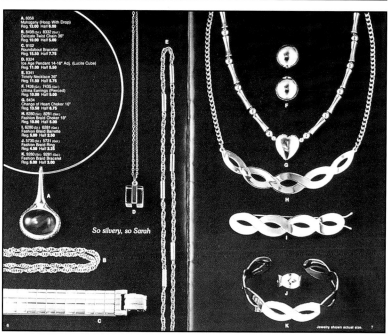

A. 8056
Mahogany (Hoop With Drop)
Reg. 12.00 Half 6.00

B. 8498 (Sil.) 8332 (Gol)
Delicate Twist Chain 36"
Reg. 10.00 Half 5.00

C. 9102
Roundabout Bracelet
Reg. 15.50 Half 7.75

D. 8324
Ice Age Pendant 14-16" Adj. (Lucite Cube)
Reg. 11.00 Half 5.50

E. 8341
Timely Necklace 36"
Reg. 11.50 Half 5.75

F. 7436 (Sil.) 7435 (Gol)
Ultima Earrings (Pierced)
Reg. 10.00 Half 5.00

G. 8434
Change of Heart Choker 16"
Reg. 13.50 Half 6.75

H. 8260 (Sil.) 8261 (Gol.)
Fashion Braid Choker 19"
Reg. 10.00 Half 5.00

I. 6280 (Sil.) 6281 (Gol.)
Fashion Braid Barrette
Reg. 5.00 Half 2.50

J. 5730 (Sil.) 5731 (Gol.)
Fashion Braid Ring
Reg. 4.50 Half 2.25

K. 9260 (Sil.) 9261 (Gol.)
Fashion Braid Bracelet
Reg. 6.00 Half 3.00

So silvery, so Sarah

Jewelry shown actual size.

Fashionably frosted

A. 8326 (Beige/Goldentone)
Fashion Frost Necklace* 36"
Reg. 10.00 Half 5.00

B. 7326 (Beige/Goldentone)
Fashion Frost Earrings
Reg. 6.50 Half 3.25

C. 8327 (Pink/Goldentone)
Fashion Frost Necklace* 36"
Reg. 10.00 Half 5.00

D. 7327 (Pink/Goldentone)
Fashion Frost Earrings
Reg. 6.50 Half 3.25

E. 8328 (Black/Silvertone)
Fashion Frost Necklace* 36"
Reg. 10.00 Half 5.00

F. 7328 (Black/Silvertone)
Fashion Frost Earrings
Reg. 6.50 Half 3.25

G. 8325 (Buck/Silvertone)
Fashion Frost Necklace* 36"
Reg. 10.00 Half 5.00

H. 7325 (Buck/Silvertone)
Fashion Frost Earrings
Reg. 6.50 Half 3.25

I. 8332 (Gol.) 8498 (Sil.)
Delicate Twist Chain 36"
Reg. 10.00 Half 5.00

J. 7393
Double Choice Earrings
(Includes Rose & Eggshell Drops)
Reg. 14.00 Half 7.00

K. 8393
Double Choice Pendant 24"
(Includes Rose & Eggshell Drops)
Reg. 17.00 Half 8.50

*2 separate strands

Jewelry shown actual size.

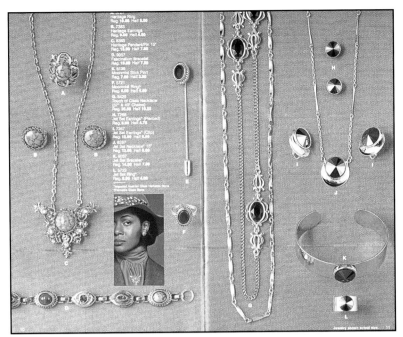

Heirlooms

A. 9837
Roman Holiday Necklace 37"
Reg. 19.00 Half 9.50

B. 6607
Tudor Cross (Drop Only)
Reg. 9.50 Half 4.75

C. 7607
Tudor Earrings (Pierced)
Reg. 9.00 Half 4.50

D. 8343 (Set) 8338 (Dst.)
Antiqued Chain Set
Reg. 6.00 Half 3.00

E. 7646
Button Pearl Earrings (Simulated)
Reg. 4.00 Half 2.00

F. 8672
Tapestry Pendant 22"
Reg. 13.50 Half 6.75

G. 8671
Grecian Pendant/Bracelet 24"
(includes clasp for Bracelet)
Reg. 19.00 Half 9.50

H. 8368
Inca Fire Pendant/Pin 20-22" Adj.
(Versatile Drops)
Reg. 19.50 Half 9.75

I. 7368
Inca Fire Earrings
Reg. 11.00 Half 5.50

J. 9586
Melody Bracelet
Reg. 11.00 Half 5.50

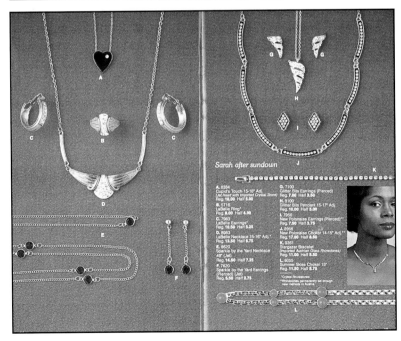

Sarah after sundown

A. 8384
Cupid's Touch 15-16" Adj.
(Jet Heart with Imported Crystal Stone)
Reg. 10.00 Half 5.00

B. 5716
LaBelle Ring*
Reg. 8.00 Half 4.00

C. 7963
LaBelle Earrings*
Reg. 10.50 Half 5.25

D. 8983
LaBelle Necklace 15-16" Adj.*
Reg. 13.50 Half 6.75

E. 8620
Sparkle by the Yard Necklace
49" (Jet)
Reg. 14.50 Half 7.25

F. 7620
Sparkle by the Yard Earrings
(Pierced) (Jet)
Reg. 5.50 Half 2.75

G. 7100
Glitter Bits Earrings (Pierced)
Reg. 7.00 Half 3.50

H. 8100
Glitter Bits Pendant 15-17" Adj.
Reg. 10.00 Half 5.00

I. 7958
New Polonaise Earrings (Pierced)*
Reg. 7.50 Half 3.75

J. 8956
New Polonaise Choker 14-15" Adj.
Reg. 17.00 Half 8.50

K. 9361
Stargazer Bracelet
(Imported Austrian Glass Rhinestones)
Reg. 11.00 Half 5.50

L. 6055
Summer Skies Choker 15"
Reg. 11.50 Half 5.75

*Crystal Rhinestones
*Rhinestones permanently set through
new methods in Austria

The many looks of Sarah

A. 7211
Golden Braids Earrings (Pierced)
Reg **10.00** Half **5.00**

B. 8953
Golden Braids Choker 16"
Reg **12.00** Half **6.00**

C. 8051
Fashion Flair Necklace
17", 24", 30" Strands
(Removable Drop)
Reg **17.50** Half **8.75**

D. 7413
Golden Rope Earrings
Reg **9.00** Half **4.50**

E. 6413
Golden Rope Necklace 24"
Reg **14.50** Half **7.25**

F. 8629 (Gol.) 8628 (Sil.)
Tassel Magic Necklace/Bracelet 30"
Reg **21.50** Half **10.75**

G. 7629 (Gol.) 7628 (Sil.)
Tassel Magic Earrings

Superstars

A. 8594
Moon Beam Pendant 16-18" Adj.
Reg **6.50** Half **3.25**

B. 8734
Moon Luv Choker 14-16" Adj.
Reg **8.50** Half **4.25**

C. 9028 (Gol.) 9029 (Sil.)
Bostonian Classic Bracelet
Reg **7.50** Half **3.75**

D. 8273 (Gol.) 8274 (Sil.)
Bostonian Classic Chain 24"
Reg **14.00** Half **7.00**

E. 8909 (Gol.) 8910 (Sil.)
Embraceable Necklace 16"
Reg **6.50** Half **3.25**

F. 6720
Star Shower Stick Pin Set
Reg **10.00** Half **5.00**

G. 8729 (Gol.) 8528 (Sil.)
Star Shower Choker 14-16" Adj.
Reg **10.00** Half **5.00**

H. 7729 (Gol.) 7528 (Sil.)
Star Shower Earrings (Pierced)
Reg **8.50** Half **4.25**

I. 8652 (Gol.) 8653 (Sil.)
Dainty Lady Chain 14-16" Adj.
Reg **4.00** Half **2.00**

J. 8335
Lucky Lady Necklace 36"
Reg **16.00** Half **8.00**

K. 8262
Jealous Heart Pendant 16-18" Adj.
Reg **7.50** Half **3.75**

L. 8101
Fly Away Necklace 14-16" Adj. (Hand Enameled)
Reg **13.00** Half **6.50**

M. 8249
Fashion Flip Bracelet (Reversible)
Reg **7.00** Half **3.50**

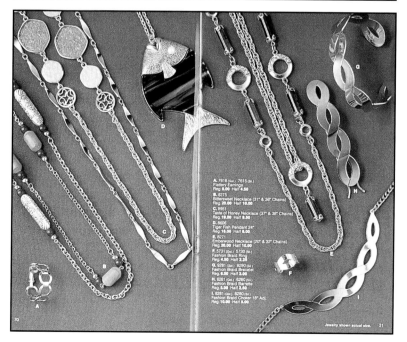

A. 7616 (Gol.) 7615 (Sil.)
Flattery Earrings
Reg **9.00** Half **4.50**

B. 8275
Bittersweet Necklace (31" & 38" Chains)
Reg **20.00** Half **10.00**

C. 8951
Taste of Honey Necklace (37" & 38" Chains)
Reg **19.00** Half **9.50**

D. 8606
Tiger Fish Pendant 24"
Reg **16.00** Half **8.00**

E. 8271
Emberwood Necklace (20" & 32" Chains)
Reg **20.00** Half **10.00**

F. 5731 (Gol.) 5730 (Sil.)
Fashion Braid Ring
Reg **4.50** Half **2.25**

G. 9281 (Gol.) 9290 (Sil.)
Fashion Braid Bracelet
Reg **6.00** Half **3.00**

H. 6281 (Gol.) 6280 (Sil.)
Fashion Braid Barrette
Reg **6.00** Half **3.00**

I. 8281 (Gol.) 8280 (Sil.)
Fashion Braid Choker 16" Adj.
Reg **10.00** Half **5.00**

Jewelry shown actual size.

20   21

When the evening is special

A. 8735
Classic Choice Choker 18"
Reg. 9.00 Half 4.50

B. 7860
Hidden Rose Earrings (Pierced)
Reg. 12.00 Half 6.00

C. 5679
Hidden Rose Ring
Reg. 13.50 Half 6.75

D. 7860
Hidden Rose Earrings
Reg. 17.00 Half 8.50

E. 8866
Hidden Rose Pendant 16-18" Adj.*
Reg. 14.50 Half 7.25

F. 8732
Simply Elegant Chain 18"
Reg. 8.00 Half 4.00

G. 8265
Mirage Choker 18"
Reg. 10.00 Half 5.00

H. 8586
Satin-Glo Necklace 14-16" Adj.
Reg. 8.50 Half 4.25

I. 7586
Satin-Glo Earrings (Pierced)
Reg. 11.00 Half 5.50

J. 7642
Sparkle by the Yard Earrings
(Pierced—Ice)
Reg. 5.50 Half 2.75

K. 8642
Sparkle by the Yard Necklace 49" (Ice)
Reg. 14.50 Half 7.25

*Exclusive Handmade German Glass Stones

22   23   Jewelry shown actual size.

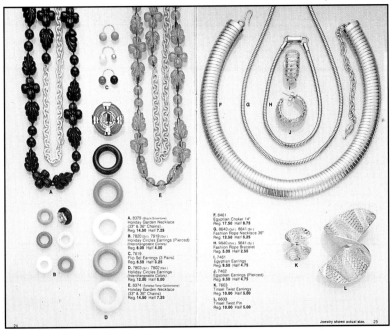

A. 8379 (Black/Silvertone)
Holiday Garden Necklace
(33" & 36" Chains)
Reg. 14.50 Half 7.25

B. 7820 (Sil.) 7819 (Gld.)
Holiday Circles Earrings (Pierced)
(Interchangeable Colors)
Reg. 8.00 Half 4.00

C. 7619
Flip Set Earrings (3 Pairs)
Reg. 6.50 Half 3.25

D. 7803 (Gld.) 7802 (Sil.)
Holiday Circles Earrings
(Interchangeable Colors)
Reg. 12.00 Half 6.00

E. 8374 (Tortoise-Tone/Goldentone)
Holiday Garden Necklace
(33" & 36" Chains)
Reg. 14.50 Half 7.25

F. 8461
Egyptian Choker 14"
Reg. 17.50 Half 8.75

G. 8640 (Gld.) 8641 (Sil.)
Fashion Rope Necklace 36"
Reg. 12.50 Half 6.25

H. 9540 (Gld.) 9541 (Sil.)
Fashion Rope Bracelet
Reg. 5.00 Half 2.50

I. 7461
Egyptian Earrings
Reg. 9.50 Half 4.75

J. 7462
Egyptian Earrings (Pierced)
Reg. 9.50 Half 4.75

K. 7603
Tinsel Twist Earrings
Reg. 10.00 Half 5.00

L. 6603
Tinsel Twist Pin
Reg. 10.00 Half 5.00

24   25   Jewelry shown actual size.

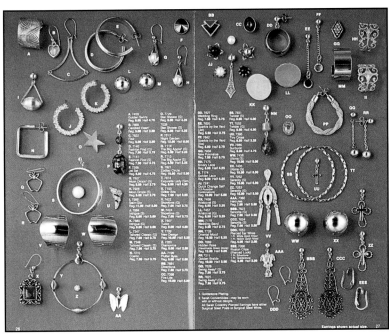

26   27   Earrings shown actual size.

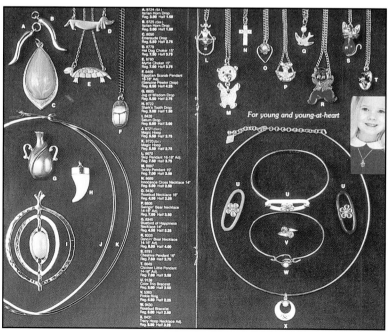

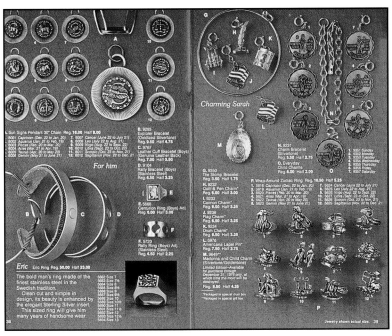

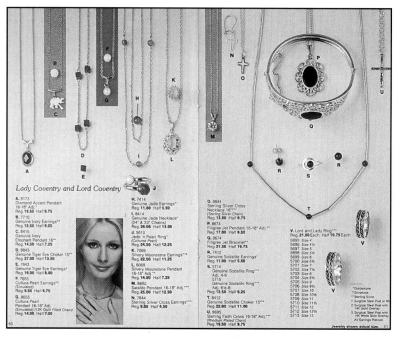

Lady Coventry and Lord Coventry

A. 8173
Diamond Accent Pendant
16-18" Adj.*
Reg **19.50** Half **9.75**

B. 7710
Genuine Ivory Earrings*²
Reg **12.50** Half **6.25**

C. 8415
Genuine Ivory
Elephant Pendant 16"**
Reg **14.50** Half **7.25**

D. 8643
Genuine Tiger Eye Choker 15"*
Reg **27.00** Half **13.50**

E. 7843
Genuine Tiger Eye Earrings¹
Reg **16.00** Half **8.00**

F. 7655
Cultura Pearl Earrings*²
(Simulated)
Reg **9.50** Half **4.75**

G. 8655
Cultura Pearl
Pendant 16-18" Adj.)
(Simulated)(12K Gold Filled Chain)
Reg **14.00** Half **7.00**

H. 7414
Genuine Jada Earrings*¹
Reg **11.00** Half **5.50**

I. 8414
Genuine Jade Necklace*
(24" & 33" Chains)
Reg **26.00** Half **13.00**

J. 5610
Jade 'n Pearl Ring*
(Cultured Pearl)
Reg **24.50** Half **12.25**

K. 7069
Silvery Moonstone Earrings*³
Reg **22.50** Half **11.25**

L. 8068
Silvery Moonstone Pendant
16-18" Adj.*
Reg **14.50** Half **7.25**

M. 8680
Saralite Pendant 16-18" Adj.***
Reg **25.00** Half **12.50**

N. 7844
Sterling Silver Cross Earrings*¹*²
Reg **9.00** Half **4.50**

O. 8844
Sterling Silver Cross
Necklace 16"***
(Sterling Silver Chain)
Reg **13.50** Half **6.75**

P. 8674
Filigree Jet Pendant 16-18" Adj.**
Reg **17.00** Half **8.50**

Q. 9674
Filigree Jet Bracelet**
Reg **21.50** Half **10.75**

R. 7412
Genuine Sodalite Earrings¹
Reg **11.00** Half **5.50**

S. 5714
Genuine Sodalite Ring***
Adj. 4-6
5715
Genuine Sodalite Ring***
Adj. 6½-8
Reg **12.50** Half **6.25**

T. 8412
Genuine Sodalite Choker 15"***
Reg **22.00** Half **11.00**

U. 8695
Sterling Faith Cross 16-18" Adj.***
(Rhodium Plated Chain)
Reg **19.50** Half **9.75**

V. Lord and Lady Ring***
Reg **21.50** Each Half **10.75** Each

5695	Size 4
5696	Size 4½
5697	Size 5
5698	Size 5½
5699	Size 6
5700	Size 6½
5701	Size 7
5702	Size 7½
5703	Size 8
5704	Size 8½
5705	Size 9
5706	Size 9½
5707	Size 10
5708	Size 10½
5709	Size 11
5710	Size 11½
5711	Size 12
5712	Size 12½
5713	Size 13

*Goldentone
**Silvertone
***Sterling Silver.
1 Surgical Steel Post or Wire
2 Surgical Steel Post with 14K Gold Overlay
3 Surgical Steel Post with 14K White Gold Overlay.
All Earrings Pierced.

Jewelry shown actual size.

40   41

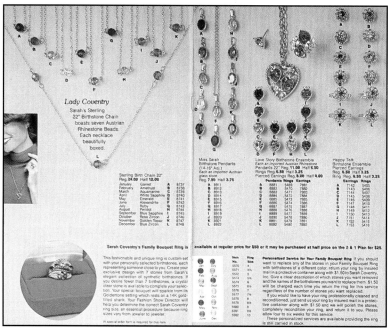

Lady Coventry

Sarah's Sterling 22" Birthstone Chain boasts seven Austrian Rhinestone Beads. Each necklace beautifully boxed.

Sterling Birth Chain 22"
Reg **24.00** Half **12.00**

January	Garnet	A	8737
February	Amethyst	B	8738
March	Aquamarine	C	8739
April	White Sapphire	D	8740
May	Emerald	E	8741
June	Alexandrite	F	8742
July	Ruby	G	8743
August	Peridot	H	8744
September	Blue Sapphire	I	8745
October	Rose Zircon	J	8746
November	Golden Topaz	K	8747
December	Blue Zircon	L	8748

Miss Sarah
Birthstone Pendants
(14-16" Adj.)
Each an imported Austrian glass stone.
Reg **7.50** Half **3.75**

Love Story Birthstone Ensemble
Each an imported Austrian Rhinestone
Pendants 22" Reg **11.00** Half **5.50**
Rings Reg **6.50** Half **3.25**
Pierced Earrings Reg **8.00** Half **4.00**

	Pendants	Rings	Earrings
A	8881	5469	7881
B	8882	5470	7882
C	8883	5471	7883
D	8884	5472	7884
E	8885	5473	7885
F	8886	5474	7886
G	8887	5475	7887
H	8888	5476	7888
I	8889	5477	7889
J	8890	5478	7890
K	8891	5479	7891
L	8892	5480	7892

Happy Talk
Birthstone Ensemble
Pierced Earrings
Reg **6.50** Half **3.25**
Ring Reg **6.50** Half **3.25**

	Earrings	Rings
A	7142	5405
B	7143	5406
C	7144	5407
D	7145	5408
E	7146	5409
F	7147	5410
G	7148	5411
H	7149	5412
I	7150	5413
J	7151	5414
K	7152	5415
L	7153	5416

Sarah Coventry's Family Bouquet Ring is available at regular price for $50 or it may be purchased at half price on the 2 & 1 Plan for $25.

This fashionable and unique ring is custom set with your personally selected birthstones, each representing someone close to you. Create your exclusive design with 7 stones from Sarah's elegant collection of synthetic birthstones. If you desire fewer than 7 birthstones, a crystal clear stone is available to complete your selection. Your special bouquet will sparkle from its Goldentone setting which rests on a 14K gold-filled shank. Your Fashion Show Director will help you determine the correct Sarah Coventry ring size, an essential procedure because ring sizes vary from jeweler to jeweler.

(A special order form is required for this item)

Item No.	Ring Size
5570	4
5571	4½
5572	5
5573	5½
5574	6
5575	6½
5576	7
5577	7½
5578	8
5579	8½
5580	9
5581	9½
5582	10

Personalized Service for Your Family Bouquet Ring if you should want to replace any of the stones in your Family Bouquet Ring with birthstones of a different color, return your ring by insured mail in a protective container along with $1.50 to Sarah Coventry, Inc. Give a clear description of which stones you want removed and the names of the birthstones you want to replace them. $1.50 will be charged each time you return the ring for this service regardless of the number of stones you want replaced.

If you would like to have your ring professionally cleaned and reconditioned, just send us your ring by insured mail in a protective container along with $1.50 and we will polish the stones, completely recondition your ring, and return it to you. Please allow four to six weeks for this service.

These personalized services are available providing the ring is still carried in stock.

A. 8683 (Gol.) 8682 (Sil.)
Fantastic Chain 50"
Reg **9.00** Half **4.50**

B. 8687
Lavender 'n Lace Necklace 54"
Reg **14.00** Half **7.00**

C. 7367
French Scroll Earrings
Reg **11.50** Half **5.75**

D. 8336 (Gol.) 8343 (Sil.)
Antiqued Chain 24"
Reg **6.00** Half **3.00**

E. 6936
Contessa Pin
(Attachment to allow wearing as Pendant)
Reg **16.00** Half **8.00**

F. 9987
Goldenrod Bracelet
Reg **16.00** Half **8.00**

G. 7997
Goldenrod Earrings
Reg **6.00** Half **3.00**

H. 8595
Outer Space Pendant 20-22" Adj.
Reg **8.50** Half **4.25**

I. 7996 (Gol.) 7998 (Sil.)
Satin Buttons Earrings
Reg **9.00** Half **4.50**

J. 8250
Duchess Necklace 24"
Reg **16.00** Half **8.00**

K. 7250
Duchess Earrings
Reg **9.50** Half **4.75**

'Round the clock with Sarah

Jewelry shown actual size.

44   45

So versatile, so Sarah

A. 7686
Sunburst Earrings (Pierced)
Reg. 9.50 Half 4.75

B. 8698
Sunburst Pendant/Pin 27"
Reg. 16.00 Half 8.00

C. 9686
Sunburst Bracelet
Reg. 14.50 Half 7.25

D. 6933
Sunburst Pin
Reg. 9.00 Half 4.50

E. 7933
Sunburst Earrings
Reg. 8.50 Half 4.25

F. 8678 (bx.) 9677 (St.)
Allure Choker
Reg. 6.00 Half 3.00

G. 7728
Golden Ice Earrings
Reg. 6.00 Half 3.00

H. 8728
Golden Ice Necklace 19"
Reg. 20.50 Half 10.25

I. 9728
Golden Ice Bracelet
(Can be attached to Necklace)
Reg. 13.00 Half 6.50

Jewelry shown actual size.

Stylish Sarah

A. 8111
Victorian Bouquet Pendant
16-18" Adj.
Reg. 7.50 Half 3.75

B. 8941
Alfa Beads Choker 14-16" Adj.
(Shades may vary)
Reg. 9.50 Half 4.75

C. 8265
Beau-Time Choker 16" Adj.
Reg. 17.00 Half 8.50

D. 8872
Golden Teardrop Hoop Necklace
Reg. 7.50 Half 3.75

E. 7716 (bx.) 7717 (St.)
Matchmaker Earrings
Reg. 7.50 Half 3.75

F. 8688
Candied Heart Choker 16"
Reg. 11.50 Half 5.75

G. 7686
Candied Heart Earrings (Pierced)
Reg. 5.00 Half 2.50

H. 7726
Oriental Mood Earrings (Pierced)
Reg. 10.50 Half 5.25

I. 9726
Oriental Mood Bracelet
Reg. 10.00 Half 5.00

J. 8726
Oriental Mood Choker 16"
Reg. 15.50 Half 7.75

Liberty Williams, starring in Walt Disney's movie "Gus"

Jewelry shown actual size.

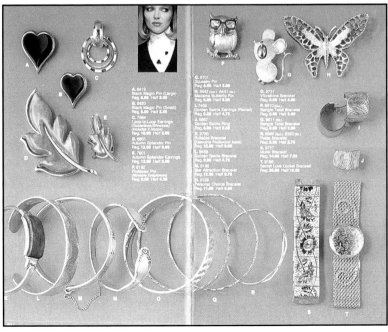

A. 6419
Black Magic Pin (Large)
Reg. 6.00 Half 3.00

B. 6420
Black Magic Pin (Small)
Reg. 5.00 Half 2.50

C. 7584
Loop-la-Loop Earrings
(Goldtone/Silvertone)
(includes 3 Holes)
Reg. 10.00 Half 5.00

D. 6601
Autumn Splendor Pin
Reg. 12.00 Half 6.00

E. 7801
Autumn Splendor Earrings
Reg. 12.00 Half 6.00

F. 6192
Professor Pin
Reg. 9.50 Half 4.75

G. 8701
Squeaky Pin
Reg. 6.00 Half 3.00

H. 6442 (bx.) 6441 (St.)
Madame Butterfly Pin
Reg. 9.50 Half 4.75

I. 7459
Golden Swirls Earrings (Pierced)
Reg. 9.50 Half 4.75

J. 5867
Golden Swirls Ring
Reg. 6.00 Half 3.00

K. 9730
Suitable Bracelet
(Genuine Fruitwood Inlaid)
Reg. 13.00 Half 6.50

L. 9458
Golden Swirls Bracelet
Reg. 9.50 Half 4.75

M. 9190
Star Attraction Bracelet
Reg. 13.50 Half 6.75

N. 9129
Personal Choice Bracelet
Reg. 11.00 Half 5.50

O. 9731
Vibrations Bracelet
Reg. 9.00 Half 4.50

P. 9510 (bx.)
Bangle Twist Bracelet
Reg. 6.00 Half 3.00

Q. 9511 (St.)
Bangle Twist Bracelet
Reg. 8.50 Half 4.25

R. 9262 (bx.) 9263 (St.)
Petite Bracelet
Reg. 5.50 Half 2.75

S. 9772
Mesh Bracelet
Reg. 14.50 Half 7.25

T. 9186
Secret Love Locket Bracelet
Reg. 30.00 Half 15.00

Timeless beauty

A. 8118
Patrician Necklace 30"
Reg.10.98 Half 5.25

B. 9359
Snowdrop Necklace 18"
Reg.6.98 Half 3.00

C. 7614
Exquisite Lady Earrings (Pierced)
Reg.8.98 Half 4.25

D. 8292
Sabrina Necklace (19" & 34" Chains)
Reg.14.98 Half 7.00

E. 5389
First Love Necklace 54"
Reg.12.98 Half 6.00

F. 8048
Memories Locket Pendant 18-20" Adj.
Reg.13.98 Half 6.75

G. 7612
Exquisite Lady Earrings
Reg.11.98 Half 5.00

H. 8612
Exquisite Lady Necklace 36"
Reg.14.98 Half 7.00

All Pearls Simulated

Jewelry shown actual size.

58   59

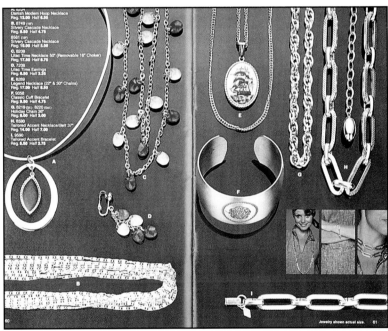

A. 8274
Danish Modern Hoop Necklace
Reg.13.00 Half 6.50

B. 8749 (18")
Silvery Cascade Necklace
Reg.9.50 Half 4.75

8581 (18")
Silvery Cascade Necklace
Reg.10.00 Half 5.00

C. 8208
Lilac Time Necklace 50" (Removable 16" Choker)
Reg.17.50 Half 8.75

D. 7208
Lilac Time Earrings
Reg.6.50 Half 3.25

E. 8269
Legend Necklace (22" & 30" Chains)
Reg.17.00 Half 8.50

F. 9358
Classic Cuff Bracelet
Reg.9.50 Half 4.75

G. 8219 (Sil.) 8220 (Gol.)
Holiday Chain 36"
Reg.6.00 Half 3.00

H. 5500
Tailored Accent Necklace/Belt 37"
Reg.14.00 Half 7.00

I. 9590
Tailored Accent Bracelet
Reg.5.50 Half 2.75

Jewelry shown actual size.

60   61

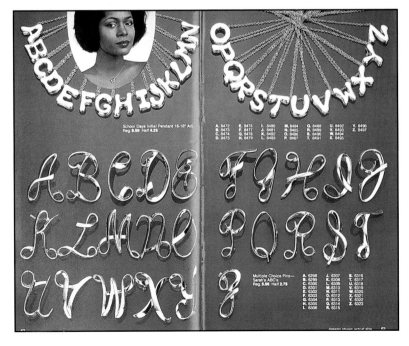

School Days Initial Pendant 16-18" Adj.
Reg.8.50 Half 4.25

A. 8472   E. 8476   I. 8480   M. 8484   Q. 8488   U. 8492   Y. 8496
B. 8473   F. 8477   J. 8481   N. 8485   R. 8489   V. 8493   Z. 8497
C. 8474   G. 8478   K. 8482   O. 8486   S. 8490   W. 8494
D. 8475   H. 8479   L. 8483   P. 8487   T. 8491   X. 8495

Multiple Choice Pins—
Sarah's ABC's
Reg.5.50 Half 2.75

A. 6298   J. 6307   S. 6316
B. 6299   K. 6308   T. 6317
C. 6300   L. 6309   U. 6318
D. 6301   M. 6310   V. 6319
E. 6302   N. 6311   W. 6320
F. 6303   O. 6312   X. 6321
G. 6304   P. 6313   Y. 6322
H. 6305   Q. 6314   Z. 6323
I. 6306   R. 6315

Jewelry shown actual size.

1978

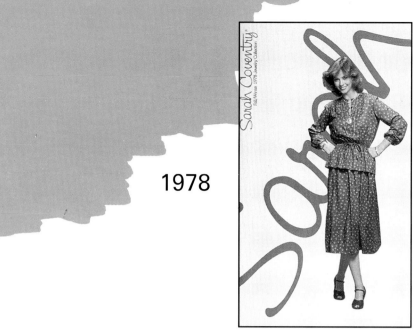

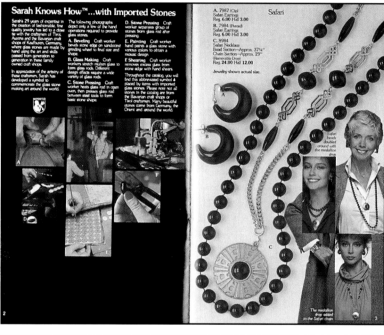

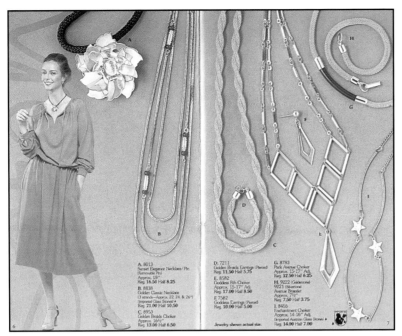

A. 8013
Sunset Elegance Necklace/Pin
(Removable Pin)
Approx. 19"
Reg. 16.50 Half 8.25

B. 8838
Golden Classic Necklace
(3 strands—Approx. 22, 24, & 26")
(Imported Glass Stones)
Reg. 21.00 Half 10.50

C. 8953
Golden Braids Choker
Approx. 16½"
Reg. 13.00 Half 6.50

D. 7211
Golden Braids Earrings (Pierced)
Reg. 11.50 Half 5.75

E. 8582
Goddess Bib Choker
Approx. 15-17" Adj.
Reg. 17.00 Half 8.50

F. 7582
Goddess Earrings (Pierced)
Reg. 10.00 Half 5.00

G. 8783
Park Avenue Choker
Approx. 15-17" Adj.
Reg. 12.50 Half 6.25

H. 9222 (Goldentone)
9221 (Silvertone)
Avenue Bracelet
Approx. 7½"
Reg. 7.50 Half 3.75

I. 8456
Enchantment Choker
Approx. 14-16" Adj.
(Imported Austrian Glass Stones)
Reg. 14.00 Half 7.00

Jewelry shown actual size.

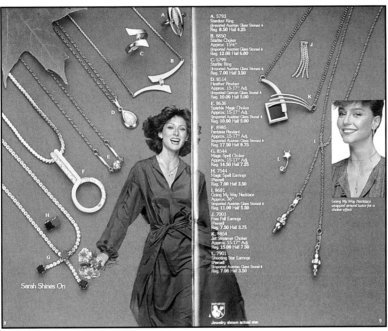

Sarah Shines On

A. 5793
Stardust Ring
(Imported Austrian Glass Stones)
Reg. 8.50 Half 4.25

B. 8850
Starlite Choker
Approx. 15¼"
(Imported Austrian Glass Stones)
Reg. 12.00 Half 6.00

C. 5799
Starlite Ring
(Imported Austrian Glass Stones)
Reg. 7.00 Half 3.50

D. 8514
Heather Pendant
Approx. 15-17" Adj.
(Imported German Glass Stone)
Reg. 10.00 Half 5.00

E. 8636
Sparkle Magic Choker
Approx. 15-17" Adj.
(Imported German Glass Stone)
Reg. 10.00 Half 5.00

F. 8985
Fantasia Pendant
Approx. 15-17" Adj.
(Imported Austrian Glass Stones)
Reg. 17.50 Half 8.75

G. 8544
Magic Spell Choker
Approx. 15-17" Adj.
Reg. 14.50 Half 7.25

H. 7544
Magic Spell Earrings
(Pierced)
Reg. 7.00 Half 3.50

I. 8681
Going My Way Necklace
Approx. 36"
(Imported Austrian Glass Stone)
Reg. 11.00 Half 5.50

J. 7003
Free Fall Earrings
(Pierced)
Reg. 7.50 Half 3.75

K. 8854
Jet Streamer Choker
Approx. 15-17" Adj.
Reg. 15.00 Half 7.50

L. 7901
Shooting Star Earrings
(Pierced)
(Imported Austrian Glass Stone)
Reg. 7.00 Half 3.50

Going My Way Necklace wrapped around twice for a choker effect.

Jewelry shown actual size.

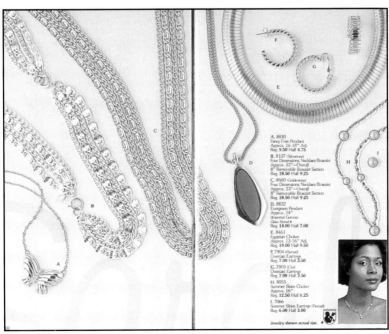

A. 8830
Fancy Free Pendant
Approx. 16-18" Adj.
Reg. 9.50 Half 4.75

B. 8107 (Silvertone)
Four Dimensions Necklace/Bracelet
Approx. 33"—Overall
8" Removable Bracelet Section
Reg. 18.50 Half 9.25

C. 8660 (Goldentone)
Four Dimensions Necklace/Bracelet
Approx. 33"—Overall
8" Removable Bracelet Section
Reg. 18.50 Half 9.25

D. 8832
Evergreen Pendant
Approx. 24"
(Imported German Glass Stone)
Reg. 14.00 Half 7.00

E. 8461
Egyptian Choker
Approx. 13-16" Adj.
Reg. 19.00 Half 9.50

F. 7904 (Pierced)
Overcast Earrings
Reg. 7.00 Half 3.50

G. 7903 (Clip)
Overcast Earrings
Reg. 7.00 Half 3.50

H. 8055
Summer Skies Choker
Approx. 16"
Reg. 12.50 Half 6.25

I. 7066
Summer Skies Earrings (Pierced)
Reg. 6.00 Half 3.00

Jewelry shown actual size.

Swarib 1978 Limited Edition
Mythology Cross

A. 8906
Gracious Lady Pendant
Approx. 20-24" Adj.
Imported German Stones
Reg. 15.50 Half 7.75

B. 8517
Silhouette Perfume Pendant
Approx. 24"
Reg. 20.00 Half 10.00

C. 8448
Omega Pendant
Approx. 24"
Imported Austrian
Glass Stones
Reg. 14.00 Half 7.00

D. 8692
Calvary Cross Pendant
Approx. 16-18" Adj.
Reg. 9.00 Half 4.50

E. 7417
Free Style Earrings
(Pierced)
Reg. 7.50 Half 3.75

E. 8699
Solitude Cross Pendant
Approx. 16½-18½" Adj.
Imported Austrian
Glass Stones
Reg. 8.00 Half 4.00

G. 9986
Delightful Bracelet
Approx. 7½"
Reg. 5.00 Half 2.50

H. 8108 (Goldentone)
Serenity Cross
Pendant
Approx. 16-18" Adj.
Reg. 11.00 Half 5.50

I. 8109 (Silvertone)
Serenity Cross Pendant
Approx. 16-18" Adj.
Reg. 11.00 Half 5.50

J. 8506
Mythology Cross
Limited Edition)
Approx. 24" Chain
Reg. 21.00 Half 10.50

Mythology
Cross
Limited Edition

Jewelry shown actual size.

12   13

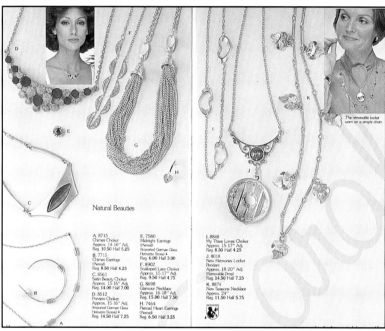

Natural Beauties

A. 8715
Chimes Choker
Approx. 14-16" Adj.
Reg. 10.50 Half 5.25

B. 7715
Chimes Earrings
(Pierced)
Reg. 8.50 Half 4.25

C. 8561
Satin Beauty Choker
Approx. 15-16" Adj.
Reg. 14.00 Half 7.00

D. 8512
Preview Choker
Approx. 15-16" Adj.
Imported German Glass
Hematite Stones
Reg. 14.50 Half 7.25

E. 7580
Midnight Earrings
(Pierced)
Imported German Glass
Hematite Stones
Reg. 6.00 Half 3.00

F. 8902
Scalloped Lace Choker
Approx. 15-17" Adj.
Reg. 9.50 Half 4.75

G. 8698
Glamour Necklace
Approx. 16-18" Adj.
Reg. 15.00 Half 7.50

H. 7464
Pierced Heart Earrings
(Pierced)
Reg. 6.50 Half 3.25

I. 8848
My Three Loves Choker
Approx. 15-17" Adj.
Reg. 8.50 Half 4.25

J. 8018
New Memories Locket
Pendant
Approx. 18-20" Adj.
(Removable Drop)
Reg. 14.50 Half 7.25

K. 8874
New Seasons Necklace
Approx. 24"
Reg. 11.50 Half 5.75

The removable locket
worn on a simple chain.

IMPORTED

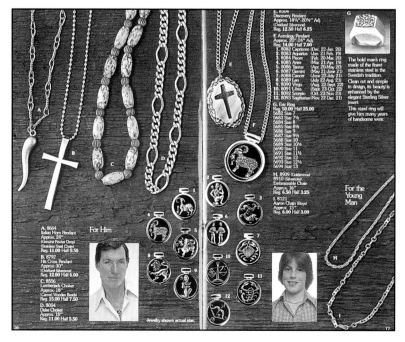

A. 8664
Italian Horn Pendant
Approx. 24"
(Genuine Pewter Drop)
(Stainless Steel Chain)
Reg. 11.00 Half 5.50

B. 8792
His Cross Pendant
Approx. 30"
(Oxidized Silvertone)
Reg. 12.00 Half 6.00

C. 8556
Lumberjack Choker
Approx. 18"
(Carved Wooden Beads)
Reg. 15.00 Half 7.50

D. 8054
Duke Choker
Approx. 18"
Reg. 11.00 Half 5.50

For Him

E. 8044
Discovery Pendant
Approx. 18¼-20¾" Adj.
(Oxidized Silvertone)
Reg. 12.50 Half 6.25

F. Astrology Pendant
Approx. 20-24" Adj.
Reg. 14.00 Half 7.00

1. 8082 Capricorn (Dec. 22-Jan. 20)
2. 8083 Aquarius (Jan. 21-Feb. 19)
3. 8084 Pisces (Feb. 20-Mar. 20)
4. 8085 Aries (Mar. 21-Apr. 19)
5. 8086 Taurus (Apr. 20-May 20)
6. 8087 Gemini (May 21-June 21)
7. 8088 Cancer (June 22-July 21)
8. 8089 Leo (July 22-Aug. 21)
9. 8090 Virgo (Aug. 22-Sept. 22)
10. 8091 Libra (Sept. 23-Oct. 22)
11. 8092 Scorpio (Oct. 23-Nov. 21)
12. 8093 Sagittarius (Nov. 22-Dec. 21)

G. Eric Ring
Reg. 50.00 Half 25.00
5682 Size 7
5683 Size 7½
5684 Size 8
5685 Size 8½
5686 Size 9
5687 Size 9½
5688 Size 10
5689 Size 10½
5690 Size 11
5691 Size 11½
5692 Size 12
5693 Size 12½
5694 Size 13

The bold man's ring
made of the finest
stainless steel in the
Swedish tradition.
Clean cut and simple
in design, its beauty is
enhanced by the
elegant Sterling Silver
insert.
This sized ring will
give him many years
of handsome wear.

H. 8909 (Goldentone)
8910 (Silvertone)
Embraceable Chain
Approx. 16"
Reg. 6.50 Half 3.25

I. 8121
Aaron Chain (Boys)
Approx. 15"
Reg. 6.00 Half 3.00

For the
Young
Man

For Him

Jewelry shown actual size.

16   17

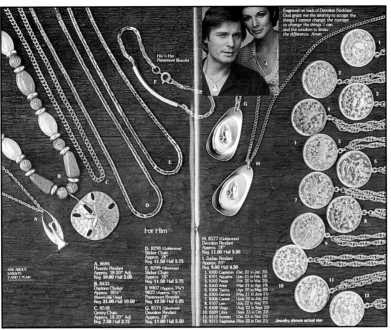

Engraved on back of Devotion Necklace: *God grant me the serenity to accept the things I cannot change, the courage to change the things I can, and the wisdom to know the difference. Amen*

For Him

ASK ABOUT
SARAH'S
2 AND 1 PLAN

A. 8694
Phoenix Pendant
Approx. 18-20" Adj.
Reg. **10.00** Half **5.00**

B. 8433
Daytona Choker
Approx. 18½"
Removable Drop!
Reg. **21.00** Half **10.50**

C. 8518
Gentry Chain
Approx. 18-20" Adj.
Reg. **7.50** Half **3.75**

D. 8298 (Goldentone)
Slicker Chain
Approx. 18"
Reg. **11.50** Half **5.75**

E. 8299 (Silvertone)
Slicker Chain
Approx. 18"
Reg. **11.50** Half **5.75**

F. 9907 (Approx. 7¼") 9827 (Approx. 7½")
Paramount Bracelet
Reg. **12.50** Half **6.25**

G. 8574 (Silvertone)
Devotion Pendant
Approx. 18"
Reg. **11.00** Half **5.50**

H. 8577 (Goldentone)
Devotion Pendant
Approx. 18"
Reg. **11.00** Half **5.50**

I. Zodiac Pendant
Approx. 20"
Reg. **9.00** Half **4.50**

1. 8300 Capricorn (Dec. 22 to Jan. 20)
2. 8301 Aquarius (Jan. 21 to Feb. 19)
3. 8302 Pisces (Feb. 20 to Mar. 20)
4. 8303 Aries (Mar. 21 to Apr. 19)
5. 8304 Taurus (Apr. 20 to May 20)
6. 8305 Gemini (May 21 to June 21)
7. 8306 Cancer (June 22 to July 21)
8. 8307 Leo (July 22 to Aug. 21)
9. 8308 Virgo (Aug. 22 to Sept. 22)
10. 8309 Libra (Sept. 23 to Oct. 22)
11. 8310 Scorpio (Oct. 23 to Nov. 21)
12. 8311 Sagittarius (Nov. 22 to Dec. 21)

Jewelry shown actual size.

For Little Sarah... and Her Teen Years

A. 8119
Frolic Pendant
Approx. 15"
Reg. **6.50** Half **3.25**

B. 8430
Rosebud Pendant
Approx. 16
Reg. **4.50** Half **2.25**

C. 6431
Tracy Barrette
Reg. **5.50** Half **2.75**

D. 5383
Pinkie Ring
Imported Austrian
Glass Stones♦
Reg. **4.50** Half **2.25**

E. 8533
Starlet Choker
Approx. 13-15" Adj.
Reg. **5.50** Half **2.75**

F. 8571
Sarah Ann Pendant
Approx. 14"
Reg. **6.00** Half **3.00**

G. 8345
Bluebird of Happiness
Pendant
Approx. 14"
Reg. **5.00** Half **2.50**

H. 8689
Innocence Cross Pendant
Approx. 14"
Reg. **5.00** Half **2.50**

J. 7375
Beachcomber Earrings
(Pierced)
Reg. **5.50** Half **2.75**

J. 7019
Luv Lee Earrings
(Pierced)
Reg. **5.50** Half **2.75**

K. 7777
Twinkle Earrings
(Pierced)
Reg. **5.50** Half **2.75**

L. 7713
Miss Anne Earrings
(Pierced)
Reg. **4.00** Half **2.00**

M. 8579
Pretty Portrait Pendant
Approx. 14-16" Adj.
Reg. **7.50** Half **3.75**

N. 8318
Young Love Choker
Approx. 15"
Reg. **6.50** Half **3.25**

O. 7318
Young Love Earrings
(Pierced)
Reg. **5.50** Half **2.75**

P. 8653 (Silvertone)
8652 (Goldentone)
Dainty Lady Chain
Approx. 14-16" Adj.
Reg. **4.50** Half **2.25**

Q. 8576
Jamie Choker
Approx. 16½"
Reg. **7.00** Half **3.50**

R. 9430
Rosebud Bracelet
Approx. 6"
Reg. **5.00** Half **2.50**

S. 9558
Little Bugger Bracelet
Adj.
Reg. **6.00** Half **3.00**

T. 9363 (Silvertone)
Petite Bracelet Adj.
Reg. **5.50** Half **2.75**

U. 9362 (Goldentone)
Petite Bracelet Adj.
Reg. **5.50** Half **2.75**

V. 9223
Sweet Hearts Bracelet
Adj.
Reg. **4.50** Half **2.25**

W. 8443
Stone Age Choker
Approx. 16½"
Reg. **6.00** Half **3.00**

Around The Clock With Sarah

A. 5650
Lovely Lady Ring
Imported German
Glass Stone♦
Reg. **9.00** Half **4.50**

B. 8266
Lovely Lady Choker
Approx. 15-17" Adj.
Imported German
Glass Stone♦
Reg. **13.00** Half **6.50**

C. 8778
Four Seasons Necklace
Approx. 54"
Reg. **13.00** Half **6.50**

D. 7255
Filigree Hoop Earrings
(Pierced)
Reg. **8.00** Half **4.00**

E. 8693
On Time Pendant
Approx. 24"
Reg. **13.00** Half **6.50**

F. 8317
Rose-Marie Pendant
Approx. 20-24" Adj.
Imported Glass
Stone♦
Reg. **14.50** Half **7.25**

G. 8501
Exclusive Pendant
Imported Stone
from Germany♦
Approx. 16-18" Adj.
Reg. **11.00** Half **5.50**

H. 5783
Exclusive Ring
Imported Stone
from Germany♦
Reg. **8.00** Half **4.00**

I. 8536
Center Attraction Pendant
(Reversible &
Removable Drop)
Approx. 24"
Reg. **11.00** Half **5.50**

Center Attraction Pendant with removable and reversible squares

Jewelry shown actual size.

22 23

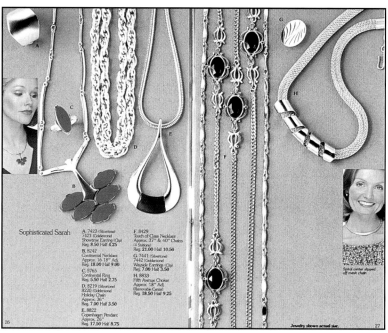

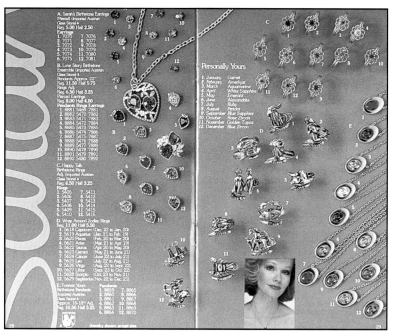

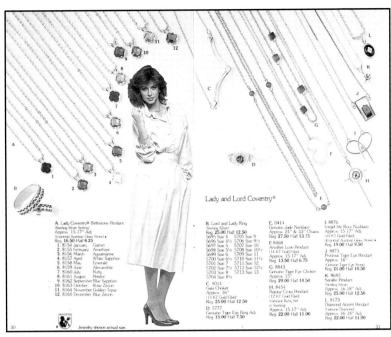

Lady and Lord Coventry®

A. Lady Coventry® Birthstone Pendant
(Sterling Silver Setting)
Approx. 15-17" Adj.
(Imported Austrian Glass Stone) ▲
Reg. 16.50 Half 8.25
1. 8154 January   Garnet
2. 8155 February   Amethyst
3. 8156 March   Aquamarine
4. 8157 April   White Sapphire
5. 8158 May   Emerald
6. 8159 June   Alexandrite
7. 8160 July   Ruby
8. 8161 August   Peridot
9. 8162 September Blue Sapphire
10. 8163 October   Rose Zircon
11. 8164 November Golden Topaz
12. 8165 December Blue Zircon

B. Lord and Lady Ring
(Sterling Silver)
Approx. 25.00 Half 12.50
5695 Size 4   5705 Size 9
5696 Size 4½   5706 Size 9½
5697 Size 5   5707 Size 10
5698 Size 5½   5708 Size 10½
5699 Size 6   5709 Size 11
5700 Size 6½   5710 Size 11½
5701 Size 7   5711 Size 12
5702 Size 7½   5712 Size 12½
5703 Size 8   5713 Size 13
5704 Size 8½

C. 8014
Gala Choker
Approx. 16"
(14 KT Gold Filled)
Reg. 25.00 Half 12.50

D. 5777
Genuine Tiger Eye Ring Adj.
Reg. 15.00 Half 7.50

E. 0414
Genuine Jade Necklace
(Sterling Silver), 24" & 33" Chains
Reg. 27.50 Half 13.75

F. 8468
Another Love Pendant
(14 KT Gold Filled)
Approx. 15-17" Adj.
Reg. 13.50 Half 6.75

G. 8843
Genuine Tiger Eye Choker
Approx. 15"
Reg. 29.00 Half 14.50

H. 8454
Rejoice Cross Pendant
(12 KT Gold Filled)
(Genuine Ruby Set in Sterling)
Approx. 15-17" Adj.
Reg. 22.00 Half 11.00

I. 8876
Forget Me Knot Necklace
Approx. 15-17" Adj.
(14 KT Gold Filled)
(Imported Autumn Glass Stone) ▲
Reg. 19.00 Half 9.50

J. 8873
Precious Tiger Eye Pendant
Approx. 16"
(Genuine Tiger Eye Stone)
Reg. 21.00 Half 10.50

K. 8680
Sarahlie Pendant
(Sterling Silver)
Approx. 16-18" Adj.
Reg. 25.00 Half 12.50

L. 8173
Diamond Accent Pendant
(Genuine Diamond)
Approx. 16-18" Adj.
Reg. 22.00 Half 11.00

30   31
Jewelry shown actual size.

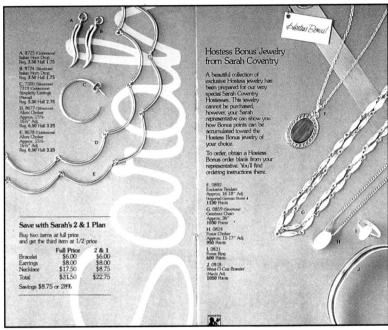

A. 8725 (Goldentone)
Italian Horn Drop
Reg. 3.50 Half 1.75

B. 8724 (Silvertone)
Italian Horn Drop
Reg. 3.50 Half 1.75

C. 7320 (Silvertone)
7319 (Goldentone)
Simplicity Earrings
(Pierced)
Reg. 5.50 Half 2.75

D. 8677 (Silvertone)
Allure Choker
Approx. 15½-16½" Adj.
Reg. 6.50 Half 3.25

E. 8678 (Goldentone)
Allure Choker
Approx. 15½-16½" Adj.
Reg. 6.50 Half 3.25

Save with Sarah's 2 & 1 Plan

Buy two items at full price
and get the third item at 1/2 price.

	Full Price	2 & 1
Bracelet	$6.00	$6.00
Earrings	$8.00	$8.00
Necklace	$17.50	$8.75
Total	$31.50	$22.75

Savings $8.75 or 28%

Hostess Bonus!

Hostess Bonus Jewelry from Sarah Coventry

A beautiful collection of exclusive Hostess jewelry has been prepared for our very special Sarah Coventry Hostesses. This jewelry cannot be purchased, however, your Sarah representative can show you how Bonus points can be accumulated toward the Hostess Bonus jewelry of your choice.

To order, obtain a Hostess Bonus order blank from your representative. You'll find ordering instructions there.

F. 0892
Exclusive Pendant
Approx. 16-18" Adj.
(Imported German Stone) ▲
1150 Points

G. 0859 (Silvertone)
Getabout Chain
Approx. 36"
1050 Points

H. 0824
Focus Choker
Approx. 15-17" Adj.
950 Points

I. 0831
Focus Ring
600 Points

J. 0818
Wrist-O-Cral Bracelet
(Mesh Adj.)
1050 Points

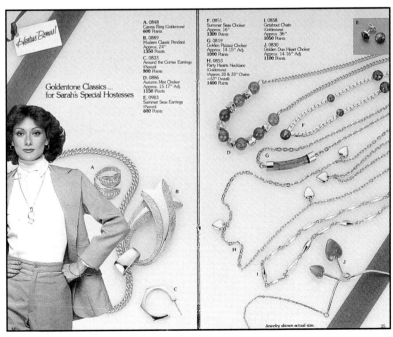

Hostess Bonus!

Goldentone Classics... for Sarah's Special Hostesses

A. 0848
Caress Ring (Goldentone)
600 Points

B. 0889
Modern Classic Pendant
Approx. 24"
1350 Points

C. 0833
Around the Corner Earrings
(Pierced)
800 Points

D. 0886
Autumn Mist Choker
Approx. 15-17" Adj.
1150 Points

E. 0983
Summer Seas Earrings
(Pierced)
600 Points

F. 0851
Summer Seas Choker
Approx. 16"
1300 Points

G. 0819
Golden Pizzaz Choker
Approx. 14-15" Adj.
1000 Points

H. 0853
Party Hearts Necklace
(Goldentone)
(Approx. 20 & 33" Chains
—53" Overall)
1400 Points

I. 0858
Getabout Chain
(Goldentone)
Approx. 36"
1050 Points

J. 0830
Golden Duo Heart Choker
Approx. 14-16" Adj.
1100 Points

Jewelry shown actual size.

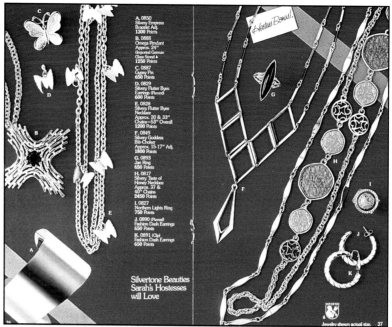

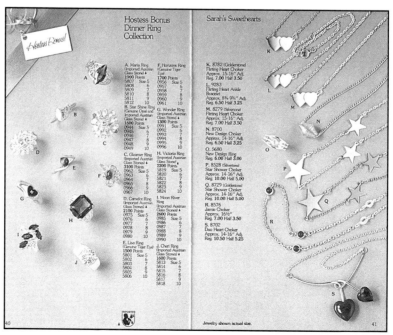

Janelle Penny Commissiong
Miss Universe 1977

A. 8559
Timeless Beauty Necklace
Approx. 22 & 30" Chains
(Removable Drop)
Reg. 15.50 Half 7.75

B. 8828
Wil'O Wrap Choker
Approx. 16"
Reg. 6.00 Half 3.00

C. 8199
Flutter Byes Necklace
Approx. 20 & 33" Chains
35" Overall
Reg. 11.00 Half 5.50

D. 7199
Flutter Byes Earrings
(Pierced)
Reg. 5.50 Half 2.75

E. 7421 (Goldentone)
7423 (Silvertone)
Showtime Earrings (Clip)
Reg. 8.50 Half 4.25

F. 8349
Sea Star Hoop Necklace
Approx. 14½-17" Adj.
Reg. 11.50 Half 5.75

G. 6349
Sea Star Stick Pin
Approx. 2"
Reg. 6.50 Half 3.25

H. 7349
Sea Star Earrings
(Pierced)
Reg. 8.00 Half 4.00

I. 5771
Sea Star Ring
Reg. 10.00 Half 5.00

Sarah Knows How™... To Brighten Up Your Day

The eternal mystery of the sea, the graceful starfish. Today, the "Ecology Collection," from Sarah Coventry. Finely crafted, exquisite in every detail, your starfish choker, ring, stickpin and pierced earrings are distinctively modern yet classically sophisticated, shimmering and warm, with the subtlety of the sea itself.

Jane Blalock defending champion of The Sarah Coventry LPGA Golf Tournament will be playing again in this year's tournament September 11-17 at Round Hill Country Club in Alamo, California.

A. 8439 (Goldentone)
Chiffon Bib-Necklace
Approx. 19¼"
Reg. 21.00 Half 10.50

B. 8404
Pandora Pendant
Approx. 15-17" Adj.
Reg. 11.50 Half 5.75

C. 9439 (Goldentone)
Chiffon Bracelet
Approx. 7¾"
Reg. 8.50 Half 4.25

D. 8594
Moon Beam Pendant
Approx. 16-18" Adj.
Imported German
Glass Stone) A
Reg. 8.00 Half 4.00

E. 5748
Moon Beam Ring
(Imported German
Glass Stone) A
Reg. 7.50 Half 3.75

F. 9057
Fascination Bracelet
Approx. 7¼"
(6 Stone Links)
(4 Imported Austrian
Glass Stone) A
Reg. 16.50 Half 8.25

G. 8929
Autumn Beauty Pendant
Approx. 22-24" Adj.
(Imported German Stone) A
Reg. 13.00 Half 6.50

H. 9445 (Silvertone)
Chiffon Bracelet
Approx. 7¾"
Reg. 8.50 Half 4.25

I. 8445 (Silvertone)
Chiffon Bib-Necklace
Approx. 19¼"
Reg. 21.00 Half 10.50

A. 8594
White Magic Choker
Approx. 16¼"
Reg. 12.50 Half 6.25

B. 5773
Duo Fashion Ring
Reg. 8.00 Half 4.00

C. 5734
Spring Fever Ring
Reg. 6.00 Half 3.00

D. 5778
City Slicker Ring
Reg. 7.00 Half 3.50

E. 7470
Pair Ups Earrings
(Pierced)
Reg. 5.00 Half 2.50

F. 8502
Perfection Necklace
Approx. 31"
Reg. 18.50 Half 9.25

G. 8524
Summer Lites Choker
Approx. 17½"
Reg. 13.00 Half 6.50

H. 7510
White Magic Earrings
(Pierced)
Reg. 6.00 Half 3.00

I. 7511
White Magic Earrings
(Clip)
Reg. 6.00 Half 3.00

White 'n Bright

A. 8245
Tradewinds Necklace
Approx. 18"
(Removable Drop)
Reg. 14.50 Half 7.25

B. 8451
Tiara Pendant
Approx. 24"
(Removable Drop)
Reg. 13.50 Half 6.75

C. 8651
Spring Bouquet Pendant
Approx. 24"
(Reversible and Remov-
able Drop)
Reg. 15.50 Half 7.75

D. 8834
Spring Moods Necklace
Approx. 40"
Reg. 7.00 Half 3.50

E. 7510
White Magic Earrings
(Pierced)
Reg. 6.00 Half 3.00

F. 8402
Paradise Choker
Approx. 15-17" Adj.
(Genuine Porcelain)
Reg. 11.00 Half 5.50

G. 8351 (Pink)
Pastel Beads
Approx. 36¾"—Overall
8" Removable Bracelet Section
Reg. 9.00 Half 4.50

H. 8352 (Blue)
Pastel Beads
Approx. 36¾"—Overall
8" Removable Bracelet Section
Reg. 9.00 Half 4.50

I. 8353 (Yellow)
Pastel Beads
Approx. 36¾"—Overall
8" Removable Bracelet Section
Reg. 9.00 Half 4.50

Reversed side of Spring Bouquet Pendant.

48

Jewelry shown actual size. 49

Beads shown with and without removable bracelet section.

A. 8101
Fly Away Choker
Approx. 14-16" Adj.
Reg. 14.00 Half 7.00

B. 8523
Garnet Twist Choker
Approx. 17½"
Reg. 12.00 Half 6.00

C. 6002
Fashion Mate Stick Pin
Approx. 2½"
Reg. 5.50 Half 2.75

D. 7823 (Goldentone)
7824 (Silvertone)
Stylish Earrings
(Pierced)
Reg. 8.00 Half 4.00

E. 8592
Limbo Pendant
Approx. 30" (Removable Drop)
Reg. 15.00 Half 7.50

F. 8410
Oriental Lanterns Choker
Approx. 15¾-17¼" Adj. (Green)
Reg. 9.50 Half 4.75

G. 8411
Oriental Lanterns Necklace
Approx. 27" (Emberstone)
Reg. 17.00 Half 8.50

H. 7387
Oriental Lanterns Earrings
(Pierced)
Reg. 8.00 Half 4.00

I. 8387
Oriental Lanterns Necklace
Approx. 33½" (Green)
Reg. 12.00 Half 6.00

Limbo Pendant doubled for a choker effect

50

Jewelry shown actual size. 51

A. 7826
Serenade Earrings (Pierced)
Imported German Glass Stone
Reg. 7.00 Half 3.50

B. 8826
Serenade Necklace
Approx. 32½" & 20¾" Chains
Imported German Glass Stone
Reg. 18.50 Half 9.25

C. 8696
First Star Pendant
Approx. 16-18" Adj.
Imported Austrian Glass Stone
Reg. 10.00 Half 5.00

D. 8632
Melissa Choker
Approx. 15-17" Adj.
Reg. 11.50 Half 5.75

E. 5781
Melissa Ring
Reg. 10.00 Half 5.00

F. 8634
Party Hearts Necklace
Approx. 20 & 33" Chains—
53" Overall
Reg. 13.50 Half 6.75

G. 5757
Heart to Heart Ring
Reg. 6.00 Half 3.00

H. 6676
Fashion Twist Stick Pin
Approx. 2½"
Reg. 6.00 Half 3.00

I. 8994
Danish Mood Pendant
Approx. 24"
Reg. 14.00 Half 7.00

J. 7441 (Silvertone)
7442 (Goldentone)
Wayside Earrings (Clip)
Reg. 7.00 Half 3.50

1978 Limited Edition Charm
Three Wise Men

K. 9506
Three Wise Men Charm
(Limited Edition)
Reg. 9.50 Half 4.75

Limited Edition charm
available for purchase
through December 31,
1978 only, at which time the
mold will be destroyed.
Packaged in a special gift
box.

Wearing just the 32½" strand, doubled around her neck.

59

Jewelry shown actual size. 53

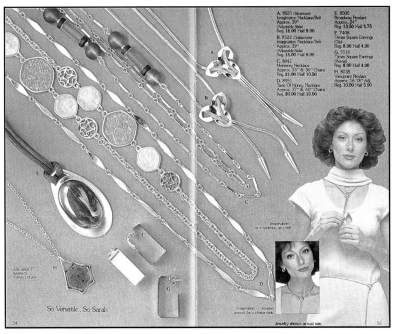

A. 8521 (Silvertone)
Imagination Necklace/Belt
Approx. 39"
(Adjustable Slide)
Reg. 16.00 Half 8.00

B. 8522 (Goldentone)
Imagination Necklace/Belt
Approx. 39"
(Adjustable Slide)
Reg. 16.00 Half 8.00

C. 8842
Monterey Necklace
Approx. 33" & 36" Chains
Reg. 21.00 Half 10.50

D. 8951
Taste Of Honey Necklace
Approx. 37" & 40" Chains
Reg. 20.00 Half 10.00

E. 8500
Broadway Pendant
Approx. 24"
Reg. 13.50 Half 6.75

F. 7408
Times Square Earrings
(Clip)
Reg. 8.00 Half 4.00

G. 7018
Times Square Earrings
(Pierced)
Reg. 8.00 Half 4.00

H. 8038
Viewpoint Pendant
Approx. 16-18" Adj.
Reg. 10.00 Half 5.00

Imagination
as a necklace, as a belt

Imagination... doubled
around, for a choker look.

ASK ABOUT
SARAH'S
7 AND 1 PLAN

So Versatile...So Sarah

54 / 55 Jewelry shown actual size.

A. 8749
Silvery Cascade Choker
Approx. 16" (Available
in two lengths)
Reg. 10.00 Half 5.00
8561
Silvery Cascade Necklace
Approx. 18"
Reg. 10.00 Half 5.00

B. 8452
Mystique Pin/Pendant
Approx. 24"
(Imported German Glass
Hematite Stone)
Reg. 10.50 Half 5.25

C. 7268
Jet Set Earrings (Pierced)
(Imported Austrian Glass
Hematite Stone) 4
Reg. 9.50 Half 4.75

D. 5723
Jet Set Ring
(Imported Austrian Glass
Hematite Stone) 4
Reg. 8.00 Half 4.00

E. 7267
Jet Set Earrings (Clip)
(Imported Austrian Glass
Hematite Stone) 4
Reg. 14.00 Half 7.00

F. 8267
Jet Set Choker
Approx. 15-16" Adj.
(Imported Austrian Glass
Hematite Stone) 4
Reg. 14.00 Half 7.00

G. 8663
Sweetheart Choker
Approx. 14-16" Adj.
(Imported Austrian Glass
Stone) 4
Reg. 14.50 Half 7.25

H. 7519 (Silvertone)
7520 (Goldentone)
Easy Going Earrings (Clip)
Reg. 6.00 Half 3.00

I. 8776
Royal Lace Bib Necklace
Approx. 15-17" Adj.
Reg. 16.50 Half 8.25

J. 7776 (Pierced)
Royal Lace Earrings
Reg. 7.50 Half 3.75

K. 8453
Dedication Cross Pendant
Approx. 16-18" Adj.
Reg. 7.50 Half 3.75

L. 8591
Papillon Pendant
Approx. 16-18" Adj.
Reg. 6.50 Half 3.25

M. 5733
Sea Treasure Ring
(Genuine Abalone Shell Stone)
Reg. 9.50 Half 4.75

N. 8551
Sea Treasure Choker
Approx. 14-16" Adj.
(Genuine Abalone Shell Stone)
Reg. 13.50 Half 6.75

Wearing the pin of
Mystique Pin Pendant

56 / 57 Jewelry shown actual size.

A. 8996
Granada Necklace
Approx. 37¼" Bead Section
Approx. 29½" Chain
Reg. 18.00 Half 9.00

B. 6995
Granada Pin
Reg. 8.00 Half 4.00

C. 6660
Floral Delite Pin
(Imported Austrian
Glass Stone) 4
Reg. 16.50 Half 8.25

D. 6349
Sea Star Stick Pin
Approx. 2"
Reg. 6.50 Half 3.25

E. 6677
Elegante Stick Pin
Approx. 2½"
Reg. 7.50 Half 3.75

F. 6139
Moon Mist Stick Pin
(Imported German Glass
Hematite Stone) 4
Approx. 2½"
Reg. 7.50 Half 3.75

G. 6676
Fashion Twist Stick Pin
Approx. 2½"
Reg. 6.00 Half 3.00

H. 6532
Carousel Pin
Reg. 7.00 Half 3.50

I. 6469
First Lady Pin
(Imported German
Glass Stone) 4
Reg. 6.50 Half 3.25

J. 6002
Fashion Mate Stick Pin
Approx. 2½"
Reg. 5.50 Half 2.75

K. 6420
Black Magic Pin (Small)
Reg. 6.00 Half 3.00

L. 6419
Black Magic Pin (Large)
Reg. 6.50 Half 3.25

M. Changing Times
Stick Pin Approx. 2"
(Includes 1 Initial,
1 Heart, and 1 Flower)
(Imported Austrian
Glass Stone) 4
Reg. 11.50 Half 5.75

A. 6006
B. 6007
C. 6008
D. 6009
E. 6010
F. 6011
G. 6012
H. 6013
I. 6014
J. 6015
K. 6016
L. 6017
M. 6018

N. 6019
O. 6020
P. 6021
Q. 6022
R. 6023
S. 6024
T. 6025
U. 6026
V. 6027
W. 6028
X. 6029
Y. 6030
Z. 6031

Pins

Granada Pin combined with
the beads.

Left—Granada beads can be doubled or worn long.
Right—Granada Pin added to the matching chain.

Changing Times
Stick Pin
Includes 1 initial, 1 heart,
and 1 flower

58 / 59 Jewelry shown actual size.

Basic Bracelets...

A. 9827 (Approx. 7¼")
9907 (Approx. 7¼")
Paramount Bracelet
Reg. 12.50 Half 6.25

B. 9841
Captive Heart Bracelet
Adj.
Reg. 6.00 Half 3.00

C. 9350
The Skimp Bracelet
Approx. 8¼"
Reg. 4.00 Half 2.00

D. 9244
Scandia Bracelet Adj.
Reg. 7.00 Half 3.50

E. 9631
Boulevard Bracelet
(Hinged Cuff)
Reg. 10.00 Half 5.00

F. 9539
Empress Bracelet Adj.
Reg. 13.00 Half 6.50

G. 9020
Congo Bracelet
(Hinged Cuff)
Reg. 15.50 Half 7.75

H. 9121
All Around Bracelet
Approx. 8".
Reg. 7.50 Half 3.75

To Mix 'n Match

I. 9283
Flirting Heart
Ankle Bracelet
Approx. 8¼-9¾" Adj.
Reg. 6.50 Half 3.25

J. 9667
Butterfly Ankle Bracelet
Approx. 8¼-9¾" Adj.
Reg. 6.00 Half 3.00

K. 9727
Mural Bracelet
Approx. 7½"
Reg. 14.50 Half 7.25

L. 9531
Classic Elegance Bracelet
Approx. 7½"
Reg. 14.50 Half 7.25

M. 9583 (Goldentone)
Young and Gay Bracelet
Approx. 7½"
Reg. 3.50 Half 1.75

N. 9733 (Silvertone)
Young and Gay Bracelet
Approx. 7½"
Reg. 3.50 Half 1.75

O. 9046 (Goldentone)
Echo Bracelet
Approx. 7½"
Reg. 3.50 Half 1.75

P. 9045 (Silvertone)
Echo Bracelet
Approx. 7½"
Reg. 3.50 Half 1.75

Q. 9222 (Goldentone)
Avenue Bracelet
Approx. 7½"
Reg. 7.50 Half 3.75

R. 9221 (Silvertone)
Avenue Bracelet
Approx. 7½"
Reg. 7.50 Half 3.75

S. 9598
Counterpoint Bracelet
Approx. 7½"
Reg. 4.50 Half 2.25

T. 9986
Delightful Bracelet
Approx. 7½"
Reg. 5.00 Half 2.50

U. 9225 (Goldentone)
Classical Bracelet
Approx. 7¾"
Reg. 7.50 Half 3.75

V. 9224 (Silvertone)
Classical Bracelet
Approx. 7½"
Reg. 7.50 Half 3.75

W. 8016
Twist About Belt
Approx. 26¼-33½" Adj.
Reg. 21.00 Half 10.50

Twist About Belt

Jewelry shown actual size.

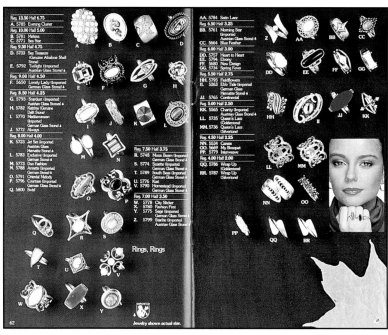

Reg. 13.50 Half 6.75

A. 5785 Evening Cluster
Reg. 10.00 Half 5.00

B. 5781 Melissa
C. 5771 Sea Star
Reg. 9.50 Half 4.75

D. 5733 Sea Treasure
(Genuine Abalone Shell Stone)

E. 5792 Twilight (Imported Austrian Glass Stone)
Reg. 9.00 Half 4.50

F. 5650 Lovely Lady (Imported German Glass Stone)
Reg. 8.50 Half 4.25

G. 5793 Stardust (Imported Austrian Glass Stone)

H. 5782 Katrina (Genuine Delft Stone)

I. 5770 Mediterranean (Imported German Glass Stone)

J. 5772 Always
Reg. 8.00 Half 4.00

K. 5723 Jet Set (Imported Austrian Glass Hematite Stone)

L. 5783 Exclusive (Imported German Stone)

M. 5773 Duo Fashion

N. 5788 Annette (Imported German Stone)

O. 5791 Oriental Melody

P. 5796 Courtesy (Imported German Glass Stone)

Q. 5800 Swirl

R. 5748 Moon Beam (Imported German Glass Stone)
Reg. 7.50 Half 3.75

S. 5774 Suzette (Imported German Glass Stone)

T. 5789 South Seas (Imported German Glass Stone)

U. 5776 Kari

V. 5790 Homestead (Imported German Glass Stone)
Reg. 7.00 Half 3.50

W. 5778 City Slicker
X. 5780 Fashion First
Y. 5775 Sage (Imported German Glass Stone)
Z. 5799 Starlite (Imported Austrian Glass Stone)

AA. 5784 Satin Lace
Reg. 6.50 Half 3.25

BB. 5761 Morning Star (Imported Austrian Glass Stone)

CC. 5664 Blue Feather
Reg. 6.00 Half 3.00

DD. 5757 Heart to Heart
EE. 5794 Ebony
FF. 5680 New Design
GG. 5734 Spring Fever
Reg. 5.50 Half 2.75

HH. 5795 Fieldflowers
II. 5263 Ebb Tide (Imported German Glass Hematite Stone)

JJ. 5765 Continental
Reg. 5.00 Half 2.50

KK. 5565 Charity (Imported Austrian Glass Stone)

LL. 5735 Queen's Lace (Goldentone)

MM. 5736 Queen's Lace (Silvertone)
Reg. 4.50 Half 2.25

NN. 5534 Carola
OO. 5669 My Bouquet
PP. 5779 Interweave
Reg. 4.00 Half 2.00

QQ. 5786 Wrap Up (Goldentone)
RR. 5787 Wrap Up (Silvertone)

Rings, Rings

Jewelry shown actual size.

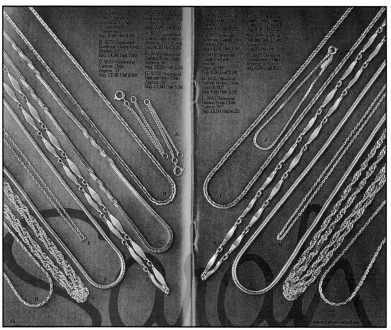

Jewelry shown actual size.

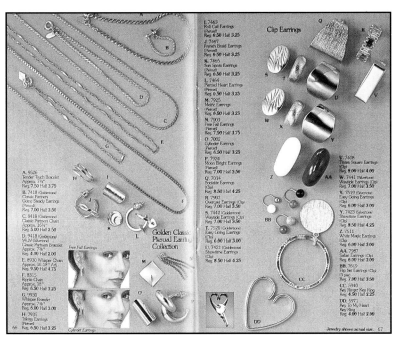

A. 9526
Tender Touch Bracelet
Approx. 7¼"
Reg. 7.50 Half 3.75

B. 7418 (Goldentone)
Classic Partners
Going Steady Earrings
(Pierced)
Reg. 7.00 Half 3.50

C. 8418 (Goldentone)
Classic Partners Chain
Approx. 16½"
Reg. 5.00 Half 2.50

D. 9418 (Goldentone)
9419 (Silvertone)
Classic Partners Bracelet
Approx. 7½"
Reg. 4.00 Half 2.00

E. 8930 Whisper Chain
Approx. 16-18" Adj.
Reg. 9.50 Half 4.75

F. 8315
Ripple Chain
Approx. 18"
Reg. 6.50 Half 3.25

GG. 9930
Whisper Bracelet
Approx. 7½"
Reg. 6.00 Half 3.00

H. 7935
Trilogy Earrings
(Pierced)
Reg. 6.50 Half 3.25

Free Fall Earrings

Cylinder Earrings

Golden Classic Pierced Earring Collection

L. 7463
Roll Call Earrings
(Pierced)
Reg. 6.50 Half 3.25

J. 7447
French Braid Earrings
(Pierced)
Reg. 6.50 Half 3.25

K. 7465
Sun Spots Earrings
(Pierced)
Reg. 6.50 Half 3.25

L. 7464
Pierced Heart Earrings
(Pierced)
Reg. 6.50 Half 3.25

M. 7925
Metric Earrings
(Pierced)
Reg. 6.50 Half 3.25

N. 7003
Free Fall Earrings
(Pierced)
Reg. 7.50 Half 3.75

O. 7002
Cylinder Earrings
(Pierced)
Reg. 6.50 Half 3.25

P. 7924
Moon Bright Earrings
(Pierced)
Reg. 7.00 Half 3.50

Q. 7014
Sociable Earrings
(Clip)
Reg. 8.50 Half 4.25

R. 7903
Overcast Earrings (Clip)
Reg. 7.00 Half 3.50

S. 7442 (Goldentone)
Wayside Earrings (Clip)
Reg. 7.00 Half 3.50

T. 7520 (Goldentone)
Easy Going Earrings
(Clip)
Reg. 6.00 Half 3.00

U. 7421 (Goldentone)
Showtime Earrings
(Clip)
Reg. 8.50 Half 4.25

Clip Earrings

V. 7408
Times Square Earrings
(Clip)
Reg. 8.00 Half 4.00

W. 7441 (Silvertone)
Wayside Earrings (Clip)
Reg. 7.00 Half 3.50

X. 7519 (Silvertone)
Easy Going Earrings
Reg. 6.00 Half 3.00

Y. 7423 (Silvertone)
Showtime Earrings
(Clip)
Reg. 8.50 Half 4.25

Z. 7511
White Magic Earrings
(Clip)
Reg. 6.00 Half 3.00

AA. 7987
Safari Earrings (Clip)
Reg. 6.00 Half 3.00

BB. 7619
Flip Set Earrings (Clip)
(3 pair)
Reg. 7.00 Half 3.50

CC. 5940
Key Ringer Key Ring
Reg. 4.50 Half 2.25

DD. 5971
Key To My Heart
Key Ring
Reg. 4.00 Half 2.00

66   67   *Jewelry shown actual size.*

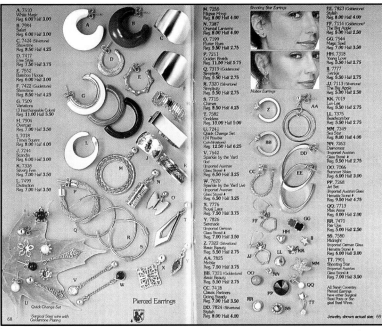

A. 7510
White Magic
Reg. 6.00 Half 3.00

B. 7984
Safari
Reg. 8.00 Half 4.00

C. 7424 (Silvertone)
Showtime
Reg. 8.50 Half 4.25

D. 7417
Free Style
Reg. 7.50 Half 3.75

E. 7552
Bamboo Hoops
Reg. 6.00 Half 3.00

F. 7422 (Goldentone)
Showtime
Reg. 8.50 Half 4.25

G. 7509
Variations
(3 Interchangeable Colors)
Reg. 11.00 Half 5.50

H. 7904
Overcast
Reg. 7.00 Half 3.50

I. 7018
Times Square
Reg. 8.00 Half 4.00

J. 7244
Scandia
Reg. 6.00 Half 3.00

K. 7338
Silvery Fern
Reg. 7.00 Half 3.50

L. 7499
Distinction
Reg. 7.00 Half 3.50

Quick Change Set
(Surgical Steel wire with Goldentone Plating)

Pierced Earrings

M. 7256
Filigree Hoop
Reg. 8.00 Half 4.00

N. 7387
Oriental Lanterns
Reg. 8.00 Half 4.00

O. 7199
Flutter Byes
Reg. 5.50 Half 2.75

P. 7211
Golden Braids
Reg. 11.50 Half 5.75

Q. 7319 (Goldentone)
Simplicity
Reg. 5.50 Half 2.75

R. 7320 (Silvertone)
Simplicity
Reg. 5.50 Half 2.75

S. 7715
Chimes
Reg. 8.50 Half 4.25

T. 7582
Goddess
Reg. 10.00 Half 5.00

U. 7241
Quick Change Set
(24 Possible
Combinations)
Reg. 12.50 Half 6.25

V. 7642
Sparkle by the Yard
(Ice)
Imported Austrian
Glass Stone) ◆
Reg. 6.50 Half 3.25

W. 7620
Sparkle by the Yard (Jet)
Imported Austrian
Glass Stone) ◆
Reg. 6.50 Half 3.25

X. 7776
Royal Lace
Reg. 7.50 Half 3.75

Y. 7826
Serenade
Imported German
Glass Stone) ◆
Reg. 7.00 Half 3.50

Z. 7322 (Silvertone)
Basic Beauty
Reg. 5.50 Half 2.75

AA. 7825
Mobile
Reg. 7.50 Half 3.75

BB. 7321 (Goldentone)
Basic Beauty
Reg. 5.50 Half 2.75

CC. 7418
Classic Partners
Going Steady
Reg. 7.00 Half 3.50

DD. 7824 (Silvertone)
Stylish
Reg. 8.00 Half 4.00

Shooting Star Earrings

Mobile Earrings

EE. 7823 (Goldentone)
Stylish
Reg. 8.00 Half 4.00

FF. 7114 (Goldentone)
The Big Apple
Reg. 5.00 Half 2.50

GG. 7544
Magic Spell
Reg. 7.00 Half 3.50

HH. 7318
Young Love
Reg. 5.50 Half 2.75

II. 7777
Twinkle
Reg. 5.50 Half 2.75

JJ. 7113 (Silvertone)
The Big Apple
Reg. 5.00 Half 2.50

KK. 7019
Luv-Lee
Reg. 5.50 Half 2.75

LL. 7375
Beachcomber
Reg. 5.50 Half 2.75

MM. 7349
Sea Star
Reg. 8.00 Half 4.00

NN. 7263
Demonoir
Imported Austrian
Glass Stone) ◆
Reg. 5.50 Half 2.75

OO. 7066
Summer Skies
Reg. 6.00 Half 3.00

PP. 7268
Jet Set
Imported Austrian Glass
Hematite Stone) ◆
Reg. 9.50 Half 4.75

QQ. 7713
Miss Anne
Reg. 4.00 Half 2.00

RR. 7470
Pair Ups
Reg. 5.00 Half 2.50

SS. 7580
Midnight
Imported German Glass
Hematite Stone) ◆
Reg. 6.00 Half 3.00

TT. 7901
Shooting Star
Imported Austrian
Glass Stone) ◆
Reg. 7.00 Half 3.50

All Sarah Coventry
Pierced Earrings
have either Surgical
Steel Posts or Surgical Steel Wires.

68   69   *Jewelry shown actual size.*

School Days Initial Pendant 16-18" Adj.
Reg. 8.50 Half 4.25

A. 8472	**I.** 8476	**L.** 8480	**M.** 8484	**Q.** 8488	**U.** 8492	**Y.** 8496
B. 8473	**J.** 8477	**J.** 8481	**N.** 8485	**R.** 8489	**V.** 8493	**Z.** 8497
C. 8474	**G.** 8478	**K.** 8482	**O.** 8486	**S.** 8490	**W.** 8494	
D. 8475	**M.** 8479	**L.** 8483	**P.** 8487	**T.** 8491	**X.** 8495	

Multiple Choice Pins—
Sarah's ABC's
Reg. 8.50 Half 2.75

A. 8298	**J.** 6307	**S.** 6316
T. 8299	**K.** 6308	**T.** 6317
C. 6300	**L.** 6309	**U.** 6318
D. 6301	**M.** 6310	**V.** 6319
E. 6302	**N.** 6311	**W.** 6320
F. 6303	**O.** 6312	**X.** 6321
G. 6304	**P.** 6313	**Y.** 6322
H. 6305	**Q.** 6314	**Z.** 6323
I. 6306	**R.** 6315	

62   63   *Jewelry shown actual size.*

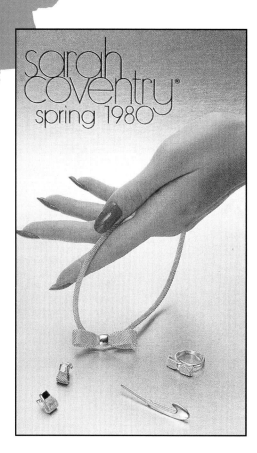

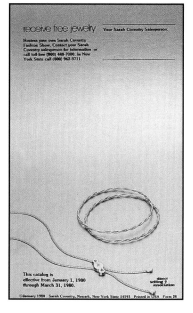

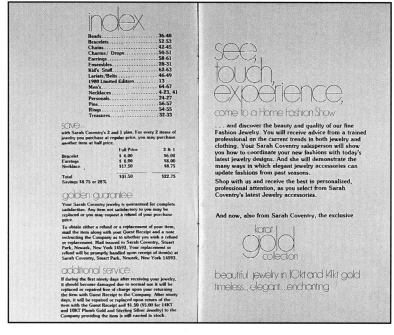

index

save...

with Sarah Coventry's 2 and 1 plan. For every 2 items of
jewelry you purchase at regular price, you may purchase
another item at half price.

	Full Price	2 & 1
Bracelet	$ 6.00	$6.00
Earrings	$ 8.00	$8.00
Necklace	$17.50	$8.75
Total	$31.50	$22.75

Savings $8.75 or 28%

golden guarantee

Your Sarah Coventry jewelry is guaranteed for complete
satisfaction. Any item not satisfactory to you may be
replaced or you may request a refund of your purchase
price.

To obtain either a refund or a replacement of your item,
mail the item along with your Guest Receipt and a note
instructing the Company as to whether you wish a refund
or replacement. Mail insured to Sarah Coventry, Stuart
Park, Newark, New York 14593. Your replacement or
refund will be promptly handled upon receipt of item(s) at
Sarah Coventry, Stuart Park, Newark, New York 14593.

additional service

If during the first ninety days after receiving your jewelry,
it should become damaged due to normal use it will be
replaced or repaired free of charge upon your returning
the item with Guest Receipt to the Company. After ninety
days, it will be repaired or replaced upon return of the
item with the Guest Receipt and $1.50 ($5.00 for 14KT
and 10KT Plumb Gold and Sterling Silver Jewelry) to the
Company providing the item is still carried in stock.

see, touch, experience,

come to a Home Fashion Show

. . . and discover the beauty and quality of our fine
Fashion Jewelry. You will receive advice from a trained
professional on the current trends in both jewelry and
clothing. Your Sarah Coventry salesperson will show
you how to coordinate your new fashions with today's
latest jewelry designs. And she will demonstrate the
many ways in which elegant jewelry accessories can
update fashions from past seasons.

Shop with us and receive the best in personalized,
professional attention, as you select from Sarah
Coventry's latest Jewelry accessories.

And now, also from Sarah Coventry, the exclusive

karat gold collection

beautiful jewelry in 10kt and 14kt gold
timeless... elegant... enchanting

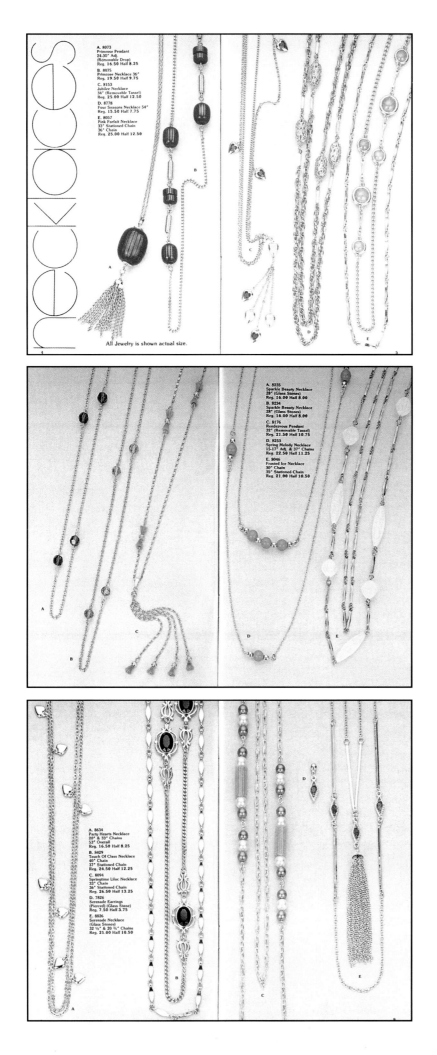

necklaces

A. 8073
Primrose Pendant
24-30" Adj.
(Removable Drop)
Reg. 16.50 Half 8.25

B. 8075
Primrose Necklace 36"
Reg. 19.50 Half 9.75

C. 8153
Jubilee Necklace
34" (Removable Tassel)
Reg. 25.00 Half 12.50

D. 8778
Four Seasons Necklace 54"
Reg. 15.50 Half 7.75

E. 8057
Pink Parfait Necklace
33" Stationed Chain
36" Chain
Reg. 25.00 Half 12.50

All Jewelry is shown actual size.

A. 8235
Sparkle Beauty Necklace
28" (Glass Stones)
Reg. 16.00 Half 8.00

B. 8234
Sparkle Beauty Necklace
28" (Glass Stones)
Reg. 16.00 Half 8.00

C. 8176
Rendezvous Pendant
32" (Removable Tassel)
Reg. 21.50 Half 10.75

D. 8253
Spring Melody Necklace
15-17" Adj. & 37" Chains
Reg. 22.50 Half 11.25

E. 8046
Frosted Ice Necklace
30" Chain
35" Stationed Chain
Reg. 21.00 Half 10.50

A. 8634
Party Hearts Necklace
20" & 33" Chains
53" Overall
Reg. 16.50 Half 8.25

B. 8429
Touch Of Class Necklace
40" Chain
37" Stationed Chain
Reg. 24.50 Half 12.25

C. 8094
Springtime Lilac Necklace
33" Chain
36" Stationed Chain
Reg. 26.50 Half 13.25

D. 7826
Serenade Earrings
(Pierced) (Glass Stone)
Reg. 7.50 Half 3.75

E. 8826
Serenade Necklace
(Glass Stones)
32 ½" & 29 ¾" Chains
Reg. 21.00 Half 10.50

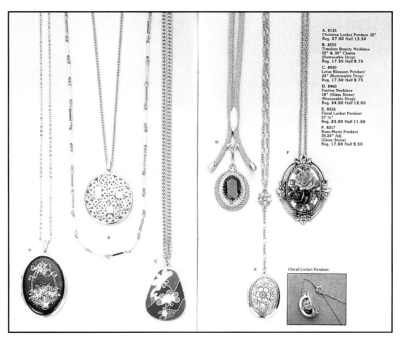

A. 9135
Christina Locket Pendant 32"
Reg. 27.00 Half 13.50

B. 8559
Timeless Beauty Necklace
22" & 30" Chains
(Removable Drop)
Reg. 17.50 Half 8.75

C. 8030
Lotus Blossom Pendant
24" (Removable Drop)
Reg. 17.50 Half 8.75

D. 8460
Festive Necklace
18" (Glass Stone)
(Removable Drop)
Reg. 24.00 Half 12.00

E. 8256
Floral Locket Pendant
27 ½"
Reg. 23.00 Half 11.50

F. 8317
Rose-Marie Pendant
20-24" Adj.
(Glass Stone)
Reg. 17.00 Half 8.50

Floral Locket Pendant.

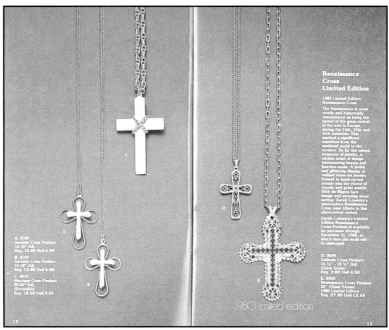

A. 8108
Serenity Cross Pendant
16-18" Adj.
Reg. 12.00 Half 6.00

B. 8109
Serenity Cross Pendant
16-18" Adj.
Reg. 12.00 Half 6.00

C. 8019
Marriage Cross Pendant
20-24" Adj.
(Reversible)
Reg. 18.50 Half 9.25

**Renaissance
Cross
Limited Edition**

**1980 Limited Edition
Renaissance Cross**

The Renaissance is most vividly and historically remembered as being the period of the great revival of the arts in Europe, during the 14th, 15th and 16th centuries. This marked a significant transition from the medieval world to the modern. As for the valued treasures of jewelry, a certain sense of design harmonizing beauty and function arose. A lavish and glittering display of radiant stone-set jewelry framed in hand-carved metals was the choice of royalty and great wealth. With its filigree lace design and stunning stone setting, Sarah Coventry's masterpiece Renaissance Cross pays tribute to this phenomenal revival.

Sarah Coventry's Limited Edition Renaissance Cross Pendant is available for purchase through December 31, 1980, at which time the mold will be destroyed.

D. 8699
Solitude Cross Pendant
16 ½"-18 ½" Adj.
(Glass Stone)
Reg. 9.00 Half 4.50

E. 8260
Renaissance Cross Pendant
28" (Glass Stones)
1980 Limited Edition
Reg. 27.00 Half 13.50

1980 limited edition

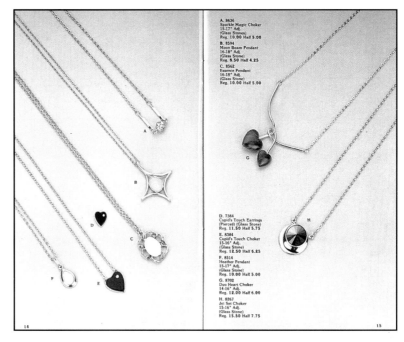

A. 8636
Sparkle Magic Choker
15-17" Adj.
(Glass Stones)
Reg. 10.00 Half 5.00

B. 8594
Moon Beam Pendant
16-18" Adj.
(Glass Stone)
Reg. 8.50 Half 4.25

C. 8562
Essence Pendant
16-18" Adj.
(Glass Stone)
Reg. 10.00 Half 5.00

D. 7384
Cupid's Touch Earrings
(Pierced) (Glass Stone)
Reg. 11.50 Half 5.75

E. 6384
Cupid's Touch Choker
15-16" Adj.
(Glass Stone)
Reg. 12.50 Half 6.25

F. 8514
Heather Pendant
15-17" Adj.
(Glass Stone)
Reg. 10.00 Half 5.00

G. 8702
Duo Heart Choker
14-16" Adj.
Reg. 12.00 Half 6.00

H. 8267
Jet Set Choker
15-16" Adj.
(Glass Stone)
Reg. 15.50 Half 7.75

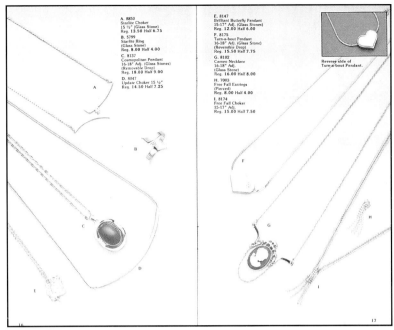

A. 8850
Starlite Choker
15 ½" (Glass Stone)
Reg. 13.50 Half 6.75

B. 5799
Starlite Ring
(Glass Stone)
Reg. 8.00 Half 4.00

C. 8137
Cosmopolitan Pendant
16-18" Adj. (Glass Stones)
(Removable Drop)
Reg. 18.00 Half 9.00

D. 8047
Update Choker 15 ½"
Reg. 14.50 Half 7.25

E. 8147
Brilliant Butterfly Pendant
15-17" Adj. (Glass Stones)
Reg. 12.00 Half 6.00

F. 8175
Turn-a-bout Pendant
16-18" Adj. (Glass Stones)
(Reversible Drop)
Reg. 15.50 Half 7.75

G. 8102
Cameo Necklace
16-18" Adj.
(Glass Stone)
Reg. 16.00 Half 8.00

H. 7003
Free Fall Earrings
(Pierced)
Reg. 8.00 Half 4.00

I. 8174
Free Fall Choker
15-17" Adj.
Reg. 15.00 Half 7.50

Reverse side of
Turn-a-bout Pendant.

16   17

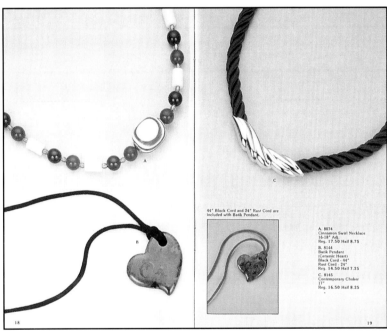

44" Black Cord and 24" Rust Cord are
included with Batik Pendant.

A. 8074
Cinnamon Swirl Necklace
16-18" Adj.
Reg. 17.50 Half 8.75

B. 8144
Batik Pendant
(Ceramic Heart)
Black Cord - 44"
Rust Cord - 24"
Reg. 14.50 Half 7.25

C. 8145
Contemporary Choker
17"
Reg. 16.50 Half 8.25

18   19

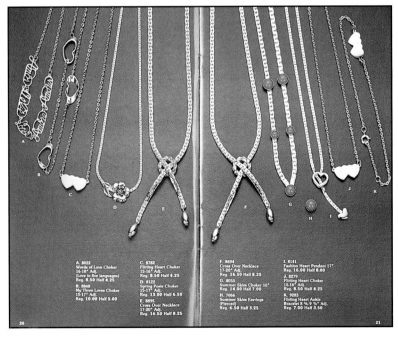

A. 8022
Words of Love Choker
16-18" Adj.
(Love in five languages)
Reg. 8.50 Half 4.25

B. 8848
My Three Loves Choker
15-17" Adj.
Reg. 10.00 Half 5.00

C. 8782
Flirting Heart Choker
15-16" Adj.
Reg. 8.50 Half 4.25

D. 8122
Springtime Posie Choker
15-17" Adj.
Reg. 13.00 Half 6.50

E. 8895
Cross Over Necklace
17-20" Adj.
Reg. 16.50 Half 8.25

F. 8894
Cross Over Necklace
17-20" Adj.
Reg. 16.50 Half 8.25

G. 8055
Summer Skies Choker 16"
Reg. 14.00 Half 7.00

H. 7066
Summer Skies Earrings
(Pierced)
Reg. 6.50 Half 3.25

I. 8141
Fashion Heart Pendant 17"
Reg. 16.00 Half 8.00

J. 8279
Flirting Heart Choker
15-16" Adj.
Reg. 8.50 Half 4.25

K. 9283
Flirting Heart Ankle
Bracelet 8 ¾-9 ¾" Adj.
Reg. 7.00 Half 3.50

20   21

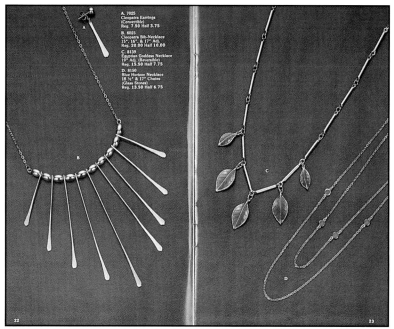

A. 7025
Cleopatra Earrings
(Convertible)
Reg. 7.50 Half 3.75

B. 8025
Cleopatra Bib-Necklace
15", 16", & 17" Adj.
Reg. 20.00 Half 10.00

C. 8139
Egyptian Goddess Necklace
19" Adj. (Reversible)
Reg. 15.50 Half 7.75

D. 8150
Blue Horizon Necklace
16 ½" & 17" Chains
(Glass Stones)
Reg. 13.50 Half 6.75

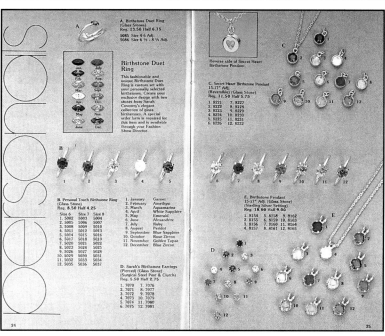

personals

A. Birthstone Duet Ring
(Glass Stones)
Reg. 13.50 Half 6.75
5085 Size 4-6 Adj.
5086 Size 6 ½ - 8 ½ Adj.

Birthstone Duet Ring

This fashionable and unique Birthstone Duet Ring is custom set with your personally selected birthstones. Create your exclusive design with two stones from Sarah Coventry's elegant collection of glass birthstones. A special order form is required for this item and is available through your Fashion Show Director.

Reverse side of Secret Heart Birthstone Pendant.

C. Secret Heart Birthstone Pendant
15-17" Adj.
(Reversible) (Glass Stone)
Reg. 11.50 Half 5.75
1. 8221   7. 8227
2. 8222   8. 8228
3. 8223   9. 8229
4. 8224 10. 8230
5. 8225 11. 8231
6. 8226 12. 8232

B. Personal Touch Birthstone Ring
(Glass Stone)
Reg. 8.50 Half 4.25

	Size 6	Size 7	Size 8
1.	5002	5003	5004
2.	5005	5006	5007
3.	5008	5009	5010
4.	5011	5012	5013
5.	5014	5015	5016
6.	5017	5018	5019
7.	5020	5021	5022
8.	5023	5024	5025
9.	5026	5027	5028
10.	5029	5030	5031
11.	5032	5033	5034
12.	5035	5036	5037

1. January   Garnet
2. February   Amethyst
3. March   Aquamarine
4. April   White Sapphire
5. May   Emerald
6. June   Alexandrite
7. July   Ruby
8. August   Peridot
9. September   Blue Sapphire
10. October   Rose Zircon
11. November   Golden Topaz
12. December   Blue Zircon

D. Sarah's Birthstone Earrings
(Pierced) (Glass Stone)
(Surgical Steel Post & Clutch)
Reg. 5.50 Half 2.75
1. 7070   7. 7076
2. 7071   8. 7077
3. 7072   9. 7078
4. 7073 10. 7079
5. 7074 11. 7080
6. 7075 12. 7081

E. Birthstone Pendant
15-17" Adj. (Glass Stone)
(Sterling Silver Setting)
Reg. 18.00 Half 9.00
1. 8154   5. 8158   9. 8162
2. 8155   6. 8159 10. 8163
3. 8156   7. 8160 11. 8164
4. 8157   8. 8161 12. 8165

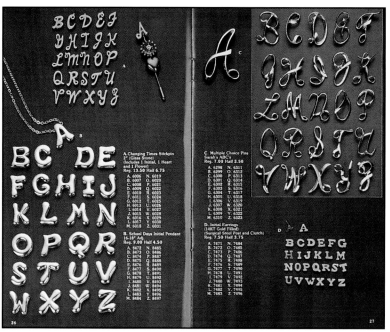

A. Changing Times Stickpin
2" (Glass Stone)
(Includes 1 Initial, 1 Heart and 1 Flower)
Reg. 13.50 Half 6.75

A. 6006   N. 6019
B. 6007   O. 6020
C. 6008   P. 6021
D. 6009   Q. 6022
E. 6010   R. 6023
F. 6011   S. 6024
G. 6012   T. 6025
H. 6013   U. 6026
I. 6014   V. 6027
J. 6015   W. 6028
K. 6016   X. 6029
L. 6017   Y. 6030
M. 6018   Z. 6031

B. School Days Initial Pendant
16-18" Adj.
Reg. 9.00 Half 4.50

A. 8472   N. 8485
B. 8473   O. 8486
C. 8474   P. 8487
D. 8475   Q. 8488
E. 8476   R. 8489
F. 8477   S. 8490
G. 8478   T. 8491
H. 8479   U. 8492
I. 8480   V. 8493
J. 8481   W. 8494
K. 8482   X. 8495
L. 8483   Y. 8496
M. 8484   Z. 8497

C. Multiple Choice Pins
Sarah's ABC's
Reg. 7.00 Half 3.50

A. 6298   N. 6311
B. 6299   O. 6312
C. 6300   P. 6313
D. 6301   Q. 6314
E. 6302   R. 6315
F. 6303   S. 6316
G. 6304   T. 6317
H. 6305   U. 6318
I. 6306   V. 6319
J. 6307   W. 6320
K. 6308   X. 6321
L. 6309   Y. 6322
M. 6310   Z. 6323

D. Initial Earrings
(14KT Gold Filled)
(Surgical Steel Post and Clutch)
Reg. 7.50 Half 3.75

A. 7471   N. 7484
B. 7472   O. 7485
C. 7473   P. 7486
D. 7474   Q. 7487
E. 7475   R. 7488
F. 7476   S. 7489
G. 7477   T. 7490
H. 7478   U. 7491
I. 7479   V. 7492
J. 7480   W. 7493
K. 7481   X. 7494
L. 7482   Y. 7495
M. 7483   Z. 7496

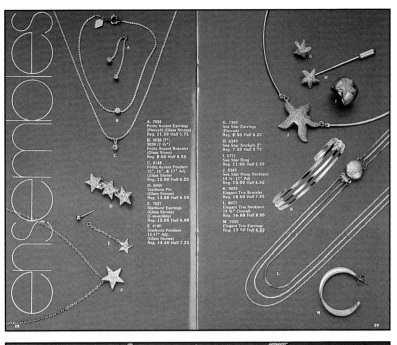

ensembles

A. 7036
Petite Accent Earrings
(Pierced) (Glass Stones)
Reg. 11.50 Half 5.75

B. 9038 (7")
9039 (7 ½")
Petite Accent Bracelet
(Glass Stone)
Reg. 8.50 Half 4.25

C. 8148
Petite Accent Pendant
15", 16", & 17" Adj.
(Glass Stone)
Reg. 12.50 Half 6.25

D. 6060
Starburst Pin
(Glass Stones)
Reg. 13.00 Half 6.50

E. 7037
Starburst Earrings
(Glass Stones)
(Convertible)
Reg. 12.00 Half 6.00

F. 6180
Starburst Pendant
15-17" Adj.
(Glass Stones)
Reg. 14.50 Half 7.25

G. 7349
Sea Star Earrings
(Pierced)
Reg. 8.50 Half 4.25

H. 6349
Sea Star Stickpin 2"
Reg. 7.50 Half 3.75

I. 5771
Sea Star Ring
Reg. 11.00 Half 5.50

J. 8349
Sea Star Hoop Necklace
14 ½- 17" Adj.
Reg. 13.00 Half 6.50

K. 9035
Elegant Trio Bracelet
Reg. 14.50 Half 7.25

L. 8077
Elegant Trio Necklace
19 ¾" Overall
Reg. 16.00 Half 8.00

M. 7035
Elegant Trio Earrings
Reg. 12.50 Half 6.25

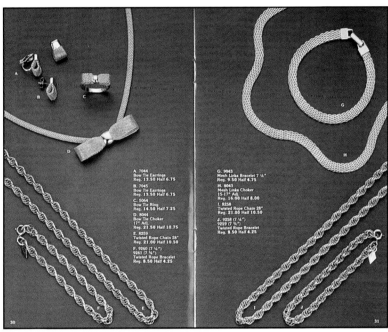

A. 7044
Bow Tie Earrings
Reg. 13.50 Half 6.75

B. 7045
Bow Tie Earrings
Reg. 13.50 Half 6.75

C. 5064
Bow Tie Ring
Reg. 14.50 Half 7.25

D. 8044
Bow Tie Choker
17" Adj.
Reg. 21.50 Half 10.75

E. 8259
Twisted Rope Chain 28"
Reg. 21.00 Half 10.50

F. 9260 (7 ¼")
9261 (7 ¾")
Twisted Rope Bracelet
Reg. 8.50 Half 4.25

G. 9043
Mesh Links Bracelet 7 ¼"
Reg. 9.50 Half 4.75

H. 8043
Mesh Links Choker
15-17" Adj.
Reg. 16.00 Half 8.00

I. 8258
Twisted Rope Chain 28"
Reg. 21.00 Half 10.50

J. 9258 (7 ¼")
9259 (7 ¾")
Twisted Rope Bracelet
Reg. 8.50 Half 4.25

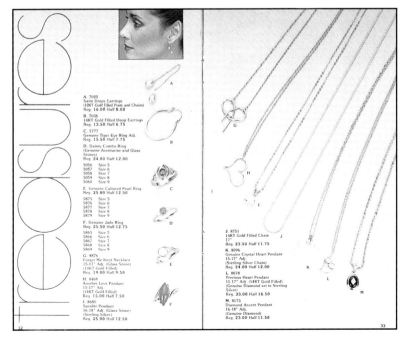

treasures

A. 7020
Satin Drops Earrings
(12KT Gold Filled Posts and Chains)
Reg. 16.00 Half 8.00

B. 7036
14KT Gold Filled Hoop Earrings
Reg. 13.50 Half 6.75

C. 5777
Genuine Tiger Eye Ring Adj.
Reg. 15.50 Half 7.75

D. Dainty Combo Ring
(Genuine Aventurine and Glass Stones)
Reg. 24.00 Half 12.00
5056 Size 5
5057 Size 6
5058 Size 7
5059 Size 8
5060 Size 9

E. Genuine Cultured Pearl Ring
Reg. 25.00 Half 12.50
5875 Size 5
5876 Size 6
5877 Size 7
5878 Size 8
5879 Size 9

F. Genuine Jade Ring
Reg. 25.50 Half 12.75
5865 Size 5
5866 Size 6
5867 Size 7
5868 Size 8
5869 Size 9

G. 8876
Forget Me Knot Necklace
15-17" Adj. (Glass Stone)
(14KT Gold Filled)
Reg. 19.00 Half 9.50

H. 8868
Another Love Pendant
15-17" Adj.
(14KT Gold Filled)
Reg. 15.00 Half 7.50

I. 8680
Satellite Pendant
16-18" Adj. (Glass Stone)
(Sterling Silver)
Reg. 25.00 Half 12.50

J. 8751
14KT Gold Filled Chain
17"
Reg. 23.50 Half 11.75

K. 8096
Genuine Crystal Heart Pendant
15-17" Adj.
(Sterling Silver Chain)
Reg. 24.00 Half 12.00

L. 8078
Precious Heart Pendant
15-17" Adj. (14KT Gold Filled)
(Genuine Diamond set in Sterling Silver)
Reg. 33.00 Half 16.50

M. 8173
Diamond Accent Pendant
16-18" Adj.
(Genuine Diamond)
Reg. 23.00 Half 11.50

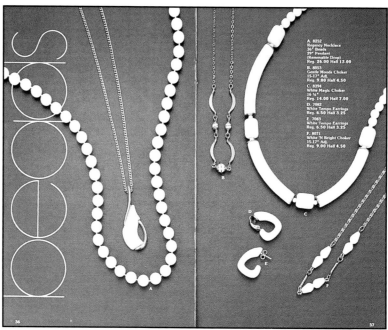

A. 8252
Regency Necklace
36" Beads
29" Pendant
(Removable Drop)
Reg. 26.00 Half 13.00

B. 8053
Gentle Moods Choker
15-17" Adj.
Reg. 9.00 Half 4.50

C. 8394
White Magic Choker
16 ¼"
Reg. 14.00 Half 7.00

D. 7082
White Tempo Earrings
Reg. 6.50 Half 3.25

E. 7063
White Tempo Earrings
Reg. 6.50 Half 3.25

F. 8071
White 'N Bright Choker
15-17" Adj.
Reg. 9.00 Half 4.50

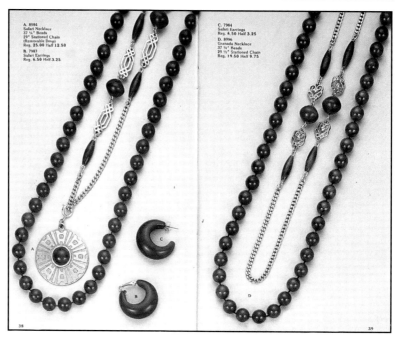

A. 8984
Safari Necklace
37 ¼" Beads
29" Stationed Chain
(Removable Drop)
Reg. 25.00 Half 12.50

B. 7987
Safari Earrings
Reg. 6.50 Half 3.25

C. 7984
Safari Earrings
Reg. 6.50 Half 3.25

D. 8996
Granada Necklace
37 ¼" Beads
29 ½" Stationed Chain
Reg. 19.50 Half 9.75

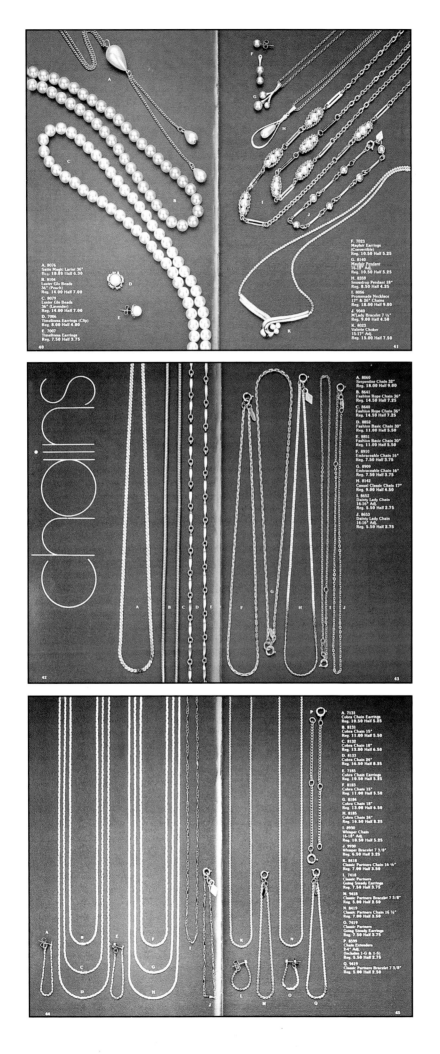

A. 8076
Satin Magic Lariat 36"
Reg. 18.80 Half 6.30

B. 8104
Luster Glo Beads
36" (Peach)
Reg. 14.00 Half 7.00

C. 8079
Luster Glo Beads
36" (Lavender)
Reg. 14.00 Half 7.00

D. 7006
Timeliness Earrings (Clip)
Reg. 8.00 Half 4.00

E. 7007
Timeliness Earrings
Reg. 7.50 Half 3.75

F. 7023
Mayfair Earrings
(Convertible)
Reg. 10.50 Half 5.25

G. 8140
Mayfair Pendant
16-18" Adj.
Reg. 10.50 Half 5.25

H. 8359
Snowdrop Pendant 18"
Reg. 8.50 Half 4.25

I. 8056
Promenade Necklace
17" & 26" Chains
Reg. 18.00 Half 9.00

J. 9040
M'Lady Bracelet 7 ½"
Reg. 9.00 Half 4.50

K. 8023
Valerie Choker
15-17" Adj.
Reg. 15.00 Half 7.50

40
41

chains

A. 8060
Serpentine Chain 32"
Reg. 18.00 Half 9.00

B. 8641
Fashion Rope Chain 36"
Reg. 14.50 Half 7.25

C. 8640
Fashion Rope Chain 36"
Reg. 14.50 Half 7.25

D. 8852
Fashion Basic Chain 30"
Reg. 11.00 Half 5.50

E. 8851
Fashion Basic Chain 30"
Reg. 11.00 Half 5.50

F. 8910
Embraceable Chain 16"
Reg. 7.50 Half 3.75

G. 8909
Embraceable Chain 16"
Reg. 7.50 Half 3.75

H. 8142
Casual Classic Chain 17"
Reg. 9.00 Half 4.50

I. 8652
Dainty Lady Chain
14-16" Adj.
Reg. 5.50 Half 2.75

J. 8653
Dainty Lady Chain
14-16" Adj.
Reg. 5.50 Half 2.75

42
43

A. 7131
Cobra Chain Earrings
Reg. 10.50 Half 5.25

B. 8131
Cobra Chain 15"
Reg. 11.00 Half 5.50

C. 8132
Cobra Chain 18"
Reg. 13.00 Half 6.50

D. 8133
Cobra Chain 24"
Reg. 16.50 Half 8.25

E. 7185
Cobra Chain Earrings
Reg. 10.50 Half 5.25

F. 8183
Cobra Chain 15"
Reg. 11.00 Half 5.50

G. 8184
Cobra Chain 18"
Reg. 13.00 Half 6.50

H. 8185
Cobra Chain 24"
Reg. 16.50 Half 8.25

I. 8930
Whisper Chain
16-18" Adj.
Reg. 10.50 Half 5.25

J. 9930
Whisper Bracelet 7 3/8"
Reg. 6.50 Half 3.25

K. 8418
Classic Partners Chain 16 ¼"
Reg. 7.00 Half 3.50

L. 7418
Classic Partners
Going Steady Earrings
Reg. 7.50 Half 3.75

M. 9418
Classic Partners Bracelet 7 3/8"
Reg. 6.00 Half 3.50

N. 8419
Classic Partners Chain 16 ½"
Reg. 7.00 Half 3.50

O. 7419
Classic Partners
Going Steady Earrings
Reg. 7.50 Half 3.75

P. 8599
Chain Extenders
3-4" Adj.
(Includes 1-G & 1-S)
Reg. 5.50 Half 2.75

Q. 9419
Classic Partners Bracelet 7 3/8"
Reg. 6.00 Half 2.50

44
45

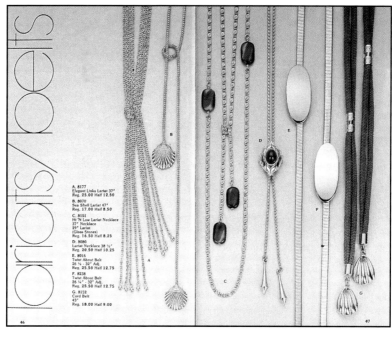

lariats/belts

A. 8177
Elegant Links Lariat 37"
Reg. 25.00 Half 12.50

B. 8070
Sea Shell Lariat 47"
Reg. 17.00 Half 8.50

C. 8151
Hi 'N Low Lariat Necklace
37" Necklace
29" Lariat
(Glass Stones)
Reg. 16.50 Half 8.25

D. 8080
Lariat Necklace 38 ½"
Reg. 20.50 Half 10.25

E. 8016
Twist About Belt
26 ¼ - 32" Adj.
Reg. 25.50 Half 12.75

F. 8238
Twist About Belt
26 ¼ - 32" Adj.
Reg. 25.50 Half 12.75

G. 8152
Cord Belt
43"
Reg. 18.00 Half 9.00

46   47

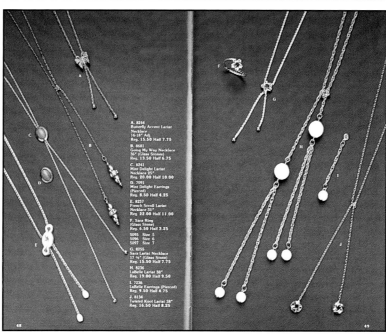

A. 8244
Butterfly Accent Lariat
Necklace
16-18" Adj.
Reg. 15.50 Half 7.75

B. 8681
Going My Way Necklace
36" (Glass Stones)
Reg. 13.50 Half 6.75

C. 8241
Mint Delight Lariat
Necklace 25"
Reg. 20.00 Half 10.00

D. 7091
Mint Delight Earrings
(Pierced)
Reg. 8.50 Half 4.25

E. 8257
French Scroll Lariat
Necklace 31"
Reg. 22.00 Half 11.00

F. Sara Ring
(Glass Stone)
Reg. 6.50 Half 3.25

5095   Size 5
5096   Size 6
5097   Size 7

G. 8255
Sara Lariat Necklace
17 ½" (Glass Stone)
Reg. 15.50 Half 7.75

H. 8236
LaBelle Lariat 38"
Reg. 19.00 Half 9.50

I. 7236
LaBelle Earrings (Pierced)
Reg. 9.50 Half 4.75

J. 8134
Twisted Knot Lariat 38"
Reg. 16.50 Half 8.25

48   49

charms/drops

A. 9008
Eagle Charm
Reg. 7.50 Half 3.75

B. 9026
Tortoise Charm
Reg. 7.50 Half 3.75

C. 9010
Lion Charm
Reg. 7.50 Half 3.75

D. 9009
Panda Bear Charm
Reg. 7.50 Half 3.75

E. 9032 (7 1/8")
9036 (7 ¾")
Charm Bracelet
Reg. 6.00 Half 3.00

F. 5971
Key To My Heart Key Ring
Reg. 5.00 Half 2.50

G. 8171
Seashore Pendant
30" (Removable Drop)
Reg. 12.50 Half 6.25

H. 8181
Amulet Pendant 30"
Reg. 17.50 Half 8.75

I. 8182
Scallop Shell Drop
Reg. 5.50 Half 2.75

J. 8239
Puffed Heart Drop
Reg. 5.50 Half 2.75

K. 8251
Egyptian Profile Drop
Reg. 5.50 Half 2.75

50   51

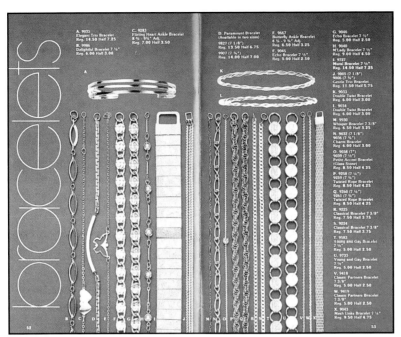

bracelets

A. 9035
Elegant Trio Bracelet
Reg. 14.50 Half 7.25

B. 9986
Delightful Bracelet 7 ½"
Reg. 6.00 Half 3.00

C. 9283
Flirting Heart Ankle Bracelet
8 ¾ - 9 ¾" Adj.
Reg. 7.00 Half 3.50

D. Paramount Bracelet
(Available in two sizes)
9827 (7 1/8")
Reg. 13.50 Half 6.75
9907 (7 ¾")
Reg. 14.00 Half 7.00

E. 9667
Butterfly Ankle Bracelet
8 ¾ - 9 ¾" Adj.
Reg. 6.50 Half 3.25

F. 9045
Echo Bracelet 7 ½"
Reg. 5.00 Half 2.50

G. 9046
Echo Bracelet 7 ½"
Reg. 5.00 Half 2.50

H. 9040
M'Lady Bracelet 7 ½"
Reg. 9.00 Half 4.50

I. 9727
Mural Bracelet 7 ½"
Reg. 14.50 Half 7.25

J. 9005 (7 1/8")
9006 (7 ¾")
Gentle Trio Bracelet
Reg. 11.50 Half 5.75

K. 9033
Double Twist Bracelet
Reg. 6.00 Half 3.00

L. 9034
Double Twist Bracelet
Reg. 6.00 Half 3.00

M. 9930
Whisper Bracelet 7 3/8"
Reg. 6.50 Half 3.25

N. 9032 (7 1/8")
9036 (7 ¾")
Charm Bracelet
Reg. 6.00 Half 3.00

O. 9038 (7")
9039 (7 ½")
Petite Accent Bracelet
(Glass Stone)
Reg. 8.50 Half 4.25

P. 9258 (7 ¼")
9259 (7 ¾")
Twisted Rope Bracelet
Reg. 8.50 Half 4.25

Q. 9260 (7 ¼")
9261 (7 ¾")
Twisted Rope Bracelet
Reg. 8.50 Half 4.25

R. 9225
Classical Bracelet 7 3/8"
Reg. 7.50 Half 3.75

S. 9224
Classical Bracelet 7 3/8"
Reg. 7.50 Half 3.75

T. 9583
Young and Gay Bracelet
7 ½"
Reg. 5.00 Half 2.50

U. 9733
Young and Gay Bracelet
7 ½"
Reg. 5.00 Half 2.50

V. 9418
Classic Partners Bracelet
7 3/8"
Reg. 5.00 Half 2.50

W. 9419
Classic Partners Bracelet
7 3/8"
Reg. 5.00 Half 2.50

X. 9043
Mesh Links Bracelet 7 ½"
Reg. 9.50 Half 4.75

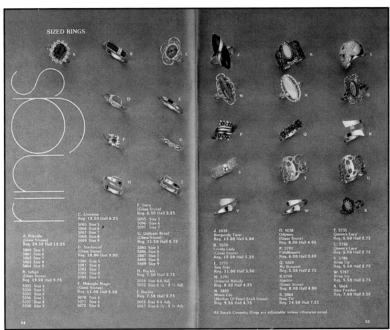

rings

SIZED RINGS

A. Priscilla
(Glass Stones)
Reg. 24.50 Half 12.25
5860 Size 5
5861 Size 6
5862 Size 7
5863 Size 8
5864 Size 9

B. Indigo
(Glass Stone)
Reg. 19.50 Half 9.75
5333 Size 4
5334 Size 5
5335 Size 6
5336 Size 7
5337 Size 8
5338 Size 9

C. Universe
Reg. 12.50 Half 6.25
5065 Size 5
5066 Size 6
5067 Size 7
5068 Size 8
5069 Size 9

D. Starbound
(Glass Stone)
Reg. 18.00 Half 9.00
5080 Size 5
5081 Size 6
5082 Size 7
5083 Size 8
5084 Size 9

E. Midnight Magic
(Glass Stone)
Reg. 11.00 Half 5.50
5070 Size 4
5071 Size 5
5072 Size 8

F. Sea
(Glass Stone)
Reg. 6.50 Half 3.25
5095 Size 5
5096 Size 6
5097 Size 7

G. Delicate Braid
(Glass Stone)
Reg. 11.50 Half 5.75
5885 Size 5
5886 Size 6
5887 Size 7
5888 Size 8
5889 Size 9

H. Buckle
Reg. 7.50 Half 3.75
5054 Size 4-6 Adj.
5055 Size 6 ½ - 8 ½ Adj.

I. Buckle
Reg. 7.50 Half 3.75
5062 Size 4-6 Adj.
5063 Size 6 ½ - 8 ½ Adj.

J. 5039
Burgundy Twist
Reg. 12.00 Half 6.00

K. 5650
Lovely Lady
(Glass Stone)
Reg. 10.50 Half 5.25

L. 5771
Sea Star
Reg. 11.00 Half 5.50

M. 5791
Oriental Melody
Reg. 8.50 Half 4.25

N. 5850
Moon Glo
(Mother Of Pearl Shell Stone)
Reg. 9.50 Half 4.75

O. 5038
Odyssey
(Glass Stone)
Reg. 8.00 Half 4.00

P. 5795
FieldFlowers
Reg. 6.00 Half 3.00

Q. 5669
My Bouquet
Reg. 5.50 Half 2.75

R. 5799
Starlite
(Glass Stone)
Reg. 8.00 Half 4.00

S. 5064
Bow Tie
Reg. 14.50 Half 7.25

T. 5735
Queen's Lace
Reg. 5.50 Half 2.75

U. 5736
Queen's Lace
Reg. 5.50 Half 2.75

V. 5786
Wrap Up
Reg. 5.50 Half 2.75

W. 5787
Wrap Up
Reg. 5.50 Half 2.75

X. 5664
Blue Feather
Reg. 7.00 Half 3.50

All Sarah Coventry Rings are adjustable unless otherwise noted.

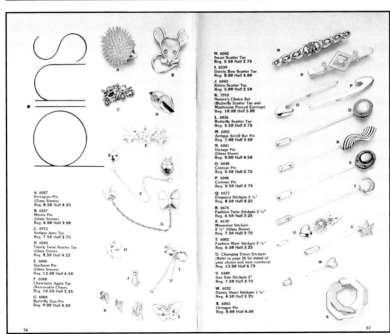

pins

A. 6047
Porcupine Pin
(Glass Stones)
Reg. 8.50 Half 4.25

B. 6037
Minnie Pin
(Glass Stones)
Reg. 6.00 Half 3.00

C. 5973
Antique Auto Tac
Reg. 7.50 Half 3.75

D. 6044
Timely Twist Scatter Tac
(Glass Stone)
Reg. 8.50 Half 4.25

E. 6040
Starburst Pin
(Glass Stones)
Reg. 13.00 Half 6.50

F. 6048
Chatelaine Apple Tac
(Removable Chain)
Reg. 10.50 Half 5.25

G. 6004
Butterfly Duo Pin
Reg. 9.00 Half 4.50

H. 6042
Swan Scatter Tac
Reg. 9.50 Half 2.75

I. 6039
Dainty Bow Scatter Tac
Reg. 8.00 Half 4.00

J. 6043
Kitten Scatter Tac
Reg. 5.00 Half 2.50

K. 7010
Nature's Choice Set
(Butterfly Scatter Tac and
Mushroom Pierced Earrings)
Reg. 10.00 Half 5.00

L. 6036
Butterfly Scatter Tac
Reg. 5.50 Half 2.75

M. 6005
Antique Scroll Bar Pin
Reg. 7.00 Half 3.50

N. 6061
Vintage Pin
(Glass Stone)
Reg. 9.00 Half 4.50

O. 6045
Contour Pin
Reg. 5.50 Half 2.75

P. 6046
Contour Pin
Reg. 5.50 Half 2.75

Q. 6677
Elegance Stickpin 2 ½"
Reg. 8.50 Half 4.25

R. 6676
Fashion Twist Stickpin 2 ½"
Reg. 6.50 Half 3.25

S. 6139
Moonmist Stickpin
2 ½" (Glass Stone)
Reg. 7.50 Half 3.75

T. 6002
Fashion Mate Stickpin 2 ½"
Reg. 6.50 Half 3.25

U. Changing Times Stickpin
(Refer to page 26 for initial of
your choice and item numbers)
Reg. 13.50 Half 6.75

V. 6349
Sea Star Stickpin 2"
Reg. 7.50 Half 3.75

W. 6032
Daisy Heart Stickpin 1 ½"
Reg. 4.50 Half 2.25

X. 6003
Octagon Pin
Reg. 8.00 Half 4.00

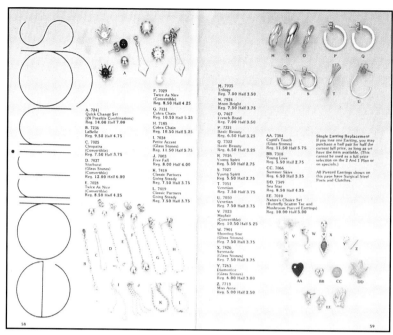

earrings

A. 7241
Quick Change Set
(24 Possible Combinations)
Reg. 14.00 Half 7.00

B. 7236
LaBelle
Reg. 9.50 Half 4.75

C. 7025
Cleopatra
(Convertible)
Reg. 7.50 Half 3.75

D. 7037
Starburst
(Glass Stones)
Reg. 12.00 Half 6.00

E. 7028
Twice As Nice
(Convertible)
Reg. 8.50 Half 4.25

F. 7029
Twice As Nice
(Convertible)
Reg. 8.50 Half 4.25

G. 7131
Cobra Chain
Reg. 10.50 Half 5.25

H. 7185
Cobra Chain
Reg. 10.50 Half 5.25

I. 7034
Petite Accent
(Glass Stones)
Reg. 11.50 Half 5.75

J. 7003
Free Fall
Reg. 8.00 Half 4.00

K. 7418
Classic Partners
Going Steady
Reg. 7.50 Half 3.75

L. 7419
Classic Partners
Going Steady
Reg. 7.50 Half 3.75

M. 7935
Trilogy
Reg. 7.00 Half 3.50

N. 7924
Moon Bright
Reg. 7.50 Half 3.75

O. 7467
French Braid
Reg. 7.00 Half 3.50

P. 7321
Basic Beauty
Reg. 6.50 Half 3.25

Q. 7322
Basic Beauty
Reg. 6.50 Half 3.25

R. 7026
Young Spirit
Reg. 5.50 Half 2.75

S. 7027
Young Spirit
Reg. 5.50 Half 2.75

T. 7051
Venetian
Reg. 7.50 Half 3.75

U. 7050
Venetian
Reg. 7.50 Half 3.75

V. 7023
Mayfair
(Convertible)
Reg. 10.50 Half 5.25

W. 7901
Shooting Star
(Glass Stones)
Reg. 7.50 Half 3.75

X. 7826
Serenade
(Glass Stones)
Reg. 7.50 Half 3.75

Y. 7263
Diamonica
(Glass Stones)
Reg. 6.00 Half 3.00

Z. 7713
Miss Anne
Reg. 5.00 Half 2.50

AA. 7384
Cupid's Touch
(Glass Stones)
Reg. 11.50 Half 5.75

BB. 7318
Young Love
Reg. 5.50 Half 2.75

CC. 7066
Summer Skies
Reg. 6.50 Half 3.25

DD. 7349
Sea Star
Reg. 8.50 Half 4.25

EE. 7010
Nature's Choice Set
(Butterfly Scatter Tac and
Mushroom Pierced Earrings)
Reg. 10.00 Half 5.00

Single Earring Replacement
If you lose one Earring, you may
purchase a half pair for half the
current half price, as long as we
have the item available. (This
cannot be used as a half price
selection on the 2 And 1 Plan or
on specials.)

All Pierced Earrings shown on
this page have Surgical Steel
Posts and Clutches.

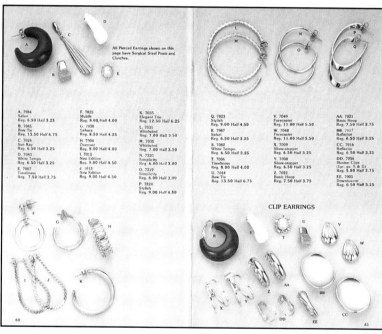

All Pierced Earrings shown on this
page have Surgical Steel Posts and
Clutches.

A. 7984
Safari
Reg. 6.50 Half 3.25

B. 7045
Bow Tie
Reg. 13.50 Half 6.75

C. 7024
Sun Ray
Reg. 6.50 Half 3.25

D. 7083
White Tempo
Reg. 6.50 Half 3.25

E. 7007
Timeliness
Reg. 7.50 Half 3.75

F. 7825
Mobile
Reg. 8.00 Half 4.00

G. 7038
Sahara
Reg. 8.50 Half 4.25

H. 7904
Overcast
Reg. 8.00 Half 4.00

I. 7012
New Edition
Reg. 9.00 Half 4.50

J. 7013
New Edition
Reg. 9.00 Half 4.50

K. 7035
Elegant Trio
Reg. 12.50 Half 6.25

L. 7031
Whirlwind
Reg. 7.00 Half 3.50

M. 7030
Whirlwind
Reg. 7.00 Half 3.50

N. 7320
Simplicity
Reg. 6.00 Half 3.00

O. 7319
Simplicity
Reg. 6.00 Half 3.00

P. 7824
Stylish
Reg. 9.00 Half 4.50

Q. 7823
Stylish
Reg. 9.00 Half 4.50

R. 7987
Safari
Reg. 6.50 Half 3.25

S. 7082
White Tempo
Reg. 6.50 Half 3.25

T. 7006
Timeliness
Reg. 8.00 Half 4.00

U. 7044
Bow Tie
Reg. 13.50 Half 6.75

V. 7049
Forecaster
Reg. 11.00 Half 5.50

W. 7048
Forecaster
Reg. 11.00 Half 5.50

X. 7009
Show-stopper
Reg. 6.50 Half 3.25

Y. 7008
Show-stopper
Reg. 6.50 Half 3.25

Z. 7022
Basic Hoop
Reg. 7.50 Half 3.75

AA. 7021
Basic Hoop
Reg. 7.50 Half 3.75

BB. 7017
Reflector
Reg. 6.50 Half 3.25

CC. 7016
Reflector
Reg. 6.50 Half 3.25

DD. 7056
Illusion Clips
(1pr. ea. S & G)
Reg. 5.50 Half 2.75

EE. 7005
Downtowner
Reg. 6.50 Half 3.25

CLIP EARRINGS

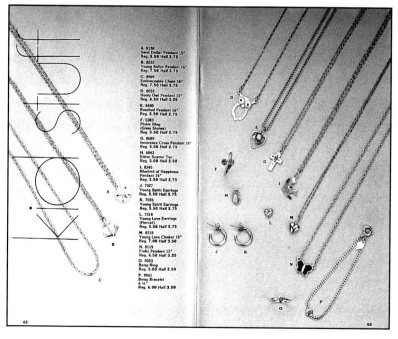

kid stuff

A. 8138
Sand Dollar Pendant 15"
Reg. 5.50 Half 2.75

B. 8233
Young Sailor Pendant 16"
Reg. 7.50 Half 3.75

C. 8909
Embraceable Chain 16"
Reg. 7.50 Half 3.75

D. 8033
Hooty Owl Pendant 15"
Reg. 6.50 Half 3.25

E. 8430
Rosebud Pendant 16"
Reg. 5.50 Half 2.75

F. 5383
Pinkie Ring
(Glass Stones)
Reg. 5.50 Half 2.75

G. 8689
Innocence Cross Pendant 14"
Reg. 5.50 Half 2.75

H. 6043
Kitten Scatter Tac
Reg. 5.00 Half 2.50

I. 8345
Bluebird of Happiness
Pendant 14"
Reg. 5.50 Half 2.75

J. 7027
Young Spirit Earrings
Reg. 5.50 Half 2.75

K. 7026
Young Spirit Earrings
Reg. 5.50 Half 2.75

L. 7318
Young Love Earrings
(Pierced)
Reg. 5.50 Half 2.75

M. 8318
Young Love Choker 15"
Reg. 7.00 Half 3.50

N. 8119
Frolic Pendant 15"
Reg. 6.50 Half 3.25

O. 5053
Betsy Ring
Reg. 5.00 Half 2.50

P. 9041
Betsy Bracelet
6 ½"
Reg. 6.00 Half 3.00

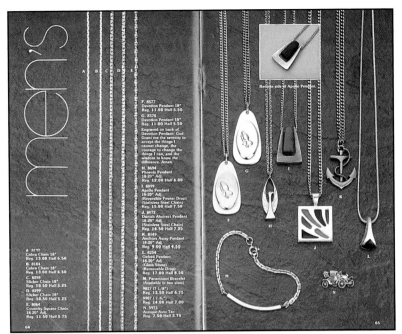

men's

F. 8577
Devotion Pendant 18"
Reg. 11.00 Half 5.50

G. 8574
Devotion Pendant 18"
Reg. 11.00 Half 5.50
Engraved on back of
Devotion Pendant: God
Grant me the serenity to
accept the things I
cannot change, the
courage to change the
things I can, and the
wisdom to know the
difference. Amen.

H. 8694
Phoenix Pendant
18-20" Adj.
Reg. 12.00 Half 6.00

I. 8599
Apollo Pendant
16-20" Adj.
(Reversible Pewter Drop)
(Stainless Steel Chain)
Reg. 15.00 Half 7.50

J. 8072
Danish Abstract Pendant
18-20" Adj.
(Stainless Steel Chain)
Reg. 14.50 Half 7.25

K. 8149
Anchors Away Pendant
18-20" Adj.
Reg. 9.00 Half 4.50

L. 8254
Oxford Pendant
18-20" Adj.
(Glass Stone)
(Removable Drop)
Reg. 17.00 Half 8.50

M. Paramount Bracelet
(Available in two sizes)
9827 (7 1/8")
Reg. 13.50 Half 6.75
9907 (7 3/4")
Reg. 14.00 Half 7.00

N. 5973
Antique Auto Tac
Reg. 7.50 Half 3.75

A. 8177
Cobra Chain 18"
Reg. 13.00 Half 6.50

B. 8184
Cobra Chain 18"
Reg. 13.00 Half 6.50

C. 8298
Slicker Chain 18"
Reg. 10.50 Half 5.25

D. 8299
Slicker Chain 18"
Reg. 10.50 Half 5.25

E. 8064
Coventry Square Chain
18-20" Adj.
Reg. 11.50 Half 5.75

Reverse side of Apollo Pendant.

64
65

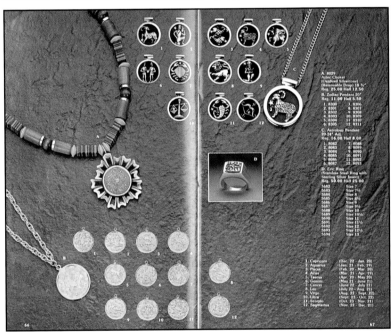

A. 8029
Aztec Choker
(Oxidized Silvertone)
(Removable Drop) 18 ½"
Reg. 25.00 Half 12.50

B. Zodiac Pendant 20"
Reg. 11.00 Half 5.50
1. 8300   7. 8306
2. 8301   8. 8307
3. 8302   9. 8308
4. 8303   10. 8309
5. 8304   11. 8310
6. 8305   12. 8311

C. Astrology Pendant
20-24" Adj.
Reg. 16.00 Half 8.00
1. 8082   7. 8088
2. 8083   8. 8089
3. 8084   9. 8090
4. 8085   10. 8091
5. 8086   11. 8092
6. 8087   12. 8093

D. Eric Ring
(Stainless Steel Ring with
Sterling Silver Insert)
Reg. 50.00 Half 25.00
5682   Size 7
5683   Size 7½
5684   Size 8
5685   Size 8½
5686   Size 9
5687   Size 9½
5688   Size 10
5689   Size 10½
5690   Size 11
5691   Size 11½
5692   Size 12
5693   Size 12½
5694   Size 13

1. Capricorn   (Dec. 22 - Jan. 20)
2. Aquarius   (Jan. 21 - Feb. 19)
3. Pisces   (Feb. 20 - Mar. 20)
4. Aries   (Mar. 21 - Apr. 19)
5. Taurus   (Apr. 20 - May 20)
6. Gemini   (May 21 - June 21)
7. Cancer   (June 22 - July 21)
8. Leo   (July 22 - Aug. 21)
9. Virgo   (Aug. 22 - Sept. 22)
10. Libra   (Sept. 23 - Oct. 22)
11. Scorpio   (Oct. 23 - Nov. 21)
12. Sagittarius (Nov. 22 - Dec. 21)

66
67

Bibliography

Ball, Joanne Dubbs. *Costume Jewelers: The Golden Age of Design*. West Chester, Pennsylvania: Schiffer Publishing Ltd., 1990.

Ball, Joanne Dubbs, and Dorothy Hehl Torem. *Masterpieces of Costume Jewelry*. Atglen, Pennsylvania: Schiffer Publishing Ltd., 1996.

Becker, Vivienne. *Fabulous Costume Jewelry*. Atglen, Pennsylvania: Schiffer Publishing Ltd., 1993.

Clements, Monica Lynn, and Patricia Rosser Clements. *Sarah Coventry® Jewelry*. Atglen, Pennsylvania: Schiffer Publishing Ltd., 1999.

Company Catalogs. Fall/Winter 1976, 1978; Spring 1980.

Cera, Deanna Farneti, ed. *Jewels of Fantasy: Costume Jewelry of the 20th Century*. New York, New York: Harry N. Abrams, Inc., and Daniel Swarovski Corporation, 1992.

Kelly, Lyngerda, and Nancy Schiffer. *Costume Jewelry: The Great Pretenders*. 3rd Edition with Revised Price Guide. Atglen, Pennsylvania: Schiffer Publishing Ltd., 1998.

Lynnlee, J. L. *All That Glitters*. Revised 3rd Edition. Atglen, Pennsylvania: Schiffer Publishing Ltd., 2000.

Newman, Harold. *An Illustrated Dictionary of Jewelry*. London, England: Thames and Hudson Ltd, 1981.

Rainwater, Dorothy T. *American Jewelry Manufacturers*. West Chester, Pennsylvania: Schiffer Publishing Ltd., 1988.

Schiffer, Nancy N. *Rhinestones!* 2nd Edition – Updated Prices. Atglen, Pennsylvania: Schiffer Publishing Ltd., 1997.

Index